Socrates:

A body, by its simple strength, and through its actions, is powerful enough
to alter even more profoundly the nature of things than whatever spirit in
its speculations and in its dreams can achieve!

Paul Valéry, *l'Âme et la Danse*

Contents

Acknowledgments

I want to express first of all my sincere gratitude to Michèle Lagny, who supervised my PhD at the University of Paris III-Sorbonne Nouvelle in Film Studies and helped me publish a French-language study in 2006 based on the research I undertook in this context.[1] After having updated this English version, she also updated the Preface for Amsterdam University Press.[2] This publication has been possible thanks to her encouragements as well as her intellectual and human generosity. I also want to thank the members of my PhD commission at the University of Paris III-Sorbonne Nouvelle: Jean-Claude Seguin, Michel Marie and Vicente Sánchez-Biosca, who offered helpful criticism that contributed to the rewriting of this manuscript. I am also grateful to Thomas Elsaesser of Amsterdam University Press for having agreed to include this book in his international series, Film Culture in Transition, which has contributed to a large extent to the institutionalisation of Film Studies in the Netherlands. Indeed, thanks to Thomas Elsaesser, academic recognition of Film as a field of study has become ever more important.[3]

Translating the French book into English was a new experience. I want to thank my Anglophone friends for improving the text. The English language can be very poetic and I am deeply honoured by the way they helped me transform this book. Thanks to their comments, their creative way of rewriting an academic text and their intelligent attitude towards analysing the subtle differences between the French and English languages, this book was born again. I want to thank Elspeth McOmish for having translated Michèle Lagny's Preface. She also participated in rewriting the Introduction and part of the first chapter, together with Sama Ky Balson and Melissa Gallo. The last theoretical part of the first chapter and the next three chapters on film analysis were edited by Lydia Inostroza, who also translated the Conclusions. I am grateful for her commitment and academic knowledge in French and English. Her creative style, which involved rewriting the description of images in the parts related to film analysis, gave a new touch to the book. The French academic language is so different and the publication of this book in English was made possible thanks to the help of these wonderful writers.

This research involved several stays in Spain and France. I would like to thank Eduardo Rodriguez Merchán (University Complutense Madrid), who guided me so well into the academic world in Spain and has supported my research projects for many years. I also want to thank Vicente Sánchez-Biosca for discussions on my research, which helped me to clarify several issues. Living in another European country meant furnishing many documents and applying for grants. I want to mention several people who supported my research project and helped me with these administrative issues: Michèle Lagny, Eduardo Rodriguez Merchán, Vicente Sánchez-Biosca, Frank Kessler, Hilde Hacquebord. Thanks to their support, I also received several Dutch, French and Spanish scholarships, which allowed me to work on this research in three countries. I am grateful to the Dutch government and several Dutch Foundations: the Prins Bernhard Fonds, Catharine van Tussenbroek Fonds and Fundatie van de Vrijvrouwe van Renswoude – which supported this project. I would also like to mention the Spanish Ministry of Foreign Affairs, which gave me a scholarship, as well as the Dutch (Nuffic, The Hague) and French Ministries of Foreign Affairs. I also received several grants from Casa Velázquez (the Ecole des Hautes Etudes Hispaniques) in Madrid, where Jean Canavaggio, Benoît Pellistrandi and François Zumbiehl created excellent working conditions. I greatly appreciated their hospitality in Madrid.

Seeing films in a period without a DVD player, I had to rely on Spanish archives. I am sincerely grateful to Marga Lobo and Trinidad del Rio for having given me access to the archives of the Spanish Film Museum in Madrid as well as to Carlos Iriart, director of the Municipal Video Library in Madrid, and José Luis Sevilla from the Film Library of Complutense University. For helping me to obtain the pictures, I would like to thank Alicia Potes and Miguel Soria (Archives of the Film Museum) as well as Pedro Almodóvar's production company, *El Deseo*. In recent years, I have presented many papers, attended many conferences and participated in a number of research projects; I would therefore like to thank the following people for the inspiring discussions I had with them on film and Spanish culture: Juan Carlos Alfeo Alvarez, Verena Berger, Nancy Berthier, Christa Blümlinger, Bénédicte Brémard, Marina Diaz, Max Doppelbauer, Kristian Feigelson, Anke Gladischefski, Camille Gendrault, Román Gubern, Françoise Heitz, Hub Hermans, Patricia Izquierdo Iranzo, Anne-Marie Jolivet, Renaud Lagabrielle, Gabriel Lago Blasco, Nuria López Blazquez, Nadia Lie, Sylvie Lindeperg, Steven Marsh, Javier Marzal, Laurence Mullaly, Itziar Muñoz Colomina, François Niney, Hilaria Loyo, Maria-Luisa Ortega, Dorota Ostrowska, Chris Perriam, Burkhard Pohl, Delphine Robic-Diaz, Sylvie Rollet, Pascale Thibaudeau, Lorenzo Javier Torres Hortelano, Dagmar Schmelzer, Clotilde Simond, Nuria Triana-Toribio, Jörg Türschmann, Dagmar Vandebosch and Belén Vidal.

I would also like to thank Paris III, the University of the Sorbonne-Nouvelle, and especially the directors of the department of Film Studies – Philippe Dubois, Michel Marie, François Thomas and Chantal Duchet – for having allowed me to lecture on Spanish cinema for many years. Students from France and all over the world showed great interest in this national cinema. As a Dutch person, it is a very inspiring experience to work with students from so many different cultures, many of whom are fascinated by Almodóvar's films and Spanish cinema in general. The students' remarks, their engagement with the topic and their international background has inspired me to undertake research and publish on this topic. Cinema is an artistic medium that raises questions about contemporary social issues. Other academic invitations have allowed me to extend this experience by lecturing in Masters courses, and I want to thank the following people for having invited me to their universities: Annie van den Oever and Barend van Heusden of Groningen University; Nicolas Blayo of the University of Paul Valéry Metz, France; Wanda Strauven and Patricia Pisters of the University of Amsterdam; Nancy Berthier of the University of Marne la Vallée; and Kathrin Sartingen and Esther Gimeno Ugalde of the University of Vienna in Austria. This European experience has illustrated once again for me that Almodóvar's characters, and indeed Spanish cinema in general, fascinate international audiences by their questioning of contemporary issues.

I want to finish this page with a special word for my family and my friends in France, Spain and the Netherlands. As the Spanish poet Antonio Machado wrote so well, "Wanderer, there is no road, by walking the road is made" ("Caminante no hay camino, al andar se hace camino"). On my road, by working and living in three countries, I met wonderful people and I would like to thank my family and friends for sharing this inspiring experience with me.

Preface

Here is a "book of passion" on the metamorphoses of post-Francoist Spain as it was catapulted into the contemporary world (1975-1995). It is a book that questions the power of myths expressed through passionate bodies, in particular those who for far too long were marginalised in traditional societies. Women trying to liberate themselves, homosexuals seeking to emerge, delinquents attempting to resist society – all are brought together and intertwined in a strange choreography of dissidence. In summary, this book is a socio-historical essay, in which Pietsie Feenstra underlines the close relationship between the transformation of the image of bodies and social rites shown in films, and that of a society that awakes from a long sleep to rush into a frenzied race – the *Movida*.

It is therefore first and foremost a book of cinema, as it considers that this latter exposes the stereotypes and expresses that which is forbidden, in particular thanks to its way of laying out the relationship between the bodies (of actors, of characters), places and the social practices that it transforms into rites by building a collective vision. Since the publication of her pioneering work *The New Mythical Figures of Spanish Cinema (1975-1995), À corps perdus* (L'Harmattan, 2006),[1] Pietsie Feenstra has enriched her research with studies, in particular by Anglo-American authors, who have all examined the importance and relevance of the question of the body.

The first originality of this book is to have taken, as a point of departure, filmic images of bodies in order to analyse the social imaginary: it is thus part of the movement that emerged from interest in the uses of constituent bodies of Marcel Mauss' "total man", and now explored in their multiple socio-historical dimensions; for example, in the *History of the Body* edited by Corbin, Courtine and Vigarello,[2] in which the title itself, and the entire research process, "placed at the 'frontier point' between the social and the subject"[3] are witness to the "quasi-invisible and yet decisive reversal [that] follows from the abandonment of traditionally-recognised sovereignty to the benefit of conscience."[4] "*A corps perdus*" is a way of speaking of this newly-found body, in particular on screen, as the cinema has played an essential role in its metamorphoses and in the "mutation of the vision" that was given to it in the 20th century, as underlined by Antoine de Baecque[5] (after Vincent Amiel, Nicole Brenez and Vicente Sánchez-Biosca). This release is enriched by the reflection developed on the homosexual body, that of women in particular (why was lesbianism considered to be less aggressive?), thanks to feminist studies that also focused on female directors in

Spain. Finally, since the year 2000, there has been new interest – both theoretical and quantitative – in the study of films on terrorism following the attack by Al-Qaeda in Madrid on 11 March 2004, giving a new face to delinquency.

The second strength is to have theorised how images of bodies are organised and their meaning expressed in the context of a visible transformation of society, by settling the traditional opposition between timeless myth and eminently time-bound history, and by presupposing that the myth itself becomes temporal and gives rise to history. Thus, alongside the stereotyped images that are a throwback to the past and presented as based on "nature" – those very stereotypes that were already being denounced by Barthes many years ago – are exemplary "prototypes". These manifest the new desires (whatever these are) in a new way, thus historicising archetypes that remain active while being transformed. This audacious use of the notion of the archetype allows us to grasp how a profound modification of the social imaginary can take place. And, so as not to hide behind theory, the author made the effort to find, through systematic viewings and a study of the reception of the films (through the quantitative analysis of the public and a qualitative analysis of the critiques) those works that could be emblematic.

But most captivating – and also most convincing – are the film analyses, founded on the idea that the choreography of bodily movements, built through film, create "thought-images" that refer back to cultural norms and values, and enable us to understand and structure the mythical figures that underlie them. Grouped according to theme – the seeking of freedom for women, of visibility for homosexuals, of recognition for the "delinquents", whose suffering sheds light on their violence – these analyses are all enlivened by sensitivity to the image that draws one in. The precision with which the shots are studied, the work on the use of mirror and the gaze, the discrepancies in voices, the choreographic forms of battle: each of these allow us to penetrate the physical intimacy of the films. For some box office successes that we believe we already know, we are encouraged to go further than the reconsideration of traditional images (that of the *femme fatale* in Saura's CARMEN) or the scandal of subversive audacity (that of the mini-skirted girls and the "always-strange boys" of Almodóvar). Other works, less well-known internationally – even if they had a certain success in Spain – by Eloy de la Iglesia (THE DEPUTY/EL DIPUTADO), Vicente Aranda (SEX CHANGE/CAMBIO DE SEXO, *El Lute*) and Imanol Uribe (THE DEATH OF MIKEL/LA MUERTE DE MIKEL, RUNNING OUT OF TIME/DÍAS CONTADOS), present the enormous advantage of revealing the vigour of the symptom analysed (the recognition of difference), without Pietsie Feenstra ever claiming to expose a mass phenomenon. I will not reveal the details here – to do so would be a shame – but I will stress that the whole publication is worth both the readings it proposes and, despite the author's passion for her subject, the measured way in which she studies it. We feel indignation for the injustices done to women and to sexual or social "deviants" and discover ideas from ethnologists, mythologists, historians, feminists and film specialists. But the arguments, developed with care, are never held sacred: despite the firmness with which the reader is directed, he or she remains free to build their own interpretation.

Michèle Lagny

Introduction

Almodóvar's swinging bodies

Pedro Almodóvar's cinema introduced new images of human bodies that have profoundly influenced the history of film. Male bodies modified by silicone, walking in a feminine manner and transforming themselves into perfect androgynes. Monstrous mothers dominating the screen (in HIGH HEELS/TACONES LEJANOS or e.g. ALL ABOUT MY MOTHER/TODO SOBRE MI MADRE), transgressing the borders of social, sexual and cultural identity. The images of these absurd, ambiguous human bodies burst through taboos and demolished traditional identities by creating new, original characters. Indeed, they illustrate the profound changes in Spanish cinema after 1975. In Almodóvar's films, this provocative director rarely reacted to dictatorship or politics. He hardly ever made a direct comment about all of the topics forbidden by censorship. However, he reacted more than any other Spanish director to the taboos of Francoism by creating new images of the body – new identities that could not be visualised during this period. In Francoist cinema, women, homosexuals or characters demonstrating violence (delinquents, gypsies, terrorists, etc.) were obviously not the main characters. They were like dissident bodies, those who were legally not allowed to be in the foreground. In direct contrast, the flamboyant director transformed them into new original protagonists. I find these new personalities thrilling and they've been an inspiration for me to write this book, focusing on how the image of their bodies created new mythological figures that refer to ancient themes. This process illustrated profound social changes in Spanish society. Another aim of this research was to gain new insights into this national cinema by familiarising ourselves with other film directors, placing Almodóvar's films in their cultural and historical context.

Spanish cinema and Film Studies

Since the 1990s, Spanish cinema has become increasingly popular in Film Studies, but research conducted by European and American scholars on the topic is quite recent. The historical situation of Spain could explain the difficulties that led to it being included only recently in European or American research programmes. Without a doubt, the films directed by Luis Buñuel or Carlos Saura made Spanish cinema world famous for its aesthetic originality. But other films did not always easily cross borders, even if the national level of production has always been significant. In his book *European cinemas. European societies 1939-1990*, Pierre Sorlin explains that since the 1950s, five countries have dominated the cinematographic scene in Europe: Germany, Britain, France, Italy and Spain.[1] Focusing on the images of national cinemas, Sorlin analysed historical and social changes in the period from 1939 until 1990. The Francoist dictatorship dominated Spanish cinema and the French scholar decided not to include this country in his historical research, underlining, however, that its level of production and aesthetic richness could be compared with that of the other four countries. Sorlin explains that the Spanish situation required a study in itself. It is clear that Spanish researchers had published on this issue before, yet we had to wait until the 1990s for European and American film scholars to begin to publish regularly on this cinema. In 1993, the American scholar Marsha Kinder published *Blood cinema: the Reconstruction of National Identity in Spain*, one of the first American studies about Spanish cinema as a national cinema from the 1950s until the 1990s. In her introduction, she commented on her ambition to convince the reader that "a knowledge of Spanish cinema alters and enriches one's understanding of world cinema."[2] Marsha Kinder was one of the first American scholars to publish on this topic, and she speaks openly of her aim to demarginalise Spanish cinema. The statements of reputable American and French film scholars illustrate the peculiar situation of the 1990s. Another explanation for having only recently included Spanish cinema in Film Studies could be the linguistic barrier, as understanding Spanish is necessary. There are already many publications in this language, but as French and English dominate Film Studies, both languages are rarely accessible for students or film scholars.

This explains my wish to translate this book into English. Linguistic borders can be crossed to stimulate the exchange of ideas setting off European debates, as approaches in Film Studies are completely different in how they focus on film as object. Indeed, research in this field has expanded only recently; national research traditions often dominate the subject. The Spanish images studied in this book therefore function due to their migrating qualities, illustrating European questions on French methods, Spanish film publications, and a Dutch approach by the author. Besides being a translation of the French edition, the book has also been extended and updated by integrating contemporary research about terrorism, female film directors and lesbianism in this new edition by Amsterdam University Press.

In addition, the aesthetic richness and originality of Spanish national cinema is increasingly appreciated, and is extremely popular today in European and American film departments. Beginning with my introduction of Almodóvar's human bodies, his name pops up again when we think about the international visibility of Spanish cinema, as he received an Oscar in 1999 for ALL ABOUT MY MOTHER. Spain was back on the international agenda. Almodóvar's recent films TO RETURN (VOLVER, 2005) and BROKEN EMBRACES (ABRAZOS ROTOS, 2009), with the Spanish film star Penélope Cruz, have reinforced his reputation. Alejandro Amenábar continued the American success story by receiving an Oscar for his film THE SEA INSIDE (MAR ADENTRO), which deals with the issue of euthanasia and is based on the real-life story of Ramón Sampedro. The fact that Spanish film directors have sent films on contemporary topics to the United States was crucial: ALL ABOUT MY MOTHER treated homosexual relationships or transsexuality, with the knowledge that homosexual marriages were legalised by law in 2005 in Spain, and not in France, while THE SEA INSIDE questioned euthanasia, relating it to religion. Contemporary issues were treated in a progressive way, transmitting a modern image of a country that had been the subject of so much pressure from the Catholic religion in its recent past. This research illustrates how the tremendous change in legislation since 1975 can be directly related to how Spanish film directors reacted to several taboos by creating new images about their culture. Cinema illustrates once again how profound changes in mentalities could already be detected in the 1970s, with the reaction to a dictatorial past. Film is a cultural and historical witness, and thanks to research we can create methods of analysing film images.

Updating myths by the human body

To illustrate my method, which is based on an historical approach to cinema, two aspects must be defined: the importance of the human body and the creation of new myths related to its historical context. The human body reveals itself as a fascinating image, able to illustrate profound changes in a cinema, indeed in a culture. Our body is like a "personal envelope"[3] and at the same time a sociological image of our culture. However, there are huge differences in the approach to analysing the human body in France, Spain and the Netherlands. The migrating implications of a national cinema illustrate important differences on how to analyse the human body. As I mentioned, this research is related to my cultural background, for example the way in which homosexuality, violence (e.g. drugs) and the position of women in society are openly and directly debated in the Netherlands. The Dutch view on these issues that are physically visible in society, in legislation or, for example, on television contrasts with the approach within French academic film studies. In the academic arena, the decision to analyse the body is inspired by French film studies of the 1990s, with an aesthetic view of the human body. Many books and articles have been published, for example those by Nicole Brenez, Vincent Amiel and Fabienne Costa.[4] The human body had already been sporadically studied or mentioned in Film

Studies, but it was not until the 1990s that this series of articles began to dominate thinking within film theory. The only questionable aspect to consider regarding the French publications is that the relationship between the body on the screen and a reflection on what it shows about the culture was rarely instigated. The body was often considered a filmic form like that of an aesthetic entity, without a focus on social backgrounds. Combining this with the Dutch context, it would have been a reduction of the richness of Spanish cinema to analyse the original bodies of Almodóvar's cinema only in the terms of their aesthetic figuration, when studying the enormous switch in the on-screen representation since 1975 of the Spanish historical context.

The "personal envelope" introduces new ideas on the screen in Spanish cinema, creating new ideas and new myths. Several studies on myths influenced my research. Theoretically I was inspired by the book *Mythologies* by Roland Barthes,[5] in which he analysed contemporary myths in daily life by examining newspaper articles from the 1950s in France. Even though his approach is very marked by an idea of power relations, his book is still of crucial importance in understanding myths today.[6] I define myths as systems of beliefs that help us structure our vision of the world. We constantly create new myths about new phenomena. The place and time in which they are constructed have a crucial impact on their final outcome. Cinema is an extremely interesting medium for communicating the renovation of myths, and I consider the image of the body to be of vital importance in this process.

To analyse the new myths in a film, I propose three concepts: the human body, the ritual, and the mythological motif or idea – the last term being grounded in the concept of the "archetype" introduced by Carl-Gustav Jung.[7] This latter defines archetypes as an original image, forming part of a collective unconsciousness, appearing to us in time and space according to the way we transform them in our dreams. Even if I do not quote the categories of Jung (*anima, animus*, etc.), I am inspired by his definition of the function of the archetypes, considering them as roots or original images. This Jungian meaning of the archetypes is still current, and we find it in several mythological themes, such as the femme fatale, motherhood and the hero. Analysing how new images of human bodies update these original ideas introduces us to the world of new mythological figures. They are constantly created, in contrast with ancient values: eternal archetypal values are transformed into something new and the contemporary language of the human body expresses this mythological thought and models its appearance. On this matter, I disagree with Gilbert Durand, who denies the existence of "new" myths.[8] Even if I assume the existence of archetypes, I define their new expressions as new mythological figures.

Reading contemporary human bodies cannot ignore their historical and cultural contexts, which determine the new expressions. I describe the representations of new identities as historicising the language of the human body. Contemporary expressions (such as songs, dialogues or gestures) update its meaning and offer connotations for the historical and cultural contexts. The historical context was therefore particularly revealing when it came to understanding what kind of new myths were created in Spain's national cinema. Alongside Almodóvar, other Spanish film directors also broke through taboos and invented a so-called new cinematographic language. The Democratic Transition (1975-1983) was a fundamental period for Spain, whose cinema communicated the euphoria of liberty. After the death of Franco, censorship was abolished in 1977 and Spanish culture entered a new period in which film directors reacted to the old regime, inventing new forms of expression.[9] The characteristics of a period of "Transition" influenced the way in which myths are constructed, as a certain perception of the past or future have been dominating ideas on-screen. The emergence of these myths can be explained by exploring the historical and cultural contexts. With the death of Franco in 1975, the dictatorship was officially finished and the political situation completely transformed. But significant confusion remained as to what life would be like in the near future. The "new" political future could not be perceived or created in a fluid way. A so-called rupture in the perception of history was felt that inspired the invention of stories about the unknown, about the future – also reacting directly to the past by breaking through taboos. The "new" period that they had to face provoked a feeling of instability and insurance. It is these characteristics of the Democratic Transition that lead to the creation of new myths, such as new stories that structure the imaginary about the unknown, in order to reduce anguish.

Embodying new ideas

Confronted with a new period and the end of dictatorship, the feeling of a new era stimulated Spanish film directors to create many new images, for example about some of the taboos of Francoism. These new ideas were often a reaction to the past. After 1975 female identities, homosexuality and delinquents became visible in a new way, representing new themes. The legislation of Francoism made them dissident bodies, protagonists of being different to the totalitarian norms of dictatorship. When legislation changed in the 1970s, their identity could be portrayed in a new way. I could have chosen several other topics for this research, but the three body images inspired the creation of new visual ideas, that questioned the norm in which sexuality and delinquency had always been the subject. Even if this research focused on the socio-historical connotations of the film, the first aspect to be studied was always film images, accompanied and reinforced by archival research (historical, sociological, anthropological and legal) to interpret their meaning in a cultural context. Several visits to

Spain were essential to carrying out this research and to viewing more than 200 films.

The 10 films studied in this book represent several dominant tendencies. First, the three social groups have a direct relationship with the repression – through Francoist legislation – of women being able to work and their sexuality, homosexuality and delinquency. At the end of the 1970s, laws were modified, censorship abolished and new ideas emerged in Spanish cinema. Second, the films received considerable attention from audiences (box offices) or through critiques in press articles. Third, my aim to convey a general idea of Spanish cinema determined the films I chose, as I wanted to avoid studying the typical prophets of marginality, such as Eloy de la Iglesia and Pedro Almodóvar. Films by a number of directors were therefore selected to analyse how the three topics were treated in several films, in a particular period, and by different directors.

To start with the first section on women, the first film analysed is not well known abroad but was extremely successful in Spain: FLUNKING OUT (ASIGNATURA PENDIENTE, 1977), by José Luis Garci. The story shows direct cinematographic references to the famous film by Chantal Akerman, JEANNE DIELMAN, 23 QUAI DU COMMERCE 1080 BRUXELLES (1975). The static life of a housewife in the Belgian film can be experienced in this Spanish box office success. The second film in this section is CARMEN (1983), by Carlos Saura. The famous ballet updates ideas of a femme fatale through flamenco dance steps. The third film, Pedro Almodóvar's HIGH HEELS (TACONES LEJANOS, 1991), shows a monstrous, selfish mother who is completely obsessed with her career, forgetting or ignoring her daughter. Concerning homosexuality, I also chose a number of films to situate this issue in its cinematographic context. SEX CHANGE (CAMBIO DE SEXO, 1977) by Vicente Aranda was certainly not a box office success. However, it introduced Victoria Abril to Spanish cinema and dealt with homophobic reactions in the 1970s based on a real-life story. On the other hand, THE DEPUTY (EL DIPUTADO, 1979) by Eloy de la Iglesia provoked strong homophobic reactions in the press, but at the same time generated a significant amount of audience interest in the country. This fiction film presented apparently new images that shocked Spanish audiences, a fact confirmed by press articles. A third film to treat homosexuality was THE DEATH OF MIKEL (LA MUERTE DE MIKEL, 1983) by Imanol Uribe, a director who also dealt with many other issues, such as the conflict with ETA. The first three films, which illustrated various aspects of homosexuality, contrast completely with Almodóvar's film LAW OF DESIRE (LA LEY DEL DESEO, 1987). The third topic – violence related to delinquency – was harder to handle from a chronological point of view; HURRY, HURRY (DEPRISA, DEPRISA, 1981) by Carlos Saura was made during a period when problems with drugs were being shown for the first time on screen. Saura, like other Spanish directors, had been working with actors who represented their own life, and thus their real-life addiction to drugs. The second film in this section, EL LUTE: RUN FOR YOUR LIFE (EL LUTE, CAMINA O REVIENTA, 1987), EL LUTE II, TOMORROW I'LL BE FREE (EL LUTE II, MAÑANA SERÉ LIBRE, 1988) by Vicente Aranda offers an historical and contemporary vision of gypsy culture, showing how El Lute managed to escape severe scrutiny by the Civil Guards in the 1950s. This story could be romanticised in cinema in the 1980s by finishing with a contemporary vision on Lute. Closely related to gypsy culture, he represents the Otherness of Spain. Archival research reveals the sociological dimension of gypsy culture during Francoism and up to today. The last film, RUNNING OUT OF TIME/ DÍAS CONTADOS (1994) by Imanol Uribe, modestly explores the question of how to visualise an ETA terrorist. It goes without saying that it is extremely difficult to make films on this topic for a Spanish public. The historical transformations of Spanish terrorism since Francoism, and its representations in national cinema, are also commented on.

The book is organised in two parts: a theoretical introduction in the first chapter, followed by three chapters demonstrating how the method presented works out inside the film image and then a chapter with conclusions. The first chapter, which is entitled "After prohibition, we clearly exhibit: how to read into these film-images?" presents the films studied in their cinematographic context and historical period (analysing two films of the 1950s, RACE (RAZA) and WELCOME MR MARSHALL! (¡BIENVENIDO MR MARSHALL!) in order to illustrate the impact of censorship in a totalitarian state, creating visual taboos). It also introduces the way in which the human body becomes a testifier and "agent" of themes that were forbidden and explains the method of analysing mythological figures in the film image. The second part of the book consists of three chapters that analyse the films, entitled: "The liberation of women", "The homosexual body on stage" and "The delinquent body out of focus." These chapters demonstrate the process of updating archetypes, inscribing them within a visual memory. This second part of the book and the Conclusions illustrate how the mise-en-scene imposes a vision of the female body, how homosexual identity is shown frontally on stage and how the delinquent is expected to stay in the social background.

I. From prohibition to clear exhibition: how to read into these film-images?

In this chapter, we will analyse two films from the 1950s to illustrate the impact of censorship on forbidden topics. It is not intended to provide a complete overview of Francoist cinema or of the political situation. Rather, we wish to illustrate some Francoist myths related to this totalitarian impact by manipulating history. Barthes' approach to myths is particularly rich for illustrating the so-called "naturalisation of history" in cinema under dictatorship, which contrasts completely with the concept of history in post-1975 national cinema.

1. Exposing prohibition

The political situation in the 1930s was determined by the 1936 electoral victory of the Republicans, followed by a military *coup d'état*, which provoked a civil war (1936-1939). After three years of war, Franco took power and imposed strict rules, installing his dictatorship. He posed as a representative of natural progression, when in fact there was no democratic process. The Spanish historian Román Gubern describes this phenomenon as a process of justification using radio and cinema; he compares this with what happened in Italian cinema under Mussolini and in German cinema under Hitler.[1] Franco appeals to a mythological discourse by referring to some archetypal aspects of the so-called "Eternal Spain": the myth of an immense Catholic country, crossing the Oceans to conquer colonies, keeping them and converting the inhabitants to Catholicism. This archetype of Spanish culture, which was born in the Golden Age (17th century), underlines the grandeur of the kingdom: it is meant to unite people under a religious dogma: Catholicism. After the Civil War, the archetype served to justify the Francoist battle, referring to superior reason, as expressed in the film RACE (1941).

RACE: imposing a Francoist myth

The propaganda film RACE (RAZA) shows a totalitarian vision. This fiction film has often been scrutinised in detail, as well as its ideological message; it was indeed Franco who devised the story and published it under a pseudonym, Jaime de Andrade.[2] Questioning this author's name, Román Gubern explains that it was related to Franco's family background. His mother came from a noble family dating back to the 14th century, the Casa de Andrade. In the narration, this link comes back directly in the name of the mother figure, "Isabel de Andrade", and the daughter's name, "Isabelita". Focusing on the female representations, Susan Martin-Márquez also relates this first name to the cult of Queen Isabella the Catholic (1451-1504), who was seriously promoted by the government after the Civil War.[3] It was under her reign that Christopher Columbus discovered the New World in 1492 and that the empire was enlarged. By using the pseudonym Jaime de Andrade,[4] Franco therefore introduces a direct historical link to the colonial past of Spain that is illustrated in the film RACE.

Directed by José Luis Saenz de Heredia, the first version of the film (1941) was replaced in 1950. As Román Gubern explains, in this second version some fundamental ideological modifications had been made: fascist salutations were cut out and the title was replaced by THE SPIRIT OF A RACE (ESPÍRITU DE UNA RAZA).[5] The political position of Spain within the international context had changed and the film images had to be adapted to this new situation. Let us therefore scrutinise some film images to situate the mythological message of this fiction film in the period after the Civil War, the 1940s.

The plot shows an exemplary family, with the father Pedro Churruca (Julio Rey de las Heras) travelling abroad to protect the Spanish colonies while his family is waiting for him at home. The whole film imposes a direct mise-en-scene and immediately shows the idea of Eternal Spain as a Crusade, particularly in the opening credits, against a background of drawings showing massive ships. The first three sequences present the issues linked to the myth by introducing the family, army and church: the three basic pillars of the Francoist regime. The Churruca family, with its parents and four children, are shown as exemplary human beings serving the fatherland. They present the idea that there is only one truth by these model children, even if their behaviour does not appear very natural (the only exception to this being the son Pedro, who is not very disciplined throughout the film).

At the beginning of the film, José, the model son, announces to his mother (Rosina Mendía) that their father will soon return home. The camera focuses directly on his mother's face in a medium close-up[6] while she gazes to heaven: her praying had been understood, her husband is finally returning home to the core of this happy, well-educated family. She then freezes, perceiving that someone behind her is shouting: Pedro, her other son, is chasing his sister to retrieve a bird that she had taken from him. This boy is rebellious; he is shouting at his sister. He had captured this animal with the intention of selling it and his mother is teaching him a lesson. She speaks of the suffering of animals: one should never let any creature suffer, not even an animal. The expressions of awe on the children's faces are astonishing. Pedro alone stands out in this atmosphere. When his father finally arrives home, he speaks to his children of the

Photo 1: The grandeur of the family (Filmoteca Española, Madrid)

importance of the homeland, and again Pedro asks inappropriate questions: is the fatherland really worth dying for? The film emphasises his clumsiness, as he is unable to understand the importance of the fatherland. Indeed, the nationalistic mission of the Churruca family is univocal. After a short stay with close family members, the father leaves again to defend the last Spanish colony, Cuba. In this battle, he will be killed.

When the Civil War breaks out in the 1930s, the children fulfil their duty by taking up arms. As a Republican, Pedro shows serious Leftist tendencies and engages with conviction in a political career. This choice is shown to be a fatal error, as if linking politics to Communism only brings disorder to the country.[7] The narration imposes a reading that the Civil War requires a military intervention to save the interests of all Spaniards. Two options are embodied: either the children are an example (like a model to be followed), or they are stereotyped in a negative way. Both readings interrogate the utility of the army, politics or religion: their activities symbolise their duty towards their country, while the masculine bodies represent the moral obligations they must undertake for society and the female represents duties linked to the home. Pedro (José Nieto) con-

Photo 2: The son José, the hero (Filmoteca Española, Madrid)

tinues to detonate in this harmonious group by choosing a political career. As Nancy Berthier comments, this actor often played evil characters in films in this period, in contrast with the character played by Alfredo Mayo, representing José. Even if they were both well known in the 1940s, their reputation differs,[8] corresponding directly to their physical portrayal in RACE. The eldest son, José, becomes a member of the military, which is presented as an exemplary voca- tion. Played by the handsome Alfredo Mayo, his body represents strength and conviction. He even stands up to death after having been shot. In a battle on the front, everyone believed he was dead. As if a miracle had taken place, he comes back to life again: his character resonates with Jesus Christ, coming to earth to save humanity against sin and evil, and giving his life to save humanity. José has now come to save the world against this "red disease", this Communist intervention: he must save Spain. The youngest son, (Luis Arroyo), a monk will be shot; the daughter Isabellita (Blanca de Sillos) is waiting for her husband to come home.

The propaganda message continues until the end of the film, as Pedro will be converted and therefore saved. Looking towards heaven, at the end of the film he abandons his political ideal to serve the fatherland. Again, José is presented as the hero in the last sequence, which shows the military parade entering Madrid. By the use of a shot/reverse shot, the daughter, Isabellita, and her son are admiring the military parade when the young boy asks his mother with enthusiasm, "How beautiful is this: what is it called, mummy?"[9] Isabellita replies with a satisfied smile, in a medium close-up, her eyes lighting up in response to this beautiful performance and with a voice that sounds deeply moved: "This is what we call the race, my son". These words were modified in the 1950's version by "the spirit of a race". The different shots of the parade place emphasis on the huge number of soldiers who had fought for the fatherland. José participates in the parade with them, straight up on his horse, touching the saddle with his hand, surrounded in the background by a marching military. His body image is that of a good-looking, young, strong man, who fought for the good cause.

At that particular moment, we again hear the words of the father in a voice-over, when he taught his children that it was a holy task for the military to accomplish their destiny fighting for their fatherland. José had listened to these words when he was a child. The shot unites the parade with these words, while we see his father's limp body when he himself died for Spain, his country.

No doubts are possible concerning the interpretation of the message of this film – and excellent studies on this issue underline its propaganda value.[10] Analysing the ideology, many researchers have already focused on the function of myths. For example, in the English publications related to Barthes' approach to myths (I refer here to Virginia Higginbotham's 1988 publication *Spanish film under Franco*). In her preface, she introduces Barthes' ideas on myths as depriving the objects of history.[11] In 1998, Barry Jordan and Rikki Morgan-Tamosunas published *Spanish contemporary cinema*, continuing in this direction by also reflecting on the concept of history in relationship to the film RACE.[12] These two groundbreaking studies particularly concentrate on the narratological function of myths, faithfully adhering to Barthes' vision. Evidently, this approach of myths is convincing for the period after the Civil War. However, in this book I will explore in depth new mythological figures in cinema after 1975, updating the method by focusing on the body image in relationship to the film material and the new political context.

Commenting on RACE, two aspects interest me in particular: the image of the human body and the concept of history in this Francoist myth. As we observed, characters serving as a model introduce the three pillars of Francoism, which are the army, religion and the family. In this way, the bodies of the characters represent the archetypal values of the fatherland and the race, justifying the Civil War. As Barthes explained, the Francoist myth thus imposes a unique vision of history by naturalising it. Often cited for his vision of history, Barthes describes myths as a negation of history, as they present facts and circumstances as being given – as part of a natural reality.[13] Based on this approach, Franco created myths to confirm his power by interpreting history: identifying with a past of grandeur and suppressing the Republican or other political visions as an error. History is naturalised and myths justify the taking of power by military intervention. It was a way of making his victory lasting, as dictatorship imposed a unique vision of grandeur, referring to the archetype of Eternal Spain.

WELCOME MR MARSHALL! (1953): questioning myths

In the process of imposing totalitarian visions, the role of censorship was crucial to studies on Francoist cinema and writings on this topic. Hans-Jörg Neuschäfer, for example, analyses the impact of censorship, indicating that not only did it limit the film directors and writers in their creativity, but the restrictions also obliged them to find a language to avoid the constraints.[14] WELCOME MR MARSHALL! by Berlanga provides a good example. Like RACE, this film has often been studied. However, as Steven Marsh illustrates, the visions of Spanish researchers and those from abroad do not always correspond. Inside the country, Berlanga's cinema has often been portrayed as typically Spanish in its sense of humour, and therefore not exportable to foreign audiences. On the other hand, Steven Marsh comments on the books by Marsha Kinder and John Hopewell, as they emphasise Hollywood's and Italian influences in his work (neo-realism, Fellini).[15] This would imply that his work could be broadcast wider into world cinema, and therefore appeal to foreign audiences. In contrast, Marsh brings to light Berlanga's focus on *the popular* as one possible reason for it not being exportable, while being so widely appreciated within Spain.

This filmmaker is still not well known abroad, yet he is a reputable filmmaker in his country. The film WELCOME MR MARSHALL! in particular is a classic in Spanish film history which reveals a reaction to some Francoist myths. Released in the same period as the second version of RACE, Berlanga proposes a comic interrogation of the myth of Eternal Spain. This film director sets in place an image of the human body, of the characters that creates another form of mythical discourse. By using humour, the filmmaker succeeded in getting around the censor, as the film was viewed by Franco and could still be projected.[16]

In contrast with RACE, which enforced a unique reading and point of view, WELCOME MR MARSHALL! begins with a distanced reading created by the voice-over introducing the story and emphasised by the mise-en-scene. On a small road in the countryside, a car approaches a village: "Once upon a time there was a Spanish village, an ordinary village". These are traditionally the first words of a fairy tale. The village is first deserted, and the voice-over (by the well-known actor Fernando Rey) provides a description. The characters then appear as if by a trick: these people represent their village through their characters, their customs, their habits; they are introduced by their social activities in a normal and poor village, *Villar del Rio*, where the quiet is disturbed by the announcement of the arrival of the Americans with their Marshall Plan. The inhabitants imagine getting rich by receiving fortunes from abroad. The mayor, Don Pablo (José Isbert), who normally sleeps when he has to work, wakes up completely and enthusiastically starts to organise a welcome party, assisted by a specialist in the Andalusian song "Manolo" (Manolo Marón). We need to know that this village is not situated in Andalusia, but that the inhabitants disguise their houses and their bodies in the hopes of pleasing the Americans, from whom they expect to receive a lot of gifts.

Three myths are exposed in this story: the myth of Eternal Spain, the Black Legend or deep Spain, and the *españoladas*. The Black Legend is opposed to the myth of Eternal Spain: it was the price to pay for all the extremely expensive expeditions that ruined the country to serve the ideals of conversion to Catholicism and to conquer the colonies. The legend had been introduced officially by Juderias in a 1917 publication in which he demonstrated that Spain was badly thought of abroad due to the Catholic fanaticism that had impoverished the country itself.[17] Part of this negative image abroad was evidently caused by the Inquisition. In 1478 the Catholic queens established the Spanish Inquisition; another form had already existed before this, but now it was imposed and directly controlled by the Spanish monarchs Ferdinand II of Aragon and Isabella I of Castilla. The negative connotation of this image is an important element of their reputation abroad, as the Inquisition only ended in 1834. On the other hand, the myth of the Black Legend can also be described as "deep Spain", where the connotations are less negative and refer more to the roots, to the profound origins of a simple country life. A third image commented on in this film is that of the *españolada*, a cliché of folkloric aspects of Spain – for example, the stereotype of a bullfighter or a flamenco dancer.[18] These three mythological images are brought to life by the bodies of the characters in the parade sequences.

The first parade creates the figure of the *españolada* presented by a group of people dressed in Andalusian costume. They hurry to the central square of the village to listen to the mayor's speech. The men are dressed in hats and trousers made of leather, the women in coloured dresses with flowers in their hair; together, they form a typical image of the Andalusian folklore. In a low angle shot, the mayor appears on the balcony of the town hall that runs onto the square. He seems, satisfied: this site of the village is still empty. The inhabitants arrive from everywhere and assemble under the balcony, in a high-angle long shot. They listen to the speech about the party and applaud. The mayor and his assistant announce the preparation of an Andalusian party. A singer, called – of course – Carmen (played by the well-known *copla* singer Lola Sevilla) will perform a *copla* of flamenco, an image so easily exported and originally linked to Andalusia.[19] They represent the *españolada* and several sequences demonstrate

Photo 3: The disguised bodies of Spain

the mise-en-scene of this Hispanic cliché: the inhabitants transform their houses into an Andalusian style, walk to the rhythm of the guitar, and a group of men repeat the names of each of the parts of the costume they have to wear. A group of women learn how to dance the Sevillanas; given the clumsiness of the movements of their arms and their bodies behind the teacher, it is evident that they are beginners in this art.

Berlanga illustrates a cliché that, in the reality of that period, was used as bait to trap foreign tourists for economic reasons. Nancy Berthier[20] explains that Francoism did not aim to introduce images of the *españolada* in its formula for the new Spain, but in the 1940s and even more so in the 1950s, it began in its national cinema to appeal to folklore where the *españolada* served to protect against the invasion of American cinema. In this way, Francoism aimed to provide a more positive vision of the country.[21] In spite of the autarchy that was officially in place until 1957,[22] it was clear to the Francoist government that the economic situation was not brilliant in Spain and the *españolada* could restore their image to some extent.

Another parade that gives an image of the deep Spain is shown in a sequence of the same crowd. The inhabitants are now wearing their usual clothes. They are queuing to express their desires. Each person may only make one wish: we

Photo 4: The mayor's body, the image of a cowboy

see faces wrinkled from the sun and labour on the countryside, humble clothes and their wishes – they embody the thought of the deep Spain. On the central square, they make a queue to attend a table where the mayor and his assistants are sitting and noting their wishes: a suit to dance on Sundays, a sewing machine, and a mirror.

Followed by the contrast between the dream of Eternal Spain and the reality of the deep Spain is illustrated by a dream-like figure. At night, the inhabitants fantasise about this event and especially about what they wish to receive. Fast asleep, the dream is witness to a kind of psychological delirium of grandeur that ends up in a nightmare. For example, the mayor of the village, who normally is not very dynamic and helpful, undergoes a metamorphosis: in his dreams he transforms into the body of a cowboy. A close-up of his sleeping face dissolves into the skirts of young girls dancing the cancan on a stage (medium close-up). Don Pablo enters a saloon dressed in a Western costume opening these small typical doors. He looks tense, creating suspense, the reason for which we know not. He turns around suddenly, ready to draw his gun, believing that he is facing an enemy who isn't behind him. In the saloon, the people are impressed by his presence and give him the place he needs when he bumps into someone when going to the bar. He orders a drink in a language that resembles American English, as he opens his mouth widely imitating these sounds; only the movements of his arms correspond to the meaning of his words.

He sits down in the middle of the room to watch a *copla* singer performing on stage: it is Carmen. A fight breaks out. He jumps on stage to save the singer and the camera frames him in a medium close-up when he falls onto her. He is touching her buttocks and her legs, one of which he is indeed stuck to. The shot dissolves into the mayor in pyjamas, waking up in an embrace with the foot of his bed. He stands up, and then goes back to bed, continuing to sleep. The voice-over consoles him, reassuring him that he will certainly get married to this girl.

The dream functions as a parody: the mayor embodies the stereotypical image of an American cowboy parodying the ideas of grandeur of the Conquistadors, like those who wanted Eternal Spain brought to life. Here it concerns a clumsy cowboy, who is not at all heroic: waking up, he is no longer a hero, but rather a dressed-up body in pyjamas who is embracing the foot of a bed. Reality also turns into a nightmare. The Americans arrive and the crowd of bodies disguised in Andalusian costume approach to greet them, singing appropriate songs for this occasion. Finally, the Marshall's delegates planned to cross the village quickly, without giving anything to anyone (corresponding to the historical reality, as Spain was not included in the Plan[23]). In this fiction, the deception is immense. The inhabitants had gathered together their last resources to organise this welcome party and now have to bring their belongings back to refund the costs. Hats are dropped on the ground and everyone redresses in their usual outfit. Life continues as in the past, with labour in the country, the narrowness of a village and poverty, but the villagers had peace again and got rid of their false beliefs. The film ends simply on this new found tranquillity. The sun is shining and rain can stimulate the harvest. Through comedy, Berlanga criticises Franco's dreams of grandeur, with the parades of people questioning the myths and the characters waking up from a physical and psychological dream. The image of Eternal Spain is transformed from a dream into a nightmare, depicting it as an outrageous expectation.

Political transition

These two films provide an incomplete description of Spanish cinema during Francoism. However, they allow us to illustrate certain myths related to a totalitarian aspect of the political situation of that period. From 1975, the national cinema, liberated from certain restrictions imposed by dictatorship, began to expose new revelations about the human body and construct new images. Related to political events that deeply moved the country, the films introduce another perspective of these historical times, as this context is essential in understanding the construction of myths.

Let us first concentrate on the political situation. The dictatorship, which lasted 39 years, carried the name of its chief: Franco's death put an end to it. This conclusion was more or less expected, as after the disappearance of Carrero Blanco no one was able to maintain this regime,[24] but it was the physical end of Franco in 1975 that marked the real end of dictatorship. As Peter Besas comments, politically this period is not considered to be a rupture, as the installed government was a continuation of the Francoist system.[25] Juan Carlos de Borbón became King of Spain and started his intentions for reform inside the existing structure. The first government was presided by Carlos Arias Navarro, former mayor of Madrid. In 1976 it was Adolfo Suárez who became prominent. He won the first elections in 1977, and sustained the King's reform policies. In this period, Spain became the scene of numerous changes in different fields and I mention only a few changes, but there were many: the first elections in 1977; the formulation of a new Constitution in 1978; a failed coup d'état in 1981,[26] the victory of the Socialist Party in 1982; the acceptance of integration into the European Community in 1983 – events that are reflected in the cinema of the Transition period and form the context for these films. The cinematographic politics in Spain changed in the same period, particularly with the removal of censorship in 1977 by Royal Decree,[27] with clear consequences. Other changes, such as the Miró law (inspired by the French model of *avance sur recette*[28]), modified the state of Spanish cinema.

Analysing the political context after 1975, the term "rupture" sparked many debates. As Peter Besas comments:

> Many had dreamed of a full *'ruptura'* or break when Franco was gone, a genuine revolution, a total about face. But their dreams had been thwarted, and it soon became clear to most observers (and certainly to the relief of the majority) that no such break would occur. *Transition* was the keyword.[29]

There wasn't a complete ideological political rupture immediately after Francoism, what led to a feeling of disenchantment (*desencanto*). I point out that the topics explored in this book, illustrate a visual and sociological rupture concerning the way they were allowed to be visualised beforehand. The political change permitted the abolition of censorship in 1977, which was a fundamental first step. But other legal changes need to be mentioned to understand this visual change. Besides the political shift, lots of legal adaptations were made, with regard to homosexuality, delinquency, the position of women. These changes were particularly reflected by the filmmakers, creating new images about these identities. I argue that this is a visual rupture, related to the legal adaptations, which was a direct consequence of the new political situation. New images on homosexuality, women, delinquency contrasted completely with what could be or was shown under Francoism, as these identities were restricted by legal descriptions on their moral behaviour, in relation to their identities.

Mentioning this distinction illustrates how we situate this research in its political context. Our research concentrates on the period from 1975 until 1995; the political and legal context is therefore related to the period when the new myths on these groups were built. Felipe González's Socialist Party governed from 1982 until 1996, with the period between 1996 and 2004 being headed by the government of José María Aznar. Concerning this latter period, new research has been done on its national cinema focusing on new representations of social issues or the past.[30] The national cinema in its political and historical context changes in the 1990s. Actually, the decision to focus on the period from 1975 until 1995 was not taken for its political unity, rather because it proposes a historical and political context rich in changes. It introduces and adapts new laws for these groups, of what cinema reflects on by introducing newly-created ideas in that period. Let us therefore further explore some of the concepts inspired by the political context that were important for the creation of new mythological figures.

The "Democratic Transition" (1975-1983) and "Transformation" (1984-1995) represent two periods that frame my study on new mythological figures: first, the birth of new themes in the cinema of the Transition period, then, in the 1980s and 1990s, the period during which democracy was increasingly implemented. This created a transformation of cinematographic topics as new concepts evolving into new groundbreaking myths. These two periods are important, as myths are linked to the historical time, as they result from political change. This led to a feeling of uncertainty, anguish for the future and the refusal of the forbidden topics from the past, as Francoist censorship was just behind them.

The term "Transition" is often used in Spain. However, the Spanish researcher José Enrique Monterde criticises it openly, emphasising that a change in the country's cinema had began prior to Franco's death:

> Surely we refuse the term 'transition' for two reasons: because it appears to be an empty term, unable to define its own content, and because it is based on a teleological vocation and determination that is highly ambiguous in the sense that neither uncertainty concerning late Francoism, nor the own development of the reform had been considered in relationship to objectives... [31]

Certainly, according to Monterde, the notion has no proper meaning. He demonstrates the vague character and tendency to presuppose clear objectives that, according to Monterde, had not taken place. From my point of view, it is not a concept without a meaning, but I prefer to state that during the Transition period a sort of emptiness was felt; in order to fill this up new ideas were born, that were expressed particularly through the films made after Franco's death. Therefore, we must define this concept in relationship to a tendency to construct new myths related to a fundamental change inside the culture.

Let us further explore the etymology of the term "transition". It means passage: from one state to another; from one situation to another.[32] In the Spanish context, this Transition period could be described as a period of passage caused by this political change. People lived "inside" an intermediate period, as if blocked because of their separation from the past due to the death of Franco and the unknown political future they faced after years of dictatorship. This "in-between" feeling is the source of the birth of myths serving to sublimate the anguish towards the current moment, trying to give "meaning" to the current situation.

Rituals of initiation correspond to this transition period and appear as ordeals that function to introduce new thoughts. Analysing Spanish cinema, the introduction of a new image of the human body will be the central focus: following this issue over a period of twenty years allows us to discover the evolution of myths. For example, in every period acts of initiation are realised and we find illustrations of them in the national cinema after 1975. Similarly certain films react against forbidden historical topics, such as, for example, THE CRIME OF CUENCA (EL CRIMEN DE CUENCA, 1979) by Pilar Miró. The issue dealt with here concerns innocent prisoners who had been tortured at the beginning of the 20th century by Civil Guards and ended up admitting a crime they had not committed. Although the film was finished in 1979, it could not be released until 1981. As censorship had been abolished in 1977, the state intervened. Indeed, the army wanted to take court action against the filmmaker as she was accused of having insulted the Civil Guards.[33] Finally, the film was able to be released without the filmmaker going on trial. It attracted at least 2.5 million spectators in 1981 and was also the film shown most often in the year of release. Wanting to show this kind of image illustrates a reaction to the many years of censorship, making public what it had been forbidden to show or to mention previously, opening up a new period. Considering the reactions, it is obvious that these were rituals of initiation through images. Another example that dates back to shortly after 1975 concerns the numerous films on homosexuality, closely related to the phenomena of transvestites or the issue of changing gender (SEX CHANGE/CAMBIO DE SEXO, A MAN CALLED AUTUMN FLOWER/UN HOMBRE LLAMADO FLOR DE OTOÑO). These images serve as a ritual of initiation, a rite of passage.[34] The Transition therefore functions as a new period in which taboos are broken.

The meaning of the term "transformation" is rather the result of a process; something that takes a different form. The new images introduced during the

Transition are founded in groundbreaking myths introduced during the Transformation. The rituals of initiation took place and allow us to approach the subject in a new manner by cementing its presence: the theme is confirmed in a groundbreaking myth. Pedro Almodóvar seems to me the best example: he started introducing multi-gendered bodies, presented as ridiculed bodies, in the 1970s. I'll define the "multi-gender" of a character by accumulating different gender aspects in the same body. For example, the role of the mother, staged by a masculine character who is a transvestite, multiplies the traditional expectations about the image of the body and therefore inspires a new reading, an untraditional interpretation. These transsexual and transvestite bodies are shown as groundbreaking myths in the 1998 feature film ALL ABOUT MY MOTHER.

In this research, I wish to distinguish the multi-gender body from the term "queer", as this latter represents a debate that is closely related to different cultural contexts. This term was born in the United States in the 1980s – using it in relation to other countries is not always appropriate as they may have another definition for or cultural reaction to it. A general definition of the term "queer" involves examining the process of socialisation of roles by men and women or the fixation on a biological aspect of origin (denouncing the social difference) that this could imply. Almodóvar does not deconstruct sexual identities, but rather constructs them in the same body.

It is challenging to refer in this context to Judith Butler, who has often been seen as representing the queer movement, thanks to her famous book on these issues *Trouble in the gender* (1991). Judith Butler criticises the naturalistic presuppositions in gender perception, which assume that there is some innate gender feelings inside the body. Scrutinising the works of Freud, Foucault, Kristeva and many others, she shows that gender is based on acts (i.e. performance). It is fascinating how Butler finishes her brilliant essay in 1991.[35] She speaks about multiplying the possibilities of gender, wondering what other local strategies of contesting the natural could lead to "denaturalising" gender in itself. Perhaps Almodóvar's cinema is an original display of multi-gender bodies.[36] It is the interaction between the Spanish audience, the perception of some characters and the repetition of the same body over several films, playing different gender roles, that creates this Almodóvarian concept of multi-gender: once again the images of the bodies invite us to enquire further or to comprehend these new creations and new visions.

Bodies in conflict

Returning to the 1970s, the human body reveals new concerns about issues that are a taboo, in reaction to the moral constraints of dictatorship. I define this Transition period in Spain's national cinema as "post-Francoism", as the bodies concerned reveal the forbidden topics of the former period. The three groups (homosexuals, women and delinquents) often present their life as a conflict within themselves or their environment. They raise questions about the forbidden topics of the past and express their thoughts through gestures and acts. To explain this visual newness, we have to situate them at least inside Spain's and perhaps even in the European cinematographical context.

The themes relating to politics and sexuality – or sexual conflicts related to political constraints such as those in THE DEPUTY (EL DIPUTADO) – correspond to a general tendency in Spain. Several press articles underline the recurrence of this topic, such as the article by Fernando Trueba in *El País* in 1979: *"Sex and politics, a potent mix that sells"*.[37] To illustrate the enormous visual contrast with the former period, Román Gubern even describes an earlier sexual phobia, referring to the absence of any type of sexual relationship in the film: "In that period the cinematographic characters fell in love, but their bodies were ectoplasm without sexuality, which caused some problems for the scriptwriters and film directors."[38] Asexual bodies. Francoism imposed this repression on sexuality with rigorous political acts, following which a new period was announced. In her book *Refiguring Spain* (1997) the American scholar Marsha Kinder describes this period as a moment of re-inscribing sexuality, which she defines as a central topic of the Transition period.[39] Sexuality was a new topic and numerous bodies demanded a new definition of its identity expressed as a "thought-image"; the image of the body expressed an idea, a thought, which was indeed to be redefined. In this tendency, the female and the homosexual body took on new meaning. This was also noticed in other European countries.

Analysing European cinema – the cinema of Italy, France, Germany and England – Pierre Sorlin concentrated on themes such as the city and women. It is revealing that he also describes the three topics of this book as changing visually in different European cultural contexts. Concerning the cities, he studied the relationship between delinquency and certain urban images. Commenting on the images of women, he also observes a change in the representation of homosexuals. For example, he notices an important modification on this topic in European cinema, in particular a more tolerant attitude towards homosexuality:

> Social standards do not evolve so quickly that what had been relevant in 1973 became obsolete less than fifteen years later. The only noticeable modification was a more tolerant attitude towards homosexuality which, still treated cautiously in the 1970s was the theme of a great many European movies in the 1980s.[40]

Sorlin then relates this modification to the new images created of women in the same period:

Few people were interested in this topic before about 1975, and everybody considered that women were simply fictional characters congruent with social models. But feminism, which had strengthened during the initial years of the decade, highlighted the problem.[41]

In summary, the new images on delinquency related to big cities and new images of the female and homosexual body relates to a European trend. All these issues became visible, in a new way, and not without debate: their new identities are shown by bodies in conflict, breaking through taboos on their private life, on intimacy, on sexuality, reacting to the concept of the family.

The family as a totem

For a very long time, the family was the basis for the organisation of intimacy.[42] It possessed a mythological value as a site of protection, security and stability for many cultures. Francoism seriously idealised the family using normative criteria. José Enrique Monterde describes the family as a micro-cosmos or totem in cinema: "This site often organises itself as a micro-cosmos representing the social; and in this micro-cosmos, the family scene is strongly privileged."[43] The family is representative of a totem for order and stability, like a myth imposed on a culture, protected by laws – because behaviour that deviated from certain principles was severely punished. For example, laws forbade, homosexual acts, sexual acts outside of marriage, the use of contraception, etc.[44] Sexuality had to serve reproduction inside the core of the family, a place dedicated to heterosexual sexuality.

The homosexual body is made visible, bearing in mind that homosexuality was not supposed to exist, as the Spanish scholar Alfeo Alvarez indicates:

> The representation of homosexuality in our cinema is relatively recent, if we compare it with the cinemas of North American, Britain and France; it is without doubt due to the weight of a dictatorship that saw a moral and social danger in sexuality exerted at the edge of the institution of marriage, and in homosexuality an aggravation that could lead the individual directly to [being charged with a] possible offence.[45]

Making a myth of the importance of the family led to the exclusion of concepts judged as deviations. The family became an enclosed space, the image of a *huis clos*; a site, in which it was difficult to enter, idealised in its presentation: this was the Francoist ideal of the family.

Enumerating several representations is not meant to entail a schematic reading of all cinema in these years. I am touching on over 40 years of contemporary cinema, introducing several crucial changes to illustrate Franco's dogma, which may explain the strong reactions in the cinema after 1975. I do not wish to encourage schematic readings, as there were certainly other images and reactions in national cinema. For example, the well-known film RAISE RAVENS (CRÍA CUERVOS, 1975) by Carlos Saura shows a clear parody of the family situation, with the children acting in the kitchen, imitating their parents. Ana (Ana Torrent) plays at being her mother, accusing her father of seeing other women and ignoring her. Her eldest sister imitates her father, in a typical macho reaction waving away all these remarks. This subversion of the ideal of the family is one of many examples that can be found, such as, for example, in POACHERS (FURTIVOS, 1975) by José Luis Borau. The incestuous mother abuses her son Angel for many years. When Angel is about to get married she is so jealous that she kills his fiancée. This obviously does not correspond to an ideal of Francoism. However, Spanish filmmakers were extremely creative in creating allegorical images, avoiding censorship and transmitting their ideas.

Discovering the body

In reaction to this Francoist ideology, there was a wish to show the sexual body outside the traditional structures of the family, which was illustrated in two streams that began in late Francoism: the *destape* (the uncovering); and the *tercera via* (the Third Way). Discovering the female body was important, but also the homosexual body. The famous *destape* appears in the 1970s as a new genre, addressing sexual issues. Naked women can be observed, but the sexual act in itself is not shown – only supposed or fantasised. The perception of the *destape* today is viewed differently. We have to relate this movement to that particular period and treat it as a sociological phenomenon. As a commercial sub-genre, the *destape* was enormously successful, although it disappeared at the beginning of the 1980s.[46]

It was like an opening and a hatching of new images during the period of the Transition, described by Gómez de Castro as a bourgeoning of new images during this period of transition: "With the opening came the *destape* and later, with the official end of censorship in December 1977, all the material that Francoism had forbidden…began to enter Spain."[47] The *destape* were films that referred to sexuality, but did not show anything; they were innovative only due to the fact that the female body could be discovered on the screen. The "Third Way" stream, which was also born during late Francoism, refers to political and sexual subjects, depicting a new elite. This stream is more intellectual, contrasting with the cinema of the *destape*, even though it also deals with sexual themes, but in a more serious tone.

Like the female body, the homosexual body is discovered by showing its sexual identity, which is updated in these films. We cannot mention the introduction of a genre in the Transition period, but the body is often visually conflicting in relation to its gender, its identity and the gaze of others. This issue of conflict recurs in several films: SEX CHANGE (1977); A MAN CALLED AUTUMN FLOWER (1978); THE DEPUTY (1979); THE DEATH OF MIKEL (1983); THE MATADOR (1986); LAW OF DESIRE (1987); THE THINGS OF LOVE (1989); STORIES FROM THE KRONEN (1994), etc.[48] The body is marked by enormous taboos in these films, particularly during dictatorship, but even more so shortly after the Francoist period.

Other taboos from the period of Francoism

Another issue important under Francoist censorship was the non-visualisation of disorder in the country; delinquency was not supposed to be represented through images. With the re-found liberty, the phenomenon appeared in Spanish culture often related to drugs that gave birth to a new genre: the police film. Vicente José Benet examines this relationship between delinquency and the emergence of police cinema during the Transition. His study covers the period until 1987 and he notices the appearance of certain movements in this genre, which would be confirmed in the 1980s.[49] The entrance of this new genre in the cinema of the Transition results in the introduction of new images of the body from the 1980s: of delinquency, youth and drugs, gypsies and terrorism.

A final topic forbidden under Francoism was history – recent history and history in general, but above all that of the Civil War. The complexity and contemporary relevance of this issue still triggers many debates and there has been a stream of new studies on these fields; even today, the Transition period is the central focus. Again, the list of publications is too long to mention, so every title selected means that the topic that is dealt with is immensely reduced. We've decided not to include this topic in this book as it deserves to be examined in a complete overview, comparing the newness of images over three decades.[50] Even though the commemoration of the historical past had already began anew during the Transition period, the complexity of the political situation and the instability of the new democracy (during the failed coup d'état of 23 February 1981 by Tejero) led the government to avoid the issue of official commemorations of victims or official judgements in the Transition period. It was the so called Amnesty Law of 1977 that had avoided every possible judgement of crimes committed under dictatorship, for both sides. This is one of the reasons for describing this period as dominated by a so-called "pacto del olvido", a pact of forgetting the past. The journalist Emilio Silva co-founded with Santiago Macías in 2000 the Association for the Recovery of Historical Memory, reacting directly to this "pact of silence" and focusing on the victims who had never received a proper burial. This sparked a massive movement of searching for family members killed, reacting to the imposed silence of the government. Silva's association became very important. However, this is only one short, reduced comment on an issue so complex that I prefer to mention some publications that dealt with the complexity of the period in detail.[51]

II. The body as witness

In this section, I will further explore the issue of representation in a given historical period. I have chosen to address issues concerning the sexual and delinquent body due to the newness of these images in Spanish cinema. These images were introduced during the Transition period and they returned during the Transformation. They hold our attention; but how they are portrayed? How to capture the imagination of the audience? Is the film image a witness to the image of the body? Based on the affluence of the audience, on the importance of the film director in the national cinema, on the appearance of a new image after 39 years of dictatorship, this research proposes a montage in which the body witnesses a change in Spanish cinema over a period of 20 years.

Female body

The big change for women in society concerning work and sexuality inspired the creation of new images of the female body. In relation to this, we will analyse three films: Flunking Out (Asignatura pendiente, 1977) by José Luis Garci, Carmen (1983) by Carlos Saura and High Heels (Tacones lejanos, 1991) by Pedro Almodóvar; and three female figures – the housewife, the *femme fatale* and the female star. These films were relatively successful, as the Spanish audience has not always been equally interested in its national cinema or indeed in cinema in general; in 1979 and at the beginning of the 1980s there was a tremendous decline in the number of spectators. As Ramiro Gómez de Castro emphasises in his research on Spanish cinematographic production until 1986, the rate of presence of Spanish productions had completely changed.[52] In 1976, 30.7% of films watched by Spanish spectators were Spanish, compared to 29.91% American (13.72% Italian, 11.13% English, 6.4% French). Ten years later, this relationship had changed completely, with 63.42% of films watched by Spanish spectators being American films, compared to 13.32% Spanish (9.14% English, 2.48% Italian and 3.28% French).[53] This change occurred in 1979, and since then the rate of the national audience has continued to decline. Carmen was made in a recession year, which might partially explain the little attention it received. This film does not appear in the Ministry's list of the top 100 box office sales – neither in 1983 nor in 1984. On the other hand, it was nominated for an Oscar, which means that a Spanish institution had chosen it to represent the country. Furthermore, the film and the ballet in itself received a lot of attention in the press and these were shown on television in 1984.[54] FLUNKING OUT (ASIGNATURA PENDIENTE) and HIGH HEELS (TACONES LEJANOS) were seen more than one and a half million times in the year of release, which was significant compared to other films; this success continued over the next few years. Each year between 1975 and 1995, a film sold more than one and a half million tickets.[55] Only in 1979, 1983 and 1986 did no film reach 1 million spectators.

The homosexual

I will discuss the issue of homosexuality up to 1987, starting with the Transition period. The scholar Alfeo Alvarez indicates four stages of representation of the homosexual body in cinema.[56] The first stage, under Franco, implied secrecy. The second stage was the Transition period with "provocative-demanding images", claiming their presence implies a ritual of initiation, bringing to light the presence of this type of body. I will focus on this second period, the Transition period, by analysing SEX CHANGE (CAMBIO DE SEXO, 1977), THE DEPUTY (EL DIPUTADO, 1979) and THE DEATH OF MIKEL (LA MUERTE DE MIKEL, 1983). For Alfeo Alvarez, there was a change after this film. The third stage began with LAW OF DESIRE (LA LEY DEL DESEO, 1987) and we have to analyse this fictional film, as after that date I did not find any films dealing with this topic in itself as the main problem of narration: from then on, homosexual relationships are represented more as secondary (STORIES FROM THE KRONEN, I WILL SURVIVE, LITTLE BIRD).[57] The period from 1996-2000 represents the fourth stage, with homosexual characters being integrated into the plot in the same way as heterosexuals.

The fiction SEX CHANGE did not sell many tickets,[58] but is an important film that treats in a direct way, visually, the issues of changing gender and homophobia. Furthermore, it was released shortly after 1975. The next film selected, THE DEPUTY, generated significant interest over two years with more than 1 million spectators.[59] THE DEATH OF MIKEL occupied third position in terms of audience the year it was released.[60] The same is true of LAW OF DESIRE, which also came third in 1987.[61] In summary, during the Transition, the theme of homosexuality in Spanish cinema interested almost a million spectators.

Delinquency

There was an increase of crime in Spain after 1975. This phenomenon also invited the construction of new images of the delinquent; in particular on certain bodies that – in different periods – were considered to be evil for society: the gypsy body, the drug addict's body, the terrorist body. These identities were introduced in Spanish cinema, making the thought-images visible. The first film to be studied, HURRY, HURRY (DEPRISA, DEPRISA, 1981) by Carlos Saura, concerns a youth gang and the use of drugs; this shows a darker side to the new freedom being experienced after 1975. Giving visibility to drugs in cinema during Francoism was not possible. Furthermore, certain drugs (such as heroin) were not consumed much during that period. The increase in the consumption of heroin in Spanish society at the end of the 1970s led to higher levels of criminality. During the 1980s, a series of films were therefore produced about youth delinquency related to drugs. Films such as STRAY DOGS (PERROS CALLEJEROS, 1978) by José Antonio de la Loma, HURRY, HURRY, (DEPRISA, DEPRISA,1981) by Carlos Saura, films by Eloy de la Iglesia including COLEGAS (MATES, 1982), EL PICO (THE SHOOT, 1983), EL PICO 2 (THE SHOOT 2, 1984), THE TOBACCONIST OF VALLECAS (LA ESTANQUERA DE VALLECAS,1986), MARAVILLAS (1980) by M. Gutiérrez Aragón, 27 HOURS (27 HORAS, 1986) by Montxo Armendáriz and, a little later, RUNNING OUT OF TIME (DÍAS CONTADOS, 1994) by Imanol Uribe, dealt with issues, such as drugs, prostitution and ETA. The fact that several filmmakers were making films on this topic, especially during the Transition period, accentuates the importance of this theme for Spanish cinema. It is evident that these critical films were not only made by a filmmaker such as Eloy de la Iglesia, known for his "tough" images of Spanish society. Carlos Saura had already made a film THE DELINQUENTS, (LOS GOLFOS, 1959) about delinquency, but not about drugs: it is the only film he directed on this issue. In the same vein, two other feature films on delinquency are EL LUTE, RUN FOR YOUR LIFE (EL LUTE, CAMINA O REVIENTA, 1987) and EL LUTE II, TOMORROW I'LL BE FREE (EL LUTE II, MAÑANA SERÉ LIBRE, 1988) by Vicente Aranda. The films about "El Lute" tell a story about a merchant who lives on the margins of gypsy society. The last film studied on this subject is RUNNING OUT OF TIME (DÍAS CONTADOS, 1994) by Imanol Uribe, which brings two worlds together: drugs and ETA.

As for productions on homosexuality, these films all attracted close to 1 million spectators.[62] During the Transition, the problems linked to delinquency retained the attention of audiences. This fact is reiterated by other films such as STRAY DOGS (PERROS CALLEJEROS, 1978) by José Antonio de la Loma, which sold 890,417 tickets in the year that it was released. Over the next few years, they attracted over 1 million of spectators. The same tendency was true of the well-known film THE SHOOT (EL PICO, 1983) by Eloy de la Iglesia. At its release in 1983, this film sold 619,568 tickets, making it second among all films (after A WOMAN IS GOOD BUSINESS. SHAKE WELL BEFORE USE/ AGITESE ANTES DE USARLA with 650,306 tickets sold).[63] In 1983, cinema experienced a crisis and few people watched Spanish films (in 1982, 23.2%; in 1983, 21.35%; in 1984, 22.14%).[64] Among the three themes examined in this book, that of the female body (FLUNKING OUT of 1977 and HIGH HEELS of 1991, for example) attracted the most spectators. The situation of women was not dealt with as an explicit denunciation, as was the case with the first films on homosexuality. This could be experienced as something difficult to watch, compared to the images of delinquency showing violence, drugs or criminality directly. As the cinema remains a place for many people to dream, this could be one of the reasons that the first theme was more attractive for audiences, even if all of the topics received considerable audience attention.

Testimonial...?

The films that will be analysed were important at their release for the Spanish, who were interested in new images created about their culture. How we may interpret the attention given to certain topics? Were they a representation of new realities or rather an emerging cultural fashion? The question of what is prevalent in films is a topic that often has been commented on – even today the theories of Bazin and Kracauer remain relevant. My aim is not to provide general theoretical reflections on this topic. However, I will examine these questions within the context of Spanish cinema: the situation following the death of Franco was a specific one, as censorship was crucial during Francoism. From 1975 onwards, the bodies bathe in sexuality and delinquency. I have already emphasised the fact that the films of the *destape*, where women's breasts and imagined sexuality dominated the plot, are an example of this aspect. This stream began in the 1970s. They were without doubt a commercial success, but lost their appeal in the 1980s. From 1975 onwards, other images of homosexuality were presented that retained the audience's attention; we can observe this in films made by Eloy de la Iglesia.

The attention that was paid to them in Spain does not simply imply that these films directly represent reality. First, they show that these images could be made after 1975 and that they aroused significant curiosity. Assessing the level of attention paid to a theme at a determined moment in time brings us back to the difference in the theoretical approaches of Bazin and Kracauer, summarised by Casetti: "For both researchers, cinema was closely linked to reality, but for Bazin this link tends towards a superposition of parts, while for Kracauer it becomes a witness to that which exists."[65] Related to this aspect from the theories by Kracauer, I emphasise that the films of the Transition represent new phenomena, as the films by Eloy de la Iglesia still illustrate. This filmmaker experienced his most important success during that period; he knew how to represent and frame social ideas and thoughts, making the spectator aware of these realities. Indeed, seeing these films induces a certain form of lucidity. Pierre Sorlin describes this function of the images:

Images reproduce – 'mirror' – what existed previously in the world but was not acknowledged as worth noticing; by framing some things, images make them visible, they help an audience to identify what was known beforehand and to learn what was not yet identified.[66]

According to Sorlin, the new images help to recognise phenomena that already existed before, which is obviously the case for homosexuality during Francoism – it was impossible to show it using a serious and honourable image. When this became possible, the curiosity for this kind of forbidden reality led to a tendency to want to see it from close by, on a big screen, in a crowd. The function of cinema is crucial in this ritual to see images: cinema proposes a possibility to see it, while the institution organises the perception of the witnesses of a society at a given moment.

Watching

Let us examine this relationship between my corpus and the culture. The films were chosen either because they appealed to a large audience, for other reasons witnessing historical pertinence, etc.), or because they are cult – this last distinction often emanating from a cinematographic institution. To illustrate the concept of "cult", I refer to Durkheim, who posits that the term "cult" carries a religious connotation and defines it as: "a system of rituals, of feasts, of diverse ceremonies that all present the characteristic of returning periodically; they reply to the need experienced by the faithful to tighten and tone, at regular intervals, the link that units them to the sacred beings on which they depend."[67] With this definition of a cult, it is tempting to note that television and cinema have become for many a form of cult, due to their regularity, which stimulates activities of ritualising it in certain places, in given circumstances and in front of a certain audience.

Two points require comments: institutionalising the perception and experiencing this "together". I will base this on the book by Ruth Friedberg (1993), *Window Shopping. Cinema and the postmodern culture*,[68] in which she comments on the fact that cinema institutionalises the activity of "watching": by going back through the history of the twentieth century, she analyses the phenomena of the perspective and describes several ways in which it exercised, such as photography, shopping, exhibitions, the circus, the theatre, museums, tourism, and finally the cinema. She theorises that the human being has a natural need to watch, and that this desire is satisfied through shopping (thus generating a desire to purchase), travelling long distances, or visiting museums. In addition, she considers that films favour the institutionalisation of our habit of watching images (*window shopping*) that are a fragmentation of realities, now become mediated.

Television generates this process in the same way as cinema, as the audio-visual media has institutionalised it: "watching" is a legal activity, which is allowed and experienced by a group of people.

More than television, the cinema-institution possesses some typical characteristics related to this activity of watching that engenders a cult phenomena or the attention of a huge audience. As far as the notion of "experiencing it together" is concerned, cinema stimulates this group ritual through the dark rooms in which it is shown, between unknown people – a fundamental dimension to giving birth to a cult phenomena. First, the obscurity of the room stimulates spectator anonymity, bringing about a certain emotional liberty. Watching, the spectator is supposed not to communicate in order not to disturb others; we live this experience through the images, alone with the film – it is rather difficult (and impolite) to observe the feelings, tears and anguish of one's neighbour. There is a contrast between this individual solitude and the fact of being in a group of people with whom we are not acquainted, each of whom is ritualising the same images: being anonymous, buried in one's private feelings, we are with many others, we experience this together, representing a ritual of "us": in the obscurity, we share deeply a feeling. These two characteristics illustrate the fact that "the institution-cinema" favours the ritual grouping of people around a film that is not necessarily cult (but that arouses interest), to experience this through a group, for example, – and this is my proposition – around images that were forbidden under dictatorship.

Cult film

Aside from the position of the cinematographic institution, which stimulates to make a film "cult" or not, a certain type of film can be characterised by its narrative myths. It is also possible for a film in itself to become, on a symbolic level, a myth. This last category refers to a cult film that testifies to a culture through the interaction between it and its audience. Certain points deserve to be explained further.

First, a cult film is supposed to be ritualised outside the direct connection between the textual contexts of the transmission in cinema or on television; the audience is "implied" in this process, in the mutation of a film into a cultobject. Let us return to Durkheim's description of the cult as an assembly of rituals, feasts and ceremonies that represent the original character.[69] This implies that a film can become a cult-symbol if these elements are ritualised regularly under different forms referring to the original character: for example, by dancing, music, haircut; a tendency to make a star of the actors; the imitation of certain forms of behaviour in everyday life, or for example the flexibility of John Travolta's knees, Madonna's haircut, the dancing of Elvis Presley or Michael Jackson. Without the audience's participation, the film cannot become a cult phenomenon; this process is not only dependent on intensive promotional advertising.

Participating in a cult phenomena, the connivance between the body of the spectator and the body in the film image is essential to demonstrate how the transfer occurs, even if the attention given to a film in particular does not automatically imply admiration – this is certainly not the case for many spectators of the film THE DEPUTY (1979) by Eloy de la Iglesia. To make clear this connection, I quote Michèle Lagny, who has written on the importance of cinema as a document to analyse society: "Cinema is part of the culture: one could consider it as a witness of ways of thinking or the feeling of a society, even as an agent that arouses certain transformations."[70] This notion of a testifier or agent indicates the presence in that period; fiction films can serve as historical documents that function as agents, an inspiring concept illustrating the role of cinema in a culture. To become a representative witness of a culture, the link with the culture must be very intense. I consider that this relationship goes even further when the film considered shows themes that are taboo. What concerns the Spanish context, the spectators, dedicate their attention to a certain phenomenon, physically, to a sensorial experience in this context, or outside the direct context of transmission, thus, they transfer this testimony. By this intensity of reciprocation between society and spectator, a cult film becomes a testimonial to society at the time.

Auteur cinema

I chose some cult films for which it is essential to grasp the importance of the auteur in relation to the issue of social representation. Certain directors are closely related to specific periods and the theme of my proposition testifies to this. I will explore more precisely this auteur concept (for example by focusing on its style of filming), which implies that these film directors construct their own world that become recognisable by themes or aesthetics. Does the fact of choosing a filmmaker in particular, oppose itself to a general representation of the ideas of a culture? Do we not risk being enclosed inside their world, their universe? It is difficult to formulate a clear answer to this question. One could consider that, besides the aesthetic point of view, the question of the auteur is related to the period in which he or she works; every director possesses his or her own characteristics related to history, but certain may seem more receptive than others to the sensibilities of a certain period.

Very good examples of putting forward cult phenomena are the works by directors Eloy de la Iglesia and Pedro Almodóvar. They illustrate the function of the body as a witness and an agent. Their cinema generated diverse reactions at first: either huge admiration or total rejection. The ambiguity of these personalities and their films meant that the Iglesia phenomenon during the Transition period and later Almodóvar during the Transformation brought about a cult in Spanish society. Why did they receive so much attention? In both cases, the theme dealt with in the historical period concerned is fundamental to understanding the attention given to their work. Both these filmmakers present themes that shake taboos, and this was done over a long period, in a systematic way. They are the most memorable Spanish film directors of marginality.

Eloy de la Iglesia

Born in 1944 of Basque origin, Eloy de la Iglesia began his career as a filmmaker during Francoism, directing Fantasy (Fantasía…3) in 1966. Since then, he has shot 22 films. In late Francoism and the Transition period, from 1970 until 1980, he directed almost one film every year. In the 1980s, he disappeared almost completely from the circuit of Spanish cinema after The Tobacconist of Vallecas (La estanquera de Vallecas) in 1986. Recently, he popped up again with Bulgarian Lovers (Los novios búlgaros, 2002), again about homosexuality. He is famous for approaching difficult themes on marginality, such as drugs, delinquency or homosexuality. When released, his films arouse strong reactions. Iglesia was most successful during the Transition period, due it would seem to the shock produced on spectators by his images, which were perceived as new after a period with Franco's particularly strict censorship.

Reactions in the press were violent. Paul Julian Smith describes the critiques on The Deputy (El diputado) as homophobic:

> To read the accumulated press files in the Filmoteca is to be exposed to an extraordinary catalogue of abuse, some of which is clearly homophobic. Interviewers constantly circle around the question of the director's own sexual preference (the secret that would "explain" the films) and repeatedly ask why he is so interested in homosexuality.[71].

Categorised as a film director of marginality, Iglesia is known for this theme of homosexuality. His work is marked by a schematic language that is provocative, almost like a pamphlet; in The Shoot (El pico, 1983) and The Shoot 2 (El pico 2, 1984) he does not hesitate to frame in a close-up the syringes injecting drugs in the veins. He knows this subject quite well as he himself was addicted to drugs for many years.[72] Iglesia's work can be described as provocative, hard-hitting, strong, radical. He was criticised strongly; as an example among many others, we can quote Casimiro Toreiro: "Simplicity, coarseness, no artistic sense, archetypal abuse, a character of a pamphlet, an absurd imitation of some codified genres by the cinema. Almost all his cinema is political, to tell the truth, almost all his work."[73] In spite of these negative critiques, many of his films were seen by a large audience. This critique, rejection or even disgust at his work marked by homophobic reactions has transformed it into a cult phenomena: the impact of these films was considerable, as were the reactions they aroused. Furthermore, forbidding the film HIDDEN PLEASURES (LOS PLACERES OCULTOS, 1976) led to the first "gay" demonstration in Spain.[74] Showing these bodies on a big screen provoked a direct link with society by the ritual of spectators, who went to demonstrate on the street, underlining the taboos of society. In this way, the cult phenomenon was shown outside the direct textual context of the perception of the public.

Iglesia's success declined strongly in the 1980s as spectators were becoming used to this theme, which was also being shown by other directors. This declining interest in his films indicates that actors, like "agent bodies" aroused, by their image, a transformation of what the public wants to see. Iglesia constructed his work on marginality using a schematic approach typical for him; he reacts to the general desire to see forbidden images from Francoism. The schematic approach simplifies the reading and imposes a unique interpretation of the "good homosexual" and the "bad rightwing politician": Iglesia incarnates the image of opposition that is too excessive, and therefore opposed to ideas in vigour under Franco.

Almodóvar

In the 1980s, another phenomenon appeared in Spanish cinema: Pedro Almodóvar (1951). His personality has marked Spanish cinema. As Mark Allinson remarks, his name carries some fascinating connotations: "Almodóvar" means place of liberty or liberating slaves, which Allinson describes as a successful coincidence when he introduces this filmmaker as an auteur of liberated Spain.[75] Born in La Mancha under Francoism, he was in his twenties when Franco died.[76] His youth was marked by excitement – at 17 years old he moved to Madrid to become a "hippie". A trip to London was an obligatory part of this training, as the city at that time represented liberty and tolerance. He was also strongly influenced by the events of May 1968 in France that inspired many young people to lead a sort of hippie culture in Spain. He lived fully through the *Movida Madrileña*:[77] he was considered a leader.[78] During that period, Almodóvar made provocative cinema and the titles of his first films illustrate a strong interest in sexuality. After his first short film dating from 1974, TWO WHORES OR LOVE STORY THAT ENDS IN A WEDDING and POLITICAL FILM, followed by THE FALL OF SODOM (1975), TRIBUTE, (1975), THE DREAM OR THE STAR (1975), WHITENESS (1975). He then directed several film trailers: WHO'S AFRAID OF VIRGINIA WOOLF (1976), BE CHARITABLE (1976), PONTE'S THREE ADVANTAGES (1977), SEX COMES, SEX GOES (1977), COMPLEMENTOS (1977), FUCK...FUCK...FUCK ME, TIM (1978) and SALOMÉ (1978).[79] In 1980, he released his first feature film: PEPI LUCI

BOM AND OTHER GIRLS ON THE HEAP. Then LABYRINTH OF PASSIONS (1982), DARK HABITS (1983), WHAT HAVE I DONE TO DESERVE THIS (1984), MATADOR (1986), LAW OF DESIRE (1987), WOMEN ON THE VERGE OF A NERVOUS BREAK-DOWN (1988), TIE ME UP! TIE ME DOWN! (1989), HIGH HEELS (1991), KIKA (1993), THE FLOWER OF MY SECRET (1995), LIVE FLESH (1997), ALL ABOUT MY MOTHER (1998), TALK TO HER (2002), BAD EDUCATION (2004), TO RETURN (2006) and BRO-KEN EMBRACES (2009).[80]

Recognition of his work in Spanish cinema lasted a long time. He was considered odd, as he did not behave in the way expected of a filmmaker, also sang in a rock band, took provocative attitudes, and provoked scandals by his presence. He became a sort of fetish, a "locomotive" that makes fashion.[81] But like Iglesia, in spite of the critiques, he also had a faithful audience in his country and significant success abroad. The Almodóvar phenomenon represents a cult in Spanish society due to the ambiguity of his personality and his work: he knows how to use publicity to stimulate a cult image of himself; the audience wants more and participates actively in its consecration.

How can one define the specificity of the Almodóvar cult phenomenon? First by the enormous amount of spectators in the 1980s and 1990s:[82] with the feature film WOMEN ON THE VERGE OF A NERVOUS BREAKDOWN, he had the same number of spectators as Berlanga's THE HEIFER (LA VAQUILLA, 1985).[83] This continued with his other films, such as HIGH HEELS (1991), THE FLOWER OF MY SECRET (1995), LIVE FLESH (1997), ALL ABOUT MY MOTHER (1998), TALK TO HER (2002), BAD EDUCATION (2002) and TO RETURN (2006). Pedro Almodóvar is simultaneously adored, well known and rejected in Spain. He is certainly recognised as a prominent filmmaker in his own country. On the other hand, he was awarded Goyas (the Spanish national film prize) only rarely in the 1980s and 1990s,[84] when he was selected by the same Academy to represent Spain abroad for the Oscars. The awards given to this filmmaker changed at the end of the 1980s, and the interaction between the Oscar and the Goya is fascinating: when his film WOMEN ON THE VERGE OF A NERVOUS BREAKDOWN was nominated for the 1988 Oscars in the category of Best Foreign Language Film, one year later he received a Goya for the same film in the category Best Script. In 1999, awarded an Oscar for ALL ABOUT MY MOTHER (Best Foreign Language Film), he began finally to be considered for the Goyas in 2000, receiving for the Goyas for Best Film and Best Director. This tendency continued, with his films then regularly being nominated for the Goyas in the category Best Film. In 2003, TALK TO HER was nominated, and in 2005 BAD EDUCATION. After these two nominations, the film TO RETURN received the Goya Award for the Best Director and the Best Film in 2007. In 2006 he also received the Prince of Asturias award, a prestigious award for the arts.

To RETURN was also internationally marked by the famous film actress Pené-lope Cruz, who received a Goya for Best Principal Female Actor in 2007. Cruz also represents a typical icon of Almodóvar's cinema. Indeed, the director knew from the beginning that it would help to create a Spanish star-system, launching a group of actors that thanks to him became famous and a cult phenomenon in itself: the girls and boys ("chicas and chicos") of Almodóvar. This refers to Antonio Banderas, Victoria Abril, Carmen Maura, Penélope Cruz, Marisa Paredes, Bibi Andersen and Rossy de Palma. Even if Antonio Banderas had already played in other films, such as STILTS (LOS ZANCOS, 1984) by Carlos Saura, it is thanks to Almodóvar's films that he became such a star and could begin a career in Hollywood. The same is true of Carmen Maura, who helped to launch Almodóvar's first films. Both were not that well known and became famous together.[85] For Victoria Abril, the situation was a little different as she was also the main actress in Vicente Aranda's cinema; however, her reputation abroad stems above all from her roles in Almodóvar's films. One might say the same of Marisa Paredes, a brilliant female actor who played in HIGH HEELS, THE FLOWER OF MY SECRET and ALL ABOUT MY MOTHER. The list also includes the beautiful Penélope Cruz, who has played in several films such as LIVE FLESH, ALL ABOUT MY MOTHER and TO RETURN. These roles stimulated her international career.

Besides these celebrities, one must not forget Bibi Andersen, present in HIGH HEELS and LAW OF DESIRE. Bibi Andersen also played in the film SEX CHANGE (1977) by Vicente Aranda, in which he had changed gender and was transformed into a very beautiful woman, apparently she is really transsexual. Bibi Andersen represents liberty as she has shown significant courage to make such a choice about her own body and to assume it openly; she is very famous in Spain. The excellent female actor Rossy de Palma, who plays, for example, in WOMEN ON THE VERGE OF A NERVOUS BREAKDOWN, TIE ME UP! TIE ME DOWN!, THE FLOWER OF MY SECRET must also be mentioned. De Palma has a cubist beauty and became a phenomenon for her face, which can be compared to the female faces painted by Picasso; she is particularly known thanks to Almodóvar's. To all these actors we must add Veronica Forque, Juliette Serrano and María Barranco, among the most famous and closely related to his cinema.

Another aspect of the cult phenomenon passes through the film's music. Most of the original soundtracks were distributed on record. Luz Casal's song *Think of me (Piensa en mi)* from HIGH HEELS was a hit in 1991-1992,[86] illustrating this secondary level of the cult ritual in Spanish society through the music. Another aspect is the "typical" character of Almodóvar's films: he was able to create an auteur cinema that makes that his productions are recognisable so that they can be decontextualised. Almodóvar's humour, the bodies of the actors and their way of behaving, the manner of describing reality, is all so personal that the perceived situation can typically be a throw-back to a scene out of Almodóvar's films. Another reason to consider his cinema as cult is the fact that it was rather provocative, particularly films from the 1980s, such as PEPI, LUCI, BOM AND OTHER GIRLS ON THE HEAP, DARK HABITS, or LAW OF DESIRE. Such a visual provocation on themes such as religion, drugs and homosexuals always provokes a reaction and attracts attention.

Visual transformation

The social and historical representation of the three main groups of this book (women, homosexuals and delinquency) will be scrutinised in the chapters on film analysis. However, focusing on the point of view of the director, the function of the filmmaker will be dealt with differently for Garci, Uribe, Saura and Aranda. Despite Imanol Uribe and Vicente Aranda treading marginally on the pushing film's boundaries, they do not make cult films. During the Transition, Eloy de la Iglesia and Almodóvar in the 1980s are exceptions as they dominated Spanish cinema, bursting through preconceived ideas on marginality. Both directors did not need words to shake the taboos; rather, they exposed this brutally by and through the bodies. Their highly provocative work is important for the representation of certain long-hidden realities in Spain. Hereby framing and representing these social thoughts, they put these characters in the foreground whose ideas were previously considered to be abnormal (e.g.: homosexuals and drug addicts, rejected during the Francoist period, previously kept in the background). Their films therefore made the spectator more lucid. They gave prominence to these human beings that in the past were hidden, now treating them as normal. This was a social provocation for society, a ritual of passage from one phase to the other, initiated through and by the bodies, by the actors of their films, viewed and celebrated by a faithful audience. These filmmakers were provocative agents of "post-Francoism": agents of the Transformation, like a phase of a visual passage, lived through by a culture.

III. Updating the archetype

Themes of rupture and liberation permeate post-Franco film. Their presence is more than ever felt in the way Almodóvar updates the archetypes reflected in his bodies, particularly the archetypes pertaining to the myth of motherhood. Almodóvar's bodies present the most revealing examples of the maternal body as well as a critique of the maternal archetype. Archetypal maternal values clearly revolve around the protection of the child: educating and nurturing are often considered typical female gestures. However, while the Almodóvarian bodies exemplify these values, they do not always do so by way of the traditional image. In LAW OF DESIRE (1987) Carmen Maura's body represents a transsexual and plays the role of the maternal character. She is accompanied by Bibi Andersen: a real transsexual playing the biological mother. In ALL ABOUT MY MOTHER (1998) it is the father who is disguised as a woman and another mother adopts his son. These transsexual and transvestite bodies undoubtedly express the feelings of motherhood; they are good mothers, confirming archetypal values. Conversely, their bodies are opposed to the norm; their atypical bodies thus function to question traditional values and interrogate conventional thoughts conjured and expressed by physical appearances. By giving a historical aspect to the myth, the relationship between the archetype and contemporary language, expressed visually by the body, illustrates the process of constructing new mythological figures. In order to better frame this exploration of archetypes, it is necessary to define certain parameters to clarify the subject.

The historical context

After having commented on it in the Introduction, let us review Jung's ideas about archetypes. Defined as original images, they are reconstructed in time and space, in every culture, by appropriated means. Archetypes are original values; they are cultural roots, images that always have a meaning about what is "evil" or "good", etc. In cinema the body updates these original values by structuring them in symbols which refer to a contemporary context and language;[87] for example, Carmen is the figure of the Spanish *femme fatale* and is often adapted and modernised to mirror the times. The same can be said with regard to the hero; Arnold Schwarzenegger in the TERMINATOR felt inspired, even outside the cinematographic context. The current image of the body thus inhabits the costume of the existing myth, giving the image of the body pertinent and updated cultural and historical connotations: the myth is thereby historicised, through the concrete expression given to it by the restructured image as seen through the body.

To define the relationship between history and myth, the distinction introduced by Paul Ricoeur between a "historical time" and "mythological time" is valuable. Historical time is that which represents the time of events. The fact that Franco died in 1975 refers to historical time. Mythological time is cyclical, as in Christmas returning every year.[88] An archetype exists in mythological time, on a latent level, and is updated at a given historical moment. The example of the femme fatale illustrates this point quite well; the archetype of the *femme fatale* exists in a mythological time in all cultures: Carlos Saura gives his version in 1983, with the film CARMEN.

The film RACE offers an example of the Barthesian analysis of myth. By providing us with a naturalistic vision of history, this propagandistic fiction uses the Francoist myth to justify the power of dictatorship. While I disagree with the Barthesian analysis which claims that all myths "naturalise" the past, I do contend that the Barthesian approach to understanding myth, one that places great importance on context, is worthy; context is of crucial significance. This well-known film demonstrates the importance of the historical context. This same film also allows for the illustration of the link between origin and mythological time. Every myth refers to it, as Mircea Eliade formulated it so well: "Knowing myths is like discovering the secret origin of things. In other words, one learns not only how things come to life but also where to find them and how to make them reappear when they disappear."[89] A myth can thus show the origin of certain phenomena and a new myth can give a new interpretation of the very same roots. Commenting on history related to a myth implies a commentary on the birth of myth. RACE interprets tendentiously the mythological concept of the origin of Eternal Spain. To justify Francoist victory, the Civil War and the taking over of power, the myth is dressed up as new in the exemplary image of the children as founders of this novel society. They function as models for the Spanish race and as the gatekeepers of Eternal Spain. The myth of Eternal Spain appears therefore as the foundation of all interpretations of history, buttressing the story as a natural and therefore inevitable evolution. This rendition of history serves the interests of those in power and through analysis points to both the origin of the myth and its opportunistic re-articulation.

In this concept of myth, history is therefore presented on two levels: by the image of the body that updates the myth to exhibit contextual symbols (the historical time) and by the interrogation of an origin (mythological time). To allow for the reading of mythological thought in a film, an analysis of the ritual is fundamental. Two phases illustrate how to analyse this process: the first consists in interrogating the archetypal values inside the given culture. The second is in constructing a new myth through the use of the image of the body. In this process, it should be made clear that the ritual and the myth are not intrinsically united; every ritualistic action is not a myth; all mythology is not ritualised. With regard to ritual proper, institutionalised and new forms must be distinguished. In both types of ritual, the body incarnates the ritual and presents it, but assumes as well a different function, which differs according to context. In the institutionalised ritual, the body submits it, conforms to it, and carries it out. On the other hand, the new ritual takes a position, which shows more initiative, and interrogates the archetypal values through its actions. A new ritual therefore not only constructs new expressions but also questions the very values which underlie its functioning.

This second step provokes cultural reactions to the phenomena introduced, because the updating of archetypal values often implies a reaction to the existing tradition. This invites us to understand the meaning of the myth as it is now juxtaposed to its refashioned form. Let us think of the reactions of rejection of the new bodies of Iglesia' cinema; making homosexuality visible in HIDDEN PLEASURES (1976) led to the prohibition of the film. The introduction of the new image of the body was cast off by censorship. Even if this visibility was done in contrast to the possibilities of expression during dictatorship, it was still not possible to represent everything. Moreover, one should mention that the protagonists in these films introduce, through inventive images of their body, their gender identity, emphasising that this identity is a social problem for them.

Therefore, when analysing these films, the idea of conflict is revealing and two concepts introduced by Claude Lévi-Strauss are useful: the binary opposition and the mediator. The binary opposition represents a conflict between two incompatible things, such as life and death, nature and culture, love and hate.[90] When introducing new phenomena, the term "new" already contains a binary opposition with the term "old", the latter representing tradition (implying areas of forbidden topics, of refusal and rejection). As demonstrated with Iglesia's cinema, introducing new phenomena is often accompanied by a reaction to an existing situation. The mediator triggers a reaction, one necessitating the recognition of binary dependence, and this is essential because both opposing concepts have some aspects in common; one cannot exist without the other. It is thus in this antagonistic context of these two opposing figures that the mediator provides his image. Mediators are characters in myths that have to find a solution to this opposition and they consequently function as negotiators in the resolution of this conflict.[91] The solution encountered illustrates the definition of the archetype in its modernised expression. The transvestite mothers and transsexuals in Almodóvar' cinema function in the same way; they are mediators and as such they live as a homosexual couple, negotiate the biological impossibility for a man to have children and express maternal feelings. Through these Almodóvarian bodies, groundbreaking mythological figures of motherhood are created by the mediator disguised as a woman and behaving as a good mother. In the context of archetypal values of motherhood, these multi-gender bodies or the presence of homosexual couples challenges traditional expectations of the family with regard to motherhood or fatherhood.

The body: a thought-image

Again it is the peculiar image of the body, which instigates a flurry of thought about oppositions and their mediators. Exploring these figures in cinema, dance becomes particularly inspiring, as it provides very interesting analyses. Accompanied by music, it is above all the body that makes the choreography speak. The dancer expresses a thought image and the body is like an expression of a thought in movement, as Paul Valéry describes it: "That woman who was there is devoured by countless faces. That body, in its glaring vigour, propositions me with extreme thoughts."[92] This image of the body, through its gestures, its actions and its expressions clearly allows for the expression of a thought. It represents an image of norms and values in a culture, which can help us to define myth. We think that our body belongs to us, but in our behaviour we are conditioned by the moral rules of our culture. Michel Bernard exposes very well this idea of the body in a society: "since all of the behaviour which we believe to be natural of our bodies, reveals itself to be not only styled by society, but also given its meaning, as a symbol of society."[93] Undeniably, the representation of the body can introduce new thoughts that refer to norms and values of a culture. The numerous bodies in Almodóvar' cinema are witnesses to this process as they break through key aspects of tradition. Even an ordinary and simple image of a body can be filled with norms: the body is like a motor for new construction when it questions, for example, traditional clichés.

The symbolic: stereotype, prototype, cliché

The interaction between the actors is another issue to explore, as several thought-images of the body will meet and be contrasted, which makes it necessary to define their figuration more precisely. In the entire narration, the mythological motif of the archetype stays present at a latent level. By the figuration of the body, it will be updated by a contemporary thought-image of the body, which can symbolise stereotypes, clichés, or prototypes, referring still on a latent level to archetypes. How can one understand this interaction of concepts through physical images? How do these thought-images of the body permit the construction of a mythological thought of the body?

Different aspects have to be defined to respond to these questions. Firstly, a culturally codified thought-image is conveyed through the symbolic of the body as reflected through its chosen gestures, movements and corporal expressions. Then this symbolic can also represent stereotyped values that have a strong link with myths: we view them as historicised codes because the cultural values are related to particular periods. These cultural values represent a sort of categorisation, reducing or even simplifying reality, serving to recognise social phenomena, but they do not imply an endorsement of the verity of these images. These cultural values are pre-conceived frames, familiar schemas typically negatively connoted.

Watching films, we are able to recognise these stereotypes of social life. Ruth Amossy describes them as a construction of a reading:

> The stereotype does not exist in and of itself. A stereotype is apparent only to the critical observer or to the spectator who can spontaneously recognise the models in their collective. The stereotype emerges once, in the selection of the characteristics or attributes of a group or situation, a familiar schema is constructed.[94]

To explore Spanish cinema, it is essential to dedicate a lot of importance to context. Firstly there is a context inside the film. When evaluating the stereotypes, can one say that the context of the image reinforces the idea that the stereotypes transmit? Or is the hackneyed representation used for the purposes of irony? In sum, what meaning is given in the film itself to the stereotype? Secondly, a cultural, historical and political context exists outside the film. How will these kinds of stereotypes be read within Spanish culture? Concerning Almodóvar's films and Carlos Saura's work after Francoism, rich in stereotypes, it is absolutely necessary to situate these productions within these two contexts of questioning.

The relationship of myth-stereotype or myth-archetype is another significant aspect of analysis to keep in mind. Ruth Amossy draws attention to the stereotype that can be transformed into a mythological model: "The fabrication of the stereotype constitutes the first phase of making myth. While it may be necessary, it is certainly not enough."[95] She begins with the construction of a familiar schema. Following her line of thinking, I consider that the stereotype provides the frame to be recognised. Then, I argue that it is also possible to establish a contrast between the stereotype and an exemplary character, a prototypical body. For example, in the Francoist myth in RACE, the son Pedro chose a political career, a choice that the Francoist thesis considered to be an error during the Civil War. In the whole film he is stereotyped as a rebellious boy, a body connoted by the negative aspects of his behaviour as he does not listen to his parents or is unable to understand the words expressed by his father. Whereas the other son, José, chose a military career and accordingly delivers the exemplary image of the prototypical body within the Francoist norm. This interaction is revealing; it is evident that a stereotype permits to recognise certain phenomena. The categorisation of the anti-Franco body is anchored by negative aspects and therefore reduces reality. The prototypical body, however, is exemplary, carrying positive attributes for the social category that the body represents. Without a doubt, behaviour, image and gestures are presented as exemplary for a social identity translating the values of vigour in the culture of that time.

The values of this historical period are so underscored by these two bodies, that, in opposing them, the difference is blatant and leads to a reflection on the norm. The stereotype shows what should be changed; the prototype is the example to be followed. Both bodies refer tacitly to archetypal values. In RACE, the archetype of Eternal Spain upholds the idea of a strong Catholic kingdom on

Spanish earth, which is made concrete during the Civil War, thanks to the heroic military actions of the son José. It is this historicised body that incarnates this myth in the film, in 1941. It is a prototypical body: the ideal to emulate. Another figuration was observed in WELCOME, MR MARSHALL! (1953): the mayor is stereotyped as an American, representing a cowboy. The positive example given at the end of the film is like waking up: one should have faith and live in reality, and not nurture ideas of greatness. These examples illustrate my approach to explore the stereotype and the prototype, by always drawing attention to the dominant ideology of the film in its historical and cultural context. The concepts utilised in this research are therefore not conceptual definitions, but always empirical, functioning inside their context.

The cliché is the last aspect to mention in defining the symbolic of the body. A cliché is a thought or a symbol on a body that is too often utilised and therefore read as a cliché-image; a cliché can be described as a predictable and overused image. Basically, a stereotypical or exemplary idea can be encountered in this image, but the reading depends on the way it is rendered and the cultural context of its presentation. The image of the bullfighter for a Spanish tourism commercial is a good example of a stereotyped image of Spain. The image allows for the immediate recognition of autochthonic symbols. It is a reduced idea of the country and thus from this point of view a stereotype; but for foreigners it can be read as a prototype of Spanish exotics. Repeating this preconceived frame converts it into a cliché-body, and the context of its reading enables us to know if we are dealing with a stereotype or a prototype. When the image is used to advertise a bullfight in Madrid at "*Las Ventas*", the bullfighter is shown to be authentic and can be seen as a prototype of a bullfighter who is very brave and well known: a model to imitate. Another reading can be made by the detractors of bullfighting who perceive this image of a bullfighter as a stereotype, as a reduced game, as a mise-en-scene of strength in a battle that is, in principle, not equal. The cliché will thus be born due to repetition. The context of its presentation is therefore fundamental to interpret its reading. Accordingly, in this book, the film analyses are constantly situated in the context of the film plot and greater Spanish culture.

The choreography of the ritual

Three concepts are essential to analyse films: the body, the ritual and mythological thought; these are analysed in the plot by focusing on the aesthetic expression of the point of view and its mise-en-scene. My research presents mainstream films, which were box office successes. This means that they are mostly based on the structure of the classical Hollywood film, introducing a problem in the opening sequence that will be resolved in the plot. Inside the narration, I'll define a mythological plot, formed around a binary opposition in which the body serves as a mediator looking for a solution as demonstrated through the rituals that take place.

With regard to rituals, the mise-en-scene of the body is fundamental; this aspect has been extensively considered. Again dance provides an inspiring example: defined by the presence of choreography, we observe bodies displacing themselves on stage, carried by music, and we focus on their movements. Seeing a film is like a reading of the actor's movements, through which they express behaviour and which subsequently allows us to understand the narration. Directing the behaviour of the actors requires the formulation of rules about how to put their expressions onto stage; the bodies move to construct a certain image, the image created is a thought, and the filmmaker hopes that the result will correspond to his own mental image. The choreography of the movements of the body, expressed by the mise-en-scene of the film, creates images in time and space that gives a structure to the mythological thought.

These expressions help in discerning the moral meaning of the conflict; the image of the body is not neutral, because the aesthetics of its mise-en-scene presupposes a point of view. I refer to an article written by Jacques Aumont, which examines the concept of the point of view in cinema.[96] He distinguishes four types. The first is based on the camera that indicates the object that is seen: it is the relationship between the camera and the object. The second concerns the captured image: here the frame is fundamental. The third is the spectator's given meaning of the second view. Finally, the fourth is the mental attitude that one attributes to the third point of view: it is the mental attitude to the object. Let us follow this reasoning: the body serves to provide a general point of view, because it is the mediator and proposes a solution at the end. The first type of point of view shows the body, the second the image that is the result of the framing imposing a thought on the body; the third point of view is based on our interpretation that is based on the way the image is shown. For example, the myth of Carmen, played by Laura del Sol, is the icon of a beautiful, seductive woman. The narrator inside the film, Gades, determines his image of her by his gaze, a gaze that is central in the plot. On the other hand, the fourth point of view can be distanced from it, remarking that in the end, the filmmaker's point of view is the camera and so it determines the entire shot. The body negotiates in this way the point of view on the conflict and illustrates its solution.

In this mise-en-scene, the rituals question two concepts: time and space. Concerning time, I already mentioned that the body connotes the concepts of the historical time. The thought-image of the body symbolises the stereotype, the prototype or the cliché and deals with this identity in relation to a certain period. The body is henceforth transformed into a sort of historical testifier. Another level of time proposed by the body questions the origin: rituals are expressed in the film, which foreground mythological time. With flash-backs or voice-over an image of the body is created that permits the questioning of the significance of this period. This is the case, for example, when a character is remembering his childhood in relation to a current problem. Cinema is very convenient for visualising the origins of a problem from the past, bringing up a problem from long ago that is still important in the current situation: a flash-back of an adult character, figuring his body as a child, makes possible the examination of the past in a mythological time of origin, relating it to the current problem of this body.

Then space frames these rituals into a specific place. This is important to capture the meaning of the mythological thought. To explain its function, space can be divided into two concepts that are closely related: a concrete space, by its material composition, and an imaginary space that is situated rather in the field of ideas, where we encounter myths, fairy tales, religion, fantasies and beliefs. This ultimate space can only be experienced in relationship to a concrete site, which has been institutionalised by social structures. One should think of the spatial organisation of a society that is constituted by concrete sites. All the edifices that represent the institutions of a society function according to a certain perspective, which makes them appear imposing. The manner of organising space, for example, through the architecture in cities, is not neutral, but rather carries in itself a cultural connotation. The concrete space is indicative of a society, which makes it a symbolic language as well.

To illustrate the link between myths and space one just has to look at the number of American films that show a court, with a jury composed of everyday people. Placing emphasis on this aspect underlines its symbolic value, affirming the importance of the justice system. Joseph Campbell[97] explains this utility of myths for a culture: by their moral contribution they glorify the unity of a country and they sustain faith in justice. According to Campbell, the Americans lack foundational myths, as the people come from different cultural backgrounds, which may explain the importance and social value attributed to the law. Another recurrent image in American cinema is the showing of "the statue of liberty and justice" in New York. It symbolises the confidence in justice in this new world, underlining the faith in justice that is represented by the jury. In a different way, and without considering it as a foundational myth, the symbol of space can be encountered in certain films of the *destape* in the Franco periods: we can mention, as an example THOU SHALT NOT COVET THY FIFTH FLOOR NEIGHBOUR (NO DESEARÁS AL VECINO DEL QUINTO, 1970) by Ramón Fernández, which was extremely successful. Most of the action was shot in the bedroom: this location is questioned concerning certain ideas, evidently in a different way to those posed in an American court. This presence marks the importance of the subject related to certain forbidden topics in the Franco periods.

The introduction of a new ritual in a place can provoke conflicts. When the body is imposing the rituals, this works almost like a dialogue with a decor, with the Other projecting his thoughts on it. Referring to dance, José Gil observes that it is particularly revealing for marking a place; when a dancer moves on stage, it is as if his body possesses space:

> It is certain that the site of the ritual can be likened to that of a stage: the transformation of space by the possessed body during ritual is similar to the transformation of space carried out by the modern dancer. Both evolve in an objective space that, through a mix, the moving body sculpts the space itself. The issue is thus to understand how objective space allows itself to be contaminated by the space and movement of the body.[98]

His analysis places the body in the foreground, dominating the site; this encounter seems to me like a dialogue with the Other. Observing the physical movements transforms a place; as a dancer transforms space with his body, an actor is doing this in a film; through his gestures, his actions, his movements, his energy transforms space by living through and experiencing a ritual. As the body moves, it encounters different sites and the images show this movement and change as a dialogue that serves to explain the negotiation of the conflict.

Body, ritual (space-time) and mythological thought are the analytical parameters used to understand the mise-en-scene of a choreography. The filmic images are always the point of departure and the body and the ritual are resolute guides. The rituals will reveal the meaning of the mythological thought. Within this framework, we will focus on the new image of gender and delinquency, which is articulated in the change in the representation of the female body and in the appearance of the homosexual and the delinquent body.

2. The liberation of women

Over a span of twenty years, the cinematographic imaginary of Spanish film underwent a perceptible and interesting change. The examination of certain myths, particularly those pertaining to work and sexuality, provide an acute perspective of this modification. Focusing on work and sexuality will allow us to study the transformation of the imaginary as well as the evolution of the legal and social background of that time. The films FLUNKING OUT (ASIGNATURA PENDIENTE), CARMEN and HIGH HEELS (TACONES LEJANOS), provide both excellent and original images, illustrating changes in the representation of women in the pre and post-Franco era.

Several traditional representations were modified. Before 1975, the question of equality was posed differently, above all about work. During the Franco period, women who worked were viewed with disdain. Unable to work without social ramifications, their situation was worsened by legal constraints. Women were required to provide proof of their husband's explicit consent, for example, to open a bank account.[1] As women could only leave their parental home to get married or to follow a religious vocation, they lived their lives in complete economic dependence, first on their parents and then on their husbands. The fiction MAIN STREET (LA CALLE MAYOR, 1957) by Juan Antonio Bardem refers to this situation. Yet there were also other legal restrictions: a woman did not have the right to travel alone. Indeed, her main and only valid task was to dedicate herself entirely to her family, to her children.[2] Furthermore, contraception was illegal. Thus, families were numerous. The mere possessing of contraception, even the seeking out for information about abortion or contraception was sanctioned by a term of imprisonment (art. 416 of the law).[3] Until 1981, still due to Franco's limiting politics, it was impossible to get divorced. This constricting legal situation clearly contrasts with the permitted liberties under the Second Republic (1931-1939) when divorce was possible and contraception was freely discussed in magazine articles.[4]

The situation changes during the Transition period: between 1977 and 1985, the use of contraception increased enormously from the moment when the Penal Code, in 1977/1978, permitted its possession.[5] The law on abortion was modified in 1985.[6] Before that, women had to go to England, France or the Netherlands to have an abortion.[7] The birth rate was the highest in the 1960s while it is currently the lowest in Europe.[8] Finally, in cases of adultery, women had been punished much more severely. For a man, he would have to impose his mistress in the family home, demanding his wife accept her, to be committing an offence before the law.[9] A modification of the Penal Code in 1977/1978 removed these inequalities.[10]

The juxtaposition of the conditions described above illustrates an important change in the area of work and sexuality, crucial topics for that period. Since the image of a woman need to be redefined and in order to encourage equality, in 1983 the Spanish government created the Women' Institute (*Instituto de la Mujer*), by the law 16/83, on 24 October. This department of the Ministry of Culture was: "charged to promote and stimulate the conditions that permit the social equality of both sexes and the participation of women in political, cultural, economic and social life."[11] Cinema reflects on this debate about repositioning and reformulating the position of women in that period.

The stereotyped body

Feminist studies have widely observed the stereotyped body in cinema. The publication by Laura Mulvey, *Visual Pleasure and Narrative Cinema*[12] is still a groundbreaking text. She often revised this work, which makes a synthesis of her reflections more difficult. The central idea of her 1975 text was that in classical Hollywood cinema, the female body was observed by a masculine gaze, set up by the camera, by the other characters and by the spectators. The exchange between these three gazes expresses patriarchal power. For her interpretations, Mulvey refers to psychoanalytical theories (Freud, Lacan). What one retains from her text is the thesis of the absence of a penis for a woman which, according to Freudian theories, provokes a fear of castration in men. This masculine anguish incites two types of behaviour: fetishism (observing a woman as a spectacle, like a star, a singer or a dancer) or submission (punishing a woman by imposing rigorous acts upon her, which lead to her death). There were numerous reactions to Mulvey's work, from criticising it to confirming her analyses in other national cinemas. All these reactions, all the articles that have been written on her work, testify to the historical value of this publication, which is unquestionable, because her thoughts have set off passionate debates on women's representation in cinema and about the masculine gaze.

According to this perspective, feminist studies have widely observed the corporal cinematographic stereotypes with the will to break through them, to denounce sexism or the passive image of submission. On this last aspect, feminist studies were strongly criticised concerning the first periods, the 1960s and 1970s. Ginette Vincendeau explains in her historical overview that the first tendencies of the feminist critiques started at the end of the 1960s with a militant feminism. She then observes an important change in the 1970s, when the mechanism of cinematographic figures was analysed, basing themes, among others, on semiotic and psychoanalytical theories (as the text by Mulvey demonstrates).[13] Nevertheless, Vincendeau underscores the importance of this first movement: "I'll add that if this kind of research was afterwards discredited, it would only be fair to recognise its value as it did fulfil the double function of launching feminist studies and provoking a re-reading of classical American cinema."[14] This movement was fundamental because a change was necessary. For a long time, this fixation on the stereotype to denounce the sexist gaze posed on women was the standard practice in cinematographic studies. Related to these first publications at the beginning of the 1970s, Francesco Casetti critiques the way many researchers got stuck on noting only this aspect, while it would have been more interesting to highlight the functionality of the concept:

> Opposing stereotype and reality does not lead anywhere: what one should question is why cinema has a mise-en-scene of fixed figures, to what extent the portraits of women are more banal than others, how factual truth can be expressed on the screen, and in what way a film is always a re-elaboration of the existent. In other words, one should ask oneself what is the function of a stereotype, before accusing it; like one should ask oneself under what condition reality can be shown before evoking it.[15]

As Casetti indicates, the functionality of fixed images is revealing. With regard to current studies, the stereotype clearly lends itself to other readings: it reveals itself to be efficient for detecting the will to change. The stereotype of the female body serves as a frame to recognising preconceived ideas: the passive, submissive and dependant woman can only be defined as being a stereotype when a change has already been achieved in society.

This chapter started with a description of the legal situation of Spanish women with regard to sexuality and work during the Franco periods. In relation to these issues, it is undoubtedly interesting to focus on the construction of new clichés of women in their national cinema. So we will examine the introduction of a stereotyped image in the film FLUNKING OUT (ASIGNATURA PENDIENTE, 1977), which demonstrates the way in which a woman wishes to change her professional life as well as how she manages her sexual freedom. Indeed, introducing the passive and submissive woman in a film during this period seems to designate a prefixed frame that demands a change; it shows the will to create new images about her social identity. By taking the perspective of the woman, a critical view is offered of the historical and cultural context. Starting with a film from 1977, then relating it to CARMEN (1983) and HIGH HEELS (TACONES LEJANOS, 1991) enables us to examine the way some fixed ideas develop over a longer period. Three functions are established: the stereotype is largely set up in 1977, interrogated in 1983, and displaced to allow other gazes in 1991. It is interesting to notice (without wishing to re-iterate the Freudian thesis put forward by Mulvey) the gendered gaze of the filmic forms. A watchful eye will notice the process of constructing new female images in the typical Spanish language of the 1970s through the *tercera vía*, flamenco dance steps and dramatic songs against a typical Almodóvar backdrop (HIGH HEELS).

The film directors

The directors of the three feature films that will be scrutinised here are known for putting a female character at the centre of the plot. The first film, which is by José Luis Garci, delivers a representative model of the stream *tercera vía*, known in the 1970s for its progressive topics, which meant staging a woman in an image which differs from the depictions of the previous period. The second film-maker, Carlos Saura, also put women at the centre of his narratives. During the Franco periods, he was married for a long time to Geraldine Chaplin;[16] they met in 1965. Between 1967 and 1980 she was the protagonist in eight of his productions. Saura comments openly on this cultural difference: "For more than ten years I shared my life and my films with Geraldine. She changed my concept of women and introduced me to the Anglo-Saxon world, so admired, so different from ours."[17] The couple's separation ended their collaboration as well. The third film, directed by Pedro Almodóvar, also gives a prominent role to women: he shows them with their desires for a professional career, their emotions, and their sexuality. As Susan Martin-Márquez comments, he is often considered a typical "women-director", and also a creator of "gay cinema."[18] Even so, she mentions explicitly the violence towards women in his cinema, so the reading of him as a "women-director" implies a diversity of reactions, viewing him at times with hostility, as much Anglo-American research confirms.[19]

In this context it is fitting to include a Dutch reading. The highly regarded film critic Hans Beerekamp shares this impression, describing Almodóvar as misogynous.[20] The Dutch film scholar, Joris Henguet explored what it could mean to describe Almodóvar as a "women's filmmaker", including Beerekamp's reactions in Dutch newspapers.[21] Scrutinising different readings about the violence committed in his films, the Anglo-American readings often focus on the rape sequence in KIKA and TALK TO HER, or the kidnapping in TIE ME UP! TIE ME DOWN!, with the victim (Victoria Abril) falling in love with her kidnapper (Antonio Banderas). These films gave the impression that Almodóvar is openly misogynous. Reactions have shown that violence is bearable when there is a rejection inside the film. The spectator feels uncomfortable when rape is shown within a comedy, as in KIKA.

In his book on Almodóvar, Mark Allinson also focuses on these films, considering that the sequence in KIKA was too long and does not work as it should have. Allinson follows this critique with an explanation of how society reacts: he comments that the refusal to rate the film in the United States was tantamount to censorship as without labelling, distribution was made impossible.[22] The second example, TIE ME UP! TIE ME DOWN! was given an X rating, associating it pornography. The third example, TALK TO HER, had an internal judgment as the protagonist, Benigno, ended up in prison for this crime.[23] The possible misogynous reading of Almodóvar's cinema is still debated by many scholars, who study these films or sequences, exploring them in order to place this label of women's director on his cinema.[24] In order to be provocative, Almodóvar may have flirted with boundaries, which led without any doubt to some misplaced sequences. As he typically creates his own artistic world, in a new and daring way, he certainly goes to the edge in terms of moral judgements. The violence against women is disturbing in the films we have cited, which contradicts the reading that a women's filmmaker uses only respectful female images, showing women in a progressive, positive way. Concerning his cinema, this label is certainly not unequivocal: indeed, women are regularly the main character in his films, these protagonists usually suffer violence and yet, fortunately, this violence is punished by an inside spectator, imposing an ethical and moralistic point of view.

Female filmmakers

After commenting on the three chosen male film directors, the next question that emerges is: why not choose films by female film directors? As this book focuses on mainstream cinema, focusing on box office successes and author recognition, this is certainly not represented by female film directors. Nevertheless it is interesting to comment on the place of women directors in Spanish cinema in order to illustrate the dominance of male filmmakers. It was only in the 1990s that a considerable number of female filmmakers emerged. Until 1988 only ten filmmakers had debuted (Rosario Pi, Helena Cortesina, Ana Mariscal, Margarita Aleixandre, Josefina Molina, Pilar Miró, Cecilia Bartolomé, Isabel Mulá, Virginia Nunes and Pilar Távora), followed by a considerable boom in the 1990s with an additional 34 female filmmakers.[25] Considering their precarious presence and their quasi-invisibility until 1988, this boom in the 1990s was impressive. Nevertheless, as Barry Jordan and Morgan-Tamosunas notice, this does not always mean that implicit attention was given to the female situation by feminist cinema, but rather that their narrative focus addressed issues of gender politics or womanhood in a new way, inscribing it into mainstream cinema.[26] A possible explanation is given by Martin-Márquez, who in the Afterword of her book portrays with enthusiasm this new boom of women film directors, also mentioning the realistic situation of being a film director:

> Of course, a boom in women directors does not necessarily produce an explosion of feminist cinema. Some of these new film-makers, hoping to get a foot firmly in the door of the national industry, are, not surprisingly, most preoccupied by the economic success of their first features; even if they find the exploration of feminist topics personally appealing, they recognize that popular audiences may not.[27]

New research has been done recently by Fátima Arranz and her research team (Esperanza Roquero, Pilar Aguilar, Pilar Pardo, …), focusing particularly on female representation in films by using a statistical approach to analyse female visibility and presence. For instance, in the 1990s there were 17.1% new female film directors, which precedes a decrease in the period from 2000-2006 to 10.4%.[28] As the Spanish female filmmaker Patricia Ferreira declared at a conference in Paris in 2008, the first feature film can succeed, but it is hard to continue, especially for women.[29] Fátima Arranz' team illustrates these difficulties by counting the number of men who are decision-makers at film festivals, or who decide who receives the Goya Award. As this film award provides explicit recognition for a Spanish filmmaker, these feminist researchers examine how the candidates are elected: until 2005 only filmmakers who had already made three feature films could vote. This has been modified since then by allowing all members of the Academy to vote. Their research project is an eye-opener about decision-making at festivals, for commissions, and Goya directions, as the representation of men is particularly dominating. I do not claim that this implies a categorical preference for their male colleagues, but if one could speak of a female imaginary, it is always much more interesting to have a realistic gamut of standpoints in society (or cinema). This issue is explored in their chapters on the representation of female visions focusing on films made between 2000 and 2006. They analyse sequences with violence done to women, shot by female or male film directors and they conclude that both genders represent it around 30%, but that the main difference is inside the film: the female film directors create an internal reaction to 100% of the depictions of violence against women. This contrasts strongly with the films made by male filmmakers: only 25% include a critical reaction and 75% a complacent reaction. This is only one of the many topics explored, differentiating between male and female filmmakers. It would be interesting to extrapolate this kind of investigation to former periods.

Female viewpoints

The issue that women make different cinema is still being debated. Various studies have tried to portray a specific aspect of their films, for example *Half of Heaven. Women directors in the 1990s*, edited by Carlos Heredero.[30] As there was an evident surge of new women filmmakers in the 1990s, José Enrique Monterde comments in this edition on their age, education and statistical presence in Spanish cinema. Other articles by Antonio Santamarina or Marta Selva Masoliver trace some characteristics of this new female point of view, followed by interviews with prominent women directors. They were invited to write on women's cinema and, for instance, the reaction of Icíar Bollaín was legendary. Entitled *Cinema with tits ("Cine con tetas")*, in it she portrays the physical gender differences of the body as the only difference in this profession. Her provocative language is a direct reaction to the repeated question: is there such a thing as women's cinema? The same tendency can be noticed in the comment *Without a title* ("*Sin título*"), written by Chus Gutiérrez, commenting that they would never ask a man how it feels to make films being a man, having a male protagonist, who represents in a typical male manner their male imagination. The female filmmakers react in this way to the eternally repeated question how is it to be a filmmaker and a woman, as this question is asked incessantly and yet it is never asked of a man to relate his film making to his gender.[31] Notwithstanding their refusal to consider a women's cinema as possessing its own characteristics, their reactions contrast with various results found by the research team led by Fátima Arranz. They scrutinise many representations such as the topic of violence, which we have already discussed. Among the many issues they consider I will mention only two. They confirm that female filmmakers have apparently more female protagonists than men, and deal with topics like the family in a different way.

A recent book published by Maria Cami-Vela, *Women behind the camera. Interviews with Spanish women directors 1990-2004*,[32] adds to the conversation by not allowing the female filmmakers to write on the issue themselves, but rather it presents their stance by interviewing each personally. She interviews well-known female filmmakers such as Icíar Bollaín, Isabel Coixet, Chus Gutiérrez and many others. The main question she asks all of them is what they think of women's cinema. A rejection of this term can be noticed in all interviews, even though they recognise now a bit more that there is something like a female point of view in some situations.

In this context a recent evolution should be mentioned. After the enthusiastic boom in the 1990s, the women directors realised that it was extremely difficult to maintain their position and to continue filmmaking. So they created the CIMA[33] in 2007, an association bringing together female filmmakers to consider their situation. As Patricia Ferreira comments, nowadays the situation is worrisome because the percentage of female presence has decreased: in the period from 1986 until 2006, 8% of films were made by women. In the period from 2000 until 2006, this figure was only 7%. In addition, the appearance of new female film directors has decreased enormously: from 2000 until 2006, only 10% new film directors were women, and in the 1990s this figure was 17%. Consequently, Patricia Ferreira joined this association for Female Film directors, with Josefina de Molina as a special member.

Commenting in this context on pioneers of the Spanish feminist cinema, Josefina Molina is a good example, forming part of the older generation. With her feminist film NIGHT FUNCTION (FUNCIÓN DE NOCHE, 1981), which was inspired by Miguel Delibes' novel FIVE HOURS WITH MARIO (CINCO HORAS CON MARIO,

1966) the protagonist speaks directly about her marriage with her husband in the dressing room. On stage she is playing the widow Carmen talking to her husband in remembrance. This film is particularly a document (inspired by *cinéma vérité*[34]) about a changing society, showing the protagonist's wish to divorce and expressing her dissatisfaction with regard to her marital, emotional and also sexual life with her husband. Another pioneer filmmaker of feminist cinema was Pilar Miró, who was also politically active for the Socialist government, having formulated the so-called Miró Law in the 1980s. Her person is described by Jaume Martí-Olivella as that of a political body, as she was a woman filmmaker as well as a political activist.[35]

In the 1990s more explicit attention was also paid to the questioning of a typical male or female spectator inside a film, which since Mulvey's text, has been ever more explored. Without having the ambition to be exhaustive in this new field, I wish to mention two new studies, both published in 1998 by Spanish female researchers. Firstly there is the book by Pilar Aguilar, published in 1998, entitled *Woman, love and sex in Spanish cinema of the 1990s.*[36] This interesting research deals with sexual issues with frankness, exemplified in the detailed analysis of the female body during the sexual act. Her daring approach works sometimes as an eye-opener of existing sexism when she proposes some role changes. Citing the film RUNNING OUT OF TIME (DÍAS CONTADOS), she describes the body of Ruth Gabriel, who usually walks in underwear or naked at home. Pilar Aguilar proposes to imagine a male character, like in this film Carmelo Gómez, who would, like her, do a striptease, and often walk naked or in underwear at home.[37] I agree that it is quite unusual and therefore challenging to see these role changes. Pilar Aguilar's direct comment on many situations is revealing in describing how we are used to seeing these images of the women's body, perceiving these same acts as unusual and funny were a male character to enact them.

Another study on the female point of view should be mentioned in this context. In a book by María Donapetry, introducing herself explicitly as being Spanish and female as a researcher, she proposes a new vision on women in Spanish culture (*The other point of view. Woman and film in Spanish culture*).[38] Her readings are fascinating, focusing on well-known films such as *Carmen* by Saura and Almodóvar's work. Her statement that Carmen is a male construction that does not correspond to any reality[39] corresponds for her to the dominance of men as filmmakers in that period. Indeed, the mainstream cinema from our research period is dominated by male film directors and our three films chosen correspond to this leading inclination.

Nevertheless we focus on how the female identity is constructed inside the filmic imagination in the period. It is therefore important to mention that the genre of the three films reflects characteristics of the melodrama or the musical.

FLUNKING OUT (ASIGNATURA PENDIENTE) is a melodrama, CARMEN a musical, and HIGH HEELS (TACONES LEJANOS) is a melodrama combined with thriller aspects. In his groundbreaking text, "Tales about sound and fury", Thomas Elsaesser analyses the American melodrama.[40] The female protagonist often suffers the repression of patriarchy with regard to her family life and sexuality. Music is particularly revealing for the emotions that soften the female character's misery. Melodramas originally had female protagonists and therefore the adaptation of their codes, accompanied by Spanish melodies, is particularly revealing for the new readings of women created by the mainstream cinema, while the situation relating to work and sexuality was changing in the 1970s.

In summary, this chapter should be read in its historical and cultural context (the 1970s), a time during which there were not a lot of female film directors. The issues explored represent mainstream Spanish cinema inside its cultural (and I am convinced also Western European) context. Let us now focus on how the female body can be found in the centre of the image and how the auteur stereotypes are introduced, transforming them into new prototypes (role models).

I.   FLUNKING OUT (ASIGNATURA PENDIENTE, 1977): breaking through a forbidden topic of the past

It is important to situate this fiction inside Spanish culture of the 1970s: FLUNK-ING OUT (ASIGNATURA PENDIENTE) by José Luis Garci is well known in Spain, but not so much abroad. It is an exemplary production of the *tercera vía*. The story is about forbidden intimacy due to the leading social conventions of the Franco periods; a man and a woman, in their thirties, meet again and wish to relive their first love with a sexual liberty that was prohibited at the time of their youth. Their unfulfilled story inspires them to pursue a love affair in an apartment in town, away from their conjugal lives, as both main characters are married and have both already built up their own family lives. In the middle of the film, the death of Franco is announced: José and his wife hear the news on the radio. The contextual change modifies the point of view on the recently re-ignited love affair: after having briefly experienced a sexual liberty that was impossible in a period of prohibition, this extraordinary love affair loses its character of transgression and thus ends up resembling their own marriages: so they decide to separate. They tried to relive a love from the past, as a way of remembering the absence of liberties, liberties they did not have when they were young; but in the advent of this new future, now waiting for them, each asks how best to face what is yet to come: this fiction also illustrates the pursuit of a lost and unattainable period, one different from those during which everything was forbidden and one less daunting then the fearsome and unknown future.

The reception of the film in Spain

The large audiences attest to its extraordinary success in the year of its release and the reactions in articles in the press were also extremely positive. The audience recognises itself in the topics touched on and attention is paid to non-experienced liberty in the areas of sexuality, politics and religion; these are key issues of the Transition.[41] The fiction emphasises the idea of a period wasted for those born during Francoism; the filmmaker José Luis Garci forms part of this generation.[42] The title symbolises the problem: *Asignatura pendiente* means that the case is pending. The word *asignatura* refers to a university course that should be passed; it is the equivalent of an "incomplete" grade. Having re-discovered their first loves, José establishes this comparison. In reality, the situation is comparable to that of a student who failed to show up for his final exam. Thus, it is as if they have not graduated and that somehow they have both been stunted by their inability to consummate their affair as youthful lovers. To be sure, their incomplete love story may mean that they will never have an intimate relationship. He often recalls that several things could not be finished or executed, as they all belonged to the forbidden. "*Nos han robado tantas cosas*": they stole from us so many things. She, from her side, regrets not having been enrolled in university.

This fiction does not seem, at first sight, to focus on the female body; but their relationship based on their adolescent romance poses a question related to the historical period of the film. The link to time is presented in a particular way: the plot begins during late Francoism, when a married woman had to dedicate herself to her family and her children to have a decent and satisfying life. But now the female character questions her life: she is clearly disconsolate to be only a mother one who was unable to realise her professional ambitions. On the one hand, the moments illustrating her relationship with her children are rare. On the other hand, her boredom is effectively and often demonstrated through the static aspect of her body. In a filmic language of the 1970s, the archetype of motherhood is updated with the creation of a stereotype of a passive, submissive woman who is bored and does not know how to change her life, even though she experiences some of the typical anguishes of that era: times are changing and she has the feeling that she missed out on many things. Adding to this is a new feeling of uncertainty concerning the future.

The actors' bodies

Related to the issues dealt with in the film, the actors chosen to play these roles are deeply anchored in the epoch and they create progressive images of politics and sexuality. Situating them inside the cinematographic context, Besas comments that: "José and Elena are now free in 1977, the prototypes of an emerging society that can live without taboos."[43] Undeniably, they are role models related to the 1970s. The actor José Sacristan is above all known for these kinds of films, those from the *tercera vía*, marked by politically loaded images; he is the prototype of an intellectual actor, inspired by speech and the act of thinking itself. He plays José, a married man, father of a son, a communist lawyer, open-minded; the colleagues at his office are like him, progressive and idealistic. During the Franco periods, as he comments, he was in prison in *"Carabanchel por rojo"* (Carabanchel is the name of a prison), and he was an absolute leftist.

Elena, played by Fiorella Faltoyano, is his first love and becomes his mistress. She assumes, by the image of her body, a double function between a stereotypical aspect and a prototypical one. Firstly the stereotype: the archetype of motherhood for a woman is updated first of all by an image of an uptight and contained body inside a decor that is repetitive; Elena establishes a thought-image that highlights the negative aspect of the life of a housewife: she is rather unhappy, without anything interesting to do; she looks depressed. To change her life, she starts an affair with this lover. She depicts a prototype in two aspects: firstly by her expression of sexual liberty as she shows herself naked. Making her extra conjugal love affair last, she realises at the end, that if her life had been a little bit more interesting she would not have started this relationship. She thus also becomes a prototype on a professional level, trying to break through the stereotype of a housewife. The press articles do not provide any commentaries on her identity – such an image was a common social figure in that period, but draw rather attention to the spectator's feelings of identification with issues related to the lost generation (sex and politics). On the other hand, Elena's despondency becomes the main theme at the end of the film plot, when she speaks up to denounce her situation.

José's wife and Elena's husband represent flat characters, as they are only there to illustrate the family situation of the two lovers. For the rest, they do not appear at all in the story of the film and they do not have an influence on the plot's evolution. "Trotsky", played by Antonio Gamero, is his work colleague (José gives him this nickname). This character therefore places emphasis on the progressive aspect concerning political liberty whereas communism was strongly repressed during Francoism.[44] Another prototypical body of political liberty is presented in the film by the actor Héctor Alterio (acting as Garcia Meana). In the 1970s, this actor was an political refugee from Argentina (1976-

1982 lasted the military dictatorship). Now in Spain he plays a Spanish political refugee incarcerated in the prison of Carabanchel. This created some difficulties for the distribution of the film in Argentina; a crucial sign about Spain's recently acquired liberty, because what could be shown in Spain then could not yet be shown in Argentina.[45]

The mythological plot

Besides the theme of time, which is a central topic in the Transition period, the film draws attention to typical questions of Spanish cinema in the 1970s about politics and sexuality. To provide a reading of the film, the plot can be divided into two parts: before and after the announcement of the death of Franco in the middle of the film. The structure of the narration of the first part concerns the past and the second one, the future. To illustrate my method, it is necessary to revisit some definitions set out in the first chapter. Inside the filmic plot there is a mythological plot, based on an insurmountable conflict. This is the case in *Asignatura pendiente*: a problem is shown about time referring to forbidden topics under the period of dictatorship. The core of the conflict is based on the binary opposition between the past (political and sexual taboos of Francoism) and the present (wishing to break through this prohibition at the end of Francoism). To read this mythological plot, the body becomes the mediator and looks for a solution by putting into place the rituals: the first love, José and Elena meet up again and become lovers. This makes them mediators: their love dates back to a period in the past and they take up again this relationship wishing to break through the taboo of that era, while still in present time. In the first part of the film, when Franco is still alive, they evoke incessantly this lack of liberty during their adolescence. In the second part of the film, after the announcement of the death of the dictator, the perception of the future changes and the woman obtains a central place in the plot. The way she feels about her life is related to her non-existent professional situation in the Spanish context of the 1970s.

Instead of defining a mythological established plot, FLUNKING OUT (ASIGNATURA PENDIENTE) questions above all taboos by demystifying them through speech and by introducing progressive characters (prototypical bodies). To analyse the mythological plot in the film images, the rituals guide our reading: the ritual can be defined as all the acts, gestures and behaviour that express the central problem of the film, questions it and tries to construct a new expression. The protagonist's bodies are set up to carry out different rituals questioning time. Not having experienced sexual liberty when they were in love for the first time, they try to catch up: they question the wasted time talking at length about everything that was prohibited, they revisit the concerned holy places, such as Miraflores, which is the village where they met when they were teenagers.

We have to go back to the first chapter where we defined the distinction be-tween "institutionalised" and "new" rituals. The first category expresses habits, by everyday gestures; for example acts or gestures in your workplace. These acts and gestures contrast with new rituals, like a second group, defined as acts and gestures that introduce new images of the body. The institutionalised ri-tuals express common ideas of the 1970s but as the film FLUNKING OUT (ASIGNATURA PENDIENTE) from 1977 is progressive for the period, referring openly to the prohibition of sexuality before marriage in the past, this imposes new, innovative rituals. In this film it is most of all about speaking openly about sexuality when referring to the fact of actually doing it. The filmic forms are closely related to that period, for example the dominant place of speech is in stark contrast to the metaphorical cinema of the Franco periods. In the multiple dialogues or monologues, often through the voice-over, the protagonists name the forbidden areas of the past in detail, and at length, to break through this taboo; on the other hand the images illustrate this gap in liberty, as this is not a public discourse expressed in a public site, but mostly in voice-over to express Jose and Elena's thoughts, or when they are alone. The lovers are therefore ne-gotiators; they negotiate between the past and the present. They are portrayed as exemplary for their progressive liberty.

The announcement of the death of Franco – at the end of the first part – leads to a change in ideas concerning the perception of time: the attempt to have a grip on the period of the past is no longer important after Franco's death. The symbolism of rupture is felt because the real problem of the current moment is posed and only then is the lack of ideas about the future considered. The whole feature film therefore offers an image of the Transition; a kind of emptiness, a rupture in time, a feeling of being blocked. These questions are expressed by a static mise-en-scene that is repetitive, and by the image of a body experiencing a meditative thought, reflecting on the past inside the historical frame of the 1970s. Only speech is there to move one's thoughts, because the rest seems im-mobile; the bodies displace a little and the colours, yellow or green, are dull, not very appealing. The camera hardly moves, or does so slowly, focusing on the character; the changing of the camera angle is also exceptionally slow. The decor also carries a double function: the protagonists show themselves as detached from their surroundings, as they live inside their thoughts, inspired by the past in the first part. In addition, the static and repetitive environment draws atten-tion to a situation that does not change for the female protagonist, particularly in the second part of the plot.

The choreography of the ritual

The film opens with everyday rituals: to situate the protagonists in their surroundings; these rituals are thus completely different for both characters, but accentuate, by the gestures of habit, an everyday reality that is not questioned, although everyone is experiencing it in their own way. The bodies perform and thus illustrate a thought about their life, about their surroundings, about time.

The first part of the film: meeting up again

From the onset, the question about time focuses on the desire to relive the past. José and Elena are introduced by a cross cutting in a decor of their conjugal apartments, which permits us to compare their dreams, which are based on the same memory. Melancholic, slow and dramatic music accompanies a high-angle extreme long shot on a city, in a tracking shot the camera approaches an apartment, accompanied by the voice-over of José: "The first time I saw Elena it was summer, in July". The memory is introduced as would a fairy tale, a magical moment to question. The image dissolves into a slight high-angle medium close-up on José who then just wakes up. While his body was fast asleep, his thoughts were expressed by the voice-over. Then we follow him inside the image; he is staring straight ahead as he reminisces about his first love. He observes his wife, who is still sleeping, the camera distances from her. He gets up and sits down on his bed. It is an ordinary image, the beginning of an ordinary day, the thoughts are somewhere else; he is in a dreamy state of mind.

Another high-angle extreme long shot on another apartment, a tracking shot to the right takes us to Elena's bedroom while the voice-over tells us about her first encounter with José. The camera slips softly on the couple, advances on Elena in a medium close-up; her husband is still asleep next to her. Her voice-over describes an image of a younger José, introduced as someone from whom one expected a brilliant future and, in a medium close-up, we observe José in front of a mirror shaving. The given thought-image of Elena' body is static: with her arms crossed in front of her body, her voice continues to accompany the noise of the shaver and a medium close-up shows her sad and melancholic face. The bodies of the two characters do not express anything concerning their direct surrounding that is there like an unmovable decor. Only the voice-over permits the recollection of their past, in a slow and melancholic rhythm, outside of the time that had been confiscated from them.

A gaze on the female body

In the next sequence, their separated lives are again united by a cross cutting: Elena leaves by car and stays then alone at home while José leaves for his work. The montage allows for a comparison of their energy and enthusiasm: the

Photo 5: Gazing at Elena

bodies of the characters establish a thought that contrasts in dynamism. We observe precise gestures: both characters stage everyday rituals. Firstly Elena who, in a medium close shot, takes a cup from the bedroom and, without doing her bed (still not tidied up), she enters into the kitchen: her body moves slowly and obeys the mechanical movements of daily life. Then, the medium close-up on a sign post for lawyers' parking place, introduces the site of work for José; the camera gets down via a tracking shot on his car, he gets out in order to enter the courthouse. José is walking in an energetic way; he is resolute and decided. The camera follows him in the same tracking shot when he approaches the building to finally frame the board "Courthouse". The sites of work are then defined and the body language is appropriating them: José enters with a lot of energy and with conviction while Elena, on whom the gaze is then posed, returns home dragging her feet.

As a spectator, we focus longer on Elena. The choreography of her movements proposes a dance of boredom, being so slow; it is even an image of depression. The daily rituals (that are not new, but completely routine) are repeated in the entire film. They convey a feeling of boredom when, in a medium close shot on the back, we see her turning on the radio in the kitchen. Her image of apathy is accompanied by the words of a masculine voice that reproaches women for the vice of wanting to work outside their home and proposes a solution: a machine for knitting that permits them to work at home. This solution does not make Elena very joyful as she sits in an armchair in the living room: we observe her tense and passive body, her arms flaccidly hanging by her side, her head dejectedly inclining forward; she feels alone and bored at home. This depressive image is amplified by a radiophonic voice that confirms the many advantages of this work; to produce unique pieces, not thinking of customers and financial gain, everything so meticulously organised, while being able to do all this within the confines of one's home. The camera zooms in slowly and frames Elena' face in a close-up; she raises her head, a tear flows on her face. The image fades out to black.

This positive message about knitting the same pieces on a machine, as a suggestion for work, confirms the stereotype about women. Supposed to feel satisfied by these domestic occupations, her body is blocked and contained in this square living room. Every movement could be a reaction to this radiophonic voice, which in fact only leads to tears: this stereotyped passive life brings only sadness.

The historic decor

The plot is situated at a precise moment because the historical date is written on the image, "1 October 1975", in a slightly high-angle long shot on a motorway, where lots of cars approach and honk; the Spanish flag brandishes through the doors. The cars approach the text, which reinforces the emphasis on that date in the frame. Historically well known, that day refers to the last parade for Franco and it is in this historical context that José and Elena meet up again. In a slight high-angle medium close shot Elena is framed in the street where she walks, reading a political pamphlet that they just gave to her: her head bowing towards this text, she is concentrated on her reading and does not hear José who is shouting from the motorway. He fidgets in all directions and gesticulates with a lot of enthusiasm leaning on a gate. Elena turns towards him and her face clears up, she recognises him immediately. They start a conversation, then in a bar they tell each other about the years that have passed. The background of the epoch is illustrated by the radio in the bar because, while they confess to each other that they have not forgotten the other's birthday, we hear the voice-over of a crowd that is shouting in a regular rhythm: "Franco, Franco, Franco". The political atmosphere is depicted by these shouting voices supporting a dictator in 1975. José and Elena do not react to this message. It is like a sound in the background, a political decor, in which they live. After this first encounter, they keep in touch, and José proposes to visit the holy places where they experienced their youthful romance: the village Miraflores, near Madrid.

Miraflores

Two aspects mark this sequence in Miraflores: their walk in the village as a couple in love and the dialogue about the past by speaking about forbidden topics. The sequence opens on a motorway showing all the clichés of happiness: the weather is beautiful, nature is lovely; José and Elena are very happy. Their faces glow with happiness; they burst out in laughter and look at each incessantly. The car approaches the camera frontally, lightened up by the sunlight, and a movement intensified by the rhythm of the song: *My love is fifteen years old*. Followed by a medium close-up from behind in the car: Elena shakes her head and is laughing. José who is driving, is gesticulating, constantly talking; a joyful couple, the sun is shining and life is smiling at them. They are the depiction of a relaxed couple during their re-encounter of a mythical love story; the song gives the rhythm to the words "My love is fifteen years old" as the images show their visit of Miraflores.

Searching for the origins of their first love in this village, the bodies of the two people incarnate and appropriate this site by their images and transform their amorous experience by projecting it on Miraflores. It is the choreography of their thought. We are supposed to watch through their eyes the little corner, the square, a house belonging to someone they knew. The images of their bodies express their radiant thoughts, happy, with a lot of young energy; they transform, with this walk, any village into a mythical place where they lived their first love affair. They deeply enjoy their retrospective walk and evoke the memories when José is climbing over a gate, and the camera follows him when he dances some rock 'n roll steps like a young boy, while Elena is waiting and laughing. It is an act of remembrance of lost places, meant to live again lost periods. Their joyful walk finishes with a high-angle long shot on a central square in Miraflores, they walk around, stop, and the voice of the song is almost shouting the words: "my loooovvvveeee".

Returning there, the memories also bring back the non-experienced: the sexual act. The next sequence expresses a different rhythm when the dialogue is concentrated on the past; they pose together, like a static painting. José, on his knees close to a stream, touches with a branch the water that flows while observing it: it is like a metaphor of time that is passing by. He is thoughtfully looking straight ahead. The camera pulls back in a tracking shot; he stands up and approaches Elena, who is sitting against a tree, closing her eyes to enjoy the sunshine. He leans against the tree, observes her and starts his monologue. These two people are represented by two immobile bodies. In a medium close-up the image shows us Elena. Her eyes still closed, Elena has a satisfied and bright expression on her face. José starts to talk: "In films they never say…., they kiss and lay down slowly on the sofa but they never say that: I want to sleep with you". These are prototypical words of the freedom of speech. Elena watches in front of her and starts to talk about her life: "Since the youngest now goes to school, I feel so alone at home. I'm thinking of enrolling into a Faculty. (–) What do you think about that?" This does not seem to be a reaction to José's remark. She wishes to change her professional life, to overcome the boredom of a house-wife's existence. The words on forbidden topics serve to somehow jolt the im-mobility, because in the whole sequence the bodies are framed in their immobi-lity, the camera moves just a little. This static situation is revealing. In this film it portrays the transitory period by showing constantly the contrast of mobility and rhythm in diverse situations.

It is hard to speak here of a dialogue between two people as they speak to each other looking in front of them; it seems more like an enunciation of a monologue about what they wish to find in life. José continues:

> They've stolen so many things of us. The times that you and me should have made love and we did not. The books that we should have read. The things we should have thought about. It's all that I cannot forgive them for. Like all these suspended cases that stay in suspense from one school year to the other, like if we never graduated and like if we're never going to.

A medium close-up on Elena's face shows her pensive expression. Making love is like recuperating lost time, and, for her, it is a means filling her long hours of boredom. In a full shot, they are face to face, the couple advances slowly to-wards the camera. For the first time they look at each other when they speak. Elena addresses directly her words to José when she asks him: "When will we settle this business...". José in a medium close-up looks at her, a little worried: "Are you serious?" Elena turns down her eyes, gives a sign with her head, and gets in the car while the music starts again. In a long shot the car is leaving Miraflores. A moment of the past has been found back on this site of their youth. Now they wish to pass the exam that stayed in suspense.....to be contin-ued.

The ellipse in Asignatura pendiente

The not yet experienced sexual act will be ritualised to recover lost time and the bodies draw attention to their liberty in a contemporary decor. These sequences are exemplary for the *tercera vía* they represent; they accentuate the naturalness of intimacy commenting on it without reluctance; a close-up on a hand that is looking for a key, a tracking from above then focusing down on the couple in front of a door. José and Elena enter, they seem tense. Elena takes a piece of paper that "Trotsky" left there for them: in a medium close-up on her, she looks extremely serious, José observes her in a worried way when she is reading: "My friends, the towels are clean", a short silence before pronouncing the end of the sentence: "I've changed the sheets so that you enjoy it in good health." She pro-

Photo 6: The exam is passed

nounces these words with hesitation, a serious and contemplative expression on her face.

José reacts telling her that she is so beautiful and takes her by the hand to show her the apartment. They are hand-in-hand when they cross first the kitchen, then the living-room and finally they enter the bedroom. These are rigid bodies. The woman does some steps in the bedroom before sitting down on the bed while José stands watching her. Elena undresses as if it was an obligatory act and José sits downs next to her proposing to leave. The telephone rings. When he comes back, we see from his point of view Elena in a medium close-up under the sheets, she looks at him in the door: "Come, come". A lateral medium close shot on Elena and frontal on José shows his stress, his worried appearance. An ellipse, a black shot and both bodies under the sheets, we see part of Elena's breast. They smoke a cigarette together (see photograph). Their bodies are then completely relaxed and demonstrably satisfied; they've made love, the act is consumed. The spectator didn't see anything. The protagonists' claimed liberty is translated in their dialogues on the topic, because physically nothing is shown. The next sequence highlights it by the way they comment on their "exam", it is necessary to situate this dialogue in the cultural context of the 1970s.

It is above all José who is holding a monologue on liberty (in a frontal medium close-up on both of them in the bed). He speaks about himself as if he were a hero: they made love, they passed the exam and *"how"*, with distinction, he affirms. It's an act of heroism, recuperating wasted time. The lovers feel more in control of their lives. When Elena takes the sheets to get up, José alludes to the films in which couples that have known each other their entire life get out of bed with a sheet around their body. He gets up and starts imitating an actress. Timidly, she looks at José and she sits down again on the bed. He speaks about this liberty (a lateral medium close-up on José's back, frontal on Elena); they were manipulated by censorship and he pulls down the sheet from Elena's body to indicate the naturalness of the image. Given the period of release of this film (1977), one can consider this sequence as a mise-en-scene of prototypical bodies that mark their sexuality with simplicity, like a "new" ritual making new images for the period. In a frontal medium close-up, both lovers walk together to the shower and are smiling: this image highlights their liberty; the breasts of the female body are uncovered, while Elena lets the sheet fall. Indeed, taking a shower together after having made love, the bodies underline once again the naturalness of this situation, without being obsessed or obscene (as this was often the case in the *destape* films).

The second part of the film: the death of Franco

The announcement of Franco's death gives the impression that time stops, like a break in time, illustrated by a contemplative sequence filmed in one long take. The announcement is done framing José and his wife fast asleep: in a static medium long shot on the couple, the phone rings in the middle of the night. The camera doesn't move, the woman gets up a little bit to answer the phone and José wakes up slowly out of a deep slumber and also sits down in the bed. They turn on the radio and listen to the broadcast of Franco's death (20 November 1975). The framing of the shot still does not change as they look straight ahead. Two reflective bodies, José smokes a cigarette, she takes one as well; they stare into emptiness. No euphoria, no comment, silence, the camera pulls back slowly from their bodies and the image fades out to black: an exemplary sequence shot to illustrate their state of mind.

Some images of the Christmas period and then a fast sequence that illustrates the radical change; the shots follow in a high, rapid rhythm with questions about the new political situation. The first image shows a woman in a swimming suit, the camera tilts down from her face towards her sex – she is spreading her legs – and in the background we hear a song *Love me forever*. This woman's body signifies sexual liberation. The historical context changes and the conflicted situation is typical for the Transition. Several fast shots accentuate the brutal change: pictures in black and white, images of coffins, incidents in

Vitoria, demonstrations for labour, new political leaders (the so-called "Bunker" as a prolongation of Franco's politics); the new situation brings with it also other melodies evoking the events. *"Como ayer"* (*Like yesterday*), the last words of the song echoes ten times on the last images: yesterday we still knew what we had; today we have only uncertainties. The rhythm and the content show in a sustained way a situation typical of the Transition: a radical change accompanied by feelings of preoccupation with the wish for a return to the past. Both sequences illustrate an idea of rupture; an intermediate period: an "emptiness" as the characters are cut off from the past by the death of Franco. It is like a split, the future is in front of them, like every future is always unknown, but this time the situation needs to be defined in political terms.

A repetitive decor

The changing of time can be seen by the mise-en-scene repeating the decors or situations by emphasising on a change in meaning. In the whole film the site of the bedroom is often present as a crucial place where decisive actions take place. For instance, to encounter the first love (José and Elena), but also to discuss calmly in intimacy: José and his wife talk from then on differently. His wife tells him an anecdote about their son. A frontal medium close-up on both of them shows how they embrace each other and make projects for their holidays. These are projects about the future, in a domestic space; it is the place of their own marriage. It was also the place where the announcement of Franco's death was heard; now it is the place to make plans for the future.

Everything seems to change but not for the framing of Elena's body since attention is drawn to the same mechanical gestures. Her life continues in different decors (her house and the apartment where she meets José) but the images emphasise the stereotype of boredom and routine by repeating her rituals. Stringing together these close-ups arouses a point of view on the monotony of her life: a close-up on a saucepan, on the gas, on the cupboard where she takes from a cup: a close-up on two hands, a tea bag that she puts into the cup with a mechanical gesture: a close-up on her face, a slight low-angle shot, she looks down, to the cup. During all these close-ups we hear the voice of José; he speaks excitedly about his work on the phone. She continues her identical rituals, establishing with her body a repetitive thought-image.

Once again, the link between the expressed gestures and a site is fundamental. The camera poses a gaze on Elena by repeating her gestures in a different setting: her house, the apartment where she meets José. These sequences of monotony make us think of the film JEANNE DIELMAN 24 QUAI DU COMMERCE 1080 BRUXELLES (1975) by Chantal Akerman. In this film a woman repeats exactly the same mechanical gestures in her domestic space for numerous sequences. The static decor is her residence in Brussels and is thus the title of the film. The emotionless aspect of the person's behaviour can certainly be compared to the demonstrated body language in FLUNKING OUT (ASIGNATURA PENDIENTE). The spectators live through many details of the domestic life, in a real perception of time, terribly stereotyped here by this woman.

In FLUNKING OUT (ASIGNATURA PENDIENTE), Elena's body expresses the same thought: she gets across the same emotion. In a frontal medium close shot, moving her spoon, she goes to the living-room where, in a dressing gown, José is caught up in a vivid telephone conversation. Elena sits down next to him (frontal full shot on Elena and lateral on José). These are images of stereotyped bodies; a working body, a serving body. Work has now also intervened in their love affair; it is like a sign of the normalisation of this relationship. The site for intimacy has become a place for work; the camera frames Elena's face, then a shot on José and they start to argue.

Revisiting Miraflores

Due to the political changes in the country, the holy sites also become less interesting: the dictator Franco is dead and José and Elena are facing the future in a new way. They return again to Miraflores to try out José's new car. But their movements are less lively. Their bodies express thought-images of soberness; they are neither joyful nor expressive. The mythical place expresses the loss of a holy aspect as is the case for the couple. They do not feel the same way as they did before. The shot, sweeping around the wet streets of melted snow, connotes sadness. It is a sombre image accompanied by melancholic music. Next, they pass along the same garden in which José danced last time some rock 'n roll steps, parodying it. In a slight high-angle long shot, they stop before the gate without the intention to enter. They cross over the village by car: it is a winter atmosphere and they do not wish to go out. They visit the same cafe. A medium close-up of Elena and José's faces, he does not speak, but smokes. She's looking in front of herself into the emptiness. They are together but they do not share the same emotions. After their visit, the car leaves from the same place as the last time, framed in a light high-angle long shot, which resembles a cold painting, accompanied by minor music. They no longer rest their heads on each other's shoulders; everything is transformed into the chilly atmosphere of a winter decor.

Repeating the gaze

The last sequence repeats the frame on the female body in a cruel way. It is a black image, little by little, dissolving into the features of Elena's face in a close-up. It is a sad face, only the body is first illuminated and the place is dark, resembling her own home when she was listening to the radio rambling on about the knitting machine; she wears the same clothes: a red and white shirt with white edges and a pair of jeans. She is sitting down at the same place in the shot. She's waiting for José. Repeating this place illustrates the repetition and persistence of her problem as it was introduced at the beginning of the film: her feelings of world-weariness.

The place then lightens up completely and José enters. In a full shot, both people face each other saying some sentences but then they are not speaking anymore; followed by an exchange of close-ups on their faces: José looks at her, she turns down her eyes. The case is closed: José does not see any point to it. Everything has changed for him. They enter into the kitchen to take a cup of tea. With the same routine gestures she prepares the tea, in a medium close-up on the back of José and on her. Now it is Elena's turn to express herself; finally she speaks up:

> You were in a bad period, bored, without any hope for anything, so then I appeared but not me but your teenager period, the epoch of the big sincerity, when there were no lies. So José came back, the one who was going to devour the world, do you remember? And it was nice to look back, most of all because there was nothing to look forward to. But now the situation has changed. You are again convinced that yours is possible.

The camera approaches and after some descriptions of her life, she concludes: "If I would have had a little bit more in life, we would not have had anything together, but women, at least most of them, we have so few things. (—) Aren't you afraid to look forward?" A medium close-up on José's face: "Like everyone because it is the reason to fight. It is the only solution". Elena replies, in a medium close-up on her face: "For you or for me?" Followed by Jose's serious and thoughtful face; he continues: "For you, for me, for both of us, for everyone".

It is the end of their first love, and in the decor of their apartment, which resembles that of Elena's, their relationship ends: "*La asignatura pendiente*" is concluded and they continue their own lives. Elena does not expect any change. José has a professional career that is waiting for him; she has a boring life. It is the end of the film, with the song *Luna de miel*, which means honeymoon, emphasising indeed that they are never going to live together. The music, with the castanets, begins. The camera pulls back. The frame of the kitchen's door is illuminated; the rest of the room goes dark: our point of view is now posed on two people, facing each other in a static decor, in a full shot; until the light turns off and the song, about this never experienced honeymoon, ends. Both protagonists find themselves in front of an open door – an image expressing a state of mind when they are facing the future.

Photo 7: Framing the future

Abundant words

At the end of the film, the film director adds a text to explain certain points: it is a melancholic discourse that evokes the idea of wasted time which had already overwhelmed the entire plot. The next fragment illustrates its tonality.

> To us, we arrived too late for everything: to childhood, being a teenager, to sex, love, and politics. To us, who lost, from one year after the other, the meaning of everything that was surrounding us, even if it were the smallest things, the less important.

> And to them who made us like that: our parents, who had also their own problems; sir Bernardo, who always gave us slaps, and father Pulido, of who we were so much afraid when he would put his arm around our neck. And to José Mallorqui and "two men so good". And to Roberto Alcázar and Pedrín, respectively the chief of "centuria" and "lèche", and to Domingo, the grocer, that would cut the chewing-gum "bazooka" with an enormous knife.

> And to Young Martin and to Fred Galiana, who we constantly annoyed because they were queer and to our rich friends who sometimes allowed us to play with their electric trains, and to all these billiards and baby-foots in Spain and to Marilyn Monroe...

and to Miguel Hernández, who died without nobody ever knowing that he had ever existed.

These words furnish a last image, already commented on in the film; they relate to a wasted period, a period to recuperate and a period to affront.

By way of conclusion: facing the future

The press reactions in 1977 draw attention to how many people recognised themselves in the issues that were dealt with, but do not insist in particular on the woman's situation. Nevertheless, FLUNKING OUT (ASIGNATURA PENDIENTE) imposes through its mise-en-scene a point of view on her life, emphasising the mechanical rituals of monotony by repeating the decors and the gestures. The archetype of the woman as a mother is made problematic by Elena, by putting into place an unsatisfied body: she insists on changing her life, by means of a stereotyped vision that functions as an appeal for a change, which she wishes for openly. For her, the professional situation has yet to be created; for a man, work was already a reality: with regard to this she feels powerless when she is facing the future. The plot does not propose an established myth but, typical of a transitory period, it emphasises a feeling of emptiness and uncertainty about the future. Some taboos on forbidden sexuality from the Franco periods are overcome, but the future is still waiting and unknown, filled undoubtedly with more issues to be resolved concerning women's professional prospects and potential.

II. The "Spanish" CARMEN by Carlos Saura

The female body brings to life the world-famous myth of Carmen. Often adapted for cinema, only twelve Spanish adaptations exist.[46] This 1983 rendition was made the same year as the Rosi, Godard and Brooks versions.[47] Saura's representation portrays the preparation of a flamenco ballet, a dance that reminds most every spectator of Spain. In his interpretation, Carlos Saura does not hesitate to emphasise this Spanish element. The protagonist, Antonio Gades, a reputed dancer and choreographer in Spain, tries to find a girl to dance the role of Carmen in a ballet that he is going to compose. He discovers Laura del Sol, a young – and above all beautiful – dancer, but one who is not as talented as Cristina Hoyos, who is also a prominent dancer. According to the choreographer, he needs a young woman for this role, even if Cristina dances much better. As Gades reflects on how to shape "his" Carmen and his version of the myth, the body of Laura del Sol is extremely exposed. Through a rhythm of steps that express feelings of revolt, Saura updates the archetype of the *femme fatale*. Fashioning this myth through the use of flamenco language, after a period of dictatorship, is a choice that deserves reflection: what reading can we make of this ambition to define a new Carmen in Spain at the beginning of the 1980s?

The Spanish reaction

While reading several reactions in press articles from 1983, we notice a strong emphasis on a political reading of the position of women in Spanish society concerning work and sexuality. Saura speaks, for example of liberated women:

> From his explanation emerges his conviction that Carmen represents a universal myth, which represents a strong liberated woman, who sleeps with a man and the day after with another, Saura thinks that in the world of gypsies in Andalusia there are still lots of things that Prosper Mérimée described in his 19th century novel. Nowadays there are still a lot of Carmens in Spain.[48]

Gades, the choreographer in the film, comments on the current discussion about women's rights in relation to this Carmen:

> So, I think it is completely relevant. Women fight for their rights. They are fighting, and they are right, because they want to obtain the same rights that men have, in human and material aspects. Because it is not correct that a waitress earns less than a barman. The efforts are the same. For this reason I think that Carmen is a completely current character.[49]

His comment is very appealing, as the film never once addresses this issue. However, Gades' reaction does illustrate the contemporaneous nature of this debate in Spanish society. Eight years after Francoism, this film was made in the same year that the socialist government created the Women's Institution. Bringing forth a frame of reference, the Institution's mandate was to encourage equality and to support the active participation of women in political, cultural and social life. Clearly, defining new ideas about women or, rather, repositioning her place in society concerning work and sexuality was a topical issue at that time. Therefore, introducing new myths or re-creating a Spanish Carmen is consonant with the discussions taking place in 1983. Moreover, Peter Evans and Robin W. Fiddian, in their article "The Europeanization of Carmen" (1988), add to this social and ideological background by situating this new Carmen in a European context, one that was witnessing the changing situation of women. The way they underline the presence and interrogation of authority is important:

Not that Saura and others are politically naïve enough to believe that the new democracy immediately ushered in Utopia, but that with the larger political issues apparently settled, artists could once again make their primary focus areas of greater intimacy – without necessarily returning to the more "dehumanizing" corners of a modernist tradition – and, equally, begin the task of interrogating the legacy of the dictatorship, particularly in the field of sexual politics.[50]

These press articles bear witness to the emergence of a new vision about work and sexuality and as Evans and Fiddian explain, the same discussion was taking place in other European countries. Within this context, this new CARMEN necessarily provokes contemporary readings. Creating a point of view inside the film is therefore an essential aspect in Saura's adaptation; he owns his "Spanish" version and explores the sources as viewpoints on a "Spanish" phenomenon: the origins of the myth are therefore essential to understanding his 1983 adaptation.

A French point of view

Two French sources have transmitted this myth to the world, both creating an image of an exotic woman who is intensely erotic. Mérimée's novel, published in 1845, is written from the point of view of an archaeologist who is travelling through Spain. He meets Carmen, describing her as an extremely beautiful gypsy of mixed background. He perceives her to be a dangerous woman; she is voluptuous, a real *femme fatale*. In Mérimée's narrative, Carmen dies at the hands of her lover José, who kills her in a jealous rage: he can no longer tolerate the fact that she is seeing other men. In the novel, the presence of a bullfighter is hardly drawn, while it is a central character in Bizet's opera (1875), first performed 30 years later in the French *opéra-comique* style.[51] Both versions emphasise the heroine's love life and her behaviour with men. The Carmen figure is often based on the stereotype of a Spanish gypsy. Yet, while Carmen's ethnic background is downplayed for both Mérimée's and Bizet's, it is more accentuated in Bizet's version. Still highly appreciated today by the public, this opera continues to be regularly performed.

Many CARMEN film adaptations from all over the world refer to these French sources, and it is this foreign point of view on a Spanish phenomenon that is worthy of note. Indeed, to remain faithful to Mérimée's understanding is to impose a foreigner's perspective on a "Spanish" myth. The character's meaning within Spanish culture itself, that is, from a Spanish position remains unknown. During my research periods in the country, it was extremely difficult to find analyses done by Spanish authors. Saura and Gades published a book on their film, which was entitled: *Carmen, the dream of absolute love*,[52] which is more a set of commentaries than it is an analysis. This book and dictionaries on myths[53] were the only publications found in the country, whereas, in the Spanish libraries, several foreign authored research projects can be found. What one can assume to be a lack of interest from the Spaniards is supported by the fact that Saura's film was not seen by a large audience[54] in Spain while it was still selected to represent Spain abroad, for the Oscars: CARMEN is an image that sells itself very well outside the borders.

It seems evident that the Carmen myth does not have the same value for foreigners as it does for the Spaniards: the outsider's stance has influenced the adaptations and provides a good example of the *españolada*. Carlos Saura declares that he abhors this Hispanic stereotype. His strong feelings explain why he distinguishes his work from that of Bizet's as he is convinced that the operatic version depicts and reinforces lifeless and typecast images of his country. According to Saura, there is a conventional false idea of Spain that is cultivated abroad. Reinforcing its bogus legitimacy, this fictitious image transforms these stereotypes into naturalised myths (according to Barthes' approach).[55]

One should not forget that the Transition' period (1975-1983) was characterised by the importance allocated to the foreign perspective as Spain was aspiring to become a member of the European Community. Spain officially joined in 1986. Saura's version puts this tension between the foreign and native viewpoint on the foreground. His mise-en-scene rejects clichés as it works with the sources and the play of bodies. By using flamenco dance, CARMEN is his attempt to restore Spanish authenticity to the myth.

The *femme fatale*

The archetype should be defined before scrutinising the film's images. The myth of Carmen is based on the archetype of the *femme fatale*, a character that is oblivious of the moral order and behaves as she wishes; it is a mythological theme that comes back in different periods and cultures. The myth is not uniquely Spanish. The myth refers to archetypal values and in its French version the myth takes place within a Spanish context. The language of its completed form deserves a more precise analysis because the Spanish version risks becoming a stereotype of the *españolada* if Carmen is understood to be simply a flamenco dancer in typical gypsy clothes.

In the first chapter, a difference was established between an "archetype" and a "stereotype". These presuppositions can be illustrated through the analysis of the image of the body. The archetype of the *femme fatale* often takes the form of a stereotyped image of the gypsy woman, one who is either a dancer or a flamenco singer. This symbolic deserves some reflection because this ethnic identity lends itself easily to the expression of liberty. The gypsies have a particular position in Spain: their presence dates back several centuries but has always been repudiated. They still live at the margins of society today.[56] Gypsies have their own culture, customs and traditions; their convictions symbolise a philosophy of liberty and independence towards authority. The gypsy figure incarnates an image of self-determination, which corresponds to Carmen's main features.

The gypsies were also the initiators of flamenco; they introduced flamenco to Spanish society. The origin of their dance and music, which is deeply rooted in their autonomous and defiant culture, directly illustrates their values. Their self-governing ethic is well demonstrated in history. In the fifteenth century this population retired to the mountains to avoid the proselytising demands of the Catholic Church. Their desire for independence was expressed by this dance and the flamenco music.[57] Saura's film was released in Spain during the establishment of Democracy. By focusing on existing visions of this myth, the film's images make plain Saura's critical stance toward authority. However, some confusion can be felt in the reading of the film. Whereas the gypsies and the flamenco express, by their music and the body of the dancers, an assertion of liberty, they can also be easily used to express stereotyped forms, particularly easy to recognise. Therefore beyond its historical reference, the dance in Saura's film is used to symbolise liberty and independence from all authority, perhaps even from the so-called legitimacy of conventional images. While closely scrutinising the film images, how can we read this updated version of 1983? How does it treat these stereotypes reinforced by the flamenco?

Updating the myth of Carmen

Referred to in the opening credits, this 1983 adaptation is inspired by Mérimée's novel and Bizet's opera. Both sources are constantly cited throughout the plot as they are incorporated into a new context of flamenco. This film does not give a continuous ballet performance, but rather emphasises the double mise-en-scene that is directed by Gades. Inside the film, Gades cuts, according to his point of view, the sessions at the dance rehearsal in order to make everything perfect. His character embodies the conflict. Gades is engrossed in the composition of his version and, using traditional and modern instruments, he struggles to make it just right. It is this double mise-en-scene that imposes his viewpoint on the rituals of realisation. His perspective, blended with Mérimée's text or mixed up with Bizet's music, is integrated into the new ballet.

Laura del Sol functions as a mediator in this process; her character has to be created through the image of her body; it must be shaped to perfection on several levels. Firstly, in the relationship between Gades and the creation of his Carmen, the myth of Pygmalion is clearly present. In this myth, the king of Cyprus is unsatisfied by the images of women that surround him. He therefore sculpts his own image of the ideal woman and immediately falls in love with it.[58] Originating in a negative and critical approach of women, this sculptured creation is thus meant to show the perfect image. The same exigencies are emphasised by Gades; surrounded by female dancers, he is not at all satisfied, as he has his own vision of the paragon Carmen. Subsequently, he falls also in love with his creation, but in 1983 the myth is formulated differently. The identity of Carmen, acted by Laura del Sol, is itself imaginary but confers an authentic air due to the actors that surround her; most of them are famed dancers and musicians from the flamenco scene. This mix of actual dancers and one fictive character creates a contemporary image, resembling a real documentary. For example Antonio Gades' character holds up this play of true and imaginary by keeping his real name, as do the musicians Paco de Lucia and the dancer Cristina Hoyos. Using their real names and not those of invented characters leads to a documentary-style reading (Odin, 1984)[59] of their identity. Indeed, the body's images represent their proper social function. In addition, filming the dance school *Amor de Dios*, and its reputed professors, with the likes of Maria Magdalena, Ciro and others, accentuates the bona fide details. This is in fact one of the most important sites of contemporary flamenco in Madrid.[60] The physical presence of the dance teachers and the site in itself roots this interpretation of the myth in a genuine Spanish context of the 1980s.

It is only Laura del Sol who carries the name of her character from whom she is supposed to create an image. Olive-skinned, exotic, shapely: she is a prototype of a Spanish woman and the mediator in Carmen's construction; her character represents different images of the body that dialogue with several sources: that of the *españolada* incarnated by Laura del Sol, that of a dancer to shape, that of a *femme fatale* who chooses the man she wants to love the moment she wishes to. Only her teachers, if this could ever be possible, dominate her. Gades' standpoint determines what we see; he lives through the conflict, which colours the entire film. He projects his interior dilemma onto her.

Creating a new version through flamenco

Creating a new version of Carmen therefore takes place in several stages. The film begins with an exchange of images of bodies, guided by Gades' point of view. He is searching for a woman, who must correspond to his own mental image: flamenco dancers here embody the myth of Pygmalion. The body expresses it: in a long shot from behind, a slightly high angle, we observe a troop of dancers guided by a man who, after a few seconds, commands the first step. "One and two (Uno y dos)", the movement of the choreography starts from the left to the right. We perceive the regularity of the feet in a cadenced and sustained rhythm; the concentrated and clean movement of the dancers is developed in a rich image full of the gleaming colours of dancing apparel. These rhythmic images determined by the flexibility of the dancing female bodies, moving in space and following the measure, possess a lot of energy and strength. The troop follows the leading man. The camera makes a medium close-up of his face: it is Antonio. He turns around, donning a serious and deep look, to better observe the dancers. The choreographer represents the current frame of the flamenco; the bodies meet each other in this dance. His viewpoint directs and observes them, accompanied by the sound of the feet that continue in the same rhythm, with the same intensity. The creator examines them severely; he is not satisfied with what he sees.

The bodies exchange some thought-images: through their dance, accompanied by the sound of their steps, the expression on their faces, the movements of their arms. The thought can be read on their bodies and Gades makes a selection: he asks some girls to dance some steps alone in front of him. These are frontal medium close-ups on the dancers that connect with a medium close-up on Gades who maintains an attentive, preoccupied expression, in spite of this demonstration of graceful female bodies, which are all well-trained and extremely concentrated. He assesses their capacities and also the dance images expressed by the bodies. His thought-image is filled up with undisclosed demands. After some auditions, he leaves: standing straight and proud, he seems decided. He joins the rest of the troop to ask Paco de Lucia if he will be going to Seville to visit some dance schools to look for a girl for the role of Carmen. Paco de Lucia is surprised that he is not satisfied. But these women do not please the creator, determined in his expectations. The myth of Pygmalion is introduced inside the current frame of the flamenco projected on the women's body. After this short sequence the opening credits appear, accompanied by Bizet's drawings and melodies.

Musical sources

The musical themes used in the sequence after the opening credits evoke the different sources already cited. The body of the dancers and the musicians expresses the themes. Gades' body's thought-image translates in a rigid manner how he is attached to, and adheres to the use, of classical music. On the other hand, the thought-images of Paco de Lucia, a contemporary musician, make us feel how contemporary music can be integrated. The conflicts between both music styles explore the link between Bizet and flamenco: the mythical figure of Carmen that is formulated through operatic music, now meets a musical figure of the flamenco. While Carmen did not dance the flamenco it will now be identified with her. This is precisely the film's outcome; it transforms Carmen into a flamenco dancer, obliging a flamenco dancer to become Carmen. This commingling of musical sources generates the new form of the myth.

The first encounter between the musical sources takes place in a hall where the flamenco dancers are rehearsing the dance steps. The spectator observes them in a tracking shot crossing over this place, a site of creation and rehearsal. During this camera movement the music begins to be heard off screen, we approach its source: a frontal full shot of the group where Paco de Lucia is playing the guitar and where Mari-Sol is singing. Then, still in the same tracking shot, a man arrives with a magnetic tape: framed by the camera, he approaches Antonio Gades sitting in the corner. He installs the tape on an old tape recorder while Paco de Lucia's music can still be heard. Obviously, the tape is that of Bizet's operatic music; at that specific moment the shot is cut. Inside the concrete space, the breaking off of the shot separates Gades and Paco de Lucia. They are also in their own heads, in their respective imaginaries. A medium close-up follows this on Gades, who is carefully listening to Bizet; he is concentrated, he is furrowing his eyebrows and his look is serious. The camera moves downwards away from his face to his hand, which is trying to clap the rhythms to compose a dance on the operatic partitions. The music sounds through this hall, not the entire melody, but some fragments, that cross each other, and then mix up with the contemporary flamenco music. Bizet's piece of music gains ascendancy and Mari-Sol stops singing.

A counter shot in a frontal medium closes up on Paco de Lucia who is playing a variation of the fragment of the opera that Gades is listening to. Then, we hear the reaction of the other musicians in a medium close-up from behind on the guitar players. The singer and Paco de Lucia are commenting that this new variation that is obviously better suited for dance than Bizet's classical music; Paco de Lucia is playing a *bulería* with some notes of the *seguidilla* of the opera. He then proposes it to Gades, who accepts it, and with Cristina Hoyos, they dance together on it *por bulería* (a lateral full shot). This sequence illustrates the first stage of the creation through the language of the music. The present time of the flamenco music assimilates a reference to Bizet's original music (1875). The creation is made thanks to the traditional sources reinterpreted inside the contemporary frames.

Mérimée describes Carmen

The new Carmen has to be constructed, but first she has to be found. Gades has precise ideas about this woman as he is also inspired by Mérimée's source dating back to 1845, from whom he cites the text directly. Several sequences underline this reference to sources, to construct the ballet. Indeed, all the aesthetic means have to be built. Both the music and the bodies of the dancers have to be defined.

Gades meticulously observes the sequence of rehearsal and he asks Cristina Hoyos to run through the steps of *por bulería* with the girls. It is a creative and free dance that can be connected by fragments. It is not a deep and heavy dance, but rather a *por burlarse*: in Spanish *burlarse* means to make fun of something, in the dance it means making the body move vivid, through the gestures and the steps.[61] This sequence shows the rehearsal. The body is framed and observed. In a long shot we see Cristina Hoyos at the head, the camera moves towards Gades who enters on the left in the shot and starts to observe and criticise. Gades places himself in front of the mirror; in this way his gaze doubles as we see him from the back and the front. This reflection frames the bodies of the dancers, who are being guided by Cristina Hoyos; several times, this frame emphasises the repetition required at their rehearsal, stressing the clumsiness of their movements and the imperfection of the images of the dancers.

The gaze of Gades dominates the scene: he observes them looking straight ahead – from the front – then turns his head towards the group to comment on their movements. In addition, he expresses his thoughts on Carmen in voice-over, talking to himself. These sentences direct quotes from Mérimée's novel but he expresses them as if they were his own words: "Carmen had a wild and strange beauty. Her lips, full but well shaped opened onto teeth whiter than almonds."[62] After this, he criticises the dancers, telling them that they should not only learn the steps, but they should observe how Cristina is working it out. In a frontal long shot, Cristina Hoyos heading the group is doing some steps, and the girls are rehearsing to reach the same effect. The dance demands concentrated practice and the masters are giving the example. Gades continues to quote in his voice-over: "Her hair was long, black and shiny, with blue glints like the feathers of a raven. Her eyes had a voluptuous but surly expression that I've never been able to find again. Gypsy eyes, wolf eyes as the Spanish saying goes,"[63] and Bizet's music connects on the thoughts of the master.

From then on, he distances himself from his direct environment to formulate his ideas on "his" Carmen. The Pygmalion effect continues. Gades lives in his own world, he dominates his environment with his acts and his way of expressing his ideas on Carmen, all the while disparaging the dancers for failing to live up to his demanding vision. The fact that his mental image is not at all corresponding to the women he observes is difficult for his to cope with. From the beginning of the plot he observes many women that leave him disappointed. In this sequence he quotes some sentences from Mérimée's novel to describe how "the Carmen" should be. Then he is searching in the famous dance school in Madrid, *Amor de Dios*. He stays in his own thoughts. When Laura del Sol enters too late in the Maria Magdalena's class, she is filmed in a medium close-up among the other dancers, and then followed by a medium close-up on Gades' face. Again he brings to bear Mérimée, expressing what he thought of her at first sight: "I looked up and I saw her. I'll never forget it. It was a Friday when I first saw her. At first I didn't like her and I went back to my work but she following the habit of women and cats, who do not come when you call but come when you do not call."[64] This expressed vision, that of the hysterical woman, the unpredictable woman, comparing her with a cat, inscribes her first impression in a larger tradition: the nineteenth century novel by Mérimée relates to a Spanish stereotype of a woman as a feline, a sexual active woman, comparing her with a female cat.[65] This animal is known for its independence and seductive qualities: when she is first visually introduced in the plot, it is the point of view that is conveyed onto Carmen.

Creating the image of the new Carmen

The woman who will incarnate Carmen has been chosen but has yet to be trained. The dance brings a contemporary expression, but this is not enough, they have to go further. The encounter with Cristina Hoyos will be revealing. She is an experienced and extremely talented dancer; she is supposed to teach Carmen how to become a good dancer. Through work on the body, she is teaching her how to behave. It is distinctly manifest that Cristina, even if she is too old for this role, is still the best. Carmen's character represents a young woman with a beautiful body, which carries in it the features of modernity, contrasting with the tradition of "the Carmen". They ask her to represent Carmen, hoping that she will simultaneously embody a tradition and place it within a contemporary context. Her way of dancing does not yet respond to this ideal.

She has to be trained according Gades' ideas: Cristina Hoyos does not really share his choice but she has to work with her. The dance is her rehearsal. Giving a strong image of her body in this dance is not easy, and Cristina Hoyos shows herself to be demanding. A beautiful sequence shows the two women in a frontal long shot, where the figure of Cristina dominating at the head of the group. Carmen finds herself in the background, trying to work on her dance. The depth of field underlines the contrasts; Cristina turns around, advances towards the camera that follows her in a tracking shot, the framing of her back fills up the image. The camera centres the back of Cristina and in the background Carmen moves in the frame, from the left to the right, while her teacher is giving severe commentaries on her gestures. Carmen searchingly watches Cristina and follows her. Filming Carmen's frontal view from Cristina's back imposes Cristina's point of view on Carmen's body. This is all the more clear because Cristina's back almost completely fills the frame, in opposition to Carmen's body, which is left in the background. Carmen focuses all her concentration on Cristina, which means that she has something to prove. When Cristina turns towards the spectator, Carmen's serious expression relaxes a little bit. The tension between the two women and the exchange of their physical images are accompanied by a deep music, the soothing part of *una farruca*, a dance that requires a lot of experience.

Gades calls Cristina Hoyos to his office and asks her to help him to improve this new Carmen. The framing of the camera emphasises their conflict. Firstly, Gades is filmed from behind, when Cristina enters. Then by a tracking shot both teachers are framed in a lateral medium close shot. In the background, a transparent mirror is placed between them, through which they still see the dancers in the classroom. The girls cannot see their teachers. At that moment Carmen approaches the one-way mirror to look at herself with a strong and convincing look, and Gades and Cristina Hoyos also look at her. This last shot of the three characters centres on Carmen's body; it is therefore a double reflection on seeing oneself and on the gaze of the other. Cristina Hoyos sketches a gesture towards her and explains that she does not understand very well why Gades is particularly attached to this girl, certainly because she is young, which is the central problem. The dancer and the director are face to face, in frontal medium close-ups and shot/reverse shots, the framing emphasises their opposition. For her, this Carmen is simply not a good enough dancer, and there are surely more talented dancers. Nevertheless, she's the one that Cristina is given to train.

Looking at the body through dance

Cristina continues and the mise-en-scene draws attention to the work on the body by the presence of mirrors: the mirrors symbolise reflection. They also furnish an effect of over-framing.[66] As Aumont affirms, this technique reinforces the impact of looking, underlining the act of viewing; the entire frame is there to be watched. The film emphasises the rehearsal to improve the dance image of Carmen's body with Cristina's guidance. Their exchange is shown in a beautiful sequence in which they dance together in front of a mirror.

The dance is an encounter of bodies during which the expression of gestures and movements declare who is master: the mirror reflects and frames this power play. In a lateral medium close-up Cristina shows a movement of her arm, around her face, around her shoulders. Frontally in the background, Carmen is placed in front of the mirrors and reflects on this exercise. Her worried and concentrated expression emphasises the difficulty. The mirror also reflects in its frame the other dancers who continue their exercises. Once again, several gazes cross each other in this mise-en-scene of the dancer's bodies; the scene draws attention to all these frames. Carmen is supposed to express through her entire person an appropriated image of the flamenco dance, thereby updating the myth. The music that accompanies the dance is a tune of the *farruca*, a sombre melody; it is the calm and intensive part (*el silencio*). The *farruca* is above all danced by men: if women dance it, they wear trousers. It is a difficult choreography, which requires from the part of the dancer an important maturity, which is expressed through the body. Before the night they make love, Antonio Gades dances a *farruca* for Carmen, with all the deep and mature feelings it

Photo 8: To discipline the body through flamenco dance

necessarily demonstrates. A young dancer who lacks the necessary experience could rarely interpret this dance.

Laura del Sol has still not reached the level of Cristina (in this sequence): during the whole film, her two teachers try desperately to train her. The images of the dancers' bodies meet each other in this gesture. Carmen tries the posture of the *farruca,* and places herself in front of the mirror; Cristina takes the position next to her. Carmen, young and struggling, executes two movements. Her style is light and lacking in emotion. Cristina shakes her head in dismay. It is interesting to see how a short step, or a slight movement of the arms, can express such a marked difference. In rehearsal, the body's image communicated through this dance declares that Carmen cannot reach the same intensity as Cristina. Cristina's gestures are perfect, controlled and show an artistic perfection. Carmen is hesitating, searching to find the same impact in this language, but does not possess her teacher's maturity: she places herself next to her and the two dancers carry on with another exercise. A gesture around the face, a tender and strong act, the camera approaches again from behind on the back of both women, while we see them in the face thanks to the mirror. Followed by a zoom in to Carmen's face who tries to reach the same effect but her face is marked by her

Photo 9: Giving birth to a new Carmen through her body

hesitation until she notices the absence of critique coming from her master; a smile of satisfaction replaces her fretful expression. She is progressing.

The rehearsal continues: *"You are the Carmen! Believe it!"*
Gades constrains himself to induce his Carmen out of Laura del Sol's body. She has to express this thought through her way of dancing. The image is shown by a lateral full shot on Carmen and frontal in the background on Gades, he gets on stage; the two bodies face each other and are marked by a distance between them on all levels. He pulls her towards the left, puts himself in front of her, his back is slightly bowed, fixing his fists, his arms are tense, all his attention is directed towards her. He looks at her as he desperately tries to pull out of her and her dance more evocative interpretations (see photograph).

He speaks severely to her, and she stays calm, despite all his admonishments: "are you marking time or dancing or what?" She replies: "I'm trying". Gades, sarcastic, watches her and continues: "trying? But you're doing all the steps the same way! Separate the times. What the hell is wrong with you? You're not concentrating!" Carmen's dance steps are technically correct, but she does not invest herself in the interpretation. Antonio Gades gets furious; he is desperately trying to shake her up by giving her the example. Counting in a loud voice, he moves on stage from the left to the right, and then approaching, he stops in front of the mirror, looks at himself and shouts to her in a pan-shot. The stairs are in the middle of the scene, the mirror in the background, his body reflects his own image underlining that she must do the same thing. The camera returns from Gades to Carmen. It is a confrontation between two bodies that affront each other, he begs her to symbolically "devour" Cristina, to dance more violently. He shouts very loudly to her, bowing his back, looking at her wildly: "you are Carmen! Believe it! If you don't, who will?" Through his words, he creates the mirror for the body of Carmen, expressing the thought she should articulate. She is there, ready to attack, she is successfully learning it because her last dance steps were done by her alone and her creator, satisfied, embraces her passionately. He wants to pull out of this Laura del Sol, the mythological image that he possesses of Carmen.

Carmen is born

The presence of the mirror is crucial during the rehearsal; this frame accentuates the image of her body. The construction is now realised. Laura del Sol becomes Carmen but she will also emancipate herself from Gades' mise-en-scene, whose gaze had guided the creation inside the film. He is now losing control. After the night of their lovemaking, Carmen becomes a real *femme fatale* as she leaves in the middle of the night, unveiling herself to be a woman who after making love nonchalantly leaves without saying goodbye. The camera follows her body half dressed in a tracking shot. As she is leaving, she bumps into something and wakes up her lover, who does not understand why she is leaving. He turns on the light and the camera displaces to him in a frontal medium close shot: the thought-image of his body is the confused expression of an abandoned lover, who is naked and alone, surprised about her leaving in secret. He asks her why she's leaving as he sits up a bit. Hair undone, she is a prototypical body of a contemporary Carmen; we distinguish the contours of the female body in the scarce light, her clothes accentuating her sensual, feminine form. Without any explanation or commentary, she re-enters the field to give him a kiss and says that she is leaving. She offers no appeasing promises of a new appointment; here we have a new Carmen without flamenco clothes, a prototype of a contemporary *femme fatale*.

Gades' body expresses the thought of being deeply moved. Shocked by the surreptitious departure of this modern Spanish lady, he gets up and walks into the dance hall. With a mirror in the background, a light vaguely brightens the room in which he starts to compose some dance steps. The camera approaches him, he moves his shoulders back, approaches the mirror that doubles his silhouette. The frontal reflection creates his thoughts by the image of his body; he makes some gestures of Carmen moving in a feminine way, wiggling his hips, embracing himself with his arms around his chest, his hands touch his shoulders and he bows to his knees. By his attitude, he establishes the thought-image of a seductive, erotic woman: hips, shoulder, kiss. He is deeply touched, without any doubt, by her. The lighting indicates that it is night, sombre: all alone, he starts to work. He feels confused.

Deeply moved by his Carmen, he returns to a traditional aspect, re-enacting the stereotypes: these are images that everybody knows, that we can classify, categorise, and control. In a medium close-up, his hands in front of his eyes, Gades puts across the idea that he knows not what to do. The choreographer approaches again the mirror, which symbolises his will to command his thoughts. At that moment, the imaginary image of Carmen arrives from the right and the opera music accompanies her: a vision of the *españolada* from Gades. A black fan concealing her face, wearing a shawl, she is dressed in an extremely stereotypical way, with all the flamenco clichés. In a medium close-up on both characters, she turns provocatively to him and looks him straight in the eye. Music accompanies this return to the cliché, because at that moment, Bizet appears. Carmen still has to be constructed, but this costume with all the typical flamenco accoutrement tortures her creator. He is well aware that these images are heralding the beginning of this woman's independence and this fact destabilizes him terribly. In a full shot, the gypsy woman sees him leaving this place while she stays there all alone, slowly waving her fan.

The stereotyped bodies have a party

The confusion between Gades and Carmen escalates after their lovemaking evening: from then on, the cutting of the acts becomes less pronounced, and the stereotyped body of Carmen is shown ever more, with all the typical flamenco attributes. For example, in the birthday sequence with the caricature of flamenco, the body refers to the *españolada* or a parody of the bullfighter. In a full shot on the group, a man is dancing *por bulería* in the middle while the other dancers clap the rhythm, *las palmas*, in order to accompany the dance. The images are cut in a medium close-up on Gades and Paco de Lucia. Gades wants to know if Carmen is seeing someone else. The party continues, and Paco de Lucia cannot tell him much about what Gades has asked. A full shot on this group is followed by a medium close-up on Carmen, who leaves the dressing room and raises her fan in the air: a cliché gesture of flamenco.

She then looks on all her sides, raising her eyebrows in a provocative manner. Her attitude expresses that of the bullfighter bravery, ready to enter the arena; hers is the arena of love in which she provokes men. Needless to say, she wears the colours of Carmen: red and black. The paso doble music of the opera dominates and accompanies her physical outlook marked by the *españolada*; the *bulería*, authentic flamenco music, is not heard anymore. In a full shot, waving the

Photo 10: Stereotyped body of the españolada

fan in front of her face, she approaches the people and sits down, turn after turn, on the knees of several men.

In a frontal full shot, Cristina reacts in order to ridicule such an image: covering her head with her skirt, she shows her buttocks to everyone there. Then, the two female bodies dressed and marked by the clothes of the *españolada*, dance face to face in a full shot. In a similar manner, they move the arms and bow their backs forward and backward in a patently exaggerated way. It is an exchange of thought-images between the dancers to parody fixed images. It is not a mise-en-scene by Gades, but a spontaneous act to celebrate a birthday. And again this image is accompanied by the operatic music. After the spectacle of the two women, another *españolada* takes place: the image of a bullfighter, in a medium close-up, wearing a typical cap. The men imitate amongst themselves a bullfight, and everyone applauds: Bizet' music accompanies them and they go outside to honour the bullfighter who has killed the bull. Another parodied image during the day; this is not a mise-en-scene anymore.

After the birthday party with the whole group, Carmen's husband is introduced. Gades wears sombre and preoccupied expression. In a medium close-up from behind on Gades, in the background, Carmen walks into the room with her husband, face to face with her lover. A close-up on Gades shows his perturbed face. He is visibly annoyed. This is followed by a medium close shot on Carmen: she kisses her husband, scoffing at Gades with her eyes. He has left prison, which she announces to Gades as if she is feeling relieved now. Still dressed up with all her attributes, also in red and black to be loyal to the symbolic colours, she incarnates a contemporary Carmen. A close-up emphasises the confusion on the face of her creator, quite discontent to see her husband reappear.

The next sequence expresses Gades' jealousy and anger during a rehearsal of footwork: *zapateados*. *Zapatos* in Spanish means shoes, in flamenco dance *zapateados* means intensive, melodic rhythmic footwork, with accents, and variations that are similar to a musical score. Originally this was a man's dance, meant to depict for virility and the dynamism of a robust character. When women dance it, they often wear trousers and a short jacket.[67] Now all dancers are executing it in a lateral medium close-up on the feet doing the *zapateados*, while Gades, in a powerful voice shouts to increase the intensity of the rhythm. The camera follows the entire group of dancers in a tracking shot, as they move from one side of the room to the other. The sound is intense and Gades' voice does not stop shouting. After this expression of anger during the rehearsal, Carmen speaks to Gades. They reconcile and continue their love story: Gades gives her some money so that her husband can leave to begin a new life somewhere else. A medium close-up shows the couple laying in bed embracing each other and, after Gades declares his love for Carmen, she says: "Antonio, *solamente quiero a ti*", "It is only you that I love", we hear again Bizet's sombre and threatening music.

Pygmalion in flamenco

The traditional version of Carmen continues to dominate the film after the love-making night. The rhythm of the film accelerates, as the music becomes ever more menacing, grave, and distressing. The danger becomes threatening as we have a premonition about the unavoidable, because it is in Carmen's nature to continue her lifestyle. It is precisely this nature that drives men like Gades completely mad. When they start their affair, he isn't able to control himself, he looses control and this loss is also visualised through the images: the "fiction" and "reality" get mixed up. The cutting between the acts is left behind, or shown at the end of the act; we do not always know on what level to situate it: is this Gades' creation or is this a rehearsal? Even on a visual level the lamp installation is less clearly indicated and the stairs and the mirrors are no longer present. Yet Carmen is trained despite all these difficulties.

When the dancers start to play cards, the mise-en-scene of the characters is ambiguous. The sequence starts after their reconciliation in a medium close-up on the husband's face, and frontally on Gades. Carmen's husband speaks about

Photo 11: Dance and fight

his stay in prison and about the joy he feels in his newly gained freedom. They play cards but thanks to Carmen, Gades discovers that her husband is cheating: a medium close-up on his face, she slightly bows her head and thus gives him a sign. This gesture provokes a fight between the two men; two enemies dance in beautiful and powerful rivalry.

In a full shot, the feet and the stick make for a full sound. The two men use the stick. The light is dim. When one man is dancing, the other replies by threatening menacing sounds. A low-angle medium close-up shot of the husband shows his anger, a tense and clenched expression, determined to affront his adversary. Acrobatic movements and a fatal strike from Gades' stick, lead to the husband's demise. A high angle shot shows a prostrate and contorted body. Carmen approaches and throws her wedding ring on the floor. In a shot on her husband's dead body, we can see the ring falling down. She places herself next to Gades and both faces are united in a medium close-up. They walk back looking at the group. This image shows the state of their couple: he has vanquished her husband. She has chosen to throw away her ring. Carmen's face is turning to him and she's smiling, indicating that the mise-en-scene is finished. At that moment, with the movement of Carmen's face, we realise the previous scene was actually a mise-en-scene of Gades' ballet. In addition, after that dance, the character that played her husband takes away the wig he was wearing. Indeed, during the scene we did not know that he was another person. This sequence is misleading as during the initial viewing, we had know way of knowing that it was one of the ballet's acts, as it seemed real. It is exactly this kind of reading, on two levels, that exemplifies the befuddlement of feelings and the Gades' composition. He is losing himself more and more in his new creation. Like the myth of Pygmalion, but this time projected onto Carmen as a flamenco dancer.

The mise-en-scene is finished and Gades is lying down on the floor. Everybody seems to have gone. Satisfied with his dance, he gets up and approaches the dressing room. The camera follows closely his face, he opens the door, and the camera shows us the costumes in a medium close-up. The camera represents his point of view. He advances a little and discovers Carmen hidden under the costumes with a new lover, a dancer of the group. She was caught by her other lover, Gades, half dressed with another man. Carmen gets up, looks straight at the camera and brings her top to her breasts. Gades is furious. Carmen quietly leaves the dressing room, calm, proud, and sure of herself. The thought her body summons up is that Gades' reaction is of no concern to her. Once discovered, she is simply annoyed to have been interrupted, but she certainly does not blame herself: the *femme fatale* shows her real character once again outside the scene.

The last dance

The last sequence starts as a party and again we are unsure as to whether this is one of Gades' mise-en-scene or not. The stereotype dominates the end of the film, backed by Bizet's music and the presence of the bullfighter. Gades and Carmen dance together a paso doble: in this dance the woman symbolises the bait for the bull, the sensual provocation that invites this virile animal to attack. The female body is like the piece of red cloth sensually waved in the arms by the toreador. Through dance, the paso doble transforms the female body into this provocative red cloth, which needs to be moved by her partner. Carmen is stunning. The bullfighter approaches her, walks around her in a medium close shot, observing her beauty with a concentrated and sensual eye and making a typical gesture with his hand, showing that he is prepared to seduce this beautiful creature. He walks like one would in an arena, master of the scene, and master of Carmen. They start dancing together when Gades intervenes in a fit of jealousy. In the arms of her toreador the body of Carmen changes into the provocative red cloth and Gades reacts. Furious, she walks away, and again her body language is impressive. She confirms her steps with grace and pride, invading the space with her presence. This woman is free and whether or not she has been created by Gades, she exists equally without him. This freedom is unfortunately hard to accept by her creator. He stabs her with a knife. She falls down (a lateral medium long shot) as Bizet's music fills the space. A dramatic cry punctuates this ungrateful end; it is a traditional finish that has been repeated ever so often. Tradition once again took what this woman wanted to live: this new Carmen is killed after having completely integrated into her body all the connotations that this myth meant to represent: sensuality, force, independence, and more tragically: actuality.

Carmen of 1983: the end?

Creating new images of women, redefining her social identity, corresponds to the issues discussed in the 1970s and 1980s and their topical nature is confirmed by the political measures during that period. Saura's film shows an actualisation of the archetype of the *femme fatale* in the Spanish language. Creating a new Carmen, the body of Laura del Sol submits to all the rituals of interrogation and the construction of a new version. She is supposed to correspond to the images of the *femme fatale*; that of Mérimée's from 1845, of the *españolada*, which refers to the 1875 version of Bizet and finally she also represents an image of a contemporary *femme fatale*, manifested in the person of a flamenco dancer of 1983. Carmen's body interrogates the historical sources of the myth and dance frames this process. Different choreographies become the ritual of the updated version, through a dance that symbolises the revolt against all authority and advocates independence. The result is a new composition in which the past still dominates; the heroine's body mirrors all these ideas and the film finishes on a traditional image of the epoch, showing how difficult it is to really liberate her from the past: Carmen dies in this new version, as in the old one.

III. High Heels (Tacones lejanos, 1991): a mother walks away

Almodóvar's High Heels (Tacones lejanos), which was released almost ten years after Saura's Carmen, is the third film to be showcased in our study. The 1990s brought a markedly changed political reality to Spain: democracy was consolidated and the country had been integrated in the European Community since 1986. Accordingly, issues concerning women had also changed since the 1970s: the right to work had become commonplace and new myths were now being projected onto the reality of combining motherhood and a professional career. High Heels (Tacones lejanos) presents this synthesis of the mother archetype. The story is about a singer, and a mother (Marisa Paredes), who encounters difficulties in meeting the requirements of her two major roles. She chooses to leave for fifteen years to pursue a prosperous singing career in Mexico, thereby forgetting or ignoring the existence of her daughter Rebeca (Victoria Abril), who consequently feels entirely forsaken. The plot begins with the mother's return and, throughout the entire film, her daughter Rebeca tries to improve their strained relationship. The acts carried out by this abandoned daughter allow us to make a reading of a ground-breaking myth about a woman who works, about a mother who is a star.

The reception in Spain

On its opening weekend, the film sold the most tickets ever for a Spanish film and its success was further confirmed by the press reactions, which commented on the enthusiasm of the audience.[68] HIGH HEELS imposes a star system: firstly, the plot was inspired by a real-life story. As several Spanish singers had lived in Mexico or in other South-American countries for long periods (Lola Flores, Rocío Durcal, Amparo Rivelles[69]), the film evoked the success of some of these Spanish stars.[70] Secondly, the film's release imitated the Hollywood model. Almodóvar had organised a parade of Spanish stars on the Gran Vía of Madrid with floats that had the form of high heels.[71]

> Madrid, at the last release, was a garbage truck and yesterday in Madrid, two enormous red floats in the form of huge heels…/…From nine o'clock in the evening to eleven o'clock on the dot, when the enthusiasm began to recede and the film could be projected – Madrid's Gran Vía was totally invaded by the non-invited of the event, those who pretended to participate while in the street, like extras of a Hollywood mega production, in the most tumultuous night of the cinematographic story. Trendy people in Gautier watched as Almodóvar, having moved on to the classics of Armani and Chanel; Miguel Bosé's admirers stood anxious to see in an "original version" of their sexual idol, one without a wig or a beard.[72]

It should be acknowledged that Almodóvar is a master at generating his own publicity and favours in this way his own cult phenomena, reinforcing his creative universe by showcasing bodies that are created by his cinema, ritualising them outside the textual context of the film's perception. As Fransisco Umbral puts it:

> Almodóvar is already a sociological phenomenon, one that develops at the margins of his own large cinematographic personality, and this can be seen at the premieres, with the Gran Via paralysed for the event, and in the very Almodóvar public, with its eternal girls in mini skirts and its boys ever so bizarre. Looking at the public is like looking at the screen: the same shiny climate is present, that of a generation that established itself through its nocturnal power. All of this is stimulating to intellectuals and ministers, like Doña Matilde. But the film does not reveal as much.[73]

As Umbral underlines, typical of cult phenomena, we are witness to both an on-screen and street-level spectacle; weird bodies walk in the street and these are as eccentric as the bodies in the films; Almodóvar has incited this imitation.

The film was subject to a lot of attention, but received also harsh critique.[74] Here is an exemplary reaction that illustrates the tone. The journalist places lots of intermediary titles, which helps to accentuate the numerous shortcomings: "In TACONES LEJANOS there is not even the minimal presence of a plot and its characters are consequently ridiculous in a pathetic way. Almodóvar made his last film with a lamentable lack of originality."[75] The author finishes his vituperative attack with this remark: "If Almodóvar did not shoot TACONES LEJANOS without motivation, he certainly did it in a state of utter creative confusion and with a lamentable lack of originality."[76] The conflict arising from the filmmaker, his work and his rejection is already an old debate in Spain: while the Academy of Spanish Cinema selected the film to represent the country for the Oscars, it itself only awarded him a Goya in 1988 for Best Script for WOMEN ON THE VERGE OF A NERVOUS BREAKDOWN. In fact, he was awarded a Goya for Best film in 2000 only, and this following international recognition of ALL ABOUT MY MOTHER, which had received an Oscar in 1999.

Star-mother: the archetype

The way in which motherhood is represented in Spanish cinema deserves some attention.[77] In the first chapter we commented on the film RACE, which portrayed a sanctimonious image of the mother figure. A mother is someone who educates children, prays to God, and supports her husband in the battles he fights abroad for the country. Her role as a procreator is a sacred aspect of her identity. In FLUNKING OUT (ASIGNATURA PENDIENTE) we also commented on a mother figure, but this time as a protagonist who has other preoccupations and concerns, or the lack thereof, as her relationship with her children is rarely shown. As one might expect, there was obviously a considerable change in figuration in Spanish cinema since the Franco periods, as Barry Jordan and Rikki Tamosunas sharply summarise: "If the castrating matriarchs of the 1970s were usually constructed in terms of their relationships with their sons, the protective and empowering influence of the benign matriarchs of the 1980s and 1990s thus often focus on mother-daughter relationships."[78] HIGH HEELS (TACONES LEJANOS) fits perfectly into this trend of displaying the relationship between a mother and a daughter.

Another aspect worth mentioning is the representation of motherhood in Almodóvar's films. Marsha Kinder analysed the strong mother figure and, when interviewing Almodóvar, she asks him why he often portrays awful mothers. His statement about them in this 1987 interview is revealing. When she asks him why these women are so repressive, like the evil one in MATADOR, the film director confirms:

> Yes, I find this kind of mother very hateful, but there are several other mothers in that film…. I feel close to the mother. The idea of motherhood is very important in Spain. The father was frequently absent in Spain. It's as if the mother represents the law, the police. It's very curious because in my next film project, I have two young girls kill their mother. When you kill the mother, you kill precisely everything you hate, all of those burdens that hang over you. In this film, I'm killing all of my upbringing and all of the intolerance that is sick in Spain.[79]

This interview was done in 1987, and the film director was already speaking about this new film, even though the main characters were two sisters. Apparently he transformed the script later on.

This mother in HIGH HEELS (TACONES LEJANOS) has indeed a lot of power and authority, but now in a modern world, she is professionally someone to admire. The film is about the life of a celebrity named Becky. As with FLUNKING OUT (ASIGNATURA PENDIENTE), this character updates the maternal archetype. Becky mediates between having children and the cluster of expectations about maternal instincts, for instance that related to protecting the child. This mother is peculiar. She is not only a woman who works but, more than that, she is a star. She is a famous singer. Becky has absolutely succeeded on a professional level; she is a body to marvel at when she is on stage; stars are to be watched and admired.

Corresponding to the main tendencies about figuring "new mothers" in the 1980s and 1990s, the conflict in the film relies on the relationship between a mother and her daughter. The daughter feels she has been abandoned: the title already establishes this reading. The meaning seems obvious, but its translation into French and English is surprising. In French TALONS AIGUILLES – in English HIGH HEELS – is linguistically quite far away from the Spanish title. High heels is more the equivalent of *"tacones altos"*. Indeed, the expression *"tacones lejanos"* does not really exist in Spanish, but the word *"lejos"* signifies *"far"*, and *"lejanos"* means "distant"; distant refers to the mother's heels as she is walking away. The film director has thus invented this linguistic construction to give a new image of the symbolic meaning that the heels might represent for the daughter: this expression furnishes the idea of a female body that is leaving. As he said in 1987 when talking about this idea: "I remember when I was a child, it was a symbol of freedom for young girls to wear high heels, to smoke and to wear trousers."[80] Often the first heels that we observe in our childhood are those of the mother and daughters often dream of wearing them one day. All children imitate the image of their parents' bodies and Rebeca imitates and tries to find an image of her mother during the long period of her absence.

The actors

Three characters are important: Rebeca, her mother Becky and the transvestite judge. All three propose by the thought of their bodies different identities that serve to understand the myth. Victoria Abril plays the character of the daughter, Rebeca. Abril knew how to create an image of a submissive daughter, one who feels abandoned and one who suffers greatly; Victoria Abril showed once more that she is able to play very different characters. The mother, Becky, played by Marisa Paredes, represents a star and the image of an unusual mother figure. Her body incarnates at once a stereotype and a prototype. Firstly, she is a prototype in light of her eminent professional life, put into image by her identity as a celebrity: Marisa Paredes, a brilliant actress, knows how to overact her feelings and creates this image of acquired fame through her gestures, her way of walking, slow sway of the hips, like the Hollywood stars are used to doing. But she is a mother as well, and this expression is stereotyped in a negative way: the narcissistic image of her character is emphasised, as she prefers to forget her child in order to accomplish her rich career abroad. She is extremely selfish.

Miguel Bosé provides the third image of a significant body; outside this filmic context, he is a Spanish sex symbol, a famous singer.[81] He embodies maternal consciousness towards Rebeca through an atypical character who has a double identity: he plays the judge Dominguez and, in addition, he imitates Becky as the drag queen Femme Letal. A mediator between mother and daughter, his duality carries the conflict and symbolises it for the abandoned daughter. Rebeca's husband (interpreted by Feodor Atkine) has little influence on the plot: his body is an issue of conflict between Rebeca and Becky, as he is the mother's ex-lover. He presents a stereotypical image of a macho man who is conservative. This is enforced by his severe traits, the angular structure of his face and his classical way of dressing.

The mythological plot

The mythological plot imposes itself in the sequences during which the daughter tries to find her mother, or is doing everything she can to accept the abandonment; she creates a presence of her mother by the intermediary of available bodies. The judge is the mediator who negotiates the conflict. How does one deal with being abandoned? How does one express or sublimate this pain? Two rituals are exercised: the presence and absence of the mother, and the private and public gaze that follow the problem. The ritual is double: Becky's body carries two identities that are difficult to assume: a mother and a star. Rebeca expresses the first ritual: to digest and cope with her abandonment, she creates a symbolic presence of her mother. The second ritual is the gaze on the abandoned child. Mother and daughter are observed by lots of people, who follow their life as a star with a child.

Childhood or the origins

The mother-daughter relationship bears the whole story. The first sequence, a flashback, illustrates the origin of the problem, which explains the myth constructed about this monstrous mother. Returning towards childhood is the first step in making this reading. This looking back makes us understand the long struggle carried out by her daughter up until the present moment.

The film begins with the mother returning after having been absent for many years. Waiting for her at the airport, the adult body of Rebeca is transformed by a flash-back into the body of herself as a child. She is recalling the events from her childhood when her mother was particularly mean to her, showing a complete lack of interest. Rebeca is extremely tense, nervous. She is sitting on a red chair in a frontal full shot, dressed up in a white Chanel, with her little red handbag in front of her. The camera approaches her thoughtful face; with the image in superimposition, she takes us with her through her thoughts to the Margarita Islands in 1972; the memories appear: no music, no sound; Rebeca, as a child, with her mother and her mother's friend are walking through a colourful market. The couple is very much in love. They kiss each other with little Rebeca next to them. Her mother is dressed in an extravagant manner, wearing a red shawl and a white hat, she has very long bright blue sleeves, a red shirt and white-framed glasses; dressed up as a star, this woman attracts a lot of attention and loves to be watched. She is buying jewellery and Rebeca asks if she may also have some white earrings. Continuing their walk, Rebeca is so happy with this gift and then she suddenly realises that she has lost a piece of jewellery; she goes back on her steps. In a static lateral full shot, two men start talking to her and Rebeca calls her mother who arrives running to her with her friend, in a tracking shot on the market, a lively sunny image.

When they are united, the men ask to buy Rebeca. Without any hesitation Becky's friend organises the sale against coconuts. The medium close-up on the couple draws attention to the mother's state of amorous devotion to the man who she is with; an atypical maternal character, watching these men, laughing with them, saying: *"but no, no"* without any conviction. The archetype of the protective mother is ridiculed with this image: her whole being exudes disinterest in her child, as a sign of absence, a pathetic rejection, which is too extreme to be taken seriously. In a reverse medium close-up, deep disappointment can be read on her daughter's face; the mother's sleeve accompanies her on the left in the shot. The child looks at her mother, who only has eyes for her friend. And the fictional sale continues. But the little Rebeca insists; in a medium close-up, she approaches again the friend's leg, her face turns towards her mother, who ignores her. Suddenly she turns round and runs away from these two monsters who want to sell her (tracking shot). And, once again, the maternal image is absurd; she reacts, annoyed: "you've traumatised her again". A long shot shows us a child running towards the camera, towards us, all alone running in a forest. The mother's voice calls her: "Rebeca, Rebeca, Rebeca..." but the call is no longer heard: the little girl is running (in superimposition) into Rebeca's adult face, (completely covered by the child's body running, and still running). The image unites brilliantly the child's grief, deep inside Rebeca's mind, with the present day adult Rebeca. Evoking this maternal voice, the shot shows again the adult woman, at the airport, the place for trips to far away.

The sequence is a return to her childhood. We see a body of a girl running away from the monstrous maternal body. A dismissive negligent mother marked this childhood, by a lack of care and selfishness. And her adult daughter still expresses this grief: she is sad, her larynx is moving, her chest shows that she is breathing rapidly, due to emotion, and her eyes look sad. Feeling uncomfortable, she moves a little and takes some earrings out of her bag: the same as in the memories of her holiday on Margarita Island. In a medium close-up, she puts them on with a little smile and looks decided with a little forced smile. This period was far from being happy.

A monstrous child

She looks downwards and another memory draws near. Once again, waiting at the airport, Rebeca is questioning the past in order to approach her mother and to construct her mother's presence through memory. For her entire life she has tried to be next to her mother, to be close to her. But her mother had other ambitions. In a flashback the image dissolves as a superimposition into a close-up of a colourful whirligig, that is turning round very rapidly, followed by a pan to the right, on a newspaper article that presents the image of a star: it is Becky, also in a close-up. The young voice of Rebeca is attentively reading the news about her mother. Even her child reads about her in the press. The thought-image of this child's body seems all nice and full of life, with this little colourful whirligig, her long hair and sweet face. She hears her mother speaking to her husband, she turns around and discretely approaches the door to listen to a conversation about Becky's professional project, for which the husband does not agree. He wants her to stay at home and she wishes to work. Madrid, 1974 was written on the screen. We know she needs her husband's permission to work. Practically walking on her tiptoes, little Rebeca goes to the bathroom where she exchanges the pills from two bottles; this young child knows what she is doing. She presents an image of being resolutely decided.

Photo 12: Monstrous child (© Mimmo Cattarinich / © El Deseo D.A., S.L.U.)

Due to this act the husband will be killed in a car crash. The medium close-up in black and white on Becky makes us understand this horrific news. With a star's facial expression, she shows her sadness for her husband's death. He fell asleep while he was driving his car. Little Rebeca feels happy. Again she is focusing on her mother's life framed by the media: when she's sitting in front of the television with another woman in a nice dress in a reverse shot, she says that her father will be happy because he did not like this new husband; her face expresses her satisfaction in a close-up when she bites, pleased with herself, into a hamburger. Her person is hiding a little monster; this nice-looking little girl, with her sweet and innocent image, is at the same time a child murderer.

Unfortunately this crime does not help her much, because her mother leaves anyway and now without her. The next sequence shows another image of the past with Becky as a star during an interview with a young journalist, Manuel, when she is speaking about a trip she is about to make. We see the little Rebeca enter through the door, to run towards her mother and then we hear the last sentence of the journalist: "so, we see each other soon in Mexico." The child also wanted to leave with her mother, but Becky changed her mind despite her promises. Her father sits down later behind Rebeca and around her head the discussion continues; the parents surround this child. A close-up on the mother's face promises her that after this film in Mexico they won't be separated ever again. This is followed by the image of Rebeca's face in close-up, replying: "I don't believe you" then that of Becky, with a sullen look; she does not know what other pretext to invent to get rid of her daughter. The selfishness of the mother is awfully accentuated by this stereotyped body. The discussion continues around the face of the child, visualising this misunderstanding, because neither the parents nor Rebeca agree; her desperate mother says that she no longer knows what to do with this child and the father promises to take care of her; the images fade to black, followed by the airport's luggage conveyor belt. We see a guitar. The star arrives, she comes back, again present in Rebeca's life, and it is a ritual of return.

An atypical maternal body

After many years, mother and daughter meet again at the airport, the place for long-distance trips. Her mother is returning from far away, very far. Following the guitar, the camera makes a tracking shot from the left to the right and shows the pink heels, it is the image of returning: the mother is again close to her child. The camera focuses then on that person dressed up in red who indicates by her gestures to someone off screen how one has to take the luggage. In the background we see Rebeca who arrives in a hurry. She bumps into her mother who, on the moment, does not recognise her and says "excuse me" with the intention to continuing to look for her luggage. But Rebeca touches her arm, looks at her with a lot of emotion, while Becky is turned completely towards her luggage. Rebeca says "mama" and Becky looks at her listening to the rest of the sentence "It's me, Rebeca". Her mother seems to be completely surprised and then they embrace each other.

After fifteen years of absence the mother has not recognised her own child: once again the stereotype of the bad mother is emphasised: she doesn't know what her own daughter looks like. Then, when they want to leave, the mother takes a little mirror to verify her make-up. An extreme close-up shows us the little mirror, particularly kitsch, with the reflection of Becky's red lips. The camera displaces to Rebeca's face in a close-up, to say that there won't be any journalists. Her mother, so disappointed about this lack of attention for her person, reacts. It is the typical image of a star that is preoccupied with her success. The idea that she had not recognised her own daughter left her unaffected; she has already forgotten the poignant episode. In a close-up, there is an exchange of looks and of emotions: Rebeca, disappointed, says that she has waited for her mother with a lot of hope. Rebeca is almost in tears. Her mother apologises. This sequence about the first re-encounter finishes with a close-up on Rebeca's sad face.

Making it present

The maternal absence is incarnated by the person of Rebeca who, questioning this maternal void, has throughout her whole life constructed a maternal presence through rituals. She has been looking for other bodies as mediators to overcome this debilitating lack. Her acts help to symbolise a sort of presence. First, she has married her mother's ex-lover, a lover who had visited her in Mexico. He had gone where she also wanted to be, with her mother. Now her mother will see this man again; he is now her daughter's husband.

The sequence shows the tense bodies, all trying to control themselves. It starts with a close-up on a television, followed by a medium close-up on Manuel's face. Manual is a man whose haughty look exudes arrogance. He is smoking a cigarette with a disdaining and cold expression. He no longer resembles the young Manuel who had wild and long hair and who was Becky's lover at that time. We hear the bell and his gaze turns to the left: Becky arrives. In a long shot we see the image of Rebeca's body running to the door to embrace her mother. Rebeca is dressed up in red, in a classical Chanel suit. Her mother is dressed up as a star, with a gold shining shirt. Both women chat together in the corridor and suddenly Becky's gaze turns to Manuel, followed by Rebeca's. Moving slowly her head, but emphasising perfectly her emotions, Becky's expression is that of a star, a theatrical body as she is making a gesture filled up with the strength of emotion, without moving too much, which accentuates the movement of her head. Hers is a manufactured and calculated appearance, which contrasts with the thought-image of Rebeca's body, which shows hers as spontaneous and more open; Rebeca's behaviour and gestures are less accentuated and she smiles with big open eyes turned towards Manuel; she seems genuinely happy. Framed in a medium close-up, her husband's expression changes. His eyes look passionate, he gets up slowly; his body vibrates to his former feelings; his mistress has come back.

A flashback image is shown to underline their shared past: two amorous bodies, the image of a blue sea, Becky is dressed in summer clothes, she throws her head back, as that of a person abandoning herself to passionate lovemaking as Manuel, with his sun-kissed brown-skinned body, stands before her. They approach each other and kiss passionately. The same image is repeated now but in a different atmosphere: Becky is at the left in the frame and Manuel enters into the field. Both approach each other and kiss, but in a distant way. Though the tension is palpable, the gestures remain polite and retained. In the background of this encounter, Rebeca is jumping between them, as a little child would while playing with her dolls. Her movements express enthusiasm as she is looking at both of them, especially at her mother. The former lovers are separated: Rebeca has tried to possess the loved object of her mother by marrying him. She imposes herself between both persons.

Photo 13: Maternal body (© Mimmo Cattarinich / © El Deseo D.A., S.L.U.)

Maternal imitation

During all those years of absence, Rebeca found her own ways of constructing a maternal presence in her life. When she missed her mother too much, she went out to see a transvestite friend, the drag queen Femme Letal, who impersonated her mother. Femme Letal is a ritual of presence because, by his body, he imitates the image of the maternal body. This makes him a mediator. After having had dinner together, Manuel, Becky and Rebeca go out to attend Femme Letal's hilarious parody.

In a medium close-up, Letal enters the room. His hair is tied up, he wears a lot of make-up, he is dressed up in red, and he dons a shirt with a mini-skirt and gloves. His exact steps accentuate his movements; his deliberate gestures give weight to the importance to his arrival. He carries himself with the attitude of a star, characterised by the movements of his hands, of his arms and a way of walking that is particularly seductive. As he moves, the slightest of his movement (a pan from the right to the left) is carried out with care. A group that is mimicking him attends him. The drag queens (Accelerated Diabetics) are in front of him and perform the same gestures with their hands, such as a movement in front of their eyes. They move in the same way and thus his presence is multiplied and felt like that of a habit; his way of possessing this place is unequivocally powerful: he imposes his body on this place and everyone, captivated, is watching him.

Femme Letal places himself then in the middle of the scene, in front of a folk-loric decor, with flamenco dancers. The stage is colourful and adorned with little white flowers. This decor of clichés contrasts with the posture of Letal, who is particularly modern, and extremely seductive. The thought of his physi-cal expression constructs the image of a modern Spain with a multiple identity; the body of Letal is that of a man, a woman, a singer (Becky) and a judge (we discover this later). These are constructed identities. The new images contrast with the folkloric cliché of the *españolada*, which are stereotyped images of Spain, reproductions of what we have seen and come to know as hackneyed images. Letal imitates Becky, the defunct maternal character, with his manufac-tured body of hips and fake breasts.

The camera stays fixed on him, but the image of his moving is very dynamic. Letal knows how to dance in an exaggerated manner, he is provocative and funny. The shot then contrasts the flamenco dancers of the decor, with their traditional movements and Letal, who constructs his own dance; a new choreo-graphy of modernity with his new body is framed. By a continuity shot we know that he dedicates his song to Becky: the next image in medium close-up on Becky's face, looking serious, surprised, impressed; her face is framed as those of the tabloid press. The comedic caricature offers a point of view on her life. The camera pans from the left to the right, stops one moment on Rebeca's face also looking at her mother with a lot of admiration. But she notices that Manuel is doing the same thing; his gaze is then immediately crossed by Rebe-ca's furious scorn to which Manual replies with a forced smile. The words of Letal's song, "Un año de amor (A year of love)" refers to the feelings between Becky and Manuel, explaining the meaning of their eye contact.

After his performance Letal joins them and they talk in a friendly way to each other. Manuel is completely cynical, when Letal is to have Becky's earrings as a present, Manuel signals that this implies a gift in return. Why not a breast? Becky is smiling and asks for the left breast, the one above the heart, which she poses then on the table. Letal thus presents a maternal symbol to Becky, as the breast is the archetype for motherly love. During her absence, he replaced the maternal image for Rebeca; now it is up to Becky to take up her maternal posi-tion again, in all of its aspects.

Focus on the star
The star's return has not passed without notice. Her public and private lives are tightly intertwined as the tabloid press and the media signal her presence, her acts and those of her family. The character of the judge's mother is used to point out to what extent Becky's life is mediatically saturated. She incarnates the stereotype of a *maruja*, someone fond of gossip. The sequence opens with a close-up on a newspaper and a voice that is commenting on the subjects: "Bull-

fights, the weather, classified ads.... Nothing. The weather goes up and down, who cares? There she is. Hand me Becky del Paramo's album, my sweet. Her first night out in Madrid", is accompanied by a photo. The place where this *maruja* lives is magnificent: in the next shot, a bed practically fills up the whole room; it is framed in the middle, in the dead centre of the room. In it we find this woman, dressed in a funny way. She wears a retro gown and her hair is tied up in an old-fashioned style. She has a lively face. This attitude presents the image of someone who does not leave the confines of her own home very often. The expansive bed seems to be the location of a great majority of her activity; however she pretends to know the "world". She is even afraid of contracting AIDS. The judge, who is her son, is sitting next to her on a chair and drinking his coffee. She has asked him to hand her Becky's album, in which she keeps, as it is with a few other stars, all of the newspaper clippings. A close-up shows some albums of Mother Teresa, of Brigitte Bardot, and of Becky who has an album dedicated to her alone. This woman lives in the world by reading the tabloid press, by watching the television placed at the foot of her bed and by religiously cutting out articles about the stars she admires. A mediatised gaze is thus constructed of "Becky's" personality, one that is worshipped by the *marujas*, among others.

Several sequences illustrate this exchange between private and public life. For example Rebeca is in prison because she has admitted to having killed her husband Manuel. He had wanted to divorce and Rebeca could not accept it. She has admitted to her crime in a public forum, during a television programme, in front of the whole world. Her desperation is theatrical. When the policemen arrive, she calmly asks them to wait a bit because she has not finished her confession. During her declaration, we see Becky's reaction in a reverse shot, her eyes bulging in disbelief. And in another exchange, in reverse shot, the judge's face in a medium close-up is shown calling the police.

The song brings together
The ritual of gazing on a public body is repeated when Becky is performing in a theatre. The montage is fundamental in this sequence to understand the exchange of gazes and the emotions between the characters. It is based on a rhythm of a dramatic song: slow, heavy, and methodical, just as a melody that develops itself softly from the beginning to the end. Rebeca is imprisoned for murder; a frontal full shot, two doors of a prison close and applause can be heard. A theatre room is presented in a high angle extreme long shot and the camera displaces itself from the left to the right: it is the image of an audience; all these people are going to live together this misfortune and these emotions. The camera moves towards the little silhouette of a lady on stage; a medium close shot from behind on Becky shows that she is spreading her arms to receive

Photo 14: Mother and star
(© MIMMO CATTARINICH / © EL DESEO D.A., S.L.U.)

the applause. She wears a green dress, red gloves, and her back is bare. It is the thought-image of an eccentric woman; her fragile body dressed up in scant fashion to accentuate her femininity. In this shot, one that is filming her back, we see that the audience is there, in front of us, for her: all these bodies in a vibrating image of emotion; a public ritual of bringing together, in reconstructing the relationship between a mother and her child.

The faces are framed and the camera is moving just a little inside the shots, only to focus on the emotion expressed by the thought-image of the body. The theatricality of this dramatic ritual is underlined by a close-up of Becky as she embraces the floor. In a frontal medium close shot, she gets up slowly, in front of the audience, with marked and exaggerated gestures. She then dedicates her song to her daughter who is sleeping in a prison cell this night. In a reverse shot we see a close-up on Rebeca who cries in prison in her bed. Hers is the image of a red and forlorn face, in tears with her hair disshevelled. She turns around and the camera follows her, she cries out when she hears a radio, asking her two cellmates to stop the music. They refuse. Sobbing, she stays in her bed and is obliged to listen to her mother. Everyone is united by Becky's voice. The star brings together the space of the prison and the space of the theatre. Becky's song guides this ritual of tears, of love, of bringing the two protagonists closer, despite their physical distance. The words of the song are simple:

> If your heart is breaking, think of me. If you feel like crying, think of me. You know I adore your divine image. Your child's mouth that being so young taught me to sin. Think of me when you suffer. And when you cry think of me too.

In a frontal medium close-up, Becky's facial expression is impressive: she shows an immense pain, a strong emotion with a hallucinatory theatricality. Becky expresses herself with her gestures towards her face, she is spreading her arms. The image of her physical performance reveals her fragility and her suffering.

Becky can hardly control herself and, framed in a close-up, we see a tear following next to the print of her red lips on the floor. It is a beautiful tear of sadness. United with her red lips, a symbol of her kiss, these two present her love; this is an image filled up with emotion. The emphasis created by the close-up continues; the gaze is posed on her face, she turns her back to the audience; her hands slightly touch her face as she tries not to disturb her make up, as she is in tears. Her gestures establish an exemplary thought of the star, overacted in all its meanings, drawing attention to every emotion by her gestures. But the spectator perceives that she is hiding it for her audience; she is covering her face by the gloved hands and cries. Slowly she turns towards the audience and the camera passes through the room in a close tracking shot on some faces that we know: the judge is among them. The ritual of bringing closer the child and the mother is lived by Becky and Rebeca, by the audience, by the radio, by her voice and the words: "*piensa en mi*". A mother who is a prototype of a star, and who comes back towards her daughter in her maternal feelings, is showing her compassion through this spectacle.

An imaginary trial

Rebeca is in prison because she killed someone, but the judge is trying hard to prove her innocence by emphasising the fact that there is no proof. His character represents maternal consciousness by organising a ritual of defence: it will be an encounter between mother and daughter to express their grief and the injustice of her abandonment. It is a violent sequence of confrontation between these characters, who are living through their conflict in a deserted court, the symbolic site of justice. For this, both women are going to direct their own process.

In a medium close-up on Rebeca's face, she enters, with a cigarette between her lips, walking in a nonchalant way with a clear air of rebellion. She looks in front of her because she does not know who is waiting for her. The camera focuses on her in a tracking shot and, in the background, we see her mother coming in, dressed in black, with a sad and tired face. She calls her daughter who approaches, putting out her cigarette; everything is shot in a medium close shot followed by a light low-angle close-up on the mother. The previous glamour of the star's appearance is no longer visible; she looks drained and tense. She is preoccupied and asks why Rebeca has killed Manuel. Framed in a frontal medium close-up, Rebeca answers in a rough tone that she hasn't done it. The confrontation starts. The mother is sitting down with her back slightly hunched. She is no longer the same woman, the woman who has stood straight and proud since the beginning of the film.

The ritual of defence starts; Rebeca moves from the bench towards her mother: her body is moving all the time, getting away and approaching. She is both the accused and the lawyer defending her own life and choices. Her mother is situated at the side of the judges. Rebeca recounts the story of a pianist who had a very ordinary daughter. All her life this child had tried to imitate and equal her mother. This was her story as well. There is a direct reference here to Bergman's film, AUTUMN SONATA (1978), with Ingrid Bergman as a star who comes home after many years, having also ignored her daughter for the sake of her career as a pianist. Here the conflict is sexualised by rivalry about the husband. Rebeca saw herself as the victor, once, married to Manuel. She was triumphant until the moment her mother comes back and makes love to him. The mother, sitting down, is listening to her and watches her with her eyes wide open; Rebeca, with a very red face, in a lateral medium close-up, is in front of her mother and is shouting. Moving back, she makes some nervous gestures pointing her finger at her mother and then at herself, as if to indicate that for once in her life she had beaten her mother with Manuel. A close-up on Becky, who is standing up, with tears in her eyes; she approaches her daughter and apologises. But Rebeca continues and says that she has to listen to her. Becky sits down again.

The defence is impressive; Rebecca vacillates between the benches, carried away by her fury. She resembles a passionate lawyer shouting for justice as she tries to defend herself for her own crimes. The reason for her acts is most clearly the grief caused by the absence of her mother. Her body occupies all the space, dominates it, incarnates it, ritualises it: she is demanding justice; she is fighting with her words, she is throwing the words into this space, with a practically discernible hurling, reinforcing her arguments by saccade gestures, with her face all the more reddening. Rebeca says that she had been only ballast for Becky. She has tried so much to obtain her love. Turning full of rage and with despair towards her mother, she says: "because I admired you" (full shot); both closed fists resting on her hips when she is watching Becky. Nevertheless we only see Rebeca in the images: we are focusing on her story. She is fighting to

Photo 15: Imaginary trial (© Mimmo Cattarinich / © El Deseo D.A., S.L.U.)

express her grief for having been deserted: an enraged child, a deeply hurt body who is struggling; she suffers but she is relentlessly combatant.

In a reverse shot, Becky's face is hanging low: she is crying; her body does not look like that of a star but rather the thought-image of a demolished and demoralised mother. At that moment Rebeca confesses to the crime that she committed when she was a child, costing Alberto, her mother's husband, his life. During her confession, we see the images of the childhood crime once again in a flashback: the little Rebeca is listening behind the door and then she exchanges the pills in the two containers. Her mother gets up; her face is violent, furious and terrified.

She approaches her daughter and slaps her face with such intensity that Rebeca falls down on to the bench. In the next medium close shot, we see her body lying down. She is wrecked. She gets back up and the camera pulls back. Rebeca is going away saying that because her mother has never held her promises, she could never forgive her (full shot, Rebeca's back). The camera approaches her mother who nervously and rapidly takes some pills that she is carrying with her. Leaning in front of her, her face is drenched in agony, her eyes glaring out into the fright of what she has just heard and understood. She is a heartbroken and sorrowful mother. The frame tightens on this broken and beaten woman. This is the image of a grief-stricken body in court; she cannot catch her breath.

The moralistic ritual concerning Rebeca's emotional and physical rejection has just taken place. The energy expressed the anguish and the disappointment in regards to a time that can never be recaptured. The ritual of approaching has been executed through the onslaught of words that have been thrown and through the bodies who even physically affronted each other. After this sequence in the court, Rebeca is liberated despite her professions, because no proof can be found. But at a latent level, the ritual of justice has taken place between these two protagonists in this site that is a symbol of the law. It is clear that her mother has been coward and oblivious towards Rebeca. A career is not an excuse to forsake a child. Becky blames herself for what she has done to her daughter and, at the end of the film; she says that she has killed Manuel, declaring herself responsible for the murder. Gravely ill in hospital, she confesses firstly to the judge, then to the priest. Then, in a house that is painted completely blue, the colour of heaven, Becky leaves for her last trip. Her daughter is lying down in the bed next to her mother. She is crying and the shot fades to black. The heels come back to leave again, and this time it's forever.

Conclusion

In the context of the 1990s, Almodóvar's film is posed as a groundbreaking myth about a woman who works. Finding a job or having the right to work is not questioned. In contemporary society women have the right to lead a professional career and at the same time they can become mothers. This combination is not always easy and invites the construction of myths. The mother in this film found an extreme solution for her maternal responsibilities: she left. Even if this fiction is very modern and absurd, it refers to an archetype: a mother who abandons or ignores her child cannot easily been forgiven. To structure this in the imagination, new myths are constructed about the maternal body who works, and about when her heels are walking away.

The archetype is actualised by a conflict between work and motherhood. Two aspects in the maternal body allow for the staging of this problem: the stereotype of a bad mother, in a prototypical body of someone who is professionally successful, a star. These are the songs and the choreographies that permit the reading of the rituals of maternal presence and absence: the extremely original interpretation that seems to hide the message of blame, often expressed about women. In Almodóvar's world the problem is exaggerated by making a star of a mother, to more easily refer to the conflict between motherhood and professional occupations. But behind this excess which the bodies represent, lies the symbolic of dealing out justice to the forgotten daughter. The filmmaker created this spectacle to show how work can make a "star" of a woman who forgets an essential part of her life: her daughter. The private problem is converted into a collective ritual, about which the world adopts a gaze implying blame.

Disguising a judge as a drag queen who is imitating a mother is absolutely humorous and disrespectful, but carries a message: this character symbolises maternal consciousness towards a child, which is the protective ethic that the archetype implies. The modernity of her parodied body exceeds all tradition, but some norms are still present: one may never abandon one's child. Even though there are not any laws about neglecting the existence of a child when the father is still alive, there subsists an archetype about maternal love. A mother who ignores and abandons her child even for work is guilty and therefore she has to pay for what she has done. If her daughter has committed some crimes, it is because she, the mother, is actually responsible. These acts were motivated by the child's desire to get closer to her mother. The maternal body loses the stereotype of selfishness by paying for her crimes, thus redeeming herself.

IV. General conclusion on the three films

To conclude the second chapter, it is important to highlight two points: the meaning of these new mythological figures as related to their cultural context and the introduction of these new images through the thought-image of the body.

The new mythological figures studied allow for the questioning of some of the archetypal values about the woman-mother and the *femme fatale*. These mythological themes were equally renewed in other national cinemas. LA MA-MAN ET LA PUTAIN (1973) by Jean Eustache provides a well-known example. The film interrogates the masculine gaze, which exists within and around the relationship between two women. The subject is dated today, but the ubiquity of the masculine gaze was a revolutionary idea at the time. Mark Allinson comments on the particularity of the Spanish context by analysing Almodóvar's cinema as opposing the Hispanic tradition of the mother to that of the prostitute.[82] The disparity between the two brings to the fore the cruel destiny associated with each option. He considers that Almodóvar recognises this contradiction for an older generation and creates at the same time a refusal through the portrayal of new Spanish women.

Indeed, the different rituals, expressed by the behaviour and the thought-image of the body, have allowed for the making of contemporary readings. Spanish cinema shows itself to be very original as it brings to life progressive characters, proclaiming their modern attributes by using speech (*tercera vía*), or showing flamenco choreographies to renovate CARMEN, or by having drag queens sing a song that delivers an idealistic image of the mother. Spain encounters itself, after thirty-nine years of dictatorship, in a period with new possibilities for women in the area of work and sexuality. It was no surprise that these original values on women, the archetypal values on her existence, were questioned in Spain's national cinema, as they were in other European cinemas.

The new images can be read thanks to the language of the body. To take up again Michel Bernard's idea (commented in the first chapter): the body very well exhibits popular societal moral prescriptions. The body becomes a symbol of the norm because what is natural is absolutely coded in a given culture.[83] The film analyses have demonstrated that the image of the body can introduce new perspectives on the norms and values of that culture. The newness opposes itself to a stereotyped idea. The contrast between the images of old and new, permits us to focus on this reading and to further define it. New images of the body are discerned through, firstly, the analysis of the gaze posed on the protagonist and, secondly, the examination of the stereotype as it is used to create the protagonist.

These new images can therefore be defined, thanks to the reading of the thought-image of the body. The stereotype delivers the preconceived frame; it is opposed to the prototypical body that inhabits the new clichés. The prototypical body highlights which ideas are invited into the creation of the myth. In the three films, the conflict of the mythological story is based on sexual liberty or the professional success of the mother. They each give a constructed imaginary of these new mythological figures: the housewife who denounces through her words her non-existent professional life, the *femme fatale* who makes her own mise-en-scene and doesn't care a stitch about her creator and finally the mother that becomes a star. These new images of the prototypical body represent subjects that are closely linked to the tremendous legal changes affecting Spanish women in the 1970s. In this way the new myths are historicised (determined by their cultural and historical context). They structure thoughts and ideas about new subjects related to a considerable change for women in Spanish society (and elsewhere in Europe), even though the plot finishes with the domination of the stereotype.

3. The homosexual body on stage

During Francoism homosexuality was forbidden. This state-enforced ban on same-sex relationships is at the basis of a number of myths about homosexuality. To be sure, when a subject is morally and legally banned, such as is typically the case for drugs or prostitution, the interdiction itself can stimulate the creation of a completely imaginary world on the subject. When homosexuality becomes clearly visible in post-Franco cinema, the taboos generated during the time of its proscription are brought to light. The feeling of social rejection is directly illustrated. The protagonist feels guilty or is doing everything to become guilty, as in MATADOR (1986) by Pedro Almodóvar. The character played by Antonio Banderas denounces himself to the police for a crime he has not committed. He suffers from an uncommon guilt complex because he is homosexual. Another example is when society denigrates the character or puts the character into a clandestine situation, as in THE DEPUTY (EL DIPUTADO): 1979, by Iglesia and THE DEATH OF MIKEL (LA MUERTE DE MIKEL): 1983, by Uribe.

To fully grasp the guilt associated with homo-erotic desire, an overview of the Spanish penal code is required. The classical penal right is normally based on two complementary aspects: the offence that has been committed and the sentence: the crime and the punishment. However, there were other possibilities with preventive laws directed against people who posed a possible threat to society. In this context, the term "danger" refers to public scandals or acts against morality, these being perpetuated by certain groups of people. Tramps and prostitutes, for example, constituted groups deserving this notorious classification (*Ley de Vagos y Maleantes*, 1933).[1] Homosexuals were also part of this category.[2] Homosexuality was considered to be a disease or a vice, one whose spread needed to be stopped, a sickness for which a cure had to be found. Various legal measures bear witness to this bigotry: in legal texts dating back to 1954, being homosexual is unmistakably considered an offence:

> In following with this kind of thinking, legislation passed against loitering not only included homosexuals who carried out sexual acts, translating their propensities into actual behaviour, but also homosexuals in and of themselves. The law of 1954 declares that homosexuals constitute a threat, as do thugs and pimps, as stated in the new stipulation of Article 2. This was our legislation until 1967.[3]

The homosexual act, even in a private setting, was thereby illegal.[4]

Replacing the former *Ley de Vagos and Maleantes*, this position was nevertheless sustained in the 1970 Law of Social Danger and Rehabilitation (*Ley de Peligrosi-dad y Rehabilitación Social*). It was yet again ratified on 4 August 1970,[5] formulat-ing two measures with regard to security and re-education.[6] The sentences of imprisonment in institutions of re-education ranged from six months to five years.[7] "Individuals considered to be dangerous are as follows: 1) loiterers 2) thugs and pimps 3) those who commit homosexual acts, (a total of fifteen groups)."[8]

A pernicious consequence was that the application of this law could lead to a certain freedom of interpretation, as Carlos María Romeo (1986) comments: "Guilt supposes a diagnosis – with a projection into the past – and the danger supposes a prognostic with a projection on the future."[9] People are thus classi-fied and judged on the possibility, the potential that they will *become* dangerous; this probability thus becomes an intrinsic quality of their character. This law led to a feeling of generalised guilt among the citizens concerned. In THE DEPUTY (EL DIPUTADO), the homosexual protagonist, Roberto, quotes Article 14 of the Spanish Constitution of 1978, recalling the equality and liberty of all Spaniards under the law: "Spaniards are equal before the law and may not in any way be discriminated against on account of birth, race, sex, religion, opinion or any other condition or personal or social circumstance (Article 14)."[10] This declara-tion contrasts with the legal measures decreed before 1978, when the film was shot, as the protagonist emphasises. It is the same story for SEX CHANGE (CAM-BIO DE SEXO, 1977).

Historicised bodies

During the Spanish Transition this restrictive legal climate changes. Through the law of 26 December 1978, the category deeming certain citizens to be a me-nace to society is removed,[11] having homosexual relationships was thereby de-clared no longer illegal.[12] In the same period, favoured by the suppression of censorship in 1977, new images of homosexuality are constructed. Clearly the introduction of new phenomena led to the creation of new mythological figures about homosexuality. These mythological figures would give homosexuality a place in the collective imagination. As we underlined in the other chapters, myths incessantly structure new themes. In this process of establishing a new view of the homosexual identity, we notice a questioning of the archetypal values relating to family and to male virility. The family, because it was tradi-tionally the place for heterosexuals, is therefore transformed through the depic-tion on new types of relationships. Virility is also expressed in a different way. As it is an archetypal image for masculinity, it is now questioned by the homo-sexual body. The homosexual character was often presented with feminine idiosyncrasies, as if being homosexual meant a certain absence of male sexuality, of male brawn. The body expresses this conception through the soft gestures of the hands, through the expression of sensitivity, of fragility even, that is often too accentuated or, then again, through the attention paid to a feminine way of talking (this set of characteristics is called the *mariquita* in Spanish cinema). This stereotype has different historical and sociological functions and is essential in the process of constructing new images.

To refer to certain historical tendencies on the subject, three important studies place emphasis on this body image. The first two studies are in English, published by Richard Dyer and by Paul Julian Smith.[13] The third study, which is in Spanish, was presented in 1997. Besides the published articles in Spain which deal with the subject in a superficial manner, we have to wait for Spanish scholar Juan Carlos Alfeo Alvarez's doctoral thesis, in which he presents the first exhaustive research on this topic, analysing the omnipresence of stereotypes.[14] As for the female body, our objective here is not to denounce this pejorative aspect, but merely to focus interest on the analysis of the sociological and historical function of this preconceived idea. Richard Dyer (1977) illustrates it in cinema in general: "It becomes reassuring to have clearly categorised homosexuality, by marking it distinctly with a well known iconography."[15] He affirms that the visualisation of the stereotyped body should be understood within the context of the stereotyped body's underlining taboo; stereotyping adds a pejorative slant to an image, which means that the image is framed as derogatory and is therefore recognised as being none other than a deprecatory image. Creating negative frames relies on the principle of control and the ability to reject something to the margins. Indeed, Dyer's book was distributed in 1977, a time in which the prejudices towards the homosexual body are made clear in clearly derogatory images of homosexuality.[16]

But an altogether different approach marks the cinema of the Transition. As was the case for the female body, the stereotyped body also plays a fundamental role of introducing new ideas. Paul Julian Smith (1998) mentions the existence of other images in the films by Eloy de la Iglesia and by Pedro Almodóvar:

> Moreover in the films I treat, de la Iglesia explicitly rejects stereotypical images of gay men, who are invariably described in the scripts as 'worthy' or 'manly'. I shall call these figures (played by sympathetic actors such as Simón Andreu and José Sacristán) 'Good Homosexuals'.[17]

Eloy de la Iglesia contrasts the stereotyped body of the *mariquita* with that of the "good homosexual". The good homosexual can be described as a role model, a prototypical body. He is an exemplary person, one who gives a positive image of the sexual category he represents.

The interaction in the film plot between several bodies, both stereotypical and prototypical, illustrates the new images on this sexual identity. Juan Carlos Alfeo Alvarez (1997) focuses on the stereotyped image of the homosexual character in Spanish cinema in the period between 1961 and 1995.[18] In his exhaustive research, he highlights the fact that a stereotype renders homosexual features more visible. This observation is extremely important when analysing the films, because the fixed model allows the recognition of homosexuality in the narration. This body makes its sexual preference legible and can be opposed to the new images of the so-called prototypical body, one exhibiting a non feminised man, who does not invite us to "suspect" his homosexuality at first sight. However, due to his relationship with a man marked with typically discernible features, his homosexuality also becomes visible. During Francoism and the Transition period, stereotyping the body expresses historical and sociological connotations meant to push this phenomenon back to the margin. In order to change these preconceived ideas, reading and defining them is fundamental. As the ideas fuelling the stereotype and even the prototypes are plain and clear, and therefore easily recognisable, it is then possible to question them.

The actor's body

Two Spanish actors have marked the films on sexuality in two streams: Alfredo Landa in the *destape* (uncovered) and José Sacristán in the *tercera vía* (third way). Chris Perriam's groundbreaking study, *Stars and masculinities in Spanish cinema* (2003)[19] is an elucidatory work in the definition of the social image of these Spanish actors. Scrutinising the social image of the most famous Spanish leading men, Perriam relates their social image to their masculinity. Perriams' conjunction is particularly interesting for this chapter on homosexuality. He focuses on different categories such as ordinariness, charisma, sex appeal, and so forth. These characteristics could then lead to audience identification.[20] Getting back to Francoism, Perriam quotes Hopewell's book on Spanish cinema:

> Hopewell (1989:421-2) makes the exaggerated but none the less useful point that the best-known and best-loved actors of the Franco era owed their success not to charisma and special, gifted qualities but rather to their ability to incarnate specific types; not to an idealised amplified individualism, but to their representation of weaknesses and failures easily recognised and identified with.[21]

Chris Perriam emphasises that the social type is valid for actors like Alfredo Landa. This actor has unquestionably demonstrated his enormous talent, having played so many different types up until today. He unequivocally represented the 70s, incarnating a character whose sexual life is fraught by failure or is non-existent, as Casimiro Torreiro (1995) explains:

The beginning of the decade marks the definitive consolidation of "landism" – from the name of the actor Alfredo Landa – archetype of the average Spaniard, more cunning than intelligent, always motivated by his limitless sexual appetite and by a certain guilt complex in his relationship with others, that he overcomes with staunch pigheadedness.[22]

Torreiro's description of Landa is absolutely correct but in this research the archetype is not defined in the same way. We examine the archetypal idea about virility and physical strength. The strong, little, macho man is therefore a hispanisation of the masculine image at a certain period. This refers to what I define as the historicised image of the body. Alfredo Landa was the 70s embodiment of the predetermined idea of the macho man. His body represents a humoristic image focusing in an obsessive way on women without having concrete relationships with them. This aspect makes his character rather silly. In THOU SHALT NOT COVET THY FIFTH FLOOR NEIGHBOUR (NO DESEARÁS AL VECINO DEL QUINTO, 1970), Alfredo Landa imitates a homosexual, a *mariquita*. His behaviour is marked by cliché womanly gestures; the effeminate movement of his hands, and his effete way of walking as he wiggles his hips accentuate his mock homosexuality. Making his body look female questions his heterosexuality, allowing him to work as a fashion designer. In his line of work, he sees a lot of naked women or women rather scantily clad. Since he imitates a typical queer by taking on the stereotypical body of one, their husbands do not mind if he watches their half-dressed or nude wives and nor do the female models.

The second actor also incarnated different types but his representations were politically charged. The exemplary body of that epoch is often brought to life by a well-known actor who is highly symbolic for the films of the *tercera vía* (such as FLUNKING OUT/ASIGNATURA PENDIENTE (1977)): José Sacristán. He is accompanied by other actors representing these "new Spaniards" shown as being progressive and modern.[23] The thought-image of the *tercera vía's'* characters can be defined as the advent of a new Spanish standard. These actors, whose political allegiances are entirely left-wing, formed a sort of social group that deliberately conveyed images meant to be imitated.

Therefore three prototypical and stereotyped bodies can be distinguished in the scrutinised period. First the filmmaker introduces the recognisable "author's" bodies, meaning that the films refer to a recognisable universe or rather to emblematic identities (Almodóvar, Iglesia, and many others). Historicised and sociological bodies make up the second group. These exist outside the filmic context, and therefore relate to broader sociological ideas (for example being an exemplary foreigner, a good pupil, a good foreign football player, etc.). Finally, related to this second case, there exists an actor's prototype or stereotype. An actor may represent in several films the same political, social, or psychological identity, perceived as exemplary during a certain historical period. While Alfredo Landa is the example of a Spanish macho man in several films, he is on the other hand also stereotyped in a negative way as he rarely realises his fantasies. Sacristán is the prototype of an intellectual, progressive actor, representing a more cerebral stream that is more politically engaged. All these images of the body will be analysed in different films to define the actualisation of masculinity's archetypical values.

And representing lesbianism?

Not having mentioned the lesbian representation in this chapter could raise some questions. Before analysing the films on male homosexuality, a short remark should be made on the subject. We already cited Alfeo Alverez's pioneering research on the representation of the male homosexual in Spanish cinema. As he mentions in a recent article published in 2008,[24] he often had to explain why he did not include the lesbian representation. Apparently this identity is particularly marked by its invisibility. Alfeo Alvarez argues that the difference in visibility is an issue that is connected to the history and the respective meaning of the public place for men and women. He contends that men always had a dominating presence in the realm of the public, implying that the conflict about a man's homosexual identity was therefore also worked out in the public arena. Whereas female sexuality has for a long time been considered as predestined for private space. When a serious lesbian image was introduced, it confirms this idea about space by filming the scenes most oftentimes in a domestic setting. Alfeo Alvarez' observations explain why Spanish cinema represents the homosexual protagonist particularly in a public site during the Transition period; the homosexual man is in any case a man – the public space is his. The conflict accordingly directly worked out in a public setting, relating it directly to political issues (the film EL DIPUTADO/THE DEPUTY and LA MUERTE DE MIKEL/THE DEATH OF MIKEL are good examples). Likewise, the historical obscurity of female sexuality impacts current research and representations.

In addition, research about lesbian representations emerged only quite recently. One reason for the late blooming nature of this research may be the existence of very different approaches to this area. Lesbian representations are often studied in Great Britain, as inspired by Cultural Studies or Queer Studies. Paul Julian Smith explains that Queer Theory is completely integrated in academic research in the United States and Great Britain, while in Spain it is only beginning.[25] Smith provides another possible reason. The recent attention for this area of research can be linked to the late emergence of (female) researchers working on this topic, most admitting that it is difficult to have their research recognised in Spanish universities. Smith's article was published in a monographic study, *Homosexual Gaze* (*la mirada homosexual*),[26] edited by the Spanish researcher Alberto Mira.[27] Alberto Mira gathers various scholars around the topic of the homosexual gaze, publishing, in Spanish, some well-known texts from the British academic world such as Babuscio's groundbreaking text about camp.[28]

Once again male homosexuality is the main issue in this publication written by reputed male scholars. As we already mentioned in the second chapter about female representation, Alfeo Alvarez also points out in his article a possible relationship between the fact that female film directors emerged quite late in the panorama of Spanish cinema. He concludes that women directors filmed only 7% of the films representing a lesbian topic. This fact is striking when contrasted with the reality that 100% of the films about homosexuality were shot by male directors exclusively. As the rate of female directors changes considerably only as of the 1990s, Alfeo Alvarez relates new representations to the late emergence of women directors.

Another reason for not analysing this topic in Queer Theory could be the cultural resistance or cultural indifference towards lesbianism (for example in France and Spain). Is it a valid to ask: is it mandatory that queer studies be the exclusive source of research dealing with homosexual or lesbian representation? Must the research have a queer point of view? Is there not a risk of new marginalisation by analysing this phenomenon from an avowed perspective? Is there not a new risk of constructing a sort of "intellectual school" that marginalises again this phenomenon by assuming the reader is familiar with at times esoteric definitions, based particularly on gender theories? Moreover, the cultural reactions towards homosexuality are certainly not the same in France, Spain, the Netherlands or the United Kingdom.[29] However, I admit that Queer Studies have introduced some challenging tools in Film Studies. Judith Butler's work on performance has been particularly productive.

Notwithstanding, also in this research I apply for a wider cultural reading. The three marginalised groups under Franco's rule are scrutinised and then compared on their new visibility in the filmic image. Body language is the central image and it is analysed in reference to the social prejudices it provokes within a specific cultural and historical context. To compare the three phenomena, the so called dissident bodies, is to examine bodies which were so persistently stereotyped during a certain period and rejected before they could transform into something new. My research is therefore directly inspired by the Spanish scholar Alfeo Alvarez, whose work I already mentioned. When he started with his PhD in the 1990s, Gender Theory or Queer Theory was not at all existent in Spanish Universities. He worked on the representation of the homosexual identity inspired by narratological theories considering the character as an existent parameter, without necessarily relating it only and exclusively to gender problematics. He therefore focused on social stereotypes from Spanish society. Irene Pelayo's PhD (2009) on lesbianism should be placed in the same frame. She presented her complete research project on the representation of lesbianism in Spanish cinema.[30] Inspired by Alfeo Alvarez's methodology on male homosexuality completed in 1997, Pelayo now updates this methodology on stereotypes or types of the lesbian representation. It is particularly interesting for this chapter on homosexuality, to compare briefly some main differences in representation by relating it to certain periods.

We already cited Alfeo Alvarez's distinction of four modalities in the representation of homosexuality relating it to four periods. The first is the so-called secret period under Francoism. This time of hiding and concealment is followed by the "provocative-demanding-images" of the Transition period. The 1980s through to the middle of the 1990s are characterized by a defocalised modality and this period is finally followed by an integrated modality from 1996 to 2000.[31] We focus indeed on an explicit filmic visibility. For example the first period under Francoism is often illustrated by quoting the film DIFFERENT (DI-FERENTE,1961) by Luis María Delgado.[32] This film had implicit references to homosexuality without ever naming it directly. However, shortly after abolishing censorship, the film reappears in Spanish cinemas with a title fitting of its 1978 debut: WHY IS BEING HOMOSEXUAL, BEING DIFFERENT? (¿POR QUÉ SER HOMOSEXUAL ES SER... DIFERENTE?).[33] Obviously, the fresh political situation allowed for the use of this title. Concerning lesbian representation, Irene Pelayo notices the same phenomenon with the film, I FEEL STRANGE (ME SIENTO EXTRA-ÑA) by Enríque Martí Maqueda released in 1977, 20 days after the abolition of censorship. Pelayo describes this film as less political than for example THE DEP-UTY (EL DIPUTADO).[34] The legal change in censorship demonstrates once more its tremendous impact on what could be visualised.

Besides the similarities during the Transition period, during which a clear visibility of the lesbian and homosexual identity is accounted for, the other periods offer no lucid opportunities for direct comparison. Pelayo defines, like Alfeo Alvarez, the same three ways of introducing the lesbian identity; the so-called "provocative-demanding-images", the defocalised and finally the integrated modality. Yet there is another category, one that is utterly distinct, of making lesbianism visible: the erotic modality. This category is directly related to the historical period of the 1970s, also represented by the *destape* films. As we commented, this period was dominated by the introduction of strong sexual images. Regarding lesbianism, some male filmmakers, such as the well-known Jesus Franco, exploited this fantasy through the use of subversive representations. Between 1977 and 1983, many of these films, (and films on homosexuality like THE DEPUTY/EL DIPUTADO in 1978), were rated S.

Daniel Kowalsky (2004) analysed the process of having a film rated S during Spain's transition to democracy.[35] When censorship was abolished in 1977, the government introduced four new cinematographic ratings. The last one was S (during the period between 1977-1982). As Kowalsky indicated, these films had explicit sexual content (porno, but also films of the *destape*). Therefore, while THE DEPUTY (EL DIPUTADO) was classified in this category, it was nonetheless projected. Between 1977 and 1982, Spain was the only European country where the category X still didn't exist (and it was introduced in 1982 only). The category S was thus used instead but without the deleterious distribution effects.

Indeed, apart from the Transition period, relating the other three modalities to a specific historical period is more difficult. For instance, the erotic modality represents films starting with the VAMPYRS in 1973 and finishing with a subversive title of 1982.[36] This period corresponds to the destape period and the S-category. The claiming modality represents films starting in 1977 and finishes with a film in 2004.[37] Now the third category, the defocalised, represents films starting with a title of 1972 and finishes with a film of 1993.[38]The last category represents films starting only in 2000 until 2005.[39]

Pelayo concludes that neither the periodisation, nor the discourse can be directly compared. The first claiming representations we cited were I FEEL STRANGE (ME SIENTO EXTRAÑA). Pelayo argues that the message cannot be compared with the first serious films about male homosexuality because these were much more political. Already the title, THE DEPUTY (EL DIPUTADO) is political. Alfeo Alvarez argues that this kind of message about lesbianism can only be found in Juan Carlos Claver ELECTROSHOCK released in 2006. This book's primary focus is on the new images introduced in a systematic way during the Transition period. In these new depictions, the homosexual identity is the real protagonist, relating the gender issues to a political discourse (THE DEPUTY, THE DEATH OF MIKEL). In the Transition period, the manner with which homosexual identity is introduced, through the image of the body, deconstructs certain patriarchal myths on the family and on male sexuality.

Similar to the second chapter on women, we are again confronted with the melodrama. This genre is an astute choice for the study of social changes inside a patriarchal structure. This time the protagonist is homosexual or suspected to be. By relying on the examination of the choreography of the body language, the first film illustrates homophobic reactions during Francoism.

I. SEX CHANGE (CAMBIO DE SEXO, 1977): rejecting the homosexual body

At first glance, SEX CHANGE (CAMBIO DE SEXO) seems to be dealing with a problem other than that of the homosexual body. However, the film is pertinent to the subject since transsexuals were often considered to be homosexual.[40] Male sexuality is questioned through the image of a male body, one that is surrounded by people who suspect it of being homosexual: José María, a seventeen-year-old young boy, has a body with a female quality to it. He is expelled from school, where the mere vision of his body incites aggressive reactions from the other pupils. His father is furious and threatens his son. A two-part punishment is imposed: a laborious exercise regimen meant to muscle-up his body and thereby boosts his masculinity and the procurement of a prostitute's services also meant to usher the reluctant boy into heterosexual manhood. The paternal reactions illustrate the consequences of the Law of Social Danger and Rehabilitation: altering the body image and initiating his son's heterosexual sex-life seems to be the best and most reasonable solution. But José María leaves his family home for Barcelona where he travesties as a girl. There, he meets Bibi Andersen who has changed gender. José María wishes to emulate her and go through with the same operation, to become a woman, and to build a relationship with Durán. The film finishes like a beautiful love story between María José and Durán; the storyline is like that of an absurd fairy tale in which a boy is transformed into a beautiful woman to finally marry her prince.

The reception of the film

Released two years after Franco's death, the credits indicate that this film is based on a real-life story. The American researcher Marsha Kinder comments that Aranda's collaborator, Carlos Durán, had read the story of a Belgian transsexual who died after surgery in 1972. When Aranda and Durán first presented their script, it was rejected. The strictures of censorship loosened, they tried once again, and successfully this time, in 1976.[41] Carlos Durán is also a main character in the film, representing José María's tutor: Durán discovers her gift for acting and later falls in love with her. Transexuality had become an innovative trend of the 1970s and Durán invented this filmic character that humanised the issue of transexuality. In the history of Spanish cinema, SEX CHANGE (CAMBIO DE SEXO) has to be related to MY DEAREST SEÑORITA (MI QUERIDA SEÑORITA, 1971) by Jaime de Armiñan. These films question sexuality through a body that can express both genders. In the film by Armiñan, the protagonist takes on the identity of a man, dressing appropriately to play the part. José Luis López Vázquez's remarkable performance allows for the convincing construction of this double identity. We are however surprised that MY DEAREST SEÑORITA was chosen to represent Spain at the Oscars; it was nominated in 1972. Apparently, besides *españoladas*, identities with a gender conflict deserve nominations abroad. In this context, it is interesting to mention Marsha Kinder's 1995 article about HIGH HEELS. She argues that the new *españoladas* are now Almodóvar's singing

transvestites, known all over the world.[42] It is fascinating to note that this inclination had already begun in the 1970s, with the nomination of this kind of film
for the mainstream and prestigious Oscar's ceremony.

Clearly, choosing such a film to represent the country is a confirmation that
these issues are considered important in 1970s Spanish cinema. Sex Change
illustrates the exploration of new topics, a break from the past, which is elabo-
rated in the press articles of the time. Before, the film director Vicente Aranda
had encountered many problems with censorship, as is indicated in *La Vanguardia Española* of the 25th of June 1977:

> The complex nature of the subject and the strong momentum that Sexology studies
> have acquired in Spain, make this movie a clear point of interest. Vicente Aranda
> tried to make this film four or five years ago, but stumbled on a series of difficulties
> with censorship. But shortly thereafter a larger trend opened up to deal with these
> problems in cinema. The film My Dearest Señorita is an example of it.[43]

The film is based on how problematic it is to change one's sexual identity and
also introduces images that address homophobic conceptions of the homosexual body under Francoism. Despite quite positive reactions in the press,[44] Sex
Change did not attract a large audience. An article from the 28th of May 1977
in *Sábado Gráfico*, supporting the film, evokes the Law of Social Danger and Rehabilitation. These historical connotations are fundamental to understand the
story:

> Aranda has treated the exception because in this country everything that refers to a
> sexuality that is not in compliance with the norm is considered – when it is not a
> taboo – to be a ridiculous act or a possible infringement of the "social danger law";
> the theme is treated neither with complacency nor with diffidence.[45]

Multiple archetypes

Conflict is ritualised during the entire narration of the film thereby allowing its
mythological aspect to dominate throughout. Through the reactions it inspires
from its environment, we slowly and painfully come to understand the body's
thought-image. Several phases make up the process of discovery, which culmi-
nates with José María's transformation into María José. The first part introduces
the problem: José María carries a feminine air about him. The stereotyped
homosexual is evoked. This is followed by an episode of attempted resolution.
The body is to be hardened, muscles are to be strengthened and grown. José
María is even confronted with the heterosexual sex act. Indeed, from the onset
of the movie, José María is continuously challenged. Finally, upon seeing Bibi
Andersen's body, José María identifies with something in his environment: he

too feels more like a woman than a man. He quickly comes to the realization that he would like to undergo a sex-change operation in a clinic. Indeed, Bibi Andersen functions as a role model, as the prototypical body.

The body expresses a myth on gender change, which was still illegal in Spain until 1983,[46] and therefore strongly idealised as a possibility. The different bodies pose the problem of different archetypes. Let us quickly review the ideas on masculinity and femininity and their respective clichés. In attempts to define them in the context of this film, we are obliged to simplify enormously because while the narration does not explore them too much, it does organise the expression of their thought-images. The masculine archetype is based on physical strength and virility. The female archetype concentrates on its ability to conceive- on its apparent fecundity, its expression of a maternal attitude and on the attention the woman pays to her appearance. Even if these descriptions are a little bit basic, an example can illustrate these archetypes more clearly: if a woman wants to imitate a man, she walks differently, talks with other gestures and shows her physical strength. Exaggerating the features of the inverse is a representation of the other gender. If a man wants to imitate a woman, he will emphasise another way of walking, swinging his hips in exaggerated fashion and touching his hair. A gamut of typical gestures and clichés, stereotypes about each gender, exists and these mannerisms help to establish an image of the other. Butler's theories on performance are confirmed here by a study of the body and its chosen movements. We witness this performance in SEX CHANGE wherein two thought-images of the body oppose one another. José María becomes María José; he will transform from a stereotyped body suspected of being homosexual into the prototype of a beautiful woman.

From a stereotype to a prototype

The characters are therefore mediators that negotiate their own gender through the image of the body. For example, José Maria negotiates the conflict of a double gender and indeed the double image of her sexuality; he is playing the role of mediator because, in principle, the binary opposition between a woman and a man cannot be adapted but, in this case, he finds his solutions. The way to establish these images needs to be commented on: the actress, Victoria Abril, knows how to create an image of a boy, one that looks innocent and young. Likewise, she easily transforms herself into a girl. And the transformation is not too visible. The thought-image of the boy's body is less dynamic, more strict and contained. Transforming into a girl, she accentuates more and more certain physical movements and the emotions expressed in her gestures are intensified. The press articles appreciate her interpretation and underline her age: she is seventeen. The fact that she is so young, and unknown, enables her body to establish a thought-image that gives birth to the idea of a double identity with more ease. A fledgling actress, her novice air reinforces her performance and no precedent work interferes with the audiences understanding of her character. Thanks to Aranda's films, and later, among others, by Almodóvar' films, she becomes a well-known actress in Spanish cinema. If at the release of SEX CHANGE viewers saw her the way they do today, it would have been difficult to appreciate the natural way with which she expresses transexuality. As is indicated in *Informaciones* of the 19th May 1977:

> The impressive revelation of the film is Victoria Abril who, as young in real life as her character, is equally convincing in the role of protagonist, as a girl or as a boy, and who does not seem female when she "is" José María no more when she forgets, when she "is" María José, to give to her movements, to her gestures, to her way of dressing, a virile resonance. And I note that, despite the support of Aranda's direction, it was an ordeal for an actress as young as she is, one who was even not seventeen years old at the beginning of the shooting.[47]

The viewer focuses on her while she struggles to transform all the while imitating her example, Bibi Andersen, José María's role model.

Bibi Andersen: the prototypical body

The appearance of Bibi Andersen's body in this film, by her transsexual identity, is extremely important. Her gender change is exhibited. Her body represents a myth about sex change, later regularly confirmed in Almodóvar's cinema. She emphasises her femininity in a convincing manner. The press' reactions underline her authenticity, as is indicated in the article already cited above:

> Bibi Andersen is a real character, present in the world of cabaret in Spain, with a regular artistic activity, circumstances that give to the film a supplementary interest and at the same time an appreciating aspect of witness. (–). Bibi Andersen is called Manuel Fernández Chica on his Identity Card, who is in some ways interpreting herself, and never makes a mistake. She acts like people who know her say she does, as in real life, like a real woman. Not like these silly transvestites from that silly cabaret, where María José-José María escapes during a moment of crisis. (–).[48]

Bibi Andersen is presented in this film under her stage name. We notice that she took a Swedish name, referring to the favourite actress of Bergman's cinema, Bibí Anderson, as an idealisation of the Swedish woman, a myth cultivated in the 1960s. Juan Eslava Galán describes this phenomenon: "From the Pyrenees until the North all women were devouring of men and all were Swedish. The passionate Spanish imagination gave birth to the myth of the Swedish woman."[49] Tourism led to an encounter with women of other cultures, during the

Franco periods when the mores were rather different. This encounter stimulated the creation of myths concerning women from the North, in particular concerning sexual freedom. These connotations of sexual freedom and the myth of the Swedish woman's beauty are incarnated in Bibi's Nordic physical features – acquired after several operations – and in her name, which itself suggests the Scandinavian legend. In SEX CHANGE she has brown hair and her face is later completely transformed into a Swedish type: long blond hair, and a thin face with fine features. This body symbolises a transformation of the myth of the Swedish woman by a multi-gendered body. In 1998 she claims again her original name: Bibiana Fernández.[50] But in Spanish cinema, from 1978 to 1998, she was known as Bibi Andersen.

But above all, Bibi was born on screen in SEX CHANGE. In this marginalised universe, other people surround her. First, Bibi Andersen shares the screen with the character of Durán – the manager of the Starlett nightclub, acted out by Lou Castel. As Kinder wrote, Carlos Durán is also Aranda's collaborator. This time an actor who is well known for Fassbinder's cinema (in for example: BEWARE OF A HOLY WHORE, 1971) represents him.[51] He looks ambiguous, with long blond hair around his face and a concentrated and direct gaze. The man's thought-image emphasises that he is familiar with the underworld. He shows himself to be tender towards his employees, among others towards José María. A rather inexpressive thought-image, we rarely see him smile. Doña Pilar, played by Rafaela Aparicio, is the landlady who rents a room to José María. She is an elderly lady who is involved in the young boy's life; she shows tolerance and comprehension with regard to his problems. Her attitude is in sharp contrast with his parents' reactions. Fernando Sancho plays his father and Montserrat Carullo plays the role of the mother. José María's sister, Lolita, acted by María Elías, is more understanding of her younger brother's problems.

The rituals of transforming the body

Several rituals allow for a reading to be made about the myth enshrouding double genders. The ritual of change begins with the restyling of appearance; first the clothes, then the wig, followed by the make-up. This first stage points directly to the idea of performativity, as Marsha Kinder links it to the Judith Butler's theories. A gender identity is based on the performance of this identity.[52] But this film goes further at its conclusion, encompassing a mythological idea about a gender change that resembles a fairy tale. The second stage already concerns the physical change: after an encounter with Bibi Andersen, José María begins hormonal treatments and aesthetic maintenance, such as waxing. The final stage is a stay at a clinic abroad. In the last images we see the victorious post-op outcome. The body has successfully changed gender thanks to medical knowledge. The sites of the body's transformation reflect marginality, returning at the end of the film to a medical facility for the operation. Here, the body is put into scene as being abnormal. Within the filmic context, these scenes reflect the protagonist's indisputable wish to change sex.

The film begins by emphasising on the social rejection he suffers: the homophobic reactions are dramatically demonstrated by the reactions to José María. Being a boy, his body's thought-image provokes problems, because he is not muscular; he is too soft, too feminine and his environment repudiates him, stereotyping him as a homosexual. Let us scrutinise the choreography of the body, constantly exposed in the film. The credits open with a small bronze doll, with two hands on its hips as if to turn up its skirt. The doll seems feminine because of its long hair and breasts, but the eyes are turned down to the floor and the hands lift the skirt slightly enough to attract our attention to the presence of a penis, and one naked breast. It is an androgynous body. A soprano accompanies these images, singing an air of Bach: the female voice carries the body. In a light high angle long shot on a boy that is walking alone, submissive and docile, we witness in the film people turning around to stare him down. The same dramatic soprano voice accompanies these images. The sound expresses mourning; it is a poignant melody heralding a tragic destiny. Above the emotional sound, the history of this classical music relates it to the storyline. In the period of Bach, young boys were castrated to reproduce these wonderfully high-pitched voices. The high voice was compared to that of an angel, a creature considered to be an asexual divine figuration.[53]

The camera in a high angle shot accompanied by this beautiful soprano voice represents a divine gaze on the destiny of this human being, born with the wrong gender. This body introduces the thought of this gender conflict. Born a boy, it is as if he is hiding a female voice deep inside himself. The camera follows him closely, and then focuses on the board indicating "hotel". José María embraces his father and helps him to serve the clients, who see him from behind and say: "Girl, bring us a bottle". José María knows that the patron is addressing him: he turns his head a little, feeling embarrassed, his eyes cast down. His father looks at those in the restaurant. Then, with a strange look, he observes his son – his eyes going up and down José María's body. The father continues his work without saying anything. The image of the boy's body distinctly effete with the long hair, a soft face the lack of a clear masculine expression all add up to make of José María a curious epicene.

At school, he is rebuffed mercilessly. The next shot shows a group of pupils in a classroom encircling José María. They shout in unison and hit on the table-tops, "Come on, cry José María", the camera approaches him. He is there, in the middle, his shoulders bowing forward as he tries to make himself invisible. His arms are crossed in front of him, he is looking at the floor; he is full of fear and intimidation. The camera approaches and we see a tear on his face, before that he gets up and leaves. At home he tells his sister that they call him *mariquita*. His body is the object of jokes about homosexuals. He is too feminine for a man and is consequently being chastised. He is sent off from school. The camera follows the schoolmaster and his mother. The former is explaining that the child is abnormal, that he could pose a threat to the other children because he causes problems. With his heavy black glasses, his male face of about fifty years old, he represents authority. He states that he wishes to not disturb the education of normal boys. They are forced, for the protection of the other, to expel José María.

At home, his father is furious. Sitting behind his desk, his body projects a powerful image, one with enormous strength despite its age. His features taut and rigid, he walks towards his son. A medium close-up focused on José Maria's face, the father enters into the frame and hits the palm of his hand, showing his force. His son's body lacks vigour. One has to efface these female features. His mother intervenes, but his father does not stop his denigrating speech; he is looking out the window because he knows he is ridiculous. His obloquy continues, he wishes to give his son: "bull ball injections. Do you hear me, a man! I will make you work to make a man out of you. Otherwise, I will kill you". José María's face, framed in a close-up, expresses terror. He cannot grasp what he has done *wrong* – he is unable to comprehend the problem; he looks anxious and is on the verge of tears.

Force and virility

His father's solution is to render his son's body more muscular, to modify this body that is too female, too soft, one that summons people's suspicions. While he is cutting wood, we see his physical fragility. To make him more masculine, his father has prepared a complete programme, based on physical force, money, alcohol and sex. His father is extremely motivated, and together they leave by car for Barcelona. When they stop at the petrol station, he gives his son some money so that he can pay the prostitute later that evening. His son is to be sexually initiated. But in a nightclub in Barcelona, José Maria is much more interested in Bibi Andersen, announced as: "The mystery of nature, the biological enigma of our century" than in any organised meeting with a prostitute. A close-up on José María's face shows his fascination for Bibi's androgynous body. A close-up on the father shows him to be looking at his son with a preoccupied mien. Bibi puts herself on a table like a tiger, showing her body in all its sensuality, she looks like a beautiful woman. A medium close-up on the father who observes again with preoccupation his son is followed by an image of Fanny, the prostitute who then enters into the field; José María does not take his eyes away from Bibi, despite Fanny's advances as she caresses his face.

Bibi undresses on stage, first the top: she is touching her breasts, and gyrating her body. She wraps herself in a red tissue, turns around again to take off her slip and lifts up the tissue: we see a penis in a medium close-up. The father, in a frontal medium close-up asks how the penis could be a part of the performer's body and Fanny explains that it is Bibi's, and that the breasts are implants. His father wants to immortalise this night, to be part of his son's rite of passage. Despite the whisky served to José María, the father's plans for sexual initiation fail. José María refuses to be touched by the hooker. His father brings him back to the lumberjack where he is put to work. He has to continue doing physical labour, and in a month they will try it again: he must absolutely become a man. These scenes illustrate the impact of the Law of Social Danger, which also proposed re-education programmes to incite change. However, despite the father's misguided efforts, José María is on his own path. His androgynous body is transforming through its proper initiatives; Jose Maria is commencing his own rituals of transformation.

Dressing up the body: changing gender

After this initiation and this so called therapy of forced labour, José María decides to leave. With unwavering will, he takes the lumberjack's daughter's clothes and packs them into a suitcase. Then, in a frontal medium close shot, he appears, dressed up as girl, leaving the metro. It is the image of an attractive female body, one that is walking in a sure and confident way. There is no doubt, this person feels good. The image created is convincing; he really looks like a girl. In a lateral medium close-up, he is buying a newspaper and is looking for a room. Then, the confrontation between his new identity and his family is presented via his sister Lolita's visit. They go out together and José María is at first the brother. His sister is crossing the street (full shot on the back), sits down in a cafe (frontal medium close-up); José María goes to the toilets. The camera is framing Lolita's face, and in the background we see someone arrive while the camera is following, we hear his sister scream and her brother's reply: "don't shout, idiot". The camera displaces on José María's face. We see a nice young girl with long hair (a wig), red lips and made-up eyes. In a medium close-up, the camera is framing the sister who approaches, sitting closer to the edge of her chair. She is gazing at her brother's features, fascinated and deeply moved. A frontal medium close-up on both of them shows two bodies of young girls as José María says that his name is María José. A man sitting close to them is flirting with them, and María José winks awkwardly. They are going to dance; we see a shot on both girls who are smiling. This is followed by several interactions of shots, showing them to be jovial as they dance.

The evening, coming back to Jose Maria's room, a medium close-up unites both faces of brother and sister. Lolita is looking directly at the camera as José

María is sitting behind her. Leaning against each other, they are very close, unified by fraternal love. They look towards the camera. They speak about the image of their bodies during that afternoon:

Lolita: What do you feel when you are dancing with a boy?
José María: I don't know, I suppose the same thing as you.
Lolita: You cannot feel the same thing as me, I am a woman.
José María: I feel like a woman also.
Lolita: You aren't.
José María: So, what am I then?

The conversation is simple and profoundly touching. Brother and sister feel very close but they are distanced by this mutual incomprehension. How can one feel like a woman with a male body? Lolita bursts out in tears and her brother tries to console her. Gender identity is interrogated by these questions, in their unadulterated simplicity and inevitable difficulty; they describe the intimate and painful problem of this human being. What am I?

Imitating a model

The encounter with Bibi Andersen announces a new chapter. At the hairdresser's, José María is helping Bibi Andersen. In a medium long shot in front of the mirror, we see their back and the reflection of their image in the mirror. Bibi is sitting down and José María is treating her hair. Both bodies are unified in the image and Bibi asks her to call her by her first name. José María, touching her hair with tenderness and admiration, offers Bibi some hair treatments (see photo).

The task of discovering the body continues: when the landlady goes out with her friend, José María stays alone at home. A medium close-up on his back displays him to be sitting in front of the bed on his knees, unpacking his suitcase. A wig, a nightgown, and ladies' clothing are laid bare: these accoutrements give his body a female allure. He is thoroughly enjoying himself as his hands touch everything softly. The ritual consists of touching objects, which belong to the realm of women, and this act of delicately grazing over the objects parallels the process of his bodily transformation. In a frontal medium close-up on her face, he is putting on a light, white dress. The camera displaces towards the mirror and frames the body that is turning around. We see a penis disappear under the dress. The mirror is drawing attention once again to the transformation of a controversial body. No details are hidden from the viewer: the body is presented naked in all its complexity, exhibiting the double gender.

The young man turns around, sits down on the bed and is listening to the radio speak about women's moment of rest. His hands are touching this nice dress, with a feminine appreciation for beauty. Sitting down like a woman who is relaxing after having done the household cleaning, he listens to a radio voice

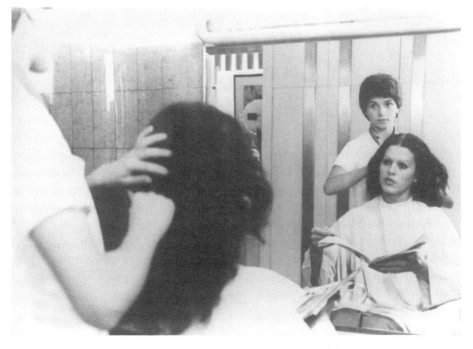

Photo 16: Bibi Andersen, a role model

discussing the importance of giving oneself attention and of finding a space of serenity; this young boy of seventeen years, puts himself into the typical role of a housewife. José María gets up, the camera is following him in a tracking shot, his steps are very light and show that he feels well in his skin, in his body. With tender gestures, he opens the window and we see him from the back in this dress, breathing the air, taking in the warmth of the sun, feeling so comfortable, moving with elegance. In this choreography of womanhood, the thought-image of the body is framed standing in front of the window. This image is a typical ritual of womanhood.

The ritual continues with a close-up on a bra, while he is putting on a red dress. The camera displaces towards his face, which is clearly happy and satisfied. A medium close-up from behind reflects his face with the wig on. The change is done once again by the mirror: the wig changes the image completely, and the mirror makes us aware of it. With the wig, the body achieves the female touch so much so that the image is transformed ever more into the other gender. In a medium long shot, José María enters into the living-room with a board for the tea. Drinking a cup of tea at home in the living-room is a ritual for women when they want to enjoy a short moment of pleasure. José Maria sits down softly, paying attention to his gestures: he arranges his skirt delicately before sitting down. His body movements intensify every gesture and the image is transformed ever more into a new form: that of a nice-looking young girl. The camera, from the point of view of the television, frames José María's face frontally in a medium close-up. His eyes are wide open: we hear a conversation about a love story, one emanating from the soap opera on the set. A couple embraces each other and the woman declares her love. This is followed by a close-up on José María's affected face. Suddenly we hear off screen the landlady coming home... José María runs into the bathroom. A girl is leaving the living-room though the landlady was under the impression that she had rented the room to a young boy!

The ritual of making this body look female continues outside. José María goes to the discotheque and once again sees the man who had been flirting with him and his sister. He asks her to go on a date. This man shows himself to be very smitten with José María, persuaded that he is talking to a woman. José María repeats the same phrases learned from television: "I feel so secure in your arms, like in a temple". The learned love discourse accompanies and reinforces the new gender identity of his body. The man is touched by her declaration, and tried to negotiate with José María as she hesitates to go on a date. He assures her he knows everything about her. José María misunderstands the man's cajoling and thinks that he is referring to his gender, but this is not the case. When they embrace, he shows his trembling hands to illustrate that he is also nervous (frontal medium close-up): he thinks that José María is still a virgin. Discovering that he is a man, he hits him and we see José-María coming home. His landlady is at home. Again the mirror is crucial. Through it we see that he is trying to amputate his body of that element that is preventing him from being a woman (see photo).

In the next shot, José María is in hospital. Bibi arrives – a medium close shot on her – she walks with grace, enters into the room and talks to José María making him promise to never start this again. The female image of Bibi is over-acted with conviction. Certainly, she is a model to imitate for José María.

The mechanical tango

A visit to his parents' place is disastrous. The meeting seems decisive for the next stage: transforming his physical outlook will now be concretised thanks to Bibi the coach. A body will be created through hormonal treatments, waxing, and by learning how to dance. Bibi is taking the boy under her protection and introduces him to the patrons of Scarlett, the nightclub, where Bibi organises a meeting with Durán. Together in the dressing room, Bibi shows his naked body. In a shot on the back on Bibi and frontal on José María, the latter is dressed up as a little lady in a chic outfit. In the background, Bibi is taking off her slip and recounting the story of her trip to Casablanca where she underwent the operation. Under the venerating expression of José María the miracle is described. In

Photo 17: Framing the destruction of the body

a frontal medium close-up on her satisfied face, we see Bibi explain, and in a comical way – her hands snipping like scissors, that her impeding member had been taken away. She is very pleased. José María reacts full of awe and enthusiasm. He approaches Bibi and embraces her tenderly in a lateral medium close-up while Bibi is saying that this is what she wanted, to be like the others.

They go out to celebrate it in the company of Durán. Bibi is dancing a tango with José María. The other clients give the floor to this original couple and the duo appropriates the spot with assurance. Their bodies press against each other; the taller Bibi guides José María who is imitating her movements. The two arms are held together to indicate the direction of their choreography: they are unified, in the image, and in a symbolic thought-image. Tango is a dance showing an image of passion and the union of bodies, but passion is expressed here by mechanical gestures in the choreography of imitation. Bibi's movements are imitated with rapt precision by José María, but with a small delay. José María's body dances like a marionette, moving his head in an automated way, from the right to the left. He resembles a robot or a doll since the movements look quite machine-like. José María is like a classical dancer who is attempting a tango for the first time. Durán observes the scene with a smile, they continue their choreography. He offers José María a job at the nightclub as a dancer. The gender transformation continues, making the body look ever more female.

The transformation process becomes ever more conclusive: the masculine body now looks like a beautiful woman. She is convincing and seductive. The movements and the thoughts of the body are transformed on stage into choreography about womanhood, referring all the while to a double code. In his show, José María has to imitate a woman. She is singing: "Am I or am I not a woman, but, shush," with the hand placed in an elegant way in front of her mouth: "shush, we don't say anything". In a frontal medium long shot, she is undressing, wraps a shawl around her body, is lying down on the sofa, pretending to sleep, and the curtains close. This gesture is successful and Durán congratulates her: he embraces her and at that moment Bibi enters with champagne glasses. Bibi feels betrayed and excluded by this new friendship; Durán says brutally that he no longer wants anything to with Bibi or María José. He leaves immediately and in the shadow of his departure it is evident that Mariá José has truly fallen in love with her tutor. This new problem will now give rise to a series of absurd choreographies, questioning once again the gender conflict through the body.

A grotesque flamenco

We bear witness to a macabre dance. Several transvestites dance flamenco, accompanied by the clapping of the hands (*palmas*) and songs. In this nocturnal atmosphere, María José is trying to dance away the pain of her broken heart and to forget the crisis about who she is. The bodies transgress in a grotesque way. The sequence begins with a medium close-up on a transvestite's outrageously made up face; the face is shocking with its red lips that are excessively accentuated and with its eyes whose blue make-up is more gaudy than it is appealing. The smile exposes the masculine identity. The camera is following this character while he approaches a group of people dancing flamenco on a stage in a bar. In a medium long shot we discover María José in a beautiful dress, in the middle of the group, dancing in a lascivious way. In a medium close-up from behind her, we see her making the typical gestures of the flamenco dance. Spellbound, she is looking at the other transvestites and twirling them around one after another, like a real flamenco choreography. Then, we see several close-ups on the transvestite's faces: they are all wearing immoderate amounts of make-up, with lips that are too red, flowers in their hair, and appealing dresses. Marked by masculine features on their proud faces, they move intensely to the music, they move their heads to the fast rhythm. María José participates in this distorted rumba: a Spanish reference, though absurd.

The dancers ask for a bottle: they attach it between María José's legs; it is lecherous flamenco choreography, carried out by transvestites and María José who dances with an enormous phallus fastened to his moving body. The intense rhythm accompanies this macabre and perverse choreography. María José's body materialises her gender crisis. As she continues to dance in the middle of all these people, she makes obscene gestures to draw attention to the presence of this enormous bottle between her legs. The choreography of the bodies' contrasts with the real gender identities: it is an absurd spectacle involving men with female features, who are overly made-up and whose muscles emphasise their actual male gender. Then a frontal medium close-up on Durán's face, entering into this spontaneous spectacle: María José escapes immediately but he follows her. In a frontal medium close-up on María José, who is looking at the camera, Durán talks to her and looks at her back: she must work, end point. She will be obliged now to do the obscene dances on another stage.

An enigmatic dance on stage

Dressed up as a little girl, José María performs on stage in a frontal full shot. He moves, jumps with the skipping rope and runs on stage singing "My little thing, I keep it hidden". While he is pronouncing the word "*tapadita*" (hidden), he is motioning towards his penis to the rhythm of the music. The choreography foregrounds the complexity of the body by these gestures, in contrast with the softness of the little girl's dress and the haircut decorated by curls and a big knotted ribbon: it is the thought-image of a childish young girl. He is touching his skirt and waving it to all sides singing: "I keep it for my love, my little thing, no." Then he turns up his skirt, a close-up frames the penis surrounded by the soft white tissue of this dress. A direct reaction of the audience is given by a frontal medium close-up on two women who turn their heads away. The spectacle is finished and José María leaves the stage. It was a forced dance, imposed by Durán who later apologises. He declares his love for her and says that he wants to marry her. In a medium close-up this announcement is made, his eyes are shining; then in a lateral long shot a plane sets off.

The film finishes in an official institution: it is the clinic. The body will be meticulously examined here before executing the sex change. First, María José has to draw up a statement about her feelings. They inject her with a serum and in a lateral medium close-up we see her sitting on a chair replying to the questions. The spontaneity of her responses is fundamental. A doctor in a white shirt is listening to the taped discourse: he is sitting behind his desk, underlining the seriousness of the act. Durán and María José enter. After this medical survey the doctor concludes that María José is not homosexual. Nowadays this hypothesis would be surprising, but as we already mentioned in this chapter, in the first periods of changing gender, transsexuals were often considered to be homosexuals.[54] In the epoch and in the film, the image of this body and the problems related to his gender gave birth to this hypothesis. The doctor explains that an operation of this type is definitive. The camera frames María José's face, then frames Durán's, who is presenting himself as her husband. The filmic fairy tale comes true. The film director Vicente Aranda invented this happy ending for commercial reasons, well aware that the everyday life of transsexuals was most often difficult,[55] and that homosexuals were socially rejected.

Conclusion: a rebirth

In our modern era, even gender can be changed. What seemed to be a myth to create a happy ending became a reality. In SEX CHANGE, the body serves to play out a ritual of rebirth, giving form to a new mythological figure that comes to be through interaction with the other key characters. José María's body is a mediator, one that negotiates the images of a stereotypical homosexuality marked by female features, through the softness of his gestures and dainty characteristics of his face. But José María is not homosexual, and the treatment meant to make him more masculine has failed. Bibi Andersen is then established as an unconditional role model and José María the direct imitation. The body reconstructs its origins and shows an image of rebirth, after a process of transforming marked by authorities: firstly the schoolmaster, who declares his abnormality, then the nightclubs that underline its marginality, ending with the clinic that will confirm the change.

The end of the film is strange: we see a close-up on María José's joyful face while the voice-over emphasises her first orgasm after six months. In a period when female sexuality was taboo, this scene is quite curious and yet shocked reactions could not be found in the press articles. Given SEX CHANGE's date of release, no more than two years after the death of Franco, everything in this film was odd for that period. This is also the case for MY DEAREST SEÑORITA (1971) by Jaime de Armiñan, which touches upon similarly peculiar themes, and which represented Spain at the Oscars. Gender issues are questioned by the image of the body in both films. We witness the birth of new myths on this subject. Indeed, the movie is a virtual fairy tale and thus presents new possibilities in the creation of future romantic love stories. Bibi Andersen is still active and appreciated today. Her physical appearance continues to represent beauty and womanhood in Spanish cinema. Her cinematographic and culturally well-known personality confirms the convincing aspect of this body. In 1977 she introduced and symbolised this new filmic myth about multi-genderness by changing gender.

II. The Deputy (El diputado, 1978): the political body

The Transition period is characterised by the continued emergence of the homosexual identity in Spanish film. During this era, distinct in its use and display of "provocative-demanding-images", the visibility of the homosexual identity is increasingly apparent. The film The Deputy (El diputado) relates the complicated negotiation between private and public life and is thus a cogent choice for review. Roberto (José Sacristán), the protagonist, narrates the tale. He is married to Carmen (María Luisa San José). They form a perfect couple: young, good-looking, and politically active within the Communist party.[56] Roberto has even been designated to represent his party for the next elections. We learn that prior to this new period of political freedom, Roberto had been imprisoned for his left-wing political stances. While incarcerated, he had an affair with a boy that was prostituting himself with other homosexual inmates. Once released, Roberto integrates political life, finds his wife, and everything seems to be forgotten. But his homosexual desires remain, deeply rooted within. One day he phones a boy who organises encounters with young homosexual prostitutes. Everything takes place in cars and, when Roberto's political career becomes more demanding, he foregoes his sexual jaunts. However, his political adversaries discover Roberto's homosexuality. They set out to trap him, paying a young hustler to seduce him. The drama begins: Roberto falls in love with the young hustler and they start a real relationship. His wife proposes to integrate this love affair into their conjugal life, pretending her husband's young lover is a relative who is living with them. She wants to keep up with appearances. The wicked adversaries come to understand that their pawn has decided to abandon the strategy agreed upon. They call upon him and murder him. Roberto encounters his lover's body in their apartment. Now, with his lover's dead body before him, he feels compelled to admit everything to the police and this the day before the legislative elections in which he is a candidate. He decides to go through with his disclosures, despite his wife's adamant resistance, who would prefer to conceal this complicating aspect of her husband's person; but it is too late.

Spanish reactions

The Deputy openly and directly represents feelings of culpability and to understand their whole import we must situate these images within the historical context: The Deputy was shot and released when the Law of Social Danger and Rehabilitation was still in place. This meant that committing homosexual acts could lead to being incarcerated in institutions of re-education for a period of six months to five years. Another historical fact should be mentioned: the first democratic elections took place in 1977, the first ever in Spain since 1936. The film refers to this politically charged situation.[57] We witness a candidate prepare for the elections. Moreover, the candidate appears to be speaking on behalf of the Communist party, a party that had only just recently been legalised. Knowing that any positive image of this political party was cinematographically censored during Francoism,[58] this new image also ushered in a groundbreaking visibility with regard to politics proper. Yet, in this historical context, with all of its political changes, mainly due to newly acquired civil freedom, homosexuality remained illegal. This makes Eloy de la Iglesia's film a political statement, unabashedly introducing new images of the homosexual body.

THE DEPUTY is thus clearly polemical for the 1970s. Its dissenting nature is illustrated in the rude press reactions of that time; the violent critiques support the idea that the images were new, shocking and destabilising. The critics focused particularly on the director's link with homosexuality. One of the most venomous grievances denounces Iglesia for exploiting the theme of homosexuality for sheer commercial purposes. Indeed, the filmmaker was often stigmatised for his preference for marginal themes. This argument is reiterated in several articles. Furthermore, the critics focus especially on the immoral and scandalous aspects of certain sequences.

I will cite some examples of these homophobic reactions: "In conclusion, an opportunistic film, gratuitously vulgar in its presentation of sexual acts, politically bias, even if it reflects a comical puerility."[59] In El Pais: "The only thing that is important to him is to sell his product, and to put within it whatever it takes to market it; sex and politics. Eloy de la Iglesia is not a good filmmaker; in his entire filmography there isn't even a single good movie. He isn't even a good cheater."[60] In Pueblo: "It is not the first time that Eloy de la Iglesia puts into his films the theme of homosexuality, which he defends with a lot of passion and conviction.... /...It is an 'S' film, needless to say, there are scenes and situations that are frankly obscene and disgusting, and in a real way, very important to De la Iglesia."[61] The reactions regarding the film focus thus on the homosexual issue and the journalists ask Iglesia why he is so interested in marginal love affairs. Several interviews are published resembling this one from *La Vanguardia*:

- Do you specialise in marginal love affairs?
- I have only made two films on this topic, out of a total of thirteen.
- But they interest you, in general, these marginal love affairs.
- Every free sexual relationship is marginal, since the "standard" relationship as it is marked by society is completely repressed, and every attempt at liberation is a form of marginalisation.[62]

And yet another reaction from the filmmaker: "I defend all sorts of sexual protests, hetero or homosexual."[63] The polemical nature of homosexuality, as it was once understood in Spanish cinema, or in Spanish society is evident in the tone echoing throughout the press reviews of that time. The film bears witness to the newness of the images. The violent reactions from the media belie the film's cult status and the existence of alternative readings stemming from other parts of Spanish culture. Variant appreciations were inspired, among others things, by curiosity: the cult aspect of the film is not only based on a positive critique, but also on the fact that this subject contrasts with the classical panorama. The public also reacted: "There is a clear divorce between the critics and the audience. That *"The Deputy"* is a success in cinema, nobody doubts: they have to put "sold out" in the cinemas where this film is projected."[64] "Thirteen feature films, which are enough for a man of thirty-five years. The feature films are frequently rejected by critics and almost always, on the other hand, attain tremendous success in the cinemas."[65] Seven years later, when it was retransmitted on Spanish television, the reactions are mitigated: "Cineaste of marginality, he approaches the theme of homosexuality.../... It is a big step and one has to continue to demand that television takes more similar steps for the freedom of expression."[66]

Indeed, Eloy de la Iglesia relates marginality to other themes. Scholars continue to write about this film, highlighting for instance his way of relating homosexuality to other marginal issues, which allowed the filmmaker to make a political statement.[67] His collocation of marginal themes made his cinema so important for the Transition periods (more than other filmmakers like Ventura Pons for example, who also treats homosexuality over several decades).[68] The body is the centre of this statement: its mise-en-scene by the filmic forms illustrates the conflict in a convincing manner relating it directly to the filmic and political language of the 1970s.

The bodies: actors, characters

The actors openly express their political allegiances. A political dichotomy is created with the left clearly anchored by the good. In fact, the visual language throughout the film expresses a conflict between the good and the bad. The good is a prototype for that period and is embodied by actors who correspond to this ideal, like José Sacristán who plays Roberto and María Luisa San José who plays Carmen or, yet again, José Luis Alonso in the role of Juanito. The conflict they face specifically arises from homosexuality. The actor Agustín González, who represents the rightwing in the filmic context, crudely evokes the bad character. The contrast between these two groups is clear and schematic: the conflict, originating in homosexuality, is at the core of the mythological narration, which pits these two groups against one another. The different images of the body will negotiate these polar antagonists and result in the creation of something new.

The character of Roberto is a prototype of common sense and intelligence. The title, THE DEPUTY, refers to Roberto's public image: his body is at once public and private. He therefore incarnates the conflict; in order to move up in his political career he must conceal his homosexuality. He is a mediator negotiating between a private life, one at the margin (because he is homosexual), and his public life (given the political situation). His body is not typically *mariquita*, but is rather the prototype for a "good" homosexual. He is supposed to hide his homosexuality and seems to succeed in doing so: his homosexuality is even dissimulated behind a marriage. Forever aware that he must keep his homosexuality secret, he consummates his desires exclusively in ephemeral spaces, further reinforcing this image of marginality. On the side of the good, an innovative image of the family is portrayed and adapted by Roberto, Carmen and Juanito/José. Their couple reflects a perfect image: Carmen, a beautiful and intelligent woman, standing proudly by a promising political man. To succeed, he needs her for what she represents; she needs him for the same reason. The images of their bodies complete each other and their private life becomes a public performance.

The situation is different inside the domestic space: they create a new structure for the family. The archetype of the family is originally represented in many cultures by a mother, a father and children. Other forms of relationships like those between lovers and mistresses are supposed to be maintained on the sly. The classical idea of a couple exists between Carmen and Roberto, but to sustain their facade, a new family has to be created to give place to his homosexual feelings. Roberto and Carmen actualise an archetype of the family and welcome Juanito to their home as Roberto's lover, while outside the familial walls they present him as a relative. This "new family" gives their bodies prototypical features of tolerance and open-mindedness. The three characters are depicted with positive qualities; their intellectual outlook, their humane behaviour and their acceptance of homosexuality are presented as being exemplary.

On the other hand, the right wing is represented by Carrés (Agustín González). The representation of "malice" is incarnated by several stereotyped bodies: a simplified categorisation that helps to recognise, classify and categorise the social phenomena in the film. Carrés wears black glasses, has a moustache and is often filmed in boxing schools or at the shooting range. His is an image of violence; he is filmed in places where people work on their physical force through, for instance, sport. This thought-image of the body contrasts completely with the prototypical body that is based on open communication, reading and rational thinking. The binary opposition, between the good and the bad, between the two camps, is therefore absolutely schematic.

Reading the ritual

In this film, a new ritual is introduced and two stages are important for the protagonist. The first stage constitutes a questioning of the origin of his homosexual feelings and the second is the integration of his homosexuality into his current life. The film opens with the first stage: examining the origins is visualised by a flashback that structures the entire narration. Roberto remembers the moment when he became aware of his homosexual feelings, and how he tried to hide them or to ignore them. In a medium close-up on Roberto, we see him in the car driving to the police headquarters to report Juanito's murder: in voice-over, he explains what happened. He begins to tell the story of his life. The flashbacks begin as he drives. Visualising the adult body as it recalls its past not only exposes the origins of this sad story but also emphasises the current relevance or state of the problem. His monologue describes the deeply repressed taboos, despite his trying to burst through them in the present tense: the discrepancy between the two tenses is illustrated by the voice-over indicating the prohibition of the past in contrast to the images of the 1970s showing political freedom. These filmic forms illustrate a transitory situation entailing a reflection on time, and the desire for change.

The mise-en-scene shows an image of the body that is blaming itself. Roberto must inform the police about the murder of his lover. He is not guilty of the crime, but is guilty only of being homosexual. His monologue is so human, foregrounding the spontaneous emergence of his feelings and their persistence. Prominence is given to the legal guilt. Already the first sequences visualise the legal consequences of his political commitments. Three sequences follow with a similar structure: first, a close-up on a drawer while someone is taking out a file on Roberto, to read aloud his police record; we see a frontal medium close-up on the person who is reading a long list of infractions in perfunctory fashion. The last sequence alludes to the fact that he defended ETA terrorists at the council of war for the Trial of Burgos. These terrorists were later condemned to death: Roberto is morally guilty for his political ideas during Francoism. The drawer is constantly opened. After this unambiguous historical reference, a link is made to his homosexuality. We see Roberto in a medium close-up in a light low angle in his toga layer, wearing glasses, talking with conviction, his eyes confident and authoritative, his hands posed assuredly on the lawyer's pulpit. It is the body of the model and idealistic lawyer, one who believes in his vocation. But then he wonders: if he were to be accused of being homosexual, would he be able to defend himself?

His voice-over commentary explores the mise-en-scene of these bodies. First a long shot showing the civil guards standing around some men. Apparently they are members of the ETA. Then, in the same position, the men are deleted from the shot: Roberto sits on the bench of the accused, bowing his head. He looks like a condemned person as he speaks about his homosexuality. He sits there in the same position as the ETA members, on the same bench, surrounded by the same civil guards. He feels guilty. In this flashback he remembers feeling guilty. As a lawyer he is less equipped to defend himself, to argue for his homosexuality than he is trained to justify a terrorist. A silent body, completely passive, he is speechless while looking uncertain. His body is indecisive. The images are strong, replete with details: during his political career he knew to plead for human rights and yet when the time to defend his homosexuality presents itself, he is left speechless.

The marriage: a facade

The flashback on his life continues through the same thought-image of the body. After this sequence in the court, he describes his encounter with Carmen, his marriage, the fact that he felt rescued from marginality. It is like a series of photographs that is shown, pictures passing fast and with intensity. We receive an enormous amount of information about Roberto's life through these images and his comment, it is almost excessive. Photographs of a close-up on Carmen, a beautiful smiling woman, several photos of her face, then the couple together in a medium close-up, Carmen in her wedding dress. The voice-over explains that this marriage served as a cover-up. But the homosexual feelings came back. While prison is a hidden space that accommodates the prohibited aspects of a society, there, at Carabanchel he meets a boy who is incarcerated for prostitution and is promiscuous with other inmates. Inez is imprisoned for "social danger" and when the two men go to the toilets, Roberto stares at Inez's penis. By an interaction of close-ups on their faces, we notice that Inez is fascinated and looks back at Roberto, who turns down his eyes. After their short love affair in prison, once liberated, Inez leaves his phone number for Roberto.

Once returned home, Roberto confesses this event to Carmen. Her reaction is given in a close-up on her face; she looks serious, attentive and calm. Understanding and comprehensive, she simply listens. Soft music accompanies this sequence as they lie in bed together. An intense emotion is visible on her face. The camera displaces from the left on him, framing both persons frontally. This intimate conjugal scene is accompanied by soft music that rhythms his words. In the image the couple is unified, he explains and confesses what he has done, she demands his sincerity. Telling him that she knew he was homosexual before getting married, she will now no less accept it. They embrace passionately, the camera approaches, the couple is reunited. Roberto was sincere with his wife and tries with his whole heart to forget his desires. Reasonable, calm and sincere: he is really trying. Roberto's voice accompanies the full shot on a telephone box while commenting his irrepressible feelings, illustrated by a camera that is

Photo 18: Homosexual desire at the margin

moving in all directions and approaching the cabin. The upheaval is strong, he cannot stand it anymore. The camera visualises his desire and gets extremely close to the telephone: a close-up on the dial, followed by an extreme close-up on the handset receiver, then on the text *monedas*, we hear the money fall down. The line is established. Inez is waiting in a garage in the basement, in a car; the two look at each other in a medium close-up on one and then the other: Inez proposes "good" boys, who won't recognise him.

The thought-image of the bodies of the young hustlers is introduced by anonymity, a smile and youthfulness. The voice-over comments on their encounters, without any dialogues. The bodies are replaced in a fast and regular rhythm in six frontal medium close-ups on six sitting boys, a rhythm that translates the regular and fast change. The camera focuses on their timid smiles, exhibiting a carefree openness, and their young, friendly faces. This is followed by a close-up on Roberto. Then the rhythm of the shots continues on six other frontal medium close-ups on boys, lying down in the car. All these shots are not commented: they are ephemeral relationships; the young boys are passive and smile for money. Roberto's voice-over concludes on this series of young hustlers with a bitter comment "For the first time clandestinity was to my benefit."

Stereotyping marginality

But Roberto has several enemies. He has no links with the social world of stereotypical homosexuals; his surreptitious encounters occur within the marginalised and discreet setting of his car. Nevertheless his enemies are interested in his inclinations. The images of numerous young bodies, of animosity declared in his rivals smiles, and of Roberto's public professional position create a play of symbols contrasting good and bad, public and private. The tension originates in the fact that he is recognised and that people wish to discover the hidden part of who he is. The good homosexual, which Roberto represents, the prototypical gay man, will be put in dialogue with the stereotypical frame of homosexuality.

The first encounter with this setting takes place in a brothel. A close-up on Juanito climaxing is followed by a high angle close-up on a bald head. The head is held on its side by hands that are heavily adorned with rings. The act of fellatio is portrayed. Different shots continue; the world of marginality marks this place by the thought-image of the stereotyped body of the homosexual, reinforced by the meaningful song about "the social danger". Juanito gets up and approaches Inez who, in a frontal long shot, is sitting completely naked in front of a man who is a perfect *mariquita*. He is looking at Inez with fascinated desire. The admirer's head moves in a feminine and soft way. Womanly, he is wrapped in a morning gown. Juanito sits down behind them and asks for work. Inez wants to introduce him to Roberto.

This site represents the visible homosexual bodies in a marginal setting, showing them during their sexual activities. These hustlers are young boys who prostitute themselves for money and exploit their own sexual desires for money. These are thought-images of the underworld. Another boy wants to introduce them to a man to earn some money, a fascist and violent politician, of the right wing. The man is everything one would expect of a bad guy: it is Carrés. A threatening face, wearing thick black glasses that dissimulate his eyes, he is bald and has a thick moustache. He has all the features of an intimidating and spiteful man. His antagonising appearance is reinforced by his discourse about the grandeur of Spain. His fascist political discourses include promises to convert these male prostitutes into real men, into unquestionable heterosexuals. The camera pulls back, frames now Inez on the left, and his friend at the right. Inez emphasises the fact that they are interested in money and behave with insolent indifference to Spain's grandeur. The stereotyped bodies of the fascist politician and the homosexual prostitute are set side by side stealthy context of underground dealings. The plan is announced. A meeting with Roberto will be organised: his prototypical image will thus be situated into this stereotyped frame, making his homosexual image visible for others. For that period that kind of revelation would be damning.

The private decor

The film contains historical references of the first post-dictatorship elections. The couple, Carmen and Roberto, is shown in a lateral shot as they vote: they are filmed, recognised, and photographed. This image represents a historical moment for Spain. Then, the difference between their private life and their political life is illustrated as we watch Carmen in her home. In a frontal full shot on the young woman, the thought-image of her body illustrates her satisfaction. She looks beautiful sitting in front of the television. A medium close-up on the screen illustrates several views of the Parliament accompanied by the voice of the king: "Today is the first day of the Monarchy's Legislative Parliament and as I preside this historic session, I see before me that attainment of a compromise that I always felt was my complete responsibility".

Several full shots and medium long shots inside the Parliament connect and in the fourth we see Roberto with the president of his party in the rows: he looks serious, gazing straight into the audience. He turns slightly to us and we recognise him immediately with his typical glasses and his suit. This point of view long shot is followed by a frontal shot on Carmen, who is proud and pleased. The montage highlights how his wife embodies the connection between his private and public life. Next to her we see a photo of her husband: she takes it, the camera approaches towards Carmen when she kisses the photograph while all around are smiling. She is proud of her husband and his career is succeeding thanks to her.

The encounter

On the other hand, there is someone preparing to ruin his prospering career, to break down this congenial family appearance. Carrés proposes to his colleagues to set up a trap. The goal is to accuse Roberto of committing a: "sex offence against minors". Framed in a frontal medium close-up at the background, we vaguely see two men who are boxing. The sound of someone giving punches can be heard. Again, these are symbols of rugged strength, of violence if necessary. Roberto's political rivals devise their destructive stratagem at a boxing school. The location's aspect of violence is reinforced by these characters that wish, by any means necessary, to take over the political power. They look menacing, stereotyped with black heavy glasses and a thick moustache. Their physique and their attitude contrast schematically with that of Roberto's. Roberto is the paragon image of rationality; his perspective is based on ideas and erudition and he shows himself to be gentlemanly in his contact with people. The bad guys meet Juanito, a frontal medium close-up shows a man who offers him a lot of money. He seems interested. The encounter is imposed without Roberto knowing it who arrives towards the camera walking, in a matter-of-fact way; he moves slowly reading at the same time, in a frontal shot. Suddenly he stops and looks ahead. Inez is waiting for him in the garage, sitting on the car. This young and virile body brings his past and his repressed desires to the surface. Yet he wishes to forget both his relationship with Inez and his homosexual desires. Inez proposes to introduce him to another young boy: Juanito.

Roberto is falling in love

In a medium close-up, Roberto approaches. Framed then at the back, it is by his gaze that we see in the background Juanito sitting on the car; soft piano music accompanies the film images in a close-up. With big open vivid eyes, Juanito watches Roberto. The thought-image of his body illustrates his feelings for this young boy. His amorous glare is intensified by the music; his hand is caressing his face, discovering it. In a close-up on Roberto is bedazzled by this magnificent creature standing next to him; his eyes, full of emotions, are transfixed by the young boy's beauty. His hands discover Juanito's body, in a high angle shot on the naked chest where Roberto's hand is caressing, hesitating, and tender. The boy's body is lying down with a professional passivity, waiting for the desire of the other. They leave together by car. It is night and little streetlamps punctuate the road. A close-up on a smiling Juanito, then a close-up on Roberto who is also laughing. In a long shot on the motorway in the dark, pierced by small lights of street lamps, a romantic atmosphere is evident. In voice-over, Roberto speaks of love, he feels so good and happy with this person. He is deeply touched by love poems that beforehand did not have the same meaning but now move him deeply. This special love affair continues then in their secret apartment: the place where they held underground political meetings before. Now it is the place to have a homosexual love affair: the filmmaker makes a direct political statement about the clandestinity of homosexuality by using this apartment, a site of past and current prohibitions.

The family as a decor

Roberto's official relationship, his marriage, is absolutely disturbed. It first functioned to keep up appearances, and now it will be transformed into a *ménage à trois*, with a homosexual element. His wife reacts again with tenderness; the rhythm of the sequence is marked by her rational reactions. She is giving an exemplary thought-image of tolerance, of being understanding; a prototype body, she speaks about everything, even when it hurts. Their dialogue is visualised in a frontal medium close-up on Roberto, followed by the same shot on Carmen. Again, nice piano music is softening the atmosphere, while he confesses his love affairs. In a lateral shot that unites them, they turn each other's back on one another, paralleling the reality of their cover-up of a relationship. He, looking out of the window, is recounting what has happened to him. She is sitting down and listening. He is unable to silence his desires, yet he still wants

Photo 19: Protective decor of the family

to pursue his political ambitions. Carmen wants to support him. The camera frames her.

We see a medium close-up on Roberto, then again on his wife as she explains that this is causing her pain. Calm-faced, sad, she shares her own thoughts, saying she believed that he would change with her. They peacefully discuss their problems, a dialogue teeming with words, in an effort to understand the feelings of the other, without tears, without yelling. But the relationship is getting more intense between Roberto and Juanito. One day Carmen knocks on the door: she meets Juanito. She wants to integrate him into their family. The next full shot on the three who are going out, presents the image of their family. Juanito discovers an environment that he is coming to like, to be committed to even. The domestic setting is changing. When the three are having a party together, they smoke a joint. Carmen is lying down on the sofa next to Juanito, on the right Roberto is sitting on a chair. She provokes Juanito, asking him to kiss her. He gets up, is looking at Roberto and she pursues her provocation making fun of him because he is asking for permission. They kiss each other, and are lying down on the floor.

Roberto gets up, looks, and bats his eyes. Next shot films him from the back: his point of view observes in a high angle his wife and Juanito who kiss each other lying on the floor. He is leaning forward and approaches them. Then, a high angle medium close-up on the three of them, a close-up zooming in ever more on the three heads, kissing each other in an acrobatic position. Franco's totem of the family is far behind us: is this the new family organised to keep up appearances?

Stereotyped body and destruction

People from the right wing spy on Juanito: the buzzing of a mosquito, a disturbing sound accompanies the images. Photos of their excursions, all three together: Juanito walked into the trap, they ask him to explain it. Dynamics and tension on the moment where they show a photo of Juanito during a meeting: the right fist straight up, a serious face. Lots of images to destabilise the young man; they give him a pistol and ask him if he is able to kill someone, like for example Roberto. Mentioning his name we see Juanito's face destabilise, in a medium close-up. They take away very quickly the pistol and get close to him. Filming Juanito from behind we see a man in front of him hitting him. The next shot is a frontal close-up on the boy's face; blood is running down from his mouth, with strayed eyes. Carrés, the man with the black glasses, blocks his head taking it by his hair, then another close-up on Juanito's face with swollen lips, that are bleeding.

Carmen and Roberto are preoccupied while waiting for him. Inez knocks at the door and says that Juanito is waiting for Roberto in the apartment. Roberto walks towards Carmen, she is filmed on the back, he frontally in a medium close shot. This shot is repeated reversely: a frontal shot on Carmen, and he is filmed on the back. Now we see Carmen in the dark, while his body is exposed in the light, then the next shot shows Roberto in front of the light of the corridor. They are together and rudely separated in their convictions: the visual interaction between shadows and light symbolise the difficulties of their choices. Carmen does not want him to go there. But for Roberto it is like assuming his homosexual choice while now leaving. He arrives in the apartment that is submerged in darkness, where the gang is waiting for him (frontal shot on them). Roberto enters and walks to the bedroom. A medium close-up on Roberto films his point of view while looking to the bed. The next shot strikes; we see Juanito's body, laid down on its back, dead, in a pool of blood. Again the camera frames Roberto's gaze, followed by a medium close shot of the victim with the shirt open, blood on his chest and on his face. Completely annihilated, he asks, pleading – dumbfounded – shocked, why? The answer is openly sadistic: they declare that it is up to Roberto to explain to the police how this body could be found in his apartment, the evening before the elections. They walk out, leaving

Roberto next to Juanito's corpse. Soft music playing in the background, the sequence finishes on an exchange of close-ups between Juanito's face, caressed by his lover's hand, and then close-ups of Roberto's anxious and devastated face. The last shot is an emotional close-up on the deceased's face while Roberto's fingers close his eyes.

The prototypical body on stage

We go back to the first images of the film, with a frontal medium close-up of Roberto driving his car. In voice-over, he confirms that he will tell the truth, the whole truth. He gets out of his car and enters the building where the Political Congress is being held. The slogan: "Socialism in freedom because socialism is freedom", is written on the building. He enters, a shot on the audience who is singing and acclaiming him. His body on stage, in a long shot on the stage, followed by long shots on the audience. The crowd is singing, with fists raised, pleased; they express force and enthusiasm to fight for this new cause. The camera frames Roberto's face with his comrades, displaces in a tracking shot on him, the fist up. We hear: *Canto a la libertad* in a voice-over, like a hymn for freedom. The camera frames Roberto's face in an extreme close-up, the voice of *Canto a la libertad* can still be heard, while we see a tear running down from his sad eyes. The image dwells upon the slight click-clack sound of a photo camera, followed by the word *"fin"* (end) on his face. He gives the image of a man who is politically free but sexually imprisoned. His body illustrates the contradiction of freedom, while he gets on stage. It is a prototypical body, exemplary for his sincere conviction: his fist raised, we understand that he intends to continue and extend the fight for freedom. The battle to live freely will continue, to live even his desires freely.

Conclusion

During the Transition period, censorship was suppressed and homosexuality became legal. In the same period there was also a new political freedom, which made it possible to express oneself openly about politics. This film bears witness to this climate by offering new images of the body. The new images are initiation rituals that struck the spirits, confirmed by the high audience turn out and the film's passionately virulent critiques. THE DEPUTY showed bodies that were traumatized due to their homosexuality. Eloy de la Iglesia is an important director of this transitory period and he created a cult phenomenon around a forbidden and taboo subject. In compliance with the law, being guilty is presented in the entire film. Roberto goes so far as to imagine himself being on the bench of the accused. This feeling is reinforced by the fact that he meets his homosexual lovers in hidden spaces, and by his wife's reaction that considers that his homosexuality can be suppressed if not overcome. In this period after the dictator-ship, the political world shows an imaginary space where liberty reigns. This prominent theme of liberty is contrasted to the lack of sexual freedom for homo-sexuals. In his professional and public life, Roberto fights for justice and liberty, and yet he is denied these values in his private and intimate space.

The archetypes of the family and the masculine body are reformulated. The actor José Sacristán questions male sexuality in a heterosexual and homosexual relationship. He is a prototype body for that period, one that is historically im-bedded, because he interprets often leftist progressive characters. La Iglesia un-derlines his normality, his virility, his rationality combined with a social status of a successful politician. It is only for his sexual life that he is obliged to meet up with marginality, with stereotyped characters (the *mariquita* and the hustlers, like Juanito). This interaction with different settings frames the love between Juanito and Roberto. But being an idealistic lawyer, this prototypical body wishes to replace the marginalised and ephemeral spaces for a stable site like a family relationship in a domestic setting.

The archetype of the family does not resemble anymore to the way Francoism made a totem of it. This traditional representation is completely demolished. The critics in the press react on this immoral aspect, when Roberto's wife kisses the lover of her husband. Several myths are destroyed: like the stereotyped images created about the bad ones, or the totem of the family. It was meant to keep up appearances for hiding homosexual feelings; the totem of the family is completely reversed. Both myths are destroyed, denouncing prohibition, be-cause the homosexual has a body and an image. The new myth is an invitation to burst through the isolation by the exemplary character finishing on stage with the fist raised. He wants to break down silence and wishes the transpar-ency in public sites, on stage, in a close-up: this mise-en-scene obliges the viewer to look at him. The imprisonment of the body was at the same time emphasised by an abundance of speech in over. This filmic language is typical for the cinema of the Transition like we have seen this with the fiction FLUNKING OUT (ASIGNA-TURA PENDIENTE, 1977); these filmic forms underline the discrepancy in time: the future has to be constructed and the voice-over, by a prolixity of words, de-signs the situation in the past, and of course, the wish for a change.

III. THE DEATH OF MIKEL (LA MUERTE DE MIKEL, 1983): becoming visible

THE DEATH OF MIKEL (LA MUERTE DE MIKEL) is another contribution in the pro-cess of making the homosexual identity more visible in Spanish cinema. The story concentrates on Mikel who shares an unhappy marriage with Begoña. During a hiatus, his wife leaves on a trip and, and upon her return, Mikel goes to pick her up at the airport. They talk in the car, then with Mikel's mother, about their conjugal problems. After a scene of domestic violence, the couple separates. Mikel then begins an affair with Fama, a drag queen. Once he admits his homosexuality, he is swiftly marginalised. The plot exhibits a ritual of initiation about the public outing of the homosexual body. As Alfeo Alvarez confirms, THE DEATH OF MIKEL ends a cycle in Spanish cinema during which homosexuality is treated as a problem, as a marginal identity.[69] Even if the story is not necessarily the tale of someone engaged in an illicit activity, in comparison to Eloy de la Iglesia's language, the message is unequivocal.

Spain at the beginning of the 1980s

Spanish society was politically transformed in the 1980s. The year of the film's release, 1983, marks the end of the Transition period and the increasing establishment of democracy. Spain enters into a new period which is politically more solid. The discussion of autonomies also receives different political interpretations. Marvin D'Lugo has written about the relationship between the New Constitution of 1978, which recognised regional autonomous communities, and the shooting of films dealing with these issues. Imanol Uribe, with his THE BURGOS TRIAL (EL PROCESO DE BURGOS, 1979) is one such example. D'Lugo also foregrounds the importance of community in THE DEATH OF MIKEL (1983).[70] Like in THE DEPUTY, homosexuality is related to political, patriarchal and social issues. In Uribe's film, homosexuality is deeply anchored in the family context and when coming out of the closet, he encounters several reactions from diverse communities: the Basque community with its ETA problems, the village community, but also the community constituted by the members of his own family.

Prohibition and intolerance characterise the atmosphere, even though the film was released six years after the suppression of the article concerning homosexuality in the Law of Social Danger. The consequences on society and cinema manifest themselves, revealing a gap between the legislation and societal views. In a human rights survey carried out in 1985, the social image of homosexuality is analysed.[71] The results are quite telling. The survey starts by quoting the Constitution's fourteenth article, which reaffirms the equality of all Spaniards before the law. But the results of the survey show that 35% of those questioned would prefer to avoid befriending a homosexual. Most of them still consider homosexuality to be a disease caused by an inadequate upbringing. In addition, some commentaries explain that one should not give too much freedom to homosexuals, lest this liberty encourage others to become homosexual as well.[72] Such an allegation implies that homosexuality is a phenomenon that can be imitated and not a specific state of being. Obviously, this survey is done on a limited group of people. However it is clear that the social proclivity for intolerance towards homosexuals was particularly strong during the Franco periods. In cinema, it is curious to observe that the homosexual protagonist lives through his feelings in absolute solitude. There is no visible identification proposed at the moment when he becomes aware that he is homosexual. Stereotyped frames stimulate in him the coming out process of his homosexuality. A complete reversal of how homosexuality was understood and represented cannot be expected a mere five years after the suppression of a repressive law. Moreover, clear signs of homophobia are detected in Spanish society, as the filmmaker Uribe explains in *El Pais*: "The film was shot at a moment when people started to denounce the threats against homosexuals and lesbians in San Sebastian."[73] The film thus confirms a tendency of overall reluctance, even if legally homosexuality was no longer considered an infraction.

This fiction shows Mikel becoming aware of his homosexuality within the core of his family and his village. It illustrates the prejudice he suffers in several spheres of his life: politics, sexuality and religion. Several themes are presented: the ETA, political protests, the civil guards, the church and homosexuality. All of these topics intertwine to create one plot. In a regular rhythm, images denoting these diverse subjects come back and determine the fibre of Mikel's life. Indeed, for a story in which intolerance provokes death, these problems provide a ubiquitously sombre backdrop. The critics were rather positive, especially in comparison to the vituperative reviews of THE DEPUTY. The filmic language, which is less combative and which is void of the sexual intimacy shown in THE DEPUTY can partly explain its more supportive reception. Another reason could be the year of the film's release. In 1983 THE DEATH OF MIKEL is described as a hymn for individual liberty.[74] What is also important to note, is that a well-known and reputed filmmaker like Uribe had chosen to make a film on this theme. The press articles comment more on his vantage point than on the delivery of opprobrium as they so readily did in Iglesia's case.

The montage of the bodies

The title does not leave any doubt: Mikel is going to die. His character bears the mythological plot. He encounters lots of problems in the process of discovering, and especially in living through, his homosexuality. The conflict he undergoes begins when he tries to let people accept and respect his homosexuality. This confrontation with his surroundings, question the ambient intolerance by portraying it within different settings. The first context of rejection is in his direct environment, composed of his wife and his mother. The parochialism is revealed and related to the weak ties he has with his wife. Mikel destroys their sexual relationship. Then he has a love affair with Fama, the drag queen, and he makes his relationship visible to his closest friends.

The actor's male identity is not innocent. In his book on Spanish stars and masculinities, Chris Perriam scrutinises the sociological aspects of some well-known Spanish film stars, like Imanol Arias who plays Mikel. He starts his analysis on him with the subtitle: Spain's sweetheart. To justify this moniker he includes press clippings:

> Part of the appeal constructed by the press, by that first television series, and by DE-MONS IN THE GARDEN/DEMONIOS EN EL JARDIN, (where his character is the object of desire of the two main screen beauties of the time, Angela Molina and Ana Belén), is sex appeal, and by extension the actor's claim to be a galán. This is, as is customary, exaggerated and adapted to readers' expectations by the press (–).[75]

As Perriam confirms, in the 1980s, Imanol Arias is definitely a well-known Spanish star, even though his career will change afterward through his acceptance of other roles, like EL LUTE, which we will scrutinise in the next chapter. His filmography shows a diversity of roles, but during the first period of his fame, in the 1980s, he certainly was Spain's sweetheart.[76]

Through his exemplary body, he expresses the thought -image of the paragon of male seduction. His gaze is firmly seated in his deep brown eyes, he has a handsome physique, tall, thin and attractive; his body offers the prototype of male beauty. His success is underlined in the press who note that the film confirms the actor's popularity:

> With the shooting of "LA MUERTE DE MIKEL" Imanol Arias definitely becomes the most popular star of Spanish cinema and the film itself is a great success. Imanol succeeds remarkably in this difficult role. He knows to give the character a just measure without having to appeal to effects or to shortcuts. Thanks to Imanol Arias, this story about social and political intolerance in the Basque country takes on a jaw-dropping tone.[77]

The actor knows to show an enclosed thought-image of his body in the way he moves and expresses himself. His rebellion against his own situation is embodied in his physical outlook. When he expresses himself, he stays calm and rational; full of held back emotions and modesty. His body shows an average human being, who keeps his problems to himself. The actor's sensitivity is particularly convincing when he is dealing with the challenges thrown at him from several communities, which each make it clear that they are not favourable to him. The core of the conflict, as the core for the mythological story, will be negotiated by Mikel. Therefore two female characters deserve attention: his wife and his mother. They represent the community of the family, and the site for heterosexual sexuality.

His wife, Begoña, acted by Amaia Lasa, is beautiful and understanding. She forgives him for the domestic violence and they separate. She is a nice and friendly woman, completely submissive to the situation and does not have any vindictive feelings towards him. Begoña represents the heterosexual relationship, an image of the family that has not worked out as Mikel's mother would have liked. The mother represents an important character in the story. Played by Montserrat Salvador, she creates a thought-image of toughness, inscribed on her face by austere and rigid features. Her body reveals the symbolic weight she carries on her shoulders in the way that she expresses herself, the way that she moves and through her behaviour. She has thin lips, a straight nose, her hair always put together; she is the personification of the strict and powerful mother. Her face does not express any flexibility or tenderness. She exemplifies the woman who is always looking out for gossip in her astute observation of others, but is horrified by the idea that she could herself become a principal character in a thrilling scandal. Their family has a central function in the community as they run a chemist in the village, in which Mikel also works.

These female bodies express a clear thought, representing the conflict of the family, but also of the community, like Marvin D'Lugo indicates. He compares the female characters as representatives of the community:

> At the outset, we see Mikel torn by a struggle between two strong female characters: his mother who embodies the narrowly defined and closed world of the small Basque community in which she lives, and Begoña, who is identified early on with geographic mobility and European culture. This duality may be read as a microcosm of the cultural and social tensions of Basque society itself, divided between closed traditionalism and a more expansive modernity. But, even more the opposing mindsets reflected by the matriarch and her daughter-in-law suggest the conflict between an intransigent world view and one that is able to accommodate itself in new and changing environments. These are, in fact, the ways that the two women will respond to Mikel's sexual crisis.[78]

This negotiation between the two female characters will question Mikel's family situation, as these two characters negotiate the archetype on virility and of the family.

The community is further represented by some secondary characters, like the brother and the doctor who is a friend. They illustrate the direct reactions of the community towards Mikel. The brother does not really agree with his politically progressive ideas. The doctor, who is a political refugee from Chile, tries not to give his opinion about Mikel, but it becomes clear that he does not really condone Mikel's homosexuality either. In contrast with the village, the city introduces the character of Fama, acted by Fernando Tellechea. He represents the homosexual, figuring the visibility through a typecast. Making this body look female is carried out by hand gestures, the way of touching his clothes and so forth. This body brings the stereotyped image of a homosexual, a drag queen, a body performing on stage. Fama's homosexual identity is clearly stereotyped and through his interaction with Fama drag queen, Mikel's homosexuality becomes visible to his community.

Myths of male sexuality

The relationships between the characters allow us to make a reading of the mythological thought. Mikel's body expresses a thought when it is questioning the relationship between Mikel and his mother, Mikel and his wife, Mikel and Fama. The interaction between these thought-images allows us to make the reading of the myth, based here on two archetypal ideas: the family and male sexuality. The representation of the family is again deconstructed. A direct reference is given to some archetypal values of the male body in the context of the family. The family represents archetypal values, which we have already defined. In general, the family is based on a heterosexual couple, which has a sexual relationship, and in most cases the family is completed with children. It is Mikel's sexuality that does not seem to function in the family. His virility is questioned and, at first, inside the family frame. In the second stage he introduces male sexuality in a homosexual setting. This prototypical body updates the archetype of the masculine body: Mikel virile body is represented in the context of homosexual love.

Several rituals take place with the introduction of his homosexuality. The rituals express a thought, an idea, and a confrontation with communities that are not receptive to homosexuality. Mikel is in the centre of all these rituals. Exhibiting this image in his village, he accomplishes a ritual of initiation by making his homosexuality visible in his community. His body figures this thought-image in a place where narrow-mindedness dominates. In the entire film, the mise-en-scene underlines intolerance from a clear point of view. Funerals are a repeating decor: they open and close the film. Mikel's funeral opens the film as a flashback (like the film *El diputado* that also started with Roberto's flashback). The ceremony takes place in the church accompanied by soprano voices. The melody is imposing, recognisable and insisting. The faces of Begoña, of his mother and his brother in the church during funeral ceremonies come back regularly in the film, foregrounding the permanent presence of death. We see no rebellion or the identification of the guilty people. The body of Mikel is never shown inside the church. He lives alone in his world and lots of full shots draw attention to his entire body, he is often filmed alone or isolated from his surroundings.

Reading the choreography of the body

The film opens with a direct gaze on Mikel. His body introduces the thought-image of the loner. In the first sequences, his environment is visualised, where bigotry and death reign. A distance can be felt between he and his family and closest friends. These strained relationships function as a sort of decor. He does not feel connected to his wife or his family. This first stage illustrates the conflict between Mikel's homosexual feelings, the village and a marriage that does not work. The different communities illustrate his cloistered off existence. Mikel is alone in his world. We see at the background of a forest a shadow, that comes closer and we recognise a man who is looking for mushrooms. He is alone in this place and his solitude is caused by an identity that he cannot express in his milieu. The body gives a static image, characterised by little emotion and re-strained movements. No smile, a serious and distracted look. He approaches a house, enters, and takes a cup of coffee with a woman, the doctor's wife. In a medium close-up on his face, he says that Begoña, his wife, is coming home from her trip. A medium close-up on the woman, who replies that he must certainly be happy. His face, again filmed in a medium close-up, shows a hesitating expression.

A plane is landing, travellers get off and the camera focuses on a woman: Begoña. In the car they speak with each other, a medium close-up on Mikel at the back, on Begoña, alternating: they exchange some phrases but no intimate or personal details. She tells him about her trip, telling him about her interesting encounters with Dutch people. Together on their balcony, in a lateral medium close shot, he keeps some distance from her but she asks him for a kiss. He feels obliged to approach. She kisses him and his body looks like a marionette while putting his arms around her in a mechanical way. His body is stiff. The camera frames a medium close shot on her back, frontal on him. He stays inert during their reconciliation as if he were submitting himself to a sort of obligation. To-gether they are going to his mother's place. The mother is very talkative. In a medium close-up on the mother, and then on Begoña, finally on Mikel, we see tense bodies, especially those of the couple. The mother is knitting and gossip-ing. Mikel wants to leave and his mother asks Begoña to stay a little longer to tell her about her trip; Begoña obeys but instead they talk about her marriage.

Strength and virility

Begoña has told her mother-in-law that their sexual relations are not satisfac-tory, even worse, non-existent. Mikel is furious; his pride is deeply hurt. The encounter with the family has taken place. The problem of Mikel's sexuality is put forward as a lack of a sexual drive. Now the next encounter will be illu-strated: the village. The next sequence illustrates a typical regional feast, which celebrates the strength of the townsmen. Mikel participates. His body demonstrates his undeniable strength. This village gathering is an important affair. Everyone is concerned as the village is small; it would be hard to avoid this type of social event. The game meant to honour the strength of the village's men begins. A long shot on a river, a boat, and a rope: we are attending the feast of geese.[79] This feast still exists in the Basque country, where many traditions revolve around showcasing the sheer strength of the male inhabitants. When the goose's head disconnects, as a consequence of force, the audience enthusiastically applauds, happy to have witnessed the display of a townsmen's power.

Mikel participates. A slight low angle shot on Mikel on the boat is followed by a lateral full shot when he approaches the goose and a low angle medium close shot when he sticks to the beast. This man is young, full of strength and energy: he pulls three times from up and down, in a long shot. A shot on the men who pull the rope, then a high angle shot on the water; then a medium long shot; the rope rises and he stops: a lateral medium up on Begoña who is applauding in the audience, proud of her husband, followed by a long shot of this scene with all the boats. The masculine bodies have shown their physical force, the spectators are applauding. Mikel is strong, young, handsome, virile, and married.

This show of strength is followed by a visit to the bar and the men are singing labour songs and clapping rhythms on the tables. It is a festive scene of alcoholism and men being men. Mikel, in good shape, seems as happy as the others. Attended by so many spectators, his act of courage symbolises his male virility. He is assuredly strong, a typical masculine archetypal value. The physical strength of a man and his sexual appetite are often linked: Mikel is feeling well. After the party, he wants to make love to Begoña. Coming home, he bumps into the furniture (full shot) and it is clear that he has drunk too much. We see him entering the door of the bedroom, then a medium close-up on her, asleep, naked, her body half covered by the sheets. Under the influence of alcohol Mikel is euphoric, he undresses, gets in the bed, and in a medium long shot, we see him groping his wife's body under the sheets before getting down to her sex. First hesitating, she starts enjoying it. Completely absorbed in this intimate encounter she gets up suddenly, with a wild shout, in a frontal medium close-up. With all her strength she is hitting Mikel under the sheets. The image is in slow motion: she does not stop hitting him, takes a bottle next to the bed and hits him several times.[80]

The next shot shows funerals, a medium close-up on the back of a priest, and at the background we notice that the church is full. The coffin in a medium long shot is followed by a medium close-up on the attendant's faces. In a pan shot from the right to the left, we see several faces: Begoña, his mother, his brother. His mother is crying, they all look so sad but without too much emotion expressed. The priest talks about the death of a man. After the last sequence, the spectator has a doubt. It could be Mikel's cadaver, because we do not see him in the church. The identity of the person is not given. The image is accompanied by voices that colour this monotonous and sad session. But it was not Mikel. His Chilean friend is visiting him. In a lateral medium close shot on both men, the last one advises him to see a psychiatrist. Mikel will follow his advice. He has destroyed the relationship with his wife and is now looking to the future.

On stage

After having consulted a psychiatrist, Mikel goes out to a nightclub and attends a performance of an original body: a man disguised as a football player. The choreography of this body is hilarious. A medium close-up on the singer shows us a masculine face wearing a considerable amount of make up; this manly face has painted red lips and eyes accentuated with shadow and mascara. His face is the picture of exaggerated womanliness. His long-haired wig is adorned with a flower and he wears a silver bandeau around his forehead. The dance and the text frame this stereotyped body of a homosexual, one that is too marked by clichés and is thus rendered too blatantly visible. The way he moves, displaces himself, and the manner with which he gestures with his hands all illustrate the gamut of typically feminine idiosyncrasies.

The show is magnificent. The song's text is sweet: he sings a song for the glory of Atlety, the local football team, moving from the right to the left in a mechanical way: "*El Atlety*, what a joy, what an emotion, when the goal is marked, they all scream, machos and gays". Even the melody is mechanical in rhythm and emotion: everything translates the body's effort to symbolise femininity; an admirable effort to camouflage his muscular body is clear. The song continues: "Crazy about football, full of passions, dreaming of the balls of all the football players". The showman is wearing Atlety's red and white football t-shirt and a pair of shorts. The hands turn with too flexible, too womanlike, a gesture. To make us laugh, this body is over codified, showing a parody of his own transvestite image imitating a football player. He announces the performance of Fama: a drag queen will now perform on stage.

In the next sequence the camera zooms onto Mikel's spellbound face. The interaction between the shots is faster and more intense, caused by the seriousness of Mikel's expression. A medium close-up on him, followed by a medium close-up on Fama, who opens delicately the curtains, before showing himself: a body made female, a drag queen with a beautiful voice. The camera approaches Mikel, followed by a full shot on Fama, walking slowly, accentuating every step with elegance. The editing of the shots draws attention to their dialogue: the body on stage illustrates the thought-image of a female body, dressed up in a

Photo 20: Fama, a visible homosexual body, on stage

beautiful dress. With sultry deliberation and a quick movement, she reveals herself from under her shawl.

The camera is approaching, reframing the gestures, thereby giving them an intimate connotation. The gestures seem much more natural, anyhow, not at all comical. This is followed by several close-ups on Mikel's face who is smiling. The dialogue is established: the montage brings together these two bodies.

Encounter

The love act is not shown: an ellipsis. A tracking shot approaches on Fama who is sleeping; in the background we see Mikel getting dressed. A nervous body evidently stressed; with some brusque gestures and in a hurry, he puts on his trousers and goes downstairs. The camera follows him through these telling mundane acts. He enters the bathroom, looks seriously at himself in the mirror, a medium close-up of the back, which illustrates the reflection of himself on himself. His face is framed twice and he seems rather unhappy. Washing his face, he takes the towels and dries himself. Once again he looks at himself, a direct and concentrated gaze, no joy, no sadness, rather upset. The mirror em-

Photo 21: A masculine body, a feminised body

phasises the gaze on his life, on the night he has spent with a man. He gets out and sits down to put on his socks. In a full shot, Fama enters into the field. Mikel continues to get dressed; he seems embarrassed. Fama asks if he is in a hurry. He wants to phone the chemist, Mikel replies. In a lateral medium close-up he phones apologising for his delay. Fama comes back in a frontal medium close shot, two persons facing each other (see photo).

A distance between them is perceptible. Fama is trying to approach his lover asking him for a kiss but Mikel refuses. The thought-image of Fama's body expresses desire, expressed by these intentionally "female" gestures: the manner with which he holds his bath gown refers to an image that is feminine in an artificial way. It looks like overacting even for a woman. This gesture confers a fragility to this body, which nevertheless is not fragile. His mannerism points to a sense of prudishness, a modesty as he stands before a man with whom he has made love and who is now in a hurry to leave. Mikel takes up a nonchalant and cool attitude: he apologises, he drank too much yesterday evening. The sexual act was of no importance; he prefers to remember it as a delirium of alcohol so as not to face the reality of the act and to avoid taking responsibility for its consequences. Fama replies: "At the beginning all the fags are the same". His lover reacts; the two men affront each other and Mikel slaps Fama. This feminised body, even when staggering from the shock, does this in a female way, leaning in front of him with little steps, and bowing his head meekly. When Mikel wants to leave, he promises to send Fama the money that he demanded later.

Returning to his village, he tries to commit suicide. Several shots express his nervous need to collide with other cars. A medium long shot of the motorway, suddenly he turns to the other side, trying to kill himself. The symbolic of the body's misfortune is expressed by the image of a motorway: he must go home, he went down the wrong path, the queer path, and it is too late to turn back. He suffers and wants to end his life. Just when he is about to bring on his own peril, he swerves back to the other side and chooses to live. A car passes in a full shot; a man gets out and runs towards Mikel. The camera follows this man, approaching Mikel who is leaning on the wheel, his head turned towards the spectator, he is crying.

Coming back to his village, he takes up again his usual life. His wife says she does not feel vindictive: she is leaving for Bilbao, to her sister's place. For him, a new period begins. His homosexuality becomes more and more visible through his encounters with Fama's femininised thought-image of the body; he returns to the city, to Bilbao, to meet again the young man who, in the evening, in the nightclub, sings for him. The men are not framed in the same shot but the montage connects and does not leave any doubt about the dialogue. It is Fama's voice that unites the feelings: in a frontal full shot, Fama is dressed all in black with a white shawl around his neck; he emanates a natural elegance and an unforced femininity. In a medium close-up on his face made up very well, he sings a love song with a soft voice. It is the famous Spanish song *Tatuaje*,[81] about a sailor, with a non-Spanish name, blond and tall, who came on a boat, who is recounting his love story about a woman he once cherished. The tattoo on his arm bears her name. A new love story started, but the sailor leaves forever without a trace. This famous song softened the spirits in Spain, like Montalbán analysed in his *Crónica sentimental de España*: a song that invited women to dream as their husbands often disappeared or were absent, because of the Civil War.[82] Now Fama interprets this song about a love leaving a deep trace in his heart.

The effect is there. In a close-up, Mikel's face looks joyful, his eyes lighten up. Again the montage frames their dialogue, their feelings: this song is a direct expression of their love. At the end, he applauds with enthusiasm, takes a cigarette and smiles. His joyful and open reaction is perceived in a medium close-up on the members of his political party, also present. They talk amongst themselves and turn their faces in his direction. Several faces approach each other, not once turning their eyes away from the object of their curiosity: Mikel applauds and smiles, he is really enjoying this performance.

In the village

Making the homosexuality visible continues: now the ritual of introducing this identity takes place in his community. We see Fama enter the chemist's: a calm and determined appearance, he is dressed up like a man but his gestures are feminine. While he is dressed like a man, the way he lives in his body remains feminine; the manner with which he puts his hands in his pockets, too softly for this body, too softly for a masculine body, are unquestionably girlish. It is a gesture that exaggerates the thought-image, expressing this stereotyped image of the homosexual. A lateral medium close shot on Mayté, who works at the chemist's and is serving a client. While gazing openly at Fama, she continues her work. Mikel enters and looks utterly horrified. The camera follows him as he speedily approaches Fama. He wants to leave immediately. But Mikel's brother enters the chemist's, and the three bump into each other in the entrance. The tension rises between the three men. Fama stays calm, but Mikel is fidgety and annoyed; he wants to leave now, while his brother is looking at them. The two leave immediately and, in the car, Mikel becomes verbally abusive; he reprimands Fama for having come to his village, telling him that he is just a vulgar transvestite, who pretends that he is normal. Mikel is furious, excited, which contrasts with Fama's calm serenity; she looks at him with pity, and asks if he must leave.

They go together to a restaurant where Fama tells him about his own difficulties to assume his homosexuality, which led to an attempted suicide. Then, they return to the village. They seem relaxed, smiling, as they come back to this insular community. An important ritual of visibility takes place through this symbolic choreography of presence: this walk through the village now makes Mikel's homosexuality visible. The people of the village pass by, follow them with their eyes. Mikel kisses Fama just before he leaves and watches the car driving away. Fama's body has introduced the thought-image of his homosexuality in this village. This quiet and innocent walk, without any physical contact between them, exhibited Mikel's homosexuality. Mikel's body did not express at first sight female features, his body did not appear homosexual. His body is on the contrary presented as the male prototype of a heterosexual and handsome man: he is virile, elegant, and masculine.

Rejected

The community reacts. The new situation is not easily accepted: Mikel is known in his village and from then on the reactions will be increasingly insolent if not violent. He will be rejected by several people or institutions. His political party, that had asked him to become their delegate, no longer needs him. His Chilean friend does not want to react, nor support him. His ex-wife and the priest in the church show themselves more tolerant but his mother refuses this new image of

her son. Leaving the church, Mikel waits for his mother with a bouquet of flowers for her birthday. She feels ashamed for him. With his brother they sit down
around a table and his mother obliges him to stay extremely discrete, because
she has the impression that the townspeople are talking about her. He asks her
if she is afraid. She replies that she is ashamed. Shortly thereafter, Mikel is accused of having been a member of the ETA in 1975. They incarcerate him for a
few days and, after several oft-violent interrogations, they finally let him go.

Nevertheless, Mikel feels happy as he is in love with Fama. His family's reaction is immediate. In a medium close-up on his mother we see her knitting with
a severe face. At the back, we see Mikel laterally, phoning his friend, telling him
about his painful experience in prison. When he adds: "I'll see you tomorrow"
we observe his mother's hands freeze in motion. She resumes her knitting, looking exceedingly tense. Framed in the same shot, mother and son are distanced
from one another. After the conversation, Mikel reclines on the sofa, where his
mother is sitting down. She is turning towards him: a close-up on her face, followed by Mikel's face. She explains to him that he is still young, that he cannot
understand everything in life. They look away from each other. His mother
turns her head asking if he has thought of the others, but Mikel replies that he
wants to live his own life. His mother turns her head away and the close-up
illustrates this scornful gesture towards her son; in a medium close-up, we see
Mikel put his hand on her shoulder. She pushes it away and looks in front of
her, pursing her lips, a bitter and severe expression on her face.

The next day, sitting at a table, his mother looks straight and concentrated in
front of her. Mikel's brother enters into the frame, announcing that he will wake
his brother up because he wants to go to Bilbao. He opens three doors; the space
where he enters is dark, after the third door the room lights up. Then we hear
the soprano voices: the funeral songs, another dirge begins. The brother comes
back nervously, approaches his mother, his arm is trembling, moving in a
strange way (see photo). He says that Mikel is dead. He walks out into the field
and calls someone to announce this horrible news. The camera zooms in on his
mother's face in a medium close-up: she turns down her eyes and closes them.
The film ends on the mother, all alone in a dark building behind a window. She
could not accept her son, she has killed him.

Conclusion: a sombre myth

THE DEATH OF MIKEL is the last film in Spanish cinema dealing with homosexuality as a social and individual problem, denouncing now the intolerance of
several communities (Basque and terrorism, the village, the family). Like in SEX
CHANGE, and THE DEPUTY, the archetypes of physical strength, of male sexuality
(virility) and the family are questioned in relation to homosexuality. These ar-

Photo 22: The mother's final decision

chetypal values are often rich in imaginary; they can be transformed into mythological stories, as lots of myths exist about male sexuality in homosexuality, about virility in general, and about what a family should represent. In this film, the body questions several conflicts, which illustrates the new reading.

Mikel's body questions the archetype on male sexuality and the archetype on the family through the image of an exemplary homosexual. Like the actor José Sacristán in THE DEPUTY, Imanol Arias is also a prototypical actor, identified with his political commitments and also for his beauty. He is Spain's sweetheart in the 1980s: handsome, virile, responsible, appreciated, intelligent and rational. He introduces in an environment nourished by prohibition, in the sombre decor of a village, in the core of his own family, a new idea about male sexuality. Observing drag queens or transvestite bodies was a way of introducing his male sexuality in a society where the heterosexual norm reigned. He is homosexual, has fallen in love, and wishes to enjoy this relationship.

The introduction of this visibility is emphasised by two rituals: in town, by the stereotyped body of Fama, the drag queen, making this body female and observing it first on stage and then in the village through the townspeople's upbraiding gaze. In the first ritual the mise-en-scene on a stage is important – like in SEX CHANGE and THE DEPUTY – this body has to be looked at and becomes visible for the others. The stereotyped body of Fama gives visibility to Mikel's homosexual feelings while they are together, first in the city, then while they walk through the village. The conflict cannot be resolved in the village: his friend, the political party and his family show that he is immediately marginalised. Fama and Mikel function as mediators: between the city and the village, between marginality and everyday life. A binary opposition is shown to us between a hidden homosexuality and a public homosexuality, between the possibility (life) and the impossibility (death) to experience this love relationship. The hidden aspect on the homosexual body disappears; the behind the doors scenes of family life are deconstructed, the myths on the absence of male sexuality for homosexuals are broken down. Mikel introduces virility in the representation of homosexuality by the image of his body. Making a body female questions the male sexuality of a man, regardless of his homosexual desires. Mikel's body experiences and shows by his thought-image his sexual identity in heterosexuality and homosexuality.

This film, released in 1983, illustrates the schism between the law and the social reactions of that time. Even if, legally, Mikel is totally within his rights to do what he is doing, socially his behaviour is rebuked and Mikel is left blamed and marginalised. We are clearly still within a context of prohibition, albeit a social one. The filmmaker promotes tolerance and expresses this point of view by the mise-en-scene of original bodies, a ubiquitous decor of death, political protests, and references to the ETA. Imanol Uribe is one of the rare filmmakers in Spanish cinema to deal with the ETA and other Basque problems. The Basque country has inspired lots of debates about independence in Spanish politics and this film expresses a hymn for liberty through the bias of a homosexual body, one that perishes in an environment of intolerance. A dark mythological story about a conflict between life and death: questioning new relationships, questioning homosexuality by making it visible in different communities, questioning virility and new visions on the family. Intolerance makes change impossible and suffocates these communities. In 1983, these mentioned social issues are historicised as it reflects in a filmic way that intolerance breaks off dialogue but that death seems at home within such a setting.

IV. Desire became the law in 1987

In Law of Desire (La ley del deseo), homosexuality is not treated as a problem. The plot relates a crazy love story, *un amour fou*, which functions as a groundbreaking myth about desire, passion, and love that is openly expressed by homosexuals. The protagonist, Pablo, is a filmmaker who has just released his latest film. His relationship with Juan is not really working, as Pablo does not feel desired the way he would like. When Juan leaves for summer, they write to each other. Then Pablo meets Antonio and they start an all-consuming love affair. But Antonio is very possessive and reading Pablo's letters, he discovers the relationship Pablo has with Juan. It makes him so jealous because he cannot bear the existence of another man in Pablo's life. Stalking Juan, Antonio kills him by accident. The police discover the truth and then Antonio takes Pablo hostage in their apartment to make love to him one last time. As Antonio says at the end of the film, he has to pay the price for his love and commits suicide. In this passionate love story between homosexuals, desiring or being desired is the main issue.

Exposing the homosexual body in 1987

The homosexual bodies are openly shown while making love, naked, wrapped around each other, but the film does not provoke reactions of rejection like Iglesia's films do. This could partly be explained by the fact that homosexuality had been legal for ten years when the film was shot. Homosexuals no longer figured on the list of menacing groups, as per the law on social danger. Moreover, the filmmaker's identity could account for its reception; Law of Desire is signed Almodóvar. This cineaste is already very well known when the film is released, which influences the reading. His films are characterised by the fact that he creates his own world wherein multi-gendered bodies are models. While his construction of clearly recognisable universes has brought him much fame, his characters have nevertheless incited some negative reactions: "As for me, I never liked Almodóvar. Not him, of course, but his cinema, his films. I find it excessively charged, excessive, and not so realistic, as if he lived in another world.'[83] Many other statements reinforce this undervaluing perception.[84] It is also important to note that, he raised the funds himself to make this film, investing his own money, that of his brother, and obtaining yet another share from a bank loan. His production company, named El Deseo, was founded with his brother Agustín. Since the shooting of this film, Almodóvar has become a producer and a filmmaker. In the published book *Conversations avec Pedro Almodóvar*, written by Frédéric Strauss, he openly comments on the adverse environment in which the film was made. He explains that even though official censorship no longer existed, there was nevertheless a moral and economical censorship.[85] This film was very dear to him and he draws attention to the fact that he never received any award for it, underlining that for almost all of his other films he did.

The Law of Desire openly exposes the body. Two types of initiation rituals introduce the homosexual identity. The first consists of making the homosexual explicitly visible through the representation of a prototypical body. Divergent with past representations, the homosexual is not dissimulated. The second initiation ritual is brought forth through an original myth. Almodóvar covers new ground by directly addressing the issues of love and desire. The core of the story is about the way passion or desire is experienced; he attempts to create love stories for multi-gendered bodies. This is new for Spanish cinema (and for other European cinemas in the same period). At that time, the heterosexual relationship constituted a hegemonic norm in cinema and was therefore the only basis for filmic portrayals of love. Accordingly, LAW OF DESIRE's filmic discourse is a myth which functions like a disparate belief system. This system restructures Spanish culture's prevalent ideas about homosexuality and multi-gendered bodies. The mythic nature of the filmic discourse is further enhanced due to the qualities of a typical Almodóvarian universe, one that presupposes a distanced reading.[86] In this research, the realistic representation of homosexuality is not questioned. Instead, we analyse the filmic imaginary about the relationships depicted.

In LAW OF DESIRE, the pioneering myth is deeply embedded in the 1980s. After having visually introduced the homosexual body in the Transition's cinema, what is new in this film is the focus on a homosexual character that experiences his love life within a domestic setting. An innovative myth is thereby created emphasising the natural, normal and the everyday life of his relationships. The researcher Paul Julian Smith describes the film as an optimistic vision, highlighting that a discrepancy exists between this fictional world and the homophobic reactions in Spanish culture.[87] Alfeo Alvarez emphasises also the purely fictional aspect of this everyday atmosphere of homosexuals living together.[88]

Meaning of the title

Desire is the motor of this ordinary plot about possessive love and a crime of passion. Let us refer once again to this famous "Law about social danger" with a category concerning homosexuals that was suppressed in 1978. Certainly a new law won't acknowledge desire, but in 1987, nine years later, a film can be entitled LAW OF DESIRE that deals with homosexual relationships. Therefore, this title marks a change. Paul Julian Smith's book (1992) appeals to the same words in his title. Exploring the representations of homosexuality, the researcher entitled his work: *The Laws of Desire. Questions of homosexuality in Spanish writing and Film 1960-1990*, clearly inspired by Almodóvar's film title. He puts into italics the word "of", desire in his Spanish version, because there are several possibilities for desire, and several laws. In the introduction he comments on the meaning: "This is why I speak about 'laws' in the plural in my title: to remind the reader that there is no monolithic struggle between power and pleasure, but rather a multiple, capillary network inflected by regional and ethnic differences."[89] His research accentuates the existing link between politics and the organisation of sexual desire in society.

Important changes occur at ten-year intervals. In 1978, the law is modified, Almodóvar's film is released in 1987 and Smith's book is published in Spanish in 1998. The 1998 edition, first published in English in 1992, is the first important study in cinema about the subject to be published in Spain. Legal adaptations, cinematographic portrayals and subsequent research activities distinguish the 1980s as the decade during which a much more open image of homosexuality prevailed. In addition, the film's title points to a rather liberal view. Desire is at the basis of human relationships and represents the law. Homosexual relationships rely, like heterosexual relationships, on desire and love for the other. Lastly, in 2005, homosexual marriage becomes legal. Almodóvar's energetic film plays a part in this evolution.

Shaking up the archetypes

Almodóvar is unique in his way of breaking apart archetypes with his characters that question virility, the family, or motherhood. Auteur prototypes exist within a distinct universe; they are valuable for Eloy de la Iglesia and Pedro Almodóvar's cinema because of their typical and recognisable universe.[90] We should therefore clarify the difference between an auteur prototype and a social prototype. A social prototype is incarnated by an exemplary body; the body bears the typical qualities of the social category that it is meant to represent (in the *tercera vía* tradition this technique was considered progressive). On the other hand, the protagonists of Almodóvar's cinema are *"auteur prototypes"*. These prototypes present model features that are linked to a sort of avant-garde view of sexuality and marginality. They are *auteur* not only because they are recognisable but also because they are specific to a particular vision. The invention of these fictive auteur's bodies proposes an exemplary idea of sexual freedom, emotional freedom and the freedom of speech. Finally, their features are exaggerated in comparison to direct reality. This technique emphasises certain aspects (like passion, desire, etc.). The filmmaker bursts through the traditional archetypal values by using these multi-gender bodies that in their excess represent models. For example in his films like HIGH HEELS, ALL ABOUT MY MOTHER, BAD EDUCATION, exaggerated identities focus on transexuality, paternalism and motherhood, forcefully challenging the mainstream understanding of these issues.

The physical appearance of these actors is also important, because they update prototypes or stereotypes with certain basic features. Homosexuals or bisexuals, these men are physically handsome, nice, virile and in love with someone of the same sex and at times with a heterosexual. And they want to enjoy

Photo 23: Carmen Maura, a transsexual adoptive mother
(© Jorge Aparicio / © El Deseo D.A., S.L.U.)

their love without any restrictions. In LAW OF DESIRE the prototypes are Pablo (Eucebio Poncela), Antonio (Antonio Banderas) and Juan (Miguel Molina). They are exemplary for their virility and beauty. Antonio Banderas is the protagonist's passionate lover, Juan is the other lover and Pablo is the cineaste inside the film. They all resemble male models, caught in this heated love triangle.

The women also appear to be exemplary. This series of characters establishes the film's "heterosexual" contingent even though they represent rather bisexual identities. Tina (Carmen Maura) and Ada's mother (Bibi Andersen) figure in the film's sub-plot. The archetype for maternal love is updated, and sometimes their heterosexual relationships are ridiculed. In addition, every spectator knows the actresses' real gender. Firstly, Carmen Maura plays the role of Tina Quintera. She plays Pablo Quintera's sister. She establishes the thought-image of a transsexual. Her female body is rigid in unduly tight dresses, which draw attention to her femininity, which is appropriate for her role. Her complicated relationships with men inspire Pablo to write a script about her. Carmen Maura is well known and nobody doubts her anatomical female gender. However, in the film she creates the image of a transsexual through the sheer masculine force that she emanates, demonstrated in the scene in which she punches a policeman.

Carmen Maura plays a transsexual adoptive mother named Tina; she plays the role of a heterosexual woman. Tina has a love affair with a beautiful woman, Bibi Andersen. Andersen has a young daughter named Ada. Tina's lesbian relationship with Ada's mother fuels a sub-plot in the film. In SEX CHANGE from 1977, Bibi Andersen began her film career introducing herself to Spain as a transsexual. In 1987, with LAW OF DESIRE Bibi Andersen establishes the thought-image of a gorgeous woman who is addicted to men and travels everywhere to follow them: her body founds its own myth through this bisexual identity. She has the role of Ada's mother, works as a model and abandons her daughter for her career and her lovers. Little Ada stays with Tina (Carmen Maura), who fully takes on the maternal role. The confusion of gender and the body's anatomical sexual identities is important: Tina is transsexual but is endowed with more maternal feelings than the supposed biological mother, Bibi. The film director opposes the gender identities and the archetypal values through the bodies of Carmen Maura and Bibi Andersen. In this way he questions ancient mythological images: the archetype of maternal love and heterosexual love; a transsexual expresses more maternal love than the real mother can.

The stereotyped body

In LAW OF DESIRE there is a contrast and a dialogue between the prototype and the stereotype, but not in the same way as in SEX CHANGE, THE DEPUTY, and THE DEATH OF MIKEL. In the aforementioned films the stereotype appeals for a change or serves to make something visible. In LAW OF DESIRE the preconceived images concern other issues, for example, the social representation of the journalist, the model, and the doctor. Indeed, their professions and their typical aspects are emphasised and stereotyped. Also, the heterosexual relationships are strongly marked by extreme situations. It is women who abandon their children or have hysterical relationships with men. In opposition, in the centre of this confusion of female bodies, the filmmaker presents a sentimental relationship between homosexuals: they behave more natural in their way of experiencing their love, (even though Antonio also becomes excessive when he falls in love). But they freely express their desire for love, their sexual desire, their emotional desire. Openly embodying these desires constructs a frame around the prototypical bodies inside a stereotyped world. This interaction between the thought-images of the bodies allows for the creation of new images about this relationship between persons of the same gender: the uninhibited desiring male identities institute a new norm.

Reading the choreography of the ritual

The filmic plot is based on a melodrama: at first sight it seems that it is only an ordinary love story. But analysing the double mise-en-scene, it becomes evident that the mythological story carries on the construction of a love discourse, based on the desire for the other. Several stages of the melodrama are illustrated: passion, possession and also abandonment. The appropriated discourses are therefore made for multi-gender bodies. Normally a love discourse is inspired or founded on heterosexual relationships. This film creates a new ritual emphasising *the creation* of this discourse for and by homosexual bodies: the creation symbolises the mythological thought. The gaze on Pablo creates the discourse, questions it; he imposes a double gaze, like a mise-en-scene, on amorous relationships. This process resembles the Carlos Saura's film CARMEN wherein the body of the femme fatale had to be trained and hispanised by flamenco dance steps, in a place of creation, e.g. in a dance room. In LAW OF DESIRE, the site of creation is the filmmaker's desk, complete with typewriter. Here the discourse to be created concerns their love and several texts will be written. In addition, the story takes place especially in Pablo, Tina and Ada's house. This site symbolises domestic and everyday life where most love stories normally take place. The other films analysed showed amorous or sexual encounters in marginalised sites. In LAW OF DESIRE, places outside the home are the same as those typically associated with a heterosexual couple: bars, the street, the beach, and so forth.

The mise-en-scene of desire

The film opens with the shooting of Pablo's film. He puts into scene the sexual desire of a man, acted by a young boy, directed by a voice-over that indicates the actions of the body. The young actor receives orders about the way of establishing the thought-image of sexual desire. It is a sexually potent sequence wherein a young man is masturbating himself in front of a mirror. But the spectator cannot stay fixed on the act itself as two voices in the background emphasise the presence of a camera, the money paid for the act, and the instructions to obey. Through its framing, the mise-en-scene gives prominence to the body's sexual desire; a gaze is created and imposed for the viewer. Then, due to the word *"fin"* (end) we know that it is the sneak preview of a film. The filmmaker, Pablo, is introduced. He is surrounded by journalists who harass him. His sister, Tina, who is herself being pursued by journalists who ask her if she is a lesbian, accompanies him. The journalists are all stereotyped. They are full of admiration for the filmmaker, absolutely indiscrete about his private life, asking weird questions that have no link to the film. Pablo returns home, accompanied by a male model, who through his physical appearance, also presents a cliché image

of his profession, underlining his beauty and his narcissism. After having listened to him, Pablo says that he would like to vomit and asks him to leave.

After this encounter, another man approaches the house. Now we see a real
passionate love affair without an accentuated mise-en-scene inside the film (like
the opening of the film). In a long frontal shot on the house, Juan (Miguel Molina) arrives at Pablo' place on his scooter, while the model is just leaving. A
medium close-up inside the house, while the song *Ne me quitte pas* plays in the
background. It is a mythical song about an imminent separation. Pablo opens
the door, and Juan appears. The music draws attention to their heartfelt reen-
counters. They kiss each other emotionally; Pablo suffers because of Juan, he is
so in love. Both men are exemplary for their beauty, for their passion and sincerity. Their love is reciprocally felt. They enter the bedroom, undress and get into
the bed together. They embrace and the song *Ne me quitte pas* takes up again
with conviction. The next day we see a romantic image of the rising sun. The
next shot shows the two naked bodies, lying down on the bed, in a high angle
shot. It is the romantic image of two embracing, intertwined bodies. Their aesthetic beauty is emphasised, they are two prototypical bodies signifying love
and passion. Juan leaves, and Pablo promises to write him or to visit him.

Juan has sent a postcard, but Pablo says that he needs something else. He
wants to receive another kind of letter and so decides to write it himself. The
typewriter and the desk where Pablo is sitting represent the site for creation.
Several images illustrate the thought of his body; he looks serious and concentrated, indicating the effort involved. The machine produces a regular and rapid
sound, which accentuates his desire to express himself. An extreme close-up on
the little iron sticks of the typewriter shows them to be jumping very fast. The
film director writes quickly and passionately on the paper: "I adore you". Pablo
has expressed how he wishes to be desired, what sort of letter he would like to
receive, how he would like to be loved. He has invented his own love story.

The possessive desire: Antonio and Pablo

When Pablo goes to town, Antonio (Antonio Banderas) introduces himself. The
two men look at each other. Pablo proposes to accompany him, but Antonio
replies that he does not sleep with boys. While Pablo pretends to walk away,
Antonio is pursuing him "You have won" he says, indicating by this that he
wanted to resist but he couldn't manage. It is the first time for him that he has a
relationship with a man. They enter into Pablo's house; Antonio with a certain
assurance is gazing all over the room. He focuses on the photograph of Tina
asking if she is a real transsexual (close-up on the back, in the background the
photo). Antonio starts to embrace Pablo after having removed a cigarette from
Pablo's mouth. Pablo retorts that he is not a washbasin that has to be unblocked.
The romanticism is slaughtered while at the same time the possessive aspect of

the kiss is underlined. Antonio asks then how it should be done and Pablo kisses him tenderly, touching his face, his body. Teaching to caress establishes a prototypical image of the amorous expression between two men. Conveying love is done though the gestures with which Pablo initiates his new lover. The two men are shown in their intimacy, discovering the sexual act together, step-by-step. The next shot is an approached tracking on two legs, the camera displaces towards the faces. The two bodies are laying down one on the other, Pablo on top, Antonio is laughing. We see the sweat on their faces, they kiss each other passionately. However, Antonio does not abandon himself completely to this passion. This ritual of initiation is expressed by Antonio's face that is marked with clear hesitation, one of waiting and clumsiness – he is learning. He is a rapt apprentice and concentrates on his initiator's gestures.

The next day, Antonio snoops around the house. He finds Juan's faked love letters, those actually written by Pablo himself, and is livid with jealousy. He writes on a piece of paper: "You are a pig, if I would have been sixteen years old and not twenty, I would have denounced you for statutory rape". He leaves, then comes back shortly after. A medium close-up on the door: Pablo opens, Antonio enters, undresses immediately, and they embrace. The passionate love between masculine bodies continues on the music of Los Panchos, *Lo dudo, (I doubt)*. The words of this song talk about a pure and strong love, one that is fiery, love like Antonio's.

Creating a love discourse

Amorous expressions vary in different cultures, but certain discourses are unprecedented. For example, in a sequence about the abandonment, a reference is made to the song *Ne me quitte pas* by Jacques Brel and to the theatre play by Jean Cocteau: *La voix humaine*.[91] These are two mythical discourses about abandonment, two groundbreaking texts. Pablo uses them as he wants to write a script based on this play for his sister Tina (Carmen Maura). Generally, abandonment is lived painfully both in the case of a child or a partner. The content of this discourse makes us comprehend the intensity of the feelings. Once again the mise-en-scene emphasises the process of creating a new version for this love discourse, representing the current ways of sustaining a relationship: communicating by phone, on stage, by letters.

The double mise-en-scene reflects the grief associated with abandonment. Tina and her adopted daughter prepare themselves for this theatre play inside the film. They portray the drama with tears, shouts, and fidgety and aggressive movements on stage. Their bodies make choreography on mythical songs like *Ne me quitte pas* during which Tina continues her telephone conversations. The female body can give a thought-image of the pain of loss, while the masculine body shows rarely in films the tears related to this problem. The girl feels abandoned by her mother, Bibí Andersen, who does not stop chasing men. Tina is on stage, a transsexual character. Bibi also abandoned her despite how deeply Tina loved her. The end of this relationship makes her suffer. She is contorted, tense, with an axe in the hand and the song *Ne me quitte pas* paralleling her movements. It is difficult for her to live through this break up. The axe symbolises the determined force, the violent effort, it will take to overcome her heartbreak and cut away her feelings of love to finally accept the separation.

Romantic photo novel

The time and aesthetic of the filmic form provide other classical references to the love discourse. A reference is made to South American soap operas (often present on Spanish television). Or, again, in reference to the aesthetics of the photo novel, faces are closely framed. These frames are used to narrate, through shots and reverse shots, a love story but this time with a homosexual couple. Pablo feels disappointed about his lover's romantic messages. Their contact is based on letters and telephone conversations. As a solution, he sends and writes the letters for Juan, those he would like to receive. Opening them, he reads them as if their arrival were a spontaneous act and as though the other in fact wrote their contents. He also writes letters to Antonio under a feminine pseudonym: Laura P. Antonio's mother cannot know that he has a male lover.

The tone is highly melodramatic. Pablo opens the letterbox. He is at home. The telephone rings, it is Juan. The framing is like that of a photo novel: the shot is on both faces, a split screen separates and unites them. Talking on the phone, their faces are turned towards each other, in two frontal close-ups. The two men look serious. Pablo is reticent and sad. Juan wants to see Pablo again. Pablo promises to come to see him. Pablo hangs up with tears in his eyes. This is an unusual image for a man on the screen, even more unusual for that period, as it concerns a love for someone of the same gender. Juan disappears by a shot dissolving the image. But like in a photo novel, on the next page another problem is announced. Pablo has two lovers: the phone rings again and this time he is listening to his answering machine. Antonio's voice is almost shouting. It is the same split screen on two faces in the same lateral close-up that is repeated, but now the two men have their backs turned on each other. Antonio talks to him severely. He wants to see Pablo again and he is fed up of Laura P. Pablo promises to write him: in a high angle shot on the typewriter and Pablo, we see him writing to Antonio that he doesn't love him. The filmmaker inside the film is creating a love discourse: he prepares the break-up, something Antonio cannot bear. The next shot on a mirror reflects Antonio, who is framed while reading this letter. His spying mother is observing him. He cannot accept to lose someone, so he will resort to act of great desperation to possess. The end of the relationship's mise-en-scene for this man is worked out in a different way: in the

Photo 24: L'AMOUR FOU *(© Jorge Aparicio / © El Deseo D.A., S.L.U.)*

middle of the night, Antonio leaves on his motorbike to see Juan. He needs to possess Pablo's lover, he is completely obsessed.

Body and abandon

The separation approaches, but Antonio cannot accept it. Tina and Ada showed their pain about loss through their acts and physical gestures. They created an image filled with tears and hysterical speeches. For men in the 1980s this is not a current filmic representation. In this film, the abandoned lover is leaving again to attack. In love there exists an archetype of the man as a chaser, who is not comparable to that of the other gender: the woman chaser has another connotation. The masculine character updates this archetype by this obsessed and possessive body that cannot deal with loss. He hunts down the other lover in jealousy. Antonio expresses his outraged reaction to being discarded. He ritualises the chase to fetishise the loved object by transference. He pursues and establishes, through Juan's body, a relationship with Pablo. He kills Juan. If you do not love me, he does not have the right to love you either. Crimes of passion are rarely realised in this form by a woman on a man. This crime is a reaction to loss and transmitted by an archetype of the love chaser.

When Pablo is told that Juan is dead, he has a car accident and loses his memory. At the hospital, his sister Tina tells him about their common past, reconstructing the events. She shows him photos and when he looks worried, she confirms that she changed gender in a clinic. Then after a period of amnesia, Pablo's memory comes back. He remembers everything, also the existence of Antonio. He also remembers the feelings of love for Juan and the sorrow he felt because of his assassination. The process is like a reality check of his feelings because his love desires reappear. There is no doubt about his homosexuality. Despite the insistence on the mise-en-scene in this film, the presence of his love desire is not at all questioned. This feeling comes back, deeply anchored in him, after an accident. It illustrates the authenticity and veracity of the homosexual desire, so often commented on as if this could be a consequence of one's upbringing or some other form of socialisation. This desire is inextricably rooted in him; it is not a learned construction.

Now he understands that Antonio is dangerous and with the police, they go to Pablo's home: in his apartment, Antonio has kidnapped his sister Tina. Antonio proposes to exchange her for Pablo so that he can live a last moment of passion with him. After making love, Antonio kills himself. We hear the song *Lo dudo*: the words illustrate the prominence of doubts, because Antonio knew all along that Pablo did not love him with the same intensity. He prefers to die than to live without his love object. At the end of the film Pablo throws his typewriter out of the window, as the symbol for evil. All of these texts led to a string of painful events. Antonio murdered Juan because of the letters he had invented himself. The typewriter created this imaginary world and expressed the intensity of passionate feelings of love between these men.

Conclusion

An innovative myth is constructed through the prototype bodies in Almodóvar's cinema: the men are handsome, virile, passionate, intelligent and charming. They update the archetypal value on masculinity and they show feelings of love for other men. An opposition with the traditional frame of society is reflected by the bodies of workers – the bodies of civil agents, like policemen, doctors, lawyers, and priests; these bodies don't express any desire; they are stereotyped and rather ordinary. A contrast is imposed with this traditional stereotyped frame and the prototypical world composed of model actors that experience different and intense love relationships. A myth is thus created about a multiplicity of love feelings, by multi-gender bodies that can represent all kinds of love relationships: between mother-daughter, father-child, woman-man, man-man, woman-woman, and so forth.

The archetype of the family was so important in the previous films about homosexuality and is now also transformed. The family no longer has the same influence. In previous periods, it was reactionary, but in this myth the family plays an integral part; the family is embodied and updated by a homosexual brother, a transsexual sister, and an abandoned daughter. The archetype of warmth and protection towards the child is expressed by the tender friendship between Tina, her adopted daughter and Pablo. This non-traditional image is a new mythological narration because the film director has completely changed the totem of the family in post-Francoist Spanish cinema. Even in his later films like ALL ABOUT MY MOTHER (1998), he confirms this idea through the image of a family reuniting multiple identities, like nuns, transvestites, drug users, and AIDS patients. This new myth created about the family is also a totem wherein the bodies, by their unexpected identities, burst through traditional expectations.

Desire is at the basis of all these situations: desire for the same gender, desire in family relationships, desire between a parent and a child. This desire does not submit a double mise-en-scene, but is rather directly experienced, and determines the relationships. In SEX CHANGE, THE DEPUTY and THE DEATH OF MIKEL, the stage was important to create a gaze on the protagonist's feelings. In LAW OF DESIRE, Antonio Banderas does not need a stage, but his homosexual love and passionate desire sets him on stage nonetheless and, with virility, he embodies the crazy lover (amour fou). The real protagonist is the desire. The creation of love discourses to express the feelings of desire still needs to be done. For example, to come back to the film SEX CHANGE (1977), José María learns cliché sentences from television, saying to his love: "I feel so safe in your arms, like in a temple." Almodóvar cites several fresh cultural sources: La voix humaine by Jean Cocteau, the mythic song by Jacques Brel: Ne me quitte pas and the song by Los Panchos: Lo dudo. To this he adds the images of soap operas and the romantic photo novel. The institutionalised discourses representing the heteronormativity are now constructed in this film for multi-gender identities (transsexuals, homosexuals, heterosexuals, bisexuals). The filmmaker creates the texts, the films, the songs, or the telephone conversations in which desire becomes the law. This fictionalised story underlines the everyday reality of these multi-gender love relationships.

However, distance in the process of creation is maintained by the double mise-en-scene, which confirms the mythological reading, as a projection of an idealised world. The narration creates a myth about these kinds of relationships, staging them in a domestic setting and emphasising everyday reality. Projecting an idealistic love discourse on it works like a belief system, like an imaginary filmic world released in 1987 in Spain. In this context it is interesting to quote an anecdote about the filmmaker,[92] speaking about his mother, who read letters for the people in the village (as many were illiterate), she often invented phrases to make the story comforting for the listener. As a child, the filmmaker told his mother that these phrases were not there in the text. Her reaction was that listeners were completely happy when they went away. Almodóvar concluded that sometimes reality needs a little bit of fiction: this film is a good example of that for 1987.

Almodóvar has been of great importance for the introduction of new images of homosexuality in Spanish cinema. These new thought-images of the body can be read as a new ritual, as was the case in Law of Desire, and a second new ritual by creating new love discourses. Heterosexual discourse was dominant in European societies in the 1980s. But Almodóvar hijacks this situation in an original and humorist manner. Citing ingenious references, he institutionalises and integrates what is new, inside what is well known and familiar. The romantic photo novel and the soap operas represent a classical discourse about heterosexual love. Available and well known in many cultures, they are often overloaded with romantic sentimentality and express the complexity of a love relationship: the desire, the joy, the emotions, the pain and the feelings of love. The clarity of these connotations is easily recognisable and entails the same discourses for homosexuals, which facilitates the reading of their affective links. But a humorist quality is present: indeed, women often held these discourses. A discrepancy can be felt in the expressed sentimentality. Due to the relentless use of hyperbole, this then connotes something entirely different. The sentimentality now expressed by men for homosexual relationship pastiches the photo novel or the soap opera. This is often hilarious and engenders at the same time a distance because everything seems real, but exaggerated. This is what we consider "Almodóvarian camp", referring to the classic text of Susan Sontag, who defined camp as the love of the unnatural or the artificial.[93] Almodóvar uses this personal auteur language also for other identities and situations.

The Almodóvarian method represents his strength and his originality. The distance created through a kind of overacting generates laughter. Without denouncing but deforming heterosexuals, he makes the situation advantageous for marginalised people. It is his way of staging some aspect of the character, by overacting, without putting someone on stage (as was the case in the other films on homosexuality). Almodóvar declares that his approach to marginality is different to that of Fassbinder for example, as this German filmmaker had a clear statement about the bad and the good. Almodóvar argues that he shows the filmic hero with all his contradictions, a hero nonetheless, but not necessarily a role model.[94]

Moreover, his work is well received all over the world, which leads to the belief that his discourse can be easily accessed by a population much larger and diverse than the frame of Spanish society. Introducing new phenomena occurs here through rituals that react to institutions (the institutionalised love discourses) or to preconceived images (the stereotypes). The newly created myths on diverse themes are then integrated into an existing tradition while at the same time maintaining a distance.

V. Masculinity and homosexuality

Finishing this chapter with a film released in 1987 was justified by the fact that LAW OF DESIRE represented a turning point in the depiction of homosexuality. It was a fundamental film in Spanish cinema about this issue. But what has happened with the representation of homosexuality since then? How did Spanish cinema and Spanish culture react to homosexuality? Before replying to these questions, we shall first shortly summarise our conclusions about masculinity and homosexuality in Spanish cinema between 1975 and 1987.

We began this chapter with a film about transexuality to illustrate homophobic reactions under Francoism. As we have already mentioned, these identities were often considered to be homosexual. Moreover, they were particularly present in Spanish cinema, and not only in Almodóvar's films. It is fascinating to note some important and pertinent legal changes. Since 1983, it has been possible to change gender in a Spanish hospital. Before, it was necessary to go abroad. In 2007 a law further modified the situation by allowing individuals who had sex changes to change their gender on their identity cards. This was impossible before, which made their social integration quite difficult, particularly in work situations. This problem was also constantly reflected in Spanish cinema: for example in the documentary DRESSED IN BLEU (VESTIDA DE AZUL, 1983) by Antonio Gimenez Rico, or even recently in the hilarious post-modern musical 20 CENTIMETERS (20 CENTÍMETROS, 2005) by Ramón Salazar.

The other films analysed represented homosexual relationships more directly. New myths were introduced on the family and on male virility. The homosexual identity became visible through a stereotyped body. By making a body female it questioned the male sexuality of a homosexual by ignoring his gender. We noticed in the three films, that the protagonists introduced the virility in heterosexuality and homosexuality by the image of their bodies, first on stage and then in a domestic setting. The identity of the actors was fundamental: José Sacristán, Imanol Arias, Antonio Banderas: prototype bodies for male sexuality, for male virility. In Almodóvar's film, Antonio Banderas is excessive in his desire, which sets him symbolically on stage in his virile quest to posses his lover. He is passionately and obsessively in love with another man but this drama takes place in a domestic setting. In sum, we noticed in this chapter that the visible stereotyped body was first marginalised in the 1970s but has now been de-marginalised in Almodóvar's 1987 film. A very virile and handsome man, the convincing actor Antonio Banderas is now like a prototype of desire staged in a domestic setting.

Spanish cinema continued to portray the male homosexual. Alfeo Alvarez already spoke about an integrated modality of representing this character, which started in 1996 and continues up to today. Chris Perriam and Santíago Fouz-Hernández also confirmed a boom of gay cinema at the beginning of the 1990s. The title of their article is revealing: desire without a law; the representation of homosexuality in Spanish cinema of the 1990s.[95] They incessantly refer to the importance of Almodóvar's film LAW OF DESIRE. They analyse several films like WITH GAIETY, MA NON TROPPO (ALEGRE MA NON TROPPO, 1994) by Fernando Colomo, EXCUSE ME DARLING, BUT LUCAS LOVED ME (PERDONA BONITA, PERO LUCAS ME QUERÍA A MÍ, 1996) by Felix Sabioso, and observe the direct influence of Almodóvar's universe. His discourse was monumental for Spanish cinema, and other filmmakers were often inspired by the way of telling stories about homosexuality.

In this chapter I focused on the homosexual representation in the Transition periods until 1987. I could not focus on the lesbian representation as women had a different way of introducing this identity. I analysed films made by Vicente Aranda, Eloy de la Iglesia, Imanol Uribe, Pedro Almodóvar, but I had to leave aside filmmakers like Ventura Pons, who also produced an impressive collection of films on this issue. Analysing new myths on homosexuality, introduced us into the world of Almodóvar's cinema. He enhances the issue: multiplying gender relationships, imposing original identities, he created a recognisable universe. The body was revealing. Almodóvar or Eloy de la Iglesia gave prominence to marginality in a broader sense: they received a lot of audience attention over several decades. In 2002, Eloy de la Iglesia released his last film: BULGARIAN LOVERS (NOVIOS BÚLGAROS), showing a homosexual relationship between a rich Spanish executive and a Bulgarian immigrant. Once again, Iglesia links marginalised identities, questioning power relationships. Making this film in 2002 introduces new identities of marginality: immigration had by now become an important issue in contemporary Spanish cinema (and of course society in general). New themes dominate the screen and the representation of homosexuality is no longer dominated by feelings of culpability or complete rejection, as it was in the 1970s.

In this context I refer again to the important consequences of legislation: homosexual marriage has been legal in Spain since 2005. Undoubtedly, legal changes have important consequences and cinema made this visible in the new way issues were treated in its national cinema since the 1970s. As Richard Dyer demonstrates with his book's illustrative title: *Now you see it. Studies on Lesbian and Gay film*[96] published in 1990. Filmmakers fulfil an important function by making them visible and by creating a positive image. We witness this process in this chapter: the marginal identity is demarginalised by making it visible, by reversing old ideas and creating new myths on traditional issues like family or male virility. Almodóvar contributed with an original artistic proposition of multi-gender characters, creating a new centre with hilarious and flamboyant bodies. Full of colour, music, and a hypnotic universe, he presented a wide range of identities that were once considered abnormal without focusing on their marginality. His discourse therefore imposes a wider reading of these identities. The next chapter will focus on a more traditional reading of marginality. In it delinquency, and those who embody it, are shown moving through history and across a variety of different sites.

4.   The delinquent's body out of focus

This chapter addresses another form of marginality by analysing real or imagined delinquency. Representing "evil" is not new, but its form and presentation were updated after 1975. Post-1975 images of delinquency refer to youngsters, drug addicts, gypsies and terrorists; these types of characters are brought into play by Spanish film directors, among others, with films such as HURRY, HURRY (DEPRISA, DEPRISA), EL LUTE, TOMORROW I'LL BE FREE (EL LUTE MAÑANA SERÉ LIBRE), and RUNNING OUT OF TIME (DÍAS CONTADOS). All four figures are emblematic of problems that are very recognisable in Spanish society. The first group – young drug users – exposes the plight of drug addiction and the simultaneous emergence of youth gangs. This theme is present in societies across Europe, linking violence and social deviation to the suburbs of big cities. The two other groups, however, represent something specific to Spanish culture: the gypsies incarnate an ethnic and cultural particularity lodged firmly within Spanish society and ETA terrorism obviously affects, first and foremost, Spain. To illustrate the relationship between the innovative images created about Spanish culture and the actual rise of delinquency in society, a statistical overview is required. Criminality was indeed extremely low during the Franco periods, but after 1975 new and distressing social phenomena emerge and become ever more important.

Drugs

Carlos Saura's film, HURRY, HURRY (DEPRISA, DEPRISA), from the 1980s, is one of a group of films (along with films by directors such as de la Loma, Uribe, Iglesia, Gutiérrez-Aragon, Montxo Armendáriz) that explore the relationship between drugs and delinquency. In the same period, certain Spanish songs also account for the significance of this societal issue: *Vamos a callar* (1977), *Sea como sea* (1977), *Libertad* (1980).[1] To better understand the emergence of this kind of film and other artistic expressions on this subject, several publications have analysed drug addiction in Spain relating it to youth gangs. In a report published in 1972 on youth delinquency, the government explains that youth criminality in Spain is much lower than in other countries.[2] However, they also note that it has increased, implying that in future it could pose a serious threat. All the same, at the end of the 1960s and at the beginning of the 1970s the number of youth

gangs (with one girl for every five boys)[3] as well as drug use increases signifi-
cantly.[4]

The subject of drug use changes in the 1970s as it is associated for the first
time with the violent means drug addicts used to obtain their fix. Juan Carlos
Usó explores this problem in Spain from 1855 to 1995 and notes that it was only
in 1976 that a drug overdose was first reported. Indeed, registering the first
victim of an overdose in 1976 seems quite late, as drugs had always existed.
Yet, it was in fact the first officially identified case in fifty years.[5] This marks a
turning point. After 1976, the situation changes considerably: between 1976 and
1977, heroin consumption proliferates, accompanied by an increasing number
of youth gangs looking for drugs.[6] Thus, the phenomenon of delinquency had
already begun prior to Franco's death but had never been explicitly related to
drugs. Nevertheless, the Transition period, which was characterised by extended freedom, accentuated this phenomenon.

The contrast with the previous period can be explained by the use of violence.
Indeed, during the dictatorship people who had sufficient financial means
could consume narcotics under medical prescription. Still, drugs were very expensive; in 1947, a kilogram of cocaine cost 60,000 pesetas on the black market
and the annual salary of a policeman was 11,900 pesetas.[7] Cannabis was considered a drug used by the military or by prostitutes.[8] In the 1960s, the hippies
received attention because they used psychedelic substances, such as LSD. As
an official reaction, the Law of Social Danger had been adapted in 1970 to include these new drug consumers.[9] At around the same time, the General Health
Direction published a report indicating that in 1962, of the 1,300 drug addicts
who had undergone rehabilitation, 800 were women. According to this research, their number decreased to 884 in 1970. Other surveys contradict these
figures, stating that in 1970 there were between 1,500 and 1,700 drug addicts.
These individuals were, above all, addicted to morphine.

After 1973, heroin dominates the situation. Its consumption is correlated with
violence, leading to rampant delinquency. According to Carlos Usó, public opinion at that time understood the problem in relation to the notorious effects
produced by heroin, but he adds that many of the consumers were known con-
victs before being identified as drug addicts.[10] Still, when in withdrawal, heroin
addicts can resort to acts of great desperation and brutality; their unhinged
search for enough money to buy their next fix was fuelled by the tormenting
and relentless symptoms of heroin withdrawal. In 1978 the Spanish government
launched a public health campaign warning against the dangers of drug use:
"Drugs are pain, drugs kill" ("La droga es dolor, la droga mata").[11] In the 1980s
the Spaniards considered drugs to be a real problem, even speaking of an epidemic between 1983 and 1986; Carlos Usó reckons that the real epidemic had
begun earlier, even if drug use intensified considerably during this period. In

the middle of the 1980s an estimated number ranging between 60,000 and 125,000 regular consumers of heroin lived in Spain.[12] The number of deaths through an overdose also surges in the 1980s, which the chart below illustrates.

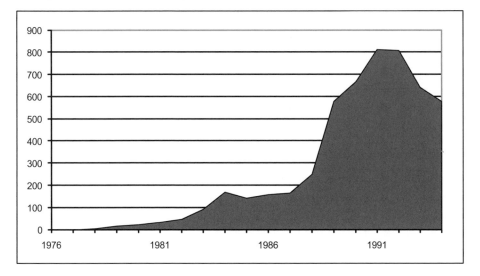

Figure 1: Number of deaths per year[13]

The graph begins with the first death through an overdose in 1976. It then shows that the rate of mortality was five times higher in 1989 than in 1983.[14] The figures provide a sombre and striking image of the rapid escalation of drug use, co-existing and accelerating the spread of delinquency. This social quandary was an issue in many European countries. For example, in the Netherlands it was only after 1972 that heroin began to dominate the drug scene and to cause the social destruction inherent in its widespread use. In response, the Dutch government adapted its legislation in 1976. Although the Netherlands has always been considered as having a direct approach to drugs, heroin became a real problem only in the 1970s. Heroin use led to such visceral and emotional dependency, and by the end of the 1970s Spain had suffered the most bank robberies in the world. Such was the extent to which drug addicts would go and at that time it was particularly easy to attack a bank and to obtain exorbitant amounts of money, allowing for the consumption of more and more drugs.[15] In fact, the recording of the first heroin overdose victim in 1976 corresponds to the main trends in other European countries in the same period. The combination of desperate violence and debilitating drug addiction was obviously a new cultural phenomenon in Spanish society. The severity of the problem and its swift propagation explains why it provided useful material for several filmmakers.

The presence of gypsies

The drug addict is not the only marginal figure; the gypsy has been margina-lised for a long time and his image was also transformed after 1975. A lack of acceptance of gypsies dates back several centuries. Without commenting on the entire history of the gypsies, it is important to clarify their status to understand the gypsy's image within Spanish culture and more particularly, how they are visualised in fictions such as EL LUTE by Vicente Aranda. To comprehend the context of the film about Lute of the 1960s it is revealing, that according to a census from 1989, 800,000 gypsies lived in Spain among a total population of 40,360,000. The number is quite high. The gypsy population of France is, in con-trast, 300,000 out of 60 million inhabitants.[16] The gypsies have been living in Spain since the 15th century.[17] At first they were compared to vagabonds and, for this reason, persecuted, hunted, and openly discriminated against. It was only under the reign of Isabelle II, in 1846, that a gypsy was for the first time considered Spanish, on condition that he or she was born in the country and was sedentary.[18] During the Franco periods, the gypsies were again considered to be vagabonds, and were again hunted down and incarcerated.

The formulation of the new Spanish Constitution in 1978 and the abolition of the law justifying persecution of gypsies[19] gave rise to a change in their status. All Spaniards were now equal by law. Since then, the treatment of gypsies has improved. Spanish politics has also changed since their arrival in Spain. Fernan-do Jordán Pemán (1991) describes this evolution as follows:

> Through a study of their history, we come to understand the official attitude toward gypsies was one of rejection, incarceration, and integration. But very quickly the Spanish state discovers that the persecution of gypsies was neither practical nor eco-nomical: it decides therefore to integrate them in the society which surrounds them, but in an authoritarian and violent way.[20]

This minority lives within the country; as this is a social fact, it would clearly be more intelligent to integrate them. A conference organised by the Association of Human Rights in 1987 comments on crucial themes, such as for instance these issues:
- The affirmation of equality rights
- The identification of alternative formulas that favour the bringing together of gypsies and 'payos'
- The clarification of the concepts of integration, assimilation, development, participation...[21]

To complete these ideas, in 1988, the government launches a social programme for gypsies: *Programma de Desarrollo Gitano*, to encourage their integration. One of the programme's measures was the enforcement of childhood education, obliging gypsy children to receive the same education as Spaniards.[22] We see in Aranda's film how the protagonist's body portrays this shift from the margin towards the centre.

ETA (*Euskadi ta Askatasuna*)

Terrorism is the last issue that needs to be explored: ETA is powerfully present in Spain's collective memory, especially the memory of its multitude of victims. In this research, we do not intend to examine the causes of terrorism. Rather, we focus on the myths that are created about this threat, which has led to so much destruction in Spain. To comment on ETA's presence in Spanish history, we have to return to Francoism. The Basque party, the PNV (*Partido Nacionalista Vasco*), was founded in 1895. During the Franco regime, several of its members were exiled.[23] The group's organised opposition was weak, and as a reaction, in 1952, a group of young people founded l'EKIN. In 1959, ETA, which means: *Euskadi ta Askatasuna*, (Patria and Liberty) was founded on the precept that their predecessors were too consenting.[24] One of ETA's ideological objectives was to reject what they viewed as a passive stance against the oppressor, and more precisely the passivity of the PNV. The PNV, in fact, respected the democratic principle, which distinguished them from ETA. From its inception, ETA was seen as a terrorist organisation. ETA's endeavours are most of all known for their violence. During the dictatorship, ETA partisans attacked government targets, the first attack taking place in 1968[25] (preceded by an "accidental" death in 1960, when a bomb exploded in San Sebastian killing a little girl who was eighteen months old[26]).

In 1970 sixteen members of ETA were judged at the Trial of Burgos. The Franco regime wanted to mete out exemplary punishment for their violent actions, sentencing them to death. This decision provoked an inverse reaction in the country and also abroad. Even the Vatican demanded clemency for the accused.[27] Public opinion forced the regime to commute the sentences to hundreds of years in prison. The objective of delivering a symbol of the government's intransigence in face of terrorism had failed. In the documentary THE BURGOS TRIAL (EL PROCESO DE BURGOS, 1979), directed by Imanol Uribe, the condemned are shown expressing themselves about this period. It should be underlined that the film director presents an idyllic vision of these first years of terrorism. The victims are presented as idealistic boys who revolted against the Franco regime. If this account were to be given today the film would evoke fierce reactions from the public. A last historical fact worth mentioning in relation to Francoism is that of the murder by ETA of Carrero Blanco. Blanco was meant to continue the Franco regime after the dictator's death. During the dicta-

torship this movement's role as an opposing power was clearly present. Nevertheless, since Franco's death, they have continued their terrorist actions and the
number of deaths has increased enormously.[28]

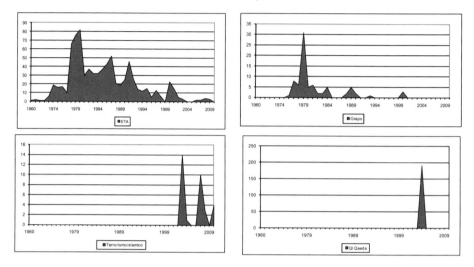

Figure 2: Number of deaths from ETA, Grapo, Terrorismo Islámico and Al Qaeda
terrorism[29]

These figures and the historical and juridical sources, bear witness to a change
in post- 1975 Spanish society. The Transition's political situation provoked an
increase in attacks around the 1980s, from groups like ETA or GRAPO (*Antifas-
cist Resistance Group October First, Grupos de Resistencia Antifascista Primer de Octubre*, a leftist revolutionary group founded in 1975, starting their actions in
1976).[30] Although GRAPO no longer received the same support in the 1980s,
their crimes heavily impacted the population in the 1970s and continued to do
so until recently. The Basque issue was also an important political topic in the
Transition period. The Constitution of 1978 was not accepted by the PNV: they
contended that the document did not allocate enough respect to Basques' rights.
In this same period, around the elections of 1977 and 1979, this stance garnered
considerable support for the PNV, which permitted them to become the most
powerful political party of the region. Moreover, even if the PNV did not want
the violence of ETA, they exploited it for their negotiations with the government
at Madrid.

In addition, ETA had a direct link (officially proved in the 1990s) with parliamentary life under the auspices of the political foundation named HB (*Herri
Batasuna*) in 1978. At the same time the terrorist group continued their struggle
for autonomy using violence, guided by principles that come close to international communism. This link with the political world was openly denounced in

1997 at a trial against the independent party, HB, which had been diffusing a video during their political campaign that justified the actions of ETA. In 2002, the government enacted a law, forbidding political parties that have links with terrorism. The law caused Batasuna's destitution in 2003 in light of the considerable financial support this party had accorded to ETA. The terrorist's intention to have themselves represented by a political party, even if surreptitiously, can be explained by the political situation of the Transition: the Spanish state almost conceded to the Basque country's demands for sovereignty. Through this undercover party, ETA could persist in its undemocratic tactics and yet continue to participate in political life. The party turned a blind eye to, and exploited, their affiliate's attacks. This combination of legitimacy, through its camouflaged relationship to HB, allowed them to follow-through with their illegal pursuits and to impose more of their power on parliamentary negotiations.

During the UCD government (1976-1981) with Adolfo Suarez, ETA had organised the kidnapping of industrialists, or politicians or other well-known personalities. Since the several UCD ministers had formed part of the Francoist movement, their subsequent democracy that was instated represented a moderated prolongation of the Francoist system. The military *coup d'état* of Tejero in 1981 provoked an important political protest by Spaniards, marching in the street, expressing their fear and resistance to the army's potential plans to return to Francoism. At the time, ETA had organised attacks against military targets.[31] During the installation of the PSOE's government in 1982 the attacks also increased against citizens. ETA denounced the democratic system as being rotten to its core. These violent actions continued in the 1990s; these numerous attacks have marked the history of ETA. To fully grasp the horror ETA perpetuated in Spanish society, one has to cite, in the long list of victims, the kidnapping of Miguel Angel Blanco, municipal counsellor of the Partido Popular, on the 10th July 1997. ETA demanded to have 460 prisoners, dispersed across different prisons in Spain, muted to the Basque prison within the next 48 hours. The country was paralysed and Miguel Blanco killed.[32] The Spanish population felt defeated and crushed. Sympathetic and disquieted concern, if not revolt, for the victims of terrorism, was manifested in large public protests. The Spaniards reacted ever more openly against ETA attacks. Still, even after 1975, the strong presence of violent actions in a political transitory situation continued and remained well into the next decades, which explains the central place of terrorism in the national imaginary. This meant ETA was considered in the 1980s and 1990s, with unemployment and drugs, as one of the most important problems for society.[33]

How was ETA represented in Spanish cinema? How to give form to terror that is uncontrollable and unpredictable? What kind of filmic character can figure this world, which frightened the Spaniards so much? A historical description over several decades reveals how films visualise terrorism.

To illustrate the visibility of the terrorist body in Spanish cinema, I cite a recent publication by Luis Miguel Carmona (2004), *El terrorismo y E.T.A. en el cine*. He presents a historical vision of its representation in national cinema. The author criticises Spanish filmmakers in the Transition periods for what he sees as a painful lack; they failed to deal with the subject of terrorism.[34] Indeed, in the 1970s, only a few films directly represent this problem. Carmona describes seven strands in the representation of the subject. He focuses on Imanol Uribe's films for an entire chapter as this film director dedicates a lot of attention to terrorism. Carmona's classification is revealing with regard to films that deal with the subject from a straightforward, serious and direct angle. Spanish cinema also includes many other references, such as Alex de la Iglesia's 1993 film ACTION MUTANTE (ACCIÓN MUTANTE), which deals with the subject in a comical and grotesque register.

His classification is categorised as part of a first group in the Transition, mentioning two films about Carrero Blanco's murder: COMANDO TXIQUIA (1977) by José Luis Madrid and OPERATION OGRE (OPERACIÓN OGRO, 1979) by Gillo Pontecorvo. Then, in the 1980s and 1990s Carmona finds two films about the organisation of ETA, four titles about the rehabilitation of ex-terrorists in Spanish society, three about the financing and five about protagonists who show remorse (SHADOWS IN A CONFLICT/SOMBRAS EN UNA BATALLA, 1993, by Mario Camus, etc.). We share his choice to leave the filmmaker Uribe aside, because his work is dedicated particularly to this subject. RUNNING OUT OF TIME (DÍAS CONTADOS) represents a masculine protagonist of ETA who shows remorse, who questions his convictions, which is typical for films that appear at the end of the 1980s and in the 1990s. The last two groups worth mentioning are two films relating the stories of real persons (YOYES, 2000, by Helena Taberna; THE WOLF/EL LOBO), 2004, by Miguel Courtois) and six documentaries about life in Euskadi like, for example, the film by Julio Medem, THE BASQUE BALL. SKIN AGAINST STONE (LA PELOTA VASCA, LA PIEL CONTRE LA PIEDRA, 2003).[35]

RUNNING OUT OF TIME (DÍAS CONTADOS) garnered much attention at its release (several cinematographic awards: eight Goyas) in comparison with the others. Then the documentary made by Medem received a lot of attention and caused an important polemic. This filmmaker is well known for fictions such as COWS (1991), THE RED SQUIRREL (1993), EARTH (1996) and LOVERS OF THE ARCTIC CIRCLE (1998), SEX AND LUCIA (2001), CHAOTIC ANA (2007) and ROOM IN ROME (2010).[36] Being of Basque origin, in 2003 he directs a documentary about terrorism and gives the floor to different people to express themselves about the Basque conflict: journalists, politicians, historians, victims of police torture, etc. He emphasises such divergent points of views on the problem that he manages to establish a difficult dialogue about the subject.[37] The documentary deserves a study in itself, because the debate at its release reveals once again the seriousness of the problem for Spanish society.

The perception of terrorist violence changes with the attack of 11 March 2004 perpetrated by Al-Qaeda. Spain had now become an international target. At the end of this chapter, we will come back to some cinematographic reactions, but the main idea of this chapter is to study *new* images of delinquency since dictatorship. Indeed, the three films chosen represent figures of violence that become visible in an innovative manner after 1975. Drugs at the end of the 1970s, a new figure of the gypsy in the 1980s and ETA in the 1990s constitute the major problems afflicting Spanish society. Giving an image to an ETA character is complicated and we will see how the protagonist's body updates archetypal values about violence, fear, and delinquency; how the thought of his image, through his incoherent acts, shows a shift in convictions that propose a different reading, resembling a projection of myths on this uncontrollable world.[38]

The figure of evil

The figure of evil is at the basis of myths about delinquency. Evil in a culture is expressed by opposing itself to the current dominating norm; liberating oneself represents an archetypal image, one of independence with regard to the traditional structures of society. We can find all kinds of examples from countless eras not only related to delinquency but also to freedom, such as the bohemian, the *femme fatale*, the cowboy, the gypsy, the drug addict. Their malicious value is expressed through the bodies that, by their nature, aspire to a liberty, which rarely corresponds to the established order or a culture's respected conventions. The Spanish filmmakers construct new images about delinquency and project it on a specific site that seems reserved for delinquent bodies (as they are the marginalised, these bodies are excluded from the centre, refusing or failing to represent the norm). High-powered movements and intense motions mark the films as they introduce the thought-image of the delinquent body through rituals of initiation. These rituals are macabre choreographies, forceful images, framed by the ubiquitous presence of violence.

In this group of films space is fragmented to accentuate the opposition between the centre and the periphery. The demarcation between the centre and its outskirts, between mainstream society and its dissidents also allows for the construction of myths about evil from a certain distance. The centre represents the norm and the images outside the norm are constructed at the margin. Even the connotation of the word *banlieues* in French underlines this modus operandi; etymologically, *banlieue* means the place for banishment. The wish to control is a constant desire for every culture. The myth about evil and its relegation to the outside also serves to reduce anguish and fear and to bolster confidence in the reproduction of the status quo. The body therefore supports a double constraint that is anchored in the mores of the outside and always in relation to its opposition to the norm. It is first located at the margin and constitutes this frame. Then, through the repetition of negative images, a stereotype is created: recognising and identifying their physical appearance helps to maintain a distance. Of course lots of bodies cannot be captured so easily, as Vicente José Benet's (1999) analysis concerning the serial form of the presentation of delinquent bodies in cinema contends. He concentrates on the psychopathic body (among others in PSYCHO (1960) by Hitchcock) showing that its difficulty to be classified is fundamental to its effective form of terror.[39] Unidentifiable, neither by its occurrence in a specific site, nor by stereotyped features, one cannot categorise the psychopath. On the other hand, the trend to serialise illustrates the function of the repetition of certain features. Through repetition, the delinquent becomes discernible. When analysing the films about delinquency, the fragmentation of space and the stereotyped bodies, are the point of departure for reading the mythological story.

Cinematographic influence

The ambition to represent themes realistically was based on certain cinematographic schools: on the one hand, the road movie, as demonstrated in EL LUTE, and on the other, the Italian neo-realism movement. The desire to explicitly show reality can be detected in Saura's film referring to ACCATONE (1961) by Pasolini and in EL LUTE by Aranda referring to SALVATORE GIULIANO (1961) by Rosi. Neorealism deeply influenced Spanish cinema during Francoism: the encounter with this Italian movement in 1951 was a revealing experience for Spanish filmmakers because the Francoist government forbade the projection of many films or the reading of specific books.[40] For a week, the Italian presenters projected their films in Madrid and Saura was delighted to discover this school.[41]

The difficulties in representing reality in film preoccupied the Spanish filmmakers. During the famous conversations of Salamanca in 1955, which brought together Spanish filmmakers and critics, this challenge was explored. This meeting illustrated that the filmmakers not only felt isolated from other national cinemas, but that they also felt isolated vis-à-vis their own reality. The filmmakers were not at all satisfied about their films and Juan Antonio Bardem affirmed without hesitation that the Spanish spectator was not at all informed about his own reality, because the transmitted vision was false. His discourse became a historical statement:

Living with its back to Spanish reality, our cinema has not been able to show us the true face of the problems, the land, or the people of Spain. This atemporal hermetic and false creation of a supposedly Spanish reality, such as it appears in our films, totally distances itself from the rich realist tradition of the Spanish novel. Right here and now, the spectator of Spanish cinema is unable to learn from a Spanish film about the Spanish style of living, how Spaniards revel or how they suffer, or what are man's conflicts, or Spanish society's. The Spanish spectator is not informed by Spanish film about his own reality. The vision of the world, of this Spanish world, portrayed in Spanish film is false![42]

Filming reality in a candid and unadulterated way during Francoism was impossible. Even though Carlos Saura had directed THE DELINQUENTS (LOS GOLFOS) in 1959 about delinquency, these images cannot be compared with those of his Italian colleagues.

During dictatorship filming reality was transformed into a highly metaphorical language. Reading this specificity of the filmic forms and the immense change of style after Francoism, it is appropriate to illustrate the language about marginality in some films. The acts of violence create a link between the space and the body. The character is often a victim or an observer, representing a metaphor for the repression that is exercised by the regime. A revealing example is given in the fiction THE HUNT (LA CAZA, 1965) by Carlos Saura. This film is not directly about delinquency but shows violence that inexplicably starts while friends are staying together on the countryside to hunt rabbits. The film's slow rhythm does not foreshadow the shift to savagery. We witness a cruel transgression: instead of chasing rabbits, they start to shoot human targets. It emerges brutally, from one moment to the other, and becomes an impressive metaphor for the Civil War when people were killing each other from one day to the next, without dialogue or explanation.

Another example of violence as critical symbol is provided in the fiction THE EXECUTIONER (EL VERDUGO, 1963) by the filmmaker Luis García Berlanga. It is a disparaging document about capital punishment. The civil servant job of executioner for the totalitarian state is open. Due to a housing issue, the current executioner gives his job to his son-in-law who accepts it, the latter hoping that he will never be obliged to actually kill someone. Waiting at home in fear, he knows the task is inescapable. Finally, he has to go to prison, and will be forced to execute the death sentence. The last sequence is frightening: the space closes in on the executioner's body, symbolising the idea of repression. The room is void of any exit; he is stuck and his choice to be the executioner is irrevocable. Several shots underline his immovability: as a symbolic prisoner, the son-in-law is filmed behind the bars pleading with his father-in-law to replace him: he refuses. Then the son-in-law is taken away and surrounded by policemen. Once again his cornered body communicates his powerlessness, even more than the actual prisoner. A long shot of an empty room and our protagonist enters into it, surrounded by men dressed in black. His little sun hat falls to the floor; it looks so white, in this sombre and cloistered place. The camera is static. His body is pushed towards the other door. He follows the prisoner who hardly resists. The doomed offender seems to be the executioner who tries with all his strength to stay out of the room, but in vain. Two groups of people cross the empty room and this site condemns the killer to execute the task. Berlanga was inspired by a real life story.[43] With this fiction, he denounces capital punishment as instated by the Franco regime: the body does not show the execution of the violence but the confined sites succeed in illustrating the regime's repression.

Visualising delinquency using metaphors changes completely during the Democratic Transition. Given the difficulties during dictatorship to shoot certain images, this incited the filmmakers even more after 1975 to push the boundaries. The filmic forms are based on a new image of the body, one inspired by neo-realistic principles. The ambition to show reality is confirmed in the choice of actors. The actors come from the social milieu they are to represent on screen; filmic drug addicts are thus veritably addicted to drugs in real life. They are filmed in natural decors with a subjective camera that focuses on the character without giving any judgement: this filmic approach comes back in Carlos Saura's fiction HURRY, HURRY (DEPRISA, DEPRISA) in 1981. Saura, like Vicente Aranda and Imanol Uribe, share the same objective: they wish to get closer to the bona fide life of the marginalised to create images about them that are respectful. The camera follows them, closely framing their particular point of view while rarely showing society's moral judgments.

Another trend after 1975 is the straightforward representation of violence. The filmmaker Eloy de la Iglesia has provided the best examples with his numerous films about drugs as well as in his accounts of prostitution or homosexuality. Indeed, a close gaze that provokes a shock effect imposes realism in this period. An observing camera, while non-judgmental, offers provocative renditions of society. The body plays, through its image, an important role. The body bears witness to the relationship between fiction and Spanish culture: in MATES (COLEGAS, 1982) by La Iglesia several delicate subjects are shown, such as illegal abortion and the traffic of babies, interpreted by Antonio and Rosario Flores, a famous real life brother and sister pair. In the 1990s, with the death of Antonio Flores, lots of rumours circulated in the tabloid press about his alleged addiction to drugs.

This new provocative image of the drugged body is clearly presented by the actor José Luis Manzano acting as Paco in THE SHOOT (EL PICO, 1983) of the same film director. Apparently a drug addict in real life, his way of acting is powerfully convincing: his body demonstrates the joy of escapism and destruction brought on by his habit. In a close-up, Paco shows the needle that he puts into his arm with the help of a friend. The thought-image of the body represents his distancing from reality, it is as if he is going somewhere else in his mind, while the sound of his beating heart can be heard in voice-over "Boom, boom, boom, can you hear the beating of your heart?" says the woman who administered the injection. The same actor delivers a compelling and persuasive performance when he tries to stop his drug habit. His mother is seriously sick and he leaves home to stay at a friend's place. His friend is a sculptor. In a moment of extreme withdrawal, a frightening sequence takes place during which he throws himself on the floor: the shots follow very rapidly, in superimposition, accompanied by the tense sound of his voice as he wildly grasps for breath; we hear him wheezing fitfully; it's like a shout for survival. His body is doubled in superimposition, he hallucinates, and his frenetic respiration shakes the images. Moving through this artist studio, throwing himself on the clay with his arms, his body motions like someone drowning, flailing his limbs, violently "swimming" through the air, convulsing on the floor in the soil, without advancing, without drowning. His friend comes home, but Paco continues like a wild animal, shouting, crying, moving, grasping for breath. He lives inside his own bubble. His drug habit is put into scene through this desperate behaviour; delivering a harrowing thought-image, he points to the real aspects of his character, which undoubtedly exist outside the filmic frame.

Another example of fresh and unsettling images that leave us silently shocked, sitting in front of the screen, is the shot of his friend dying from an overdose. The mise-en-scene of this action makes the spectator feel helpless in the face of his death. We feel as though we are the only testifiers to this scene. Sitting on a chair, with a naked chest, with extremely pale white skin, he tries to put the needle in his vein. Paco is staring out the window and their friend just left the room. The viewer lives vicariously through Paco's gaze, as if we are the only spectators, in front of this body of a young drug addict who, in a close-up, introduces the syringe, but suddenly something blocks. The syringe is stuck in his vein, in his arm; he breathes nervously, quickly, and then calms down. Then he stops breathing. Several shots follow up on him revealing a still chest. We watch with horror through a medium close shot and several close-ups on his pallid face. Only then does Paco and his friend realise that he is dead. Paco touches his body, the needle moves but stays stuck in his arm. This thought-image of a sudden death, the naked and white chest, the pale and young face and the needle that is still planted in his veins, shows the irreversible destruction provoked by seeking out pleasure in heroin. A camera observes it closely and with unwavering close-ups the body. These are the kinds of images that constitute the Spanish neorealist code of the Transition. Marginality is figured in a body exposed in a matter-of-fact manner, alongside the brash displaying of violent images.

I. Hurry, Hurry, (Deprisa, deprisa, 1981): faster than time

Violence is powerfully introduced in Hurry, Hurry (Deprisa, deprisa). Carlos Saura describes the film as a love story situated within a delinquent setting,[44] the whole story is centred on an amorous relationship between Mini and Angela; this couple and two other boys form a gang in which the girl disguises herself as a boy, wearing a moustache and hiding her hair. Together they look for money to live their rumba of liberty, complete with drugs and music; they are young and want to enjoy life. The fiction depicts an updated portrait of delinquency in the country. The press reactions are positive and emphasise most of all the realistic aspect of the actors' presence: these youngsters' performances are candid and validated by reactions such as this one from *Diario 16*:

> The Spanish filmmaker was successful in his film, which had to become a commercial success, because he definitely treats a current problem: juvenile delinquency. Saura seriously investigated the environment on which he based his film, in an effort to come close to the language and the situations in which these young marginal people find themselves while living at the periphery of Madrid, 'but who could very well be living in any other large Spanish city' as the filmmaker said yesterday in Berlin.[45]

The film director became well acquainted with these young people's lives, listening to their music, visiting their bars and nightclubs. He concluded that the difficulties these young people of the suburbs were facing were rooted in the ethos of consumerist society. The media shows them an abundance of luxurious items that they cannot possibly afford. In addition, Saura argues that the decriminalisation of drugs would diminish their consumption.[46]

The film's forthright and realistic effect provoked reactions abroad: in France, the commission responsible for censorship proposed – in vain – to limit the screenings by labelling it with an X rating, claiming that these youth gangs presented an inimical example.[47] The film received the Golden Bear of Berlin and provoked a heated debate about the choice of actors; journalists in Berlin accused Saura of having "exploited" these young people as objects. The actors were present and replied that they really liked the film.[48] Since the characters in the film expose a Spanish and contemporary rendition of delinquency, it's important to note that José Antonio Valdelomar – who plays the main character, and who has two names in the film, El Mini and Pablo – had been veritably incarcerated before the film's release in Spain. The press magazines commented on his family's distress upon his imprisonment.[49] During a press conference, the producer Elías Querejeta explained that he regretted Valdelomar's detention and that he resolutely refuted every insinuation that his incarceration was actually a publicity stunt.[50] Nevertheless, Valdelomar embodies the delinquent, both on film and in his real life. In a two-page article in *Diario 16*, the event is described:

> When the police proceeded with the identification of the two delinquents, they discovered that they were José Antonio Valdelomar González, "el Mini", age twenty-four, protagonist of Carlos Saura's latest film, one that had won the Golden Bear, the Cinematographic Festival of Berlin's Grand Prize, and Manuel Solal Téllez, age twenty-three. José Antonio Valdelomar was in possession of the movie's film contract when he was arrested, the very film contract that had made him famous.[51]

The actor's body confirms the reality of the cultural context; sensationalist newspaper articles commingle the filmic universe and reality; this boy becomes once again the protagonist of his own life, ending up now in prison.

A fast body's rhythm

DEPRISA, DEPRISA, delivers an exemplary document for the Transition, as it insists on the question of time. Life should be fast and intense, as the title makes clear. *Deprisa* in English means "hurry". It implies a sense of urgency. The film was released under the title HURRY, HURRY, FASTER, FASTER and FAST, FAST. The characters reflect the acceleration of time through the frenetic rhythm of their life. Firstly, their "work" obliges them to act quickly. From their lawless perspective, their criminal activities are considered to be their work. Accordingly, during their larcenies and other crimes, they often repeat *deprisa*, particularly at the beginning and the conclusion of their attacks. Their work prevents them feeling at ease in public spaces. Holding up armoured-courier vehicles, banks and other targets, these four youngsters work quickly, very quickly. Their patent opposition to convention is demonstrated in their unusual schedules and in their flippant approach to acquiring money. Finally, furthering their structural antipathy for tradition, their solution is inspired by a fast-forwarded vision of the future; they don't want to wait for years to have the money to buy a car, an apartment or a television. The Transition is characterised by an "in between" feeling (Francoism-future), which illustrates this questioning of time and authority. These youngsters want to build their own life immediately and outside the traditional sphere that loomed so omnipresently in the past. For example, Angela and Mini live together after their first encounter, without getting married; why should they wait? They find a way to make their life together possible. Through armed robberies they take possession of huge amounts of money to thereby live their life in an intense rhythm punctuated by drug use and flamenco rock music. They don't question themselves about their activities: their life style is completely and simply *deprisa*.

The mythological plot is illustrated through the juxtaposition of the vigorous rhythm of their criminal activities and the more languid pace with which they live other parts of their lives. The mythological conflict is set between these polar cadences. All throughout, they are antagonistic to the order of the status quo and the rules governing society. This opposition is demonstrated in the sequences during which they question and build their professional independence, carrying out different burglaries. On the other hand, a slow rhythm permeates the sequences that show them enjoying their liberty in dance, drugs and trips, etc. The attack sequences represent the encounter with the other, with societal norms, mise-en-scène at *Cerro de los Angeles (Hill of the Angels)*. The contrast of tempos brings the conflict and the stereotyped bodies to the fore. The interaction with other people or institutions demonstrates their conflict with tradition, with imposed rules that they try to ignore or to break.

The archetype: a figure for liberty

Myths about unlimited freedom have always existed: in every society the established order is based on the reproduction of a norm. Behaviour that fails to reproduce the dominant order risks being marginalised. After many years of dictatorship in Spain the totalitarian norm is replaced by an openness that stimulates the emergence of new forms; delinquency is a ritual that establishes independence towards work. The delinquent body actualises in this manner a figure of independence and liberty, which represents an updated archetype about freedom for the Transition period. The film critic Julián Marías describes, in the *Gaceta Ilustrada*, their behaviour as "*señoritismo*", as a feeling of superiority towards the obligation of working:

> Sociologically, the characters are defined by their aversion to work. My father told me that during his childhood there was a drunk in Zaragoza, who walked in the streets proclaiming aloud: "Pedro Martín does not work, even if the government wants it". Angela works in a bar, but at Pablo's first inquest, she goes to live with him and takes advantage of her idle time by vagabonding.[52]

This theme of being above work is also emphasised in other films, such as Ac-catone by Pasolini and El Lute by Aranda. Hurry, Hurry brings it to life in a scene where the characters comment on the unpleasant life of people who work; they disdain a regular life led according to the traditional norm and they invent their own jobs by becoming criminals. Julian Marias describes violence as a solution to maintain this attitude of superior stance:

> Society nowadays renders the "passive señoritismo" difficult, enabled, for example through an inheritance: a variant has been introduced, according to which access to the disdaining "club" is obtained by the appropriation of the inaccessible through violence.[53]

They wish to escape the strictures of conventional life and so employ violence to obtain their money, therefore defining their illicit acts as work. The youngster's perspective testifies to their myth about independence by accelerating time. Outside mainstream ideals, they invent their own lifestyle and their own rhythm. The film director does not judge their behaviour but rather offers a close view of it. Having worked with the actors, Saura comments on their viewpoints:

> They allowed me to see the other side of the coin, they made me understand something obvious, that goodness or badness can be found amongst marginal people, just as much as it can among the oppressors, with one exception, that repression is a cold bureaucratic machine, full of deafening sirens and mysterious calls from the radio. Moreover, there exists most often only an irrepressible anguish to live, to live in another way, to live fast in a marginalisation that is an inverted form, one condemned from the beginning to be catastrophic. All this for this almost mythical desire for freedom... [54]

Their mythic view of independence underpins their wild behaviour: based on their ideas, which spring forth from their absolute belief in this kind of freedom, the filmmaker illustrates their mythological thought.

Actors

The characters re-enact this image of escaping throughout the film. The four youngsters are all unknown: Mini (José Antonio Valdelomar), Meca (Jesús Arias Aranzueque), Sebas (José María Hervás) and Angela (Berta Socuéllamos). Mini/Pablo is the gang's leader; through a visit at his grandmother's home, we come to understand that he was in reformatory school, but the rest of his origins are left unknown. We only see the current moment. The thought-image created by his body is that of a young boy, that shrugs his shoulders symbolically about a lot of things. Ignorant, he wants to live in his own way. He meets Angela and they decide to live with each other immediately, without paying respect to the proprieties of marriage or to making their link official.

Meca, who is sometimes called Susi, establishes the same thought-image by his "couldn't-give-a-damn" attitude; he makes scornful comments about the life of working people. He wants to live in his own way. Sebas, the third member of the gang, is the only one who is at first reticent about integrating a girl in their work team. He is the most talkative but in general the boys do not discuss much but simply live their life. Angela does not belong to this milieu but she will participate in it in a convincing manner. Nothing is known about her origins neither in life, nor in the film. The girl is the mediator, negotiating several worlds through the image of her body; she is initiated after the boys and she is the only one who survives. Coming from outside this setting, she becomes a new element in this gang, entering the group and living with them as Mini's girlfriend. No conflict of origin is shown, for example with her parents. In addition, she is the sole survivor and reintegrates society once they disband; she therefore represents a sombre image, leaving and entering several frames without considering the consequences or showing any remorse. Her body represents a young and nice appearance; she looks like a friendly young girl.

Creating a stereotype

Several films were made with this type of authentic character, creating recognisable thought-images. This stimulates the creation of a stereotype on the body as a social construction that can be identified, because the stereotype brings a sort of categorisation that helps to recognise and classify social phenomena. Repeating the visualisation of a delinquent in the current moment by the same type of character stimulates this process. Moreover, the real life aspect of it is emphasised, which allows the detection of recognisable features to have an even better grip on the problem. The filmmaker works with boys that play out, in a way, their own life. Their bodies incarnate an image of Spanish reality, a marginalised reality. As we commented already, the actor José Antonio Valdelomar attempted a bank robbery at Rios Rosas, in the centre of Madrid, and was subsequently jailed.[55] The film had not yet even been released in Spain; the protagonist thus could not view the film. In August 1981, the police reprimanded the actor Jesus Arias Aranzueque (who plays the part of Susi, the pyromaniac boy in the film). He also attempted a bank robbery in Madrid.[56] The actor, a drug addict of many years,[57] a habit he had during and after the shooting of the film, continued his way of surviving.[58] According to a press article in *El Pueblo* in 1983, two years later, the actors were arrested anew by the police for having committed bank robberies to buy their drugs.[59] The two boys died later of overdoses.[60]

The realistic aspect of the characters' life is pertinent, and striking. In the film the gang is killed by the police. Saura comments that it corresponds to reality and describes their conflict: "They declared a war, basic if you want, but a real war, cruel, with the police: the first candidate that we had as a protagonist died under police gunfire during an altercation with the police, before the beginning of the shooting."[61] The boy refused to stop and the police started to shoot as in the film.[62] The film, as in the reality it reflects, is about a war declared between two camps.

Choreography of the ritual

The characters create myths about their liberty accelerating time as they wish, imposing another time schedule: a violent, dynamic, and intense timetable replaces the workaday life of mainstream society. Their ritual of a fast work rhythm structures their perspective: *deprisa*, if they hurry up they can maintain their liberty. Two aspects are therefore important in the mise-en-scene of the body: the displacement from nature towards culture and the choreography of the ritual carried by the music.

Firstly, this displacement from a natural setting to culture illustrates the increasing risks that the youngsters are willing to take and to impose on others. The outskirts of Madrid resemble the countryside. The environment is natural and deserted. There is an absence of urban structures and it is in these isolated conditions that they take most of their risks. The film begins on the street and finishes on the street: a site that belongs to everyone, where the dominant rules can be changed radically because it is an open space. It is very difficult to oppose or to stop them because they prepare their attacks: with their body's gestures they transform the image of the street into a Wild West where bullets are fired in all directions.

They begin at the margins: the first offence, stealing a car, is shown in the first sequence and is set in the suburbs. The second attack is on a building located in the middle of a desert. Then they attack an armoured vehicle transporting funds, also in a deserted area on a motorway. The last action shows them coming closer to culture. They attempt to rob a bank and this ends catastrophically. The police invade the street in a few seconds. The forces of order do not hesitate to shoot and even accidentally kill a passer-by. Their destruction is the result of their own initiative; the police react by imposing law and order in the site of culture, which must figure civilisation. The street, this street, does not belong to these hoodlums and their bodies are completely destroyed.

The second aspect is illustrated through music. The bodies express the ritual as a choreography that looks like a wild dance. The music intensifies the rhythm of their attacks, as movements for destruction. They do not hesitate to fire bullets. These rituals of aggression allow them to keep their liberty and their independence, musically accompanied by the sounds of flamenco rock. A new stream in flamenco music, influenced by rock, this type of music made its debut in Spain in the 1980s. In flamenco it represents a modernisation of the deep *"jondo"* music: this form is lighter, and therefore less authentic. The song of *Los Chunguitos, Ay que dolor* became a huge success in Spain in that period. This rumba provides an added element of speed to the youngsters' fight. *Ay que dolor*, a deep text, for an important battle: the rhythm of time is difficult to change but in this fiction these youngsters are trying by any means to accelerate it as they wish.

Imposing themselves by violence

The film emphasises a mise-en-scene that is distanced since they are filmed mostly inside their frame. As this distance does not represent the central focus of the frame, it makes the contact between their cosmos and the rest of society all that more unpredictable and violent. They know how to become the centre of the image through wild and violent choreographies. Nothing is questioned; everything is imposed by the youngsters. The first sequence emphasises already the contradictory movement: the frames are opposed. The opening of the film is marked by the camera that moves in a tracking shot from the right to the left, in contrast with the traditional occidental reading of left to right. The strong and powerful rhythm of the song *Ay que dolor* by *Los Chunguitos* can be heard. The camera fixes itself in a medium close-up on the windows, to focus frontally on a yellow car: inside it we perceive two faces, looking down in rapt concentration at what they are doing. Electric cables inside the car are shown in a close-up and we understand that the characters are trying to start the car without a key. The camera does not stop moving and moves in a tracking shot on the other cars, to a long shot on a building behind. Then we return to the car: a medium close-up shows a boy, his face seems stressed as if in a hurry. He turns towards his neighbour and says: "Have you forgotten how to do it?"

In a close-up, the hands establish the contact and the car starts. At the same moment a family leaves the building, looking relaxed, talking about a birthday: they represent a standard couple. Their thought-image is traditional: the man in a suit, the wife next to him in a skirt, they are talking about parties they will organise and smile. They are like role models of a united and normal family. Suddenly the man sees his own car starting and his face looks frightened. His wife is calling out for help and completely panicking, they shout around them, dash forward to the car, the owner visibly outraged. The camera provides a lateral medium close shot, in which the man signals to another car to block the exit. All these men, dressed in suits with a tie, aged forty years or more, appear to be coming straight out of work. They surround the car and start to hit from all sides on the windows. When the tapping on the vehicle becomes too strong, Mini takes his pistol. He looks calm when pointing it in all directions, to the left and to the right and in a reverse shot, we observe the men's fear. Suddenly these working men are standing there, completely immobile and speechless, fear can be read on their faces. The car starts. Bouncing along and hitting some trash-cans, it rushes away to the motorway at a dangerous speed. In a close-up on the radio *Ay que dolor* can be heard; the car vibrates to this music that accompanies the young people, accentuating the rhythm of their speed and of their intensity while they enjoy their escape. In a long shot on the periphery of Madrid we see them arriving; the camera follows them laterally then films them on the back. At top speed they overtake all the other cars. They are the winners.

The film begins with this first sequence that presents two young impassive boys, who morally scoff at car owners. They take as they wish and they are not afraid to use arms. Their behaviour confirms the stereotype of a typical criminal who does not worry about the reactions of others: the victim represents on the contrary the traditional thought-image of the family and of those coming home from work. It is the beginning of the film and the spectator has been introduced to the gang members and their lifestyle, characterised by its violence, dynamism and an accelerated, excessive speed.

Love inside their frame

The two friends enter into a bar and Mini feels attracted to the girl who works there, Angela. Quietly they take their beer: Mini is in love, and his eyes send a dreamy gaze to Angela, while his friend turns on the music, so we can listen to a romantic song about a butterfly. The sweet text is accompanied by an exchange of shots on Mini and Angela's faces. The moment their eyes meet, it is only a very short moment, and he gets up immediately and invites her to go out with him. In the nightclub where they meet later, he asks her if she wants to be his girlfriend. They kiss; a love story begins when they return to his flat. In his small apartment she tells him that she is a virgin, and he is surprised. The cam-era closes up on her face when she demands his fidelity, and he swears on his liberty to be faithful to her. This is the most important promise he can make and it is the utmost representation of their commitment. After this initial encounter and first night of lovemaking, the three youngsters drive to the countryside to practice shooting. In a full shot, we see Mini who places a can. In a light low-angle medium close-up on Mini and Angela, he shows her how to use a weapon (see photo).

A snapshot of rural youth in love, they smile happily as the countryside spreads around them. But this idyllic picture is countered by their original choice of a pastime. The image of Angela's body, of this young, nice-looking girl, is quickly modified to that of a professional shooter. She looks concentrated and her gestures are appropriately deliberate. She shoots once, and once again, without missing her target. She feels no need to speak about what is happening, nor does she question what they are up to. Without any hesitation, she shows herself to be an adept marksman. Young people normally symbolise the future,

Photo 25: Teaching and initiating her body

as do these young people, which makes the scene all the more frighteningly aberrant. The police arrive and they flee the scene in haste. They always run away at a bolting rate when the forces of law and order arrive.

Angela wishes to join the gang but the presence of a woman arouses problems. A third member of the gang is supposed to give his opinion. In a lateral medium close-up we see Mini and Susi playing at a video game machine, shooting targets; the two young people are enjoying themselves. Angela is waiting next to the bar and seems to be nervous. The *rasguado* sound of a guitar, a typical flamenco touch of guitar music, is heard: it underscores Angela's tension. In a medium close-up on Angela's face we see her anxiously waiting for the other youngster to arrive, drawing attention to the importance she has attributed to her admittance to the gang. The three boys discuss, we hear them talking, and we see Angela's tense face brighten up when they give her permission to participate in their "work".

Preparing and transforming one self

Before leaving for their first job the couple prepares themselves at home. A medium close shot from outside on the apartment gives us a view on Angela who opens the shutters and then on the inside of the apartment. Apparently, they already live together. Mini lies down on the bed in a high angle medium close shot; he is thinking of his "work", saying that he always sleeps poorly before

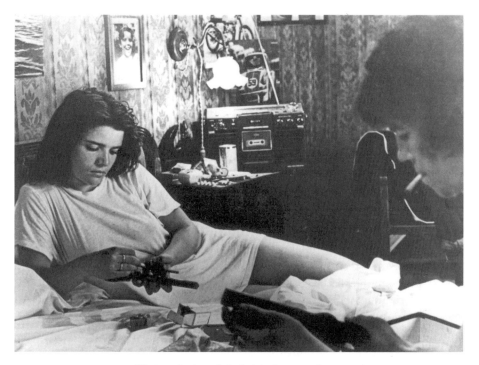

Photo 26: Angela's initiation continues

going "to work". It is the only comment he makes. His physical attitude also reveals his apprehension as he does some exercises in front of the mirror. Moving his naked torso as if to imitate a boxer, this little young man is not very athletic or muscular. With a wild and brutal face, he is physically training his body for the rhythm that will follow. She places herself in front of him, covering her face behind her hands. Then she shows her moustache: he laughs and kisses her tenderly, telling her that it's ticklish. Once again her body is easily transformed, from a girl gang member into one of a male gangster's body. They prepare the weapons. Angela and Mini sit down on the bed and in a close-up we see how experienced she is loading the arms. In a frontal medium close shot we see her load a gun (see photo).

The young people talk about the project: they act natural and skilful. When Angela has finished, she directs the pistol toward Mini. The image of this young girl's face quickly reshapes to that of a dangerous criminal. Seeing her concentrated gaze, we remember her talent as a shooter. She directs the weapon straight toward him and maintains this position for some seconds. A medium close-up on Mini's face, looking serious and tense: "Angela, it is the devil who loads the weapons". This is followed by a frontal medium close-up on Angela who does not falter. Another frontal shot on the other face shows he's worried, he repeats: "it is the devil that loads up the weapons". Smiling nicely she puts down her weapon, poses it on the bed. Her young and lively face reappears, completed by this new transformation: the image of her body demonstrates so easily her delinquent appearance, she is used to arms, she changes easily into this new body thought-image without questioning herself.

The first job

In a long shot they arrive, slowly, accompanied by the intense rhythm of the flamenco *rasguado*, an explosive and cacophonic accompaniment. In a high angle long shot we see their car that arrives at a parking lot, they drive slowly, very slowly, while we hear Mini's voice give instructions. His message finishes with the slogan: "*deprisa, deprisa*", accompanied by guitar music that announces once again an explosive, violent action. When the attack begins, the music stops. No musical support for this moment of intense speed: these are tense and sharp bodies in action. The sound of silence is remarkable; it accentuates the tension of the agitated movements that will follow. All four youngsters jump on the security guard and threaten him with their weapon: it is Angela's role to stay with him while the others are looking for the money. It is a strong sequence, during which Angela's face constitutes the central image. Her presence imposes her force and her domination on the guard in a silence that seems to last forever. Her determined attitude is exposed in a frontal medium close shot. She keeps the guard under control and directs her pistol to his face (see photo).

We feel the interminable silence, as if nothing is happening, all too aware that Angela is waiting. Her gestures express that she's counting time, she touches her moustache a little, looks behind her and we see from far away a truck that passes. This place looks like a desert; there is nobody in sight. The guard is shown frontally, he looks tense with worry, his face contorted and behind him we see Angela, concentrated on her task. The two persons are unified in a shot displaying the power imbalance, which could be potentially fatal for the guard. He provokes her, saying: "Your friends, they have abandoned you". She reacts: "You're going to shut up", pushing the pistol brutally against his face to make him ever more aware of the threat of death that is weighing on him. But he replies: "You're all sons of bitches"; his annoyed face on the bottom of the shot looks very small in the image; at the background, tall and powerful, he is opposed to the girl's furious face with a pistol prominently present. She pulls him by his hair, shaking his little head around: "What did you say?" He replies: "Nothing", and she: "I thought so". He is completely paralysed in his helpless position; his head is stuck in Angela's menacing grip. In a close-up on his face, the pistol changes position and we observe then that she is also moving: the others arrive and they get out.

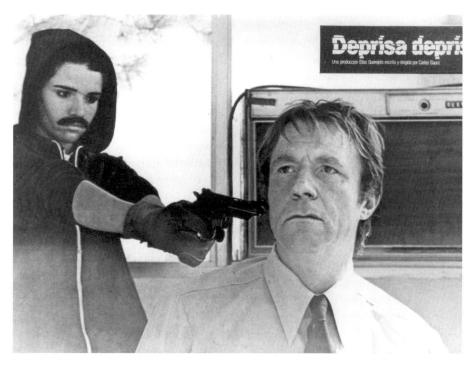

Photo 27: Angela's initiated body

They escape again by car, at top speed. The last shot shows a gate, with a sign indicating that the place is closed. However this does not stop these thugs as they can still open the gate. They enter. In a frontal medium close-up we see the four youngsters in a car while they share the money. Angela looks in the mirror and takes off her moustache. She looks calm and satisfied and is a little circumspect. The music *Ay que dolor* marks the rhythm of victory after this successful crime.

Victory: Angela initiated

One of the boys in the gang is heard announcing: "Ladies and gentleman, here we are, at the geographical centre of Spain" and we see in a long shot the monument of *Cerro de los Angeles (Hill of the Angels)*. Then, in a frontal medium close shot framing our gang in the middle we watch them comment on the passers-by. The youngsters are filmed frontally in a medium close shot, together, and in the background we see the same statue. This monument located on a hill close to Madrid symbolises the protection of the city like the basilica of the Sacré-Cœur in Paris. The history of the site is important for a reading of the mytholo-

gical thought. The gang confirms here an idea about their freedom: they perform with their bodies their idea about liberty, their asserted irreverence is symbolised at this site. At the beginning of the twentieth century the pious Spaniards showed a particular devotion to the *"Sagrado corazón de Jésus"*. They
built a monument on the site, officially inaugurated by King Alfonso XIII in
1919. In 1936, during the Civil War, the monument was destroyed.[63] During
Francoism a new monument was constructed in front of the old one and inaugurated by Franco in 1965. The statue shows Jesus with open arms, inviting
people to come towards him. At this historical and religious site we find our
gang, its members are marking the site with a ritual of presence.

The teenagers walk around: they are approaching the camera slowly in a
frontal medium close shot. They look relaxed and talk joyfully. In the background the pillar of the statue remains visible as they discuss among themselves. They are five today as one of Angela's girlfriends has joined them. Their
acts of heroism are evoked, talking about their first experiences. They congratu-
late Angela in a medium close-up first on Sebas who is talking about his first
job, then on Meca and finally on Mini, all cut by medium close-ups on a smiling
Angela, who feels satisfied, appreciated and of course, integrated in the gang
because of these reinforcing comments. The camera passes behind them when
they approach the statue. No music but a sequence filled up by smiles and
heroic stories of these boys, proud of what they are able to do. They appropriate
the space, a protected place that is now invaded by new elements – by juvenile
delinquents.

In this frame we witness a negative interpretation of their actions; these exter-
ior reactions are also stereotyped. They will clash with the older generation. A
full shot on the statue, two old ladies deplore the degradations that it suffered
during the Civil War: these older ladies are thought-images of conventional women who coif their hair in a predictable fashion, holding their purses correctly
under their arms, talking about this statue with a respectful tone. They miss the
anterior authority and complain about the destruction. Then they meet the
young people: in a tracking shot from the right to the left the camera approaches again the youngsters. They wonder what the monument represents.
This thought-image is that of young rebels who are mockingly contemplating
the statues merits; their glib attitude contrasts with the serious and respectful
gestures of the two older ladies.

In a frontal medium close-up, Meca asks the ladies what the statue refers to,
and once again the camera displaces from the right to the left, as to illustrate an
image that goes against the established order. For only a few seconds, his body
is inside the same frame as the lady, and the effect is explosive. The old lady
comments with gravity about what happened, expressing with her gestures an
unmistakable dignity while insisting on the statue's significance, saying that it

represents Jesus but that a part had been destroyed by *"los rojos/the reds"* during the war. Together in the same shot, the thought-image of Meca contrasts with her serious appearance: he doesn't even listen to half of what she says and makes a rude joke about the fact that there was certainly a good reason to destroy these stones. Moreover, he adds that he wonders what war she is talking about. The two women leave immediately; they walk off grumbling to each other, shaking their heads in disapprobation. Both identities are stereotyped in their behaviour. Once the paragons of conservative values leave, the youngsters immediately burst out in raucous laughter. We see the police arriving in a subjective long shot. The boys must present their identity cards, after that they can leave without any problem.

At this site of *Cerro de los Angeles* three events intervene: the homage of Angela's victory, the confrontation of the youngsters with the Catholic religion and the existence of a past (or a Civil War), and the encounter with the police who ask for their identification. These three issues are explored in a site that represents the heart of Spain, meant to be a protected spot: an essential part of the country is touched, invaded by a new group. These youngsters symbolise, by their age, the future. They appropriate the site and make clear their absolute rejection of not only traditions, but also of the past's meaning; they transgress this site with their mere presence.[64] This confrontation between the two generations is convincing through the mixing of two thought-images of the bodies. Both groups are overloaded with stereotypes, from one extreme to the other, from the tradition represented by the elderly conservative generation to the rebellious attitudes of youngsters who express a disturbing levity for the past.

Second job

The second attack with the gang begins with a long shot on a dry and abandoned landscape dotted by small houses far away in the background. Then there is a lateral medium close-up on the car and then on Angela. She looks concentrated and serious with her moustache: being disguised points to the fact that the gang is preparing another heist. The image is accompanied by a tango of flamenco, profound and lively, sung by a female voice. The camera frames Mini on the back: "There they are. Let's go, we will do it". In a reverse shot, we see the deserted landscape; a white van enters into the field, followed by their blue car. A frontal shot on the small van, we then see the blue car pass it and block the van's way: all four jump out of their car, ready to attack; in a light low-angle medium close shot on the young people, we see their savage choreography. Their faces are hidden under black masks and with an athletic and fast movement they direct their weapons to their victims; their violent gestures dominate the scene. The camera moves quickly, the action lasts only a few seconds: the two passengers get out, their hands in the air, the young people take the money and leave at top speed.

The van's driver also has a weapon, and shoots at them. A medium close-up in the car on Angela who turns round, she is furious, and asks to get back to the driver. At top speed they approach the van again, the man is running into the fields as fast as he can, but Angela gets out: a frontal medium close-up on her, she looks decided, concentrated on her target, she shoots. She doesn't hesitate a second, she executes her gestures with the detachment of a professional killer. One, two, and the third time we see the body falling down; he does not get up off the ground anymore. The gang escapes. They argue violently between them. Sebas, who had reservations about admitting the girl to the gang, admonishes her loss of control. It is clearly a nervous atmosphere one in which Angela remains silent, her eyes gazing blankly ahead.

Their frame

Nevertheless the gang stays united. In Mini and Angela's new apartment, they share the money. Sitting around a table, they start to drink and toast to their happiness. Sebas is watching in front of him, in a lateral medium close-up, and then we see Angela. In a shot on her face, he affirms: "*siempre amigos*" ("for ever friends"). Sebas has now also fully accepted Angela as a gang member. Angela has accomplished an initial act to be admitted; she has shown her strength, her will, her cold-blood and her determination. For the rest of the film there are rarely any conflicts between them as they are friends: they repeat all the time the slogan "*siempre amigos*". Harmony governs them and they laugh and enjoy themselves. They drink together festively and in a medium close-up on the young people, we watch each share a wish. Meca: "That we will always be together." Mini: "Yes, and that we will enjoy life. There is still so much to do." They turn on Meca's favourite music, *Ay que dolor*, and begin to dance in the apartment as Sebas prepares a dose of drugs. Angela continues to dance a little. Her boyfriend embraces her asking her if everything is okay. She regrets her action: "I've killed him, you know". Together they go out on the balcony. In a medium close-up the young couple is filmed on the back, on the background we see Madrid: they are united in their view. We listen to Mini's reaction: "Moreover, he was looking for it. Don't think about it anymore Angela, you didn't kill anyone." Bodies unified in their convictions, they are filmed in the same frame from behind looking together towards the world.

Opposing frames

During the entire plot the young people are filmed in their milieu giving their viewpoints on the world, proclaiming their opinions on life. They lean on each other with camaraderie and watch from a distance the motorway, observing the

Photo 28: A picture of their myth for independency

cars that pass in a subjective long shot. This image is connected to a medium close-up in a light low-angle shot on them. They are united in the image and unified in their opinions. Framing a light low-angle illustrates visually their feeling of superiority: they feel above the world and express their convictions about liberty and independence. Without any obligations or constraints, they feel free and together. It looks like an idyllic picture, like a photograph of a happy family as this group expresses their opinion on how to live, and above all about the working life of other people: what a waste of time! (See photo).

They believe in their rejection of convention, they justify their ideological stances, their mythological thought. Susi starts to talk and in a reverse shot the motorway is framed with the countless cars that rush away into the distance: "Look at them…they're rushing like fools. Look at them, they can't wait to get home, that their wife opens the door, gives them a kiss and says: how was it at work? And the guy all sweaty: Good, a bit tired." A monologue by Susi, a continuity shot on the youngsters, and the motorway in a long shot. He continues: "Then they turn on television and the children arrive. A slap for the kid. I will knock them down. I would kill them all. I'll swear it, I would kill them tired." They demonstrate their disdain towards a traditional life with so many rules and obligations and their complicity is illustrated by their laughter to Susi's speech. Moreover, during this monologue, the joint circulates from one to the other: drugs intensify the perception and the pleasure of the current moment listening to commentaries about people who squander their time with work. The camera displaces to Mini in a low-angle, he gets up and announces that he is going to the sea. Angela hugs him and they decide to leave. They live to have fun and that's all. They feel free to live as they wish.

In the city

But they take greater and greater risks. Despite their commentaries about the city and the stress it entails, they want to infiltrate the city's culture, of course in their own manner. Their "work" continues; the last attack takes place without any music or rumba and everything finishes very badly. There is not even a musical introduction for this last attempt in the centre of the city. The choreography illustrates the destroyed bodies by gunfights, with plenty of blood: the macabre dance is finished without music. This time, violence and blood dominate. The policemen hunt them as if they were wild animals and do not hesitate to shoot them; the same risks exist for other people that were too close. Violence comes from two sides, but the young people pay the most elevated price: Sebas will be killed in the bank, Mini taken back home to die later and Susi, while burning the car, will also be killed by the police.

Angela is sitting alone in the apartment next to her friend's body as she watches the news: the images show that Sebas is dead. She is alone; her partner is nearly dead. She will be the gang's sole survivor. People's reactions are rapidly shown as shocked by the ferocious violence. The camera frames them in extreme close-ups on parts of their faces; like talking heads, the facial features cannot be identified, but they look like huge mouths that are moving and speaking. Again the reactions are stereotyped by these bodies representing mouths and faces. The reactions are predictable: "Horrible, it was horrible. You cannot imagine how afraid we were." The microphone passes from one mouth to the other: "It is terrible not knowing what to do. They did not stop. They were jumping from one place to another." The last close-up on the enormous microphone in the frame is extremely close to a man's lips, only the emotions can be felt: "I say that we have had enough with terrorism. What we want is to be left alone and to live in peace. It can't continue like this." Violence and terrorism are confused, which is understandable in light of the late 1970s and the beginning of the 1980s context. The filmic voices represent a chain of horrified words from men and women of all ages. These images are followed by a frontal medium close-up on Angela who is touching her arm, feeling uneasy in her solitude. She is staring out in front of her, in the general direction of the TV set, with a forlorn and pensive look.

A young body, once again we emphasise that young people are the archetypes for the future. This thought haunts the scene and makes it quite unsettling. Angela stays alone next to her friend. In a lateral close-up the camera shows Mini lying down, with his mouth open and with a contorted face, he groans in pain. The camera focuses on the body from the head, filming then the feet where Angela is sitting, framing her face, with her sad and melancholic eyes. His moaning can still be heard but then suddenly stops. Then, from Angela's point of view the camera provides a light high angle shot on Mini's corpse with his mouth open: he is no longer breathing. A continuity shot follows as an extreme close-up on Angela's face. She leaves, putting the stolen money in a bag, then her pistol, she hesitates about the photo of her and Mini, then decides to take it as well. The music *me he enamorado (I've fallen in love)* begins. It is their song. She walks out into the night, the camera focusing on her in a slight low-angle medium close-up.

Conclusion

Images of youth are conducive to the construction of myths about innocence and naivety: in this fiction the image of youth is completely opposed to that typical conjunction. Hurry, Hurry updates an archetype of liberty using a group of delinquents, which relates a frightening image. These young criminals show little remorse and self-introspection with regard to their relentless use of violence. Moreover, the film finishes with a troubling image. After the shot on Angela's back leaving into the night, the image fades out into black. Her body disappears and the spectator has no idea where she will go. What is she? The film showed us thought-images of her body that were extremely violent, very changing. The voices of children that play and shout accompany this black shot; the sound of youth is also an image for the future: these young bodies incarnate and represent the future. Finishing a film with this kind of image is not new in Saura's filmography: already Raise Ravens (Cría cuervos, 1975) finishes on a shot on Ana Torrent who goes to school and we see a little girl – often an image of innocence – who we know to be obsessed with death, having tried to kill several people. This was also a final image of a story that left us with many doubts and questions about the young girl's archetype of innocence and naivety. In Hurry, Hurry, the spectator experiences the same effect when presented with the shocking Angela. Her body created the image of a young girl in love, looking friendly and smiling. But from one moment to the next she is able to show with her body the thought-image of a dangerous delinquent who without hesitation shoots a bullet to kill someone.

The film introduced a new mythological figure based on an archetype of liberty by questioning the perception of time. The problematic is embodied by the youngsters who oppose themselves to the previous generation. The young delinquents construct their own idea about freedom, distancing themselves from traditions and they receive stereotyped reactions by representatives of social order on their behaviour. Just to repeat some examples: Angela and Mini don't want to get married. She explains that it is only a piece of paper. Their rejection expresses also a reaction against the importance of religion, illustrated by the generation gap in front of the statue of *Cerro de los Angeles*, the geographical centre of Spain. Another example, there doesn't exist a traditional schedule for work for this gang that has created its own agenda filled with illegal and violent activities. The thought-image of these youngsters seems distanced from any tradition, they turn their back towards traditional society, to the past, and more exactly to work, marriage, and religion. But the repetition of the thought-image filming them inside their own frame confirms the stereotyped image of a new delinquent in Spanish society. The delinquent body is at the margin, an image that is to be suppressed, or eliminated. The filmic frame and the mise-en scène confirm that a certain distance is still sustained: they are filmed in their own milieu, without any real or current interaction with other people. Due to several films on this topic, their bodies can be more easily identified which establishes their stereotype.

Made during the Transition period, this fiction symbolises a period of initiation in Spain; these youngsters, like society, are approaching another phase, that of democracy. But all this is not done without friction. The country is not united, the enemy comes once again from within and this time it is the youngsters: the fledgling generation that is expected to build this new Spain. These young people want everything, immediately, but at the same time it is astonishing that their dreams are so basic: what they want is an apartment, some plants, a television, to go to the sea, etc. These are ordinary dreams, but maybe they were difficult to realise in Spain in the 1980s when unemployment among young people was particularly acute.[65] To live their own life in complete liberty, they take charge of their future: through their rituals they play out a violent and macabre choreography. These youngsters were born under dictatorship and did not live during the Civil War or many years of dictatorship. They don't like waiting and realise their dreams in their manner: it is their myth at the margin. They actualise and present a new mythological figure about liberty.

The plot allows a double reading of the myth: the youngsters' personal convictions and the image made of them by the filmmaker. Obviously the entire film is conceived from Saura's point of view. Indeed, familiarising himself with their way of life, working with drug addicts as actors, emphasises a wish to become acquainted with their myths, their ideas that illustrate an image of liberty inspired by everyday dreams. The filmmaker humanised these human beings and transmits this filmic thought through their bodies in 1981, during the Transition: a myth that sublimates the anguish in the face of new uncertainties and an unclear future. Most of all, the film is a testament to the emergence of these new forms of violence in Spanish society.

II. El Lute: a mythological figure is born in the 1960s

Eleuterio Sánchez (1942), also known as Lute, was sentenced to thirty years in jail for his involvement in a jewellery store robbery. Imprisoned for 18 years (until 1981), he wrote and published two autobiographical books: *El Lute, Run for Your Life* (*El Lute, camina o revienta*, 1977) and *Tomorrow I'll be Free* (*Mañana seré libre*, 1979). Each of these publications inspired a film by Vicente Aranda: El Lute Run for Your Life (El Lute, camina o revienta, 1987) and El Lute II, Tomorrow I'll be Free (El Lute II, mañana seré libre, 1988). The first film paints the picture of his life prior to the robbery, recounting the trials of a poor merchant. Portraying a life on the edges of legality, one characterised by its desperation and lack of resources, we watch as he and his wife are incarcerated for stealing some chickens. The film also depicts the robbery of a jewellery store situated on Bravo Murillo street. While Lute undoubtedly plays a role in the crime, accompanied by two other young men, his part is negligible. However, since a guard is killed during the hasty altercation, Lute, despite his tertiary role, is condemned to death in 1965. Due to public outrage, General Franco commuted his death sentence to thirty years of imprisonment. Nonetheless, Lute is unable to accept this damning verdict and focuses all of his energy on an eventual escape. The next film, *El Lute II, mañana seré libre*, starts with his second breakout. Helped by his brother he escapes with his whole family and attempts to rebuild his life in spite of the two manhunts on him guided by the civil guards.

The film is based on a real-life story which begins in the 1960s and continues well beyond the 1970s; the saga spans the periods of Francoism all the way to the *Movida*, as "El Lute" stays in prison until 1981. He was judged by a military court during Francoism, and therefore fell under the law of bandits and terrorism (*Ley de bandidaje y terrorismo*).[66] Due to this Francoist law, which concerned certain groups, he could not be amnestied in 1977 whereas others were granted immunity. Political prisoners were released. Yet Lute had to wait until 1981 to be pardoned by a Ministry Council. In 2009, Lute reappears in the Spanish press with headlines announcing his demand to have his trial cancelled. His objective was to be amnestied, not only pardoned, appealing to a newly accepted law 52/2007, known as the Historical Memory Law.[67] Being a lawyer himself, he found fault with the Military Council of War for imprisoning him, criticising their legitimacy since they were not lawyers. To this day, Lute is a well-known figure in public life; Lute is still very present in the media. Moreover, his tale has crossed borders. Even international pop groups like Boney M were inspired by his story composing a hit single about *El Lute Gotta Go Home* in 1979.[68]

Within Spain it was his real life story that became a myth from its despondent beginnings in the Francoist periods. El Lute is a hero, admired for his fearless and successful escapes from prison. Twice he valiantly dared to challenge the civil guards, representative of daunting Francoist authority. However, if Eleuterio Sánchez is the person represented in the myth "El Lute", there nevertheless remains a difference between the tone and interpretation of his problems in his autobiographical novels and their cinematographic adaptation. In his books he introduces and explains his origins, how hard it was to survive as an individual born into want and exclusion. He describes a life of such flagrant paucity that robbery appears to be the only way out: "I want to take advantage of mass media to shout from the rooftops where my life came from, what everyday life was, the sad lot of the poor, the marginalised, the shantytowns, the itinerant merchandisers, the gypsies."[69]

He dedicates particular attention to the terminology of marginality in Spain. He elucidates the difference between a gypsy, a *payo* and a *quinqui*, the last term often used to describe him. The gypsies have their own culture, based on customs and traditions, while a *quinqui* is a member of a marginalised group,[70] without a specific folklore. The films do not delve into these linguistic nuances, which makes the translation of the term sometimes tricky. For example, in the book *Spanish contemporary cinema*, Barry Jordan and Rikki Morgan-Tamosunas write about this film relating the term directly to criminality: "The films concern the legendary *quinqui* (delinquent)."[71] This understanding of the word is further confirmed at an exhibition organised in Barcelona in 2009 about *Cine quinqui*, bringing together films on youth delinquency between 1978 and 1985, as more than 30 films had been made on the topic (STRAY DOGS, EL TORRETE/ PERROS CALLEJEROS, EL TORRETE).[72] In Spain, the term is also related to marginalised groups who make their living illegally or at the fringes of mainstream society.

Nevertheless this term has other origins, representing nomadic groups or travellers with their own individual background. Doubtless, the word *quinqui* is pejorative and the films definitely testify to this derogatory stereotype, which makes the biographies written by Eleuterio Sánchez even more interesting. As he explains, he earned his living as a scrap dealer. On the other hand he writes about the *payo*, whom he defines as an integrated person in society: someone who works and earns his living with a regular job; he is the everyman. Lute clearly presents himself as a *quinqui* that connected himself to gypsy culture through his second marriage. His first marriage is carried out following the purest form of the *quincallera* tradition. His ex-wife affirms that it was indeed a ritual.[73] The second marriage was celebrated by a *rito gitano*.[74] The second film illustrates this gypsy matrimonial ceremony. Lute, joined in wedlock to adjacent though disparate groups, represents therefore a mixed marginalised category, made up of *quinquis* and gypsies. Born poor, he describes his life as a path that brought him to robbery:

> My whole life I saw misery, hunger, brutality, cruelty…I saw my mother dying slowly little by little by lack of care. The same thing happened to my father…And slaps for everyone. Nor bread, clothes or school, or a roof….Nothing….Nothing but the boot of a civil guard that would throw us his leftovers and would piss on our neck to joke around. When you free an aggressive dog, one cannot know who he will bite. But if he bites someone, whose fault is it? That of the dog's or of the soul's? So we were, those named the *quinquis*, so did the merchants suffer. To survive, I had to beg. I had to, later, steal (and what kind of robbery), and at twenty-two years old, I found my-self brutally separated from my life, from my closest friends and family, to be, more than anyone, locked up, buried in a dark pit, in the prison El Puerto de Santa Maria for the rest of my life.[75]

Even though he describes in great detail his life of misery in his autobiography, the films not only give prominence to this difficult past but also emphasise it to create an emotional atmosphere when explaining his background. In the new edition of 1987, Eleuterio Sánchez comments on his first books. He explains that he had written them for several reasons but especially to "deconstruct the myth about my person as much as I could."[76] One can certainly doubt if his books have reached this objective. His two autobiographies validate Lute's background, making the meagre origins of his life apt material for a myth about the struggle for emancipation, first from indigence and then from jail. His myth, a brave battle for freedom, is enduringly poignant until today.

Reactions

The two films attracted a large audience in Spain[77] and garnered exceedingly positive reviews in the press. Concerning CAMINA O REVIENTA, the critiques fo-cused especially on his ex-wife's reaction. His ex-wife, known as *La Chelo*, lodged a complaint in reaction to what she considered to be a disrespectful im-age of her person. She is shown bathing naked or depicted showing her breasts to her husband in prison, etc.[78] The tabloid press is highly present in Spanish society and has published several interviews with Chelo about her "real life."[79] Lute then reacted, retorting that he had never wanted to prejudice the mother of his children. According to him, the images are not at all degrading but represen-tative of a couple's relationship.[80] Despite her insistence, Chelo was dismissed from court.[81] The critiques of EL LUTE II, TOMORROW I'LL BE FREE, concentrate especially on Imanol Arias's acting talent as he proficiently embodies the main role of Lute. The critics also comment on the lighter tonality of the film.

Two films for one mythological story

While the two films illustrate the myth of the 1960s, they differ in rhythm, structure and meaning. Their titles guide their readings: EL LUTE, CAMINA O REVIENTA means symbolically: "Lute, sink or swim". This title evokes the image of a body in movement, walking wearily, drained of all energy but forced to keep on moving if it is to remain free. In English it was released as EL LUTE, RUN FOR YOUR LIFE. The second title, EL LUTE II, TOMORROW, I'LL BE FREE portrays Lute's obsession with escaping prison, a fixation which began from the very first moments of his incarceration. He never accepted the verdict: the death sentence commuted to thirty years of imprisonment. He escaped and, after a year and a half on the run, he is again locked up and this time for good. He is only liberated after the death of Franco; the freedom he so dearly and so persistently coveted is only then finally his. Lute cannot be dissociated with the idea of courage. His audacious character is clearly expressed in his name, Lute, a derivative of *luchar*, which means "fighting" in Spanish. Lute is thus the name of a national hero, one who represents a paragon of strength and determination. He is undeniably a Spanish hero of the 1960s.

Archetype of a hero

Lute's body updates the archetype of a hero. Through his marriage with Frasquita, a gypsy, he also represents gypsy culture. It is difficult to separate the thought-image of a scrap dealer from that of a gypsy in the film because the cultures are so intertwined; this mixture of stereotypical images brings about a new idea of the body. Gypsies have their own culture, their own customs and traditions.[82] Freedom and a feeling of independence are monumental (as in the myth of Carmen, who is also of gypsy origin; gypsies are often figures of freedom). Several negative images were projected on them. For example, to warn disobedient children: "If you do not behave well, the gypsies will come to get you."[83] The same image recurs in the film when Lute goes to look for his own children.

The whole film evokes a social context of scarcity: living in shantytowns, earning his life as an itinerant salesman, frequently having parties, drinking and sleeping (the character Lute in RUN FOR YOUR LIFE) with a wife that seems to be forever pregnant (Victoria Abril in RUN FOR YOUR LIFE). This life is opposed to that of the everyday working man. The *payos* (the employed), do not live in the grottos, perpetually evading authorities, etc. These are the stereotyped clichés about gypsies, a life of revelry and want, and the actors, through the thought-image of their bodies, reproduce this culture's image.

The actor's bodies

Lute is the main narrator. Imanol Arias plays the role of Eleuterio Sánchez, the personification of "Lute". He is a highly esteemed actor. Chris Perriam describes him as Spain's sweetheart. Arias is as treasured for his riveting performances as he is known for his repertoire, which includes some national histories.[84] In this film, his character represents the *quinqui*, a man living at the margins of conventional society. His family earns their living in the second hand trade, by stealing chickens to then sell them in order to make just enough to feed themselves. They live in the slums. His character brings together opposing features. Indeed, his person brings forth the juxtaposition between the freedom of a gypsy and the secure frame of the payo life. This tension is the basis of Lute's myth. In the film, Lute announces that he wants to live like the employed do: the image of his body is that of a mediator, one negotiating between freedom and prison, between the gypsy milieu and the desire to live like the *payos*.

Lute unmistakably demonstrates his ambition to be free. The other characters serve as a decor for his escapes. The civil guard incarnate the enemy- the unyielding hunters. Chelo is played by Victoria Abril, an actress that had then already acted in many films. In EL LUTE, RUN FOR YOUR LIFE, she is Lute's wife, and together they have two children. Chelo's parents are also merchants who travel and move throughout Spain. The father is played by José Cerro, the mother by Margarita Calahora. Lute's sister, Esperanza, is nearly absent in the first film but in the second she is an omnipresent figure, faithfully standing by her brother. In the first film she is played by Diana Penalver who, unable to take up the role in the second film, is replaced by Pastora Vega (Imanol Arias' wife in real life). Lolo, Lute's brother, is interpreted by Angel Pardon. His character is hysterical. Due to his separation from his wife he has fits of anger. These attention grabbing scenes of raucous disorder endanger the entire group. The civil guards are consequently alarmed and Lute returns once again to prison. Toto, Lute's younger brother, is interpreted by Jorge Sanz, a reputed actor of Aranda's films. In the second film he gets married to a gypsy, as does Lute who remarries Frasquita (interpreted by Silvia Rodriguez). She is a gypsy of the *los gatos* family.

The brothers are much more present in TOMORROW I'LL BE FREE in which we no longer see his first wife, Chelo (Victoria Abril), who has left for Valencia after having left her children with her parents in Madrid. The actors' depiction of this marginalised culture is commendable. The way they emphasise their language, their way of moving, and their behaviour in general is true to life. In Spanish cinema we often encounter these same actors, but in completely different roles.

Victoria Abril's, Imanol Arias' and Jorge Sanz's acting skills are remarkable. Through their bodies, they create an accurate image of this group. In addition to the fact that the actor puts himself in the skin of another person, the actors of TOMORROW I'LL BE FREE imitate the gypsies and the merchandisers accurately, authentically creating the image of this Spanish cultural minority. Victoria Abril and Imanol Arias were recognised for the quality of their acting at the festival of San Sebastian.

What is thus this stereotyped image? As José Angel Garrido analysed in his book about the representation of the gypsy ethnic group, there is a stereotypical representation in Spain's national cinema[85]. He provides his readers with some descriptions of these cliché attributes. Gypsies are violent, they are thieves, etc. A sort of speech is also associated with gypsies. In El Lute the gypsies and the *quinquis* rightfully employ this characteristic way of speaking or expressing themselves; they speak in a monotonous and ordinary way, frequently dropping the last letter of words; they cry with expression, shout with conviction, etc. In addition to their speech idiosyncrasies, there are some physical characteristics. There is a sequence at the market that believably illustrates the physical stereotype through the body image. Victoria Abril alias Chelo, is selling stolen chickens, a child on her left arm, a chicken in the other hand: she is trying to persuade two women to buy it. Her hair is pulled back in a ponytail, she is wearing a bright blue dress and an apron. She speaks like a gypsy merchant with a typically straightforward manner, without pronouncing the last part of the word, all the while expressing herself with melodic gypsy intonations. But the chickens are stolen so the police take her to the police station. When they want to take her child, she fights, with all her force, in a savage, wild way: she screams and shouts- she even kicks the guard. These are not typical feminine gestures and her violence foregrounds her savagery, showing the image of an emotional and aggressive character. The cineaste creates through her body this highly stereotyped image of a gypsy woman who can fight like a man and who cares nothing at all for the pretence of politeness and pays no homage to authorities. It is fascinating to watch Victoria Abril's convincing performance as she constructs through her gestures and her behaviour a thought-image of a marginalised woman, a merchandiser and a gypsy.

Creating a prototype?

Lute's life seems to be an eternal struggle. He fights incessantly to improve his situation: he is a prototype of someone who wishes to change. His body expresses his desire to become a *payo*, an employee with a stable financial situation. Different actions illustrate his ambition to integrate mainstream society. His attempts to escape and his subsequent choices demonstrate his wish to lead a traditional and conventional life. The film director comments on the second film:

> His rehabilitation was not done in prison, like some would like to believe. There, no-body is rehabilitated unless they escape. With his intelligence and his skills he is able to build a family, with his fridge, his house and his television with the same ambition as everyone else.[86]

It seems that this change of the body image is confirmed in real life, as Aranda describes it in a press article:

> In this second part, Eleuterio is completely different. Five years have passed and his personality has changed a lot. He has left behind his "quinqui" accent to speak an impeccable Spanish with a Venezuelan accent; he spends his time with people from the coast who represent an important social category: he assumes for good that he is a leader of marginality.[87]

Becoming a leader, he is a role model for the social group he represents.

Birth of the myth

The first film Run for Your Life is a chronicle that introduces the birth of the myth of Lute. He is the protagonist from the onset. His body questions the mythological time of the archetype of this *quinqui* hero of the 1960s. The images accompany the historical titles when the commentaries in voice-over emphasise the historicity of his life: the crime he committed in the 1960s and the civil-guard led manhunt. The myth is founded on an antagonism between the strictures of the historical context and his relentless ambitions. The prison, for example, offers education but he wishes to be free. Several rituals express the meaning of the myth centred on this vague attempt for freedom and his aspiration to be settled down. He does everything to achieve his desires but several institutional and cultural restrictions prevent him from realising his wish: the prison and the gypsy culture. The two stories illustrate Lute's fight to realise his ideals.

The myth is born with Lute's refusal to accept neither the death sentence nor the thirty years of imprisonment for the act of breaking a window. In a slight low-angle medium close-up, he is sitting on a motorbike with two friends. Lute is in the middle. The three young men seem sure of themselves, rebellious, and courageous. They smile, looking with enthusiasm in front of them. The shot focuses on the three bodies on an old motorbike. On the road, they pass in front of a jewellery store and one of them proposes to rob it. The image of Lute on this motorbike with his friends is the thought-image of a young body that is wild and insufficiently prepared for a career of crime. In haste they decide then and there to commit the crime.

One of them pretends to be doing his hair and checks to see if there are people in the shop. In a reverse shot, they discover a site with stones and decide to go there in front of everybody. In a lateral medium long shot, Lute's friend throws the first stone. Lute hesitates and looks behind him before throwing a stone himself. He throws the stone and breaks the window. These impulsive gestures mark the spontaneous image of the crime: they quickly abscond with some jewellery. A guard suddenly comes out of the shop. A fight with Lute's friend ensues and a shot is fired. Lute jumps on the motorcycle and joins his friend. Later, they hear on the radio that the guard is dead. It was a spontaneous crime; the burglary was not premeditated and the spoils of the burglary were negligible. Nevertheless, Lute becomes the object of a manhunt led by the civil guard. While he did play a role in a robbery, he also only broke a window. He repeats this reasoning over and over again throughout the film.

Tortured body

When Lute is incarcerated, he is interrogated by the civil guards. The images of Lute's body, tortured and humiliated, are extremely degrading. In several gradual steps, his executioners try to destroy his force, his virility, all the typical values of masculinity and courage. The fact that he resists, without saying anything, symbolises his strength. The first sequence of torture is shown to us in a close-up. He is naked and his hands are handcuffed on his back. Lute is blocked; he cannot do anything. The camera moves with a tracking shot to a face in a lateral close-up and, frontally on his scowling interlocutor. It is a dark and sombre room. The camera makes a tracking shot around Lute and then focuses frontally on Lute, while we see next to him another interlocutor with a callous face. The interlocutors want to know who fired the shot, but Lute refuses to say anything. He is naked, his hands are tied, he has no defences and he is surrounded by hate.

A scene of explicit sadism begins: during a frontal close-up on Lute, a man kicks him in the back. Lute crumbles forward, in this dim and gloomy room, and he is encircled by several men who attack him, each kicking and hitting him. The camera frames the executioners' faces. They are civil guards. A close-up grasps their disdaining grimaces as they look at helpless Lute on the floor. The power imbalance is clear and yet these guards try to destroy this young body with unmeasured force. They try to break down all his strength, all his energy. Abruptly, a man standing behind the door enters and tells them to stop. Through the door we see six men leaving. The room is still dark; we can only vaguely see the bodies of the executioners who are leaving the premises. The chief asks Lute where his friend is hiding and wants to know the name of the person who fired the pistol. He replies that he doesn't know anything. In a close-up, we see his face is drenched in blood; he is utterly enervated.

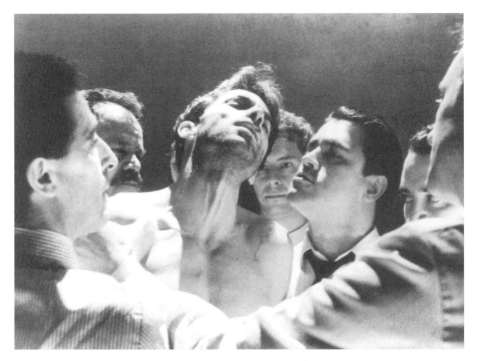

Photo 29: Tortured body, body of a victim

The sessions of torture start again. The next sequence shows Lute's naked body, with his hands tied at the ceiling. He is whipped by his executioners who laugh as they beat him. The sound of the whip is a musical rhythm for them. His tormentors have one objective only: to humiliate him, torture him and destroy him. These are extremely violent images; the images of their attempt to destroy his human dignity are sincerely disgusting. Nevertheless, despite their relentlessness, this method fails to make Lute speak. His body still expresses his courage in its resolute silence, despite the torture. Then, in the last sequence of torture, Lute is tied by his genital parts. They pull a rope to make him jump on his knees: in a full shot from behind, a man puts the rope as the other is waiting. To complete the image of brutality, Lute is still handcuffed. Destroying his force, his virility, his power, they take him by his most intimate parts to debase him as much as possible. They wanted to obliterate him at all costs, but Lute, remarkably, survives.

Domestication in prison
Lute is condemned to the death sentence. Thanks to the intervention of a priest, General Franco commutes his sentence to thirty years of imprisonment. Lute understands the sentence as the greatest and most obvious injustice; all of this

Photo 30: Lute aspires to freedom

castigation for breaking a window. Lute endlessly repeats his logic. The prison becomes a school. In a panoramic shot from the left to the right, the camera follows the teacher who is dictating, then frames the prisoners' faces. These are well-behaved and submissive pupils; they look like serious school kids, learning to write. The camera focuses on Lute in a medium close-up. With a hardworking and intense expression, he is trying to write. Through his gestures, his body shows that this is a novel activity for him. His is clearly deliberate and puts a lot of effort into controlling his pencil. His motions are a little clumsy and insisting. This is a domestication of Lute's vital force – the disciplining of his brain power; he was illiterate before his incarceration. This image shows the beginning of the process of becoming a *payo*, an employee. But Lute still dreams of escaping. When he must testify at his friend's trial, he is transferred to Madrid. Before getting on the train, one of the guards shows Lute the bullets of his machine-gun, make it clear that if he were to try to escape, one of the bullets would just as swiftly follow him. But Lute, in yet another demonstration of his boundless courage, manages to jump off the train despite the two guards.

The founding ritual of his myth begins at that very instant. His successful escape, the mere audacity of attempt to escape, especially with a menacing civil guard so close to him, reiterates his impervious bravery. He runs unafraid, even as bullets are fired in his direction.

To stay free

The dream of freedom becomes a reality in the second film, EL LUTE II, TOMORROW I'LL BE FREE, which is a composed genre because the story, in its narrative structure, can be compared to a western and to a road movie. Lute's body expresses the image of a hunted down cowboy muddling through difficult situations. Indeed, because of his identity, he cannot integrate any community: when he does finally settle down and gets married, he is recognised and must then leave immediately. Following the traditions of the western, the hero does not have the luxuries of a sedentary life; the wanted cowboy can never stay in one place and is cursed to living on the run. Just as in a road movie, his body is always on the road incessantly trying to evade the civil guard. He incarnates the rhythm of the road as he moves fast and dynamically. Lute's life is an endless confrontation, either present or latent, with the civil guard. The film opens with our protagonist standing between two civil guards. His body reflects his heroism as he stands proud. The arm he broke when he jumped out of the train in his escape is pre-emptively held by a watchful civil guard (see photo).

Lute is then put back into prison. He holds his head high. His left arm, even when it is broken, is still taken by the guard, a sign that one should never let Lute out of sight- this brave one; he is too dangerous for the guards who surround him. In voice over we hear his sentencing: fifty-one years, for stealing chickens, mattresses, etc. He will spend his life in prison. But Lute's is appropriately named Lute. As a heroic symbol, he will fight for his freedom even if it means risking his life. The doors of the prison are shown in a long shot; they are solid and close behind the car transporting him to the place of imprisonment. The next sequence shows his jailbreak, on 24 December 1971. The prisoners are having a party. He takes advantage of the noise from the festivities to break a part of the wall with help of other co-prisoners. He then sneaks out a window to join his brother's car that is waiting for him outside. Getting out of the window Lute accidentally touches the wall and a stone falls down, alerting security. The civil guard sounds the alarm immediately and fires shots in the dark. He climbs the wall, manages to pass it and escapes. Again he has escaped and again the hunt for him begins.

His athletic body expresses the features of a wild animal. He is ready to do anything to attain his freedom. In a long shot, we see the image of a forest with lots of civil guards in uniform around him: it is as if there are as many guards as trees. Their presence draws a threatening picture: a vast green landscape that is encroached by dozens of civil guards who are wearing dark green capes over their green uniforms. Their uniforms camouflage into the trees and grass, but

Photo 31: Heroic body

the silhouette of their bodies, through their movements towards the camera, allow us to distinguish them ever more clearly as they approach their sole target. They pass in front of the camera placed next to a tree, a tight medium close-up frames the face of a guard and the camera moves slowly upwards in a tracking shot. In a low-angle full shot, in the middle of the branches, we perceive Lute's face. The pallid colour of his face, which is contorted and concentrated, outlines a dash of difference amongst the green of the forest and the green of the moving soldiers. These images are forcefully dynamic because Lute is so close to his enemy. He remains completely still but this immobility only highlights the strikingly proximate and active hunt for him. The shot is continuous: the two bodies are reunited inside the frame. Lute's appearance expresses the thought of a wild animal trying to remain still and completely silent. Sought after, his face is attentive and tense. He holds himself with all his strength around the tree trunk. The silence of his body expresses the dynamism.

Framed together

The threat of the civil guard obliges Lute to move incessantly. After his second prison break, Lute and his family take up a normal life and they try to settle again. With a false passport, Lute tries to change money that he had taken from a safe. Despite his suit, his tie and glasses, he is recognised and the civil guards show up at the bank. Lute turns round and tells them that they are mistaken (medium close shot). This gesture only shows the thought of his body. It is again an act of courage, or despair, in hopes of retaining his freedom. Two threatening pistols are pointed at him: his body is again a target. A close-up on Lute with a pistol pointed at his face, shows him looking to the right then to the left. He says that he is on holiday and wants to take his passport from his left inner pocket. The bodies are framed together but, with a rapid gesture Lute manages to take the guard under the threat of the pistol. He pushes the guard towards his colleague. This scene is impressive considering the direct threat of pistols directed at him hardly more than a metre away. His daring brings its fruits as he manages to escape. The civil guards then shoot at him. As he runs we see him get shot and injured.

We see Lute running to us. His body is writhing in pain when the bullets reach him. He throws his head back at every impact, even if limping he does not stop running. His is a chased body. There is no respect for his life. He looks like a hurt animal, he is crunched forward in pain, and he turns the corner of the street and leans against the wall. The camera approaches his back and shows his wound; on his jacket we see the trace of blood. But he continues his evasion in the next street. The tracking shot focuses on Lute's body, limping and bending forwards. Pain and suffering are expressed by his movements, but he doesn't give up. The camera films the same route again, but this time following the guards. Lute then jumps on a wall of more than two metres: his is an acrobatic body in a desperate choreography of survival, he is absolutely heroic. Surviving all these attacks, he is an exemplary figure of archetypal values: he has the strength and bravery; we are invited to idolise his intrepid persistence as he faces the civil guards.

The body of a cowboy

Several sequences show this confrontation with the civil guards; each demonstrates how potentially fatal his battle with them is. This dialogue with death reinforces his heroic connotations: he continues to fight to be free. After his last injury, Lute successfully finds his family who nurse his injuries. In the next sequence, he wants to recuperate "his" car but a rainfall of shots is waiting for him. The civil guards are installed everywhere. When he gets into the car and tries to start it, shots are fired on him from all sides. Several shots reach the frontal window. He dives to the right and the next image shows us Lute in a

Photo 32: Cowboy body

low angle medium close-up. The window breaks and the glass shatters onto his face, his mouth and his teeth; he tries hard to hold on. The windscreen shatters.

Enclosed by civil guards, Lute cannot escape this onslaught. The camera illustrates the mortal choreography by framing the bodies of the guards around Lute. A tracking shot from the left to the right shows long shots, not focusing on the image of one person but jumping around the car and stopping only one short moment on a person to continue towards the next person. The camera moves on three men rapidly, like three jerking movements that foreground the mortal threat. In this chasing ritual, Lute is definitely in an inferior position. The confrontation makes the sequence dynamic; the bodies of the civil guards dominate the setting, making the unambiguous point that there is no exit for Lute. It is a murder ritual expressed by destructive, direct and brutal gestures; they are trying to kill him at any price.

Several breaks of bullets are fired and the tracking shots insist on the different characters in the fight. This is followed by a shot on the bullet-whole ridden car, more and more followed by other camera movements, another tracking shot now from the right to the left. These are "jumping movements" from the camera framing three men without a face but a chest, it is an anonymous body. The framing focuses on the machine gun, the shotgun or the pistol making fall a flood of bullets on the car. It is a monstrous image; the bodies resemble robots both in their anonymity and unquestioned firing assail on Lute. And the confrontation continues illustrated in another round by a tracking shot; once again we see the initiators of this mortal dance. This time the camera shows the bodies of the guards and their faces as they stop shooting. Lute's car is shown laterally from the right in a medium close-up. The window is broken. The civil guards have stopped firing bullets. An eerie silence permeates the scene. The spectator expects that battle to be over. The sudden contrasting quiet only gives more force to the prior sound of the machine guns.

Seeing this sequence, it is difficult to believe that Lute could survive such an attack. But Lute passes his pistol through the window (a close-up on the barrel and a part of his face) and he starts to shoot at them, two or three times. Apparently they no longer have any bullets. The guards are then shown running for their lives in a long shot. Once again Lute's body is heroic; he is the archetype of someone who is invincible. He gets of the car. The frame tightens on his savage face and the pistol is pointed to the sky. He looks straight in front of him, towards his enemies, his hand and the pistol in the iconic gesture of a cowboy, shooting in a symbolic manner a shot in the air to hunt his enemies. A tracking follows him, showing him as he starts to run again. He shoots into the air, leaning forward, advancing with all his strength. His gait resembles that of a cowboy. His body is obliged to move. And the hunting continues as it would in a road movie. In a new car, the brothers try to escape. Again on the road, a transient site for a transient body; there is no safe place for Lute to settle. On the road they cross the civil guards. They don't stop and the enemy fires ad lib on them. Hunted by a helicopter, they still successfully evade their pursuers.

Between his full speed escapes, Lute forms clear ideas about his transformation: he wants to settle down and adapt the image of his family. Lute announces to his family that he wants to become a *payo* (employed) or would like to have, at least, a *payo* image. In a shot inside the house, Lute gets worked up and declares new and strict measures. He speaks like a gypsy eating half of the words, with a stressed intonation. His family listens to him and asks him about this transformative process. Lute answers that they have to learn to read and to write at the very least. Another sequence shows Lute reading in a frontal medium close-up. He pronounces the words correctly not forgetting the last syllable. At the same time, we hear the voice of his brother reading like a beginner: hesitating, slowly pronouncing the words, like a child that is learning to read. The next shot shows his sister and his two brothers sitting at the table and writing. The way that his brother takes the pencil in his hand expresses the newness of this activity: he pushes down too much and looks serious while writing. They have to change their lifestyle and this alteration invariably changes the image of their bodies. Lute is at the origin of this revolution.

Francoism

In the 1960s, the Francoist government was strongly criticised beyond the borders of Spain. In one sequence of the first film a civil servant argues on the phone saying that foreign reactions do not interest him. Another civil servant then enters and announces that there are protests in several universities throughout Spain. They discuss together and while they are informed about the helping hand of Lute, the first one chooses to transmit the news. It is more interesting to speak about delinquency than it is to discuss international reactions; the myth of Lute is instrumentalised to avoid conversations about internal politics. Subsequently, all the writing staffs of newspapers favour the creation of this national myth. Lots of people are interested in his plight: the more he stays in freedom, the more he becomes a hero. Every confrontation with the civil guard reinforces this mythological thought. The newspapers provoke a strong public interest, duly reporting his sightings, which reinforce his powerful position and uphold his mythological strength, despite his desire to live below the radar. The newspapers transmit the point of view of the civil guard and create this common enemy, feeding their own psychosis of being powerless before Lute. This instrumental narrative feeds the Spanish imaginary. He becomes the figure that dared to defy the civil guard. This myth of being a dangerous dissenter is projected on his body when he is in freedom.

Lute becomes a folk hero but he also serves as a threat for the education of children. In France, the same kind of characters exists, but they are imaginary: Croquemitaine, for example, has the reputation of kidnapping children. When Lute hears from a gypsy that Chelo, his ex-wife, now lives in Valencia and that his children are in Madrid, he decides to look for them at their grand parents' home. At night he goes with his brother in an old car to Madrid and they enter into the shantytown area. He enters an iconic setting of poverty- a stereotypical image of the gypsies dwelling place. When he arrives in the house, the grandmother strongly resists the children's departure. Her body, in particular her face, expresses her hysteria and grief: she shouts and sobs because Lute is taking away her grandchildren. The presence of Lute's body provokes an immediate public reaction: the next sequence shows the newspaper headlines about this episode. As the media creates a buzz, the reality is still quite simple: Lute only wanted to recuperate his own children.

Gypsy culture

His life on the run lasts quite a long time and Lute buys a house with his family in Granada. Having become "Don Manuel", he introduces himself as a

Photo 33: Lute's prototype body and the gypsy culture

Venezuelan, wears a suit and a tie, glasses, and a beard. This body thought-image does not reiterate the scrap dealer who has escaped from prison but rather becomes the active prototype of a man who wants to found a family and settle down. However, despite this new physical image, to find a young woman and complete his settling, he looks to the gypsy community buttressed by the idea that his brother Toto is getting married to a gypsy. Lute then marries Frasquita who is a gypsy. Lute merges with distinct identity groups. He dresses and acts like a conventional fellow and he looks to the marginal gypsy community for his wife, exploiting his adaptive abilities to his gain. Dressed up as a businessman, he participates in traditional rituals, like the test of Frasquita's virginity. Lute sits down with his sister and his two brothers next to the tent; Frasquita wears a white dress and has to lie down on a sofa. Several persons are sitting down in front of the tent, among others her father who is looking nervous. The exchange of gazes of the characters outside the tent and inside translates the importance of the ceremony. The silence outside reinforces the girl's shouts of pain, that causes a smile of satisfaction on the father's face. After the test, the woman shows the handkerchief to Lute, now marked with blood. She turns then, in the same medium close-up, to the father who expresses his joy by the thought-image of his body: he is so proud that he tears off his white shirt, starts to shout savagely and to sing. The music begins, people sing and the men take the fiancée out of the tent and carry her in their arms. The wedding party starts according the gypsy traditions. But Luke is in a hurry to leave, because he is afraid that people will recognise him. After this marriage a new period of living on the run begins because Lute's sister is recognised by the police.

National hero

After some time they settle again in an apartment and Lolo, his brother, cannot keep himself under control anymore: he wants to see his wife Maria, who is imprisoned in Valence. Approaching the car, followed by Lute who tries to calm him down, they are taken by the police. Lute's bout of freedom, is once again brought to an end. He will be re-incarcerated but this time at Cartagena, in *la caja fuerte*, which is a maximum security prison. We see the images of Lute, a convoy of cars and motorists take him to the new prison. The voice-over explains that he is escorted as though he were a chief of state. The real chief of State dies two years later and, in 1981, Lute is finally pardoned. The film ends on some photos of Lute surrounded by the civil guards, with his broken arm. This is a well known image and the camera zooms in on it. The next photo shows in a close-up a smiling Lute next to a smiling policeman and the camera pulls back. A voice-over confirms that today he lives like a normal citizen: like a prototype that has surpassed the stereotype of the marginal, like a hero of a real life fairytale about a Spanish *quinqui*.

Conclusion

Lute's body brings together opposed elements that allow for the construction of a mythological thought. In this process, the historical time has a symbolic meaning about two periods: the 1960s for the birth of the myth and the 1980s to give a new image to it with the last sequence of the film.

First his body has ritualised a binary opposition in time. His struggle begins during a politically repressive period. Indeed, he was a hero, due to his audacity and proclaimed wish to be free regardless of what the state thought right. For the Spanish people of the 1960s, Lute encompassed exemplary characteristics. But this cinematographic reading could not be made during dictatorship because of the image that was given of the civil guards, the main pillar of Francoism. Lute was no more than an insurgent from the state's perspective; Lute was able to flout Francoist authority twice. He is therefore a historical Other; a hero for the Spaniards in that period incarnating this desired and fantasised freedom. It is a groundbreaking myth because the heroic aspect is unquestionably confirmed. The films released in 1987 and 1988, as the two biographies released in 1977 and 1979, could never be diffused under dictatorship because of the sequences of torture among other reasons. The film POACHERS (FURTIVOS, 1975), by José Luis Borau, was the first that could give an ironical image of civil guards.[88] Torture had already been shown in THE CRIME OF CUENCA (EL CRIMEN DE CUENCA), by Pilar Miró, released in 1979 and was delayed by military censorship until 1981.[89] In 1987, twelve years after Franco's death, it was possible to show the atrocities committed by the civil guards.

The second historical level of Lute's body image is his mythological value in the 1980s. It is a myth about what has become of a person with a marginal identity, a petty thief of the 1960s who has become a lawyer, a *payo*. Lute was a scrap dealer, forming part of these marginalised groups who were a minority in Spain. They were rejected and poorly integrated into society. He is furthermore reinforced as a marginal when he gets married to a gypsy. Indeed, emphasising the normality of Lute's life in the 1980s delivers therefore another reading: the second film, TOMORROW I'LL BE FREE finishes with this sentence: "Today he leads a completely normal life." In addition, several press articles highlight the same reading in the 1980s: "The story about a *quinqui* that manages to become a myth."[90] "Eleuterio Sánchez, today a respected lawyer, writer and lecturer, was the emblematic hero of the 1960s in the eyes of the public opinion, he became a myth about delinquency through his great ability to escape…"[91] "Today we see the life of 'El Lute', the illustrious *quinqui*, who had become a veritable myth under Francoism and who, thanks to his fierce energy and his unquestionable personal skills lives today like a totally normal person."[92]

He converted into a *payo*. He is an exemplary body for a marginalised group as he demonstrates that he could integrate Spanish society, thanks to the education he acquired in jail (he studied law). In this manner the oppositions between two historical periods (1960s/1980s) and inside the culture (gypsy/*payo)* brought about a resolution. His body is a mediator. The only place where he was lodged, nourished and educated was in a cell without any light. It is from inside the penitentiary system that he could realise his dream and become a *payo*. He benefited from his punishment. Moreover, his jailbreaks permitted him to become a hero in liberty, showing his immeasurable courage. Another opposition: to construct a new identity of a businessman he doesn't hesitate to look for a wife in the gypsy milieu. His body navigates therefore between different poles that are the historical and cultural 'Other': the Francoist prison and the gypsy culture, his periods of evasion allow him to construct himself as he wishes. The binary oppositions so typical for the construction of a myth are brought together by the thought-image of his body over different periods and in different cultural places; they concretise themselves into a new mythological thought in the 1980s. The contradictions reunite themselves inside this reading and are historicised by the context. Press articles explain that he is invited to conferences to discuss the issue of gypsy marginalisation in Spanish society and marginalisation in general. He is a lawyer and a well-known writer in Spain.[93] He has undoubtedly proved his good will, which was an essential prerequisite for his successful integration. He was like a marginal cowboy but the stereotyped idea of Lute's body during this film gets rid of this thought-image and is idealised by a prototypical image: the lawyer that wears glasses, the exemplary integrated gypsy.

III. Running out of Time (Días contados, 1994): drug addiction and terrorism

In the 1990s, images of evil are re-defined in Spanish culture. ETA terrorism, through its destructive and traumatising acts, had become the principal representation of danger. Uribe's film, Running Out of Time (Días contados), echoes societal apprehension and, as does Saura in Hurry, Hurry, (Deprisa, deprisa), he frames this frightening social phenomenon with a love story. Charo, an eighteen-year-old drug addict who prostitutes herself, falls in love with Antonio, who is thirty years old, and who has chosen to dedicate himself to terrorist ambitions. Along the narrative we come to understand that he questions his involvement. Their love story brings about an encounter between two crepuscular worlds. Their lifestyles are destructive and their days are counted. Uribe's film, thus, depicts the myth of a love story, taking place within an environment dominated by destructive forces.

This milieu, at the margin, directly represents the Basque country. The press critiques focus particularly on the terrorist body. While the film was not so well received in the Basque country itself, it nevertheless obtained the Concha de Oro award for the best film at the festival of San Sebastian in 1994.[94] The press reactions categorise Running Out of Time as a good film and the film director's commentaries are often cited. In an interview, he explains his interest in this theme:

> Perhaps it comes from the fact that I am Basque and that I never lived there. It is a way to renew my link to my roots. My first three films respond to the need to make contact with cinema and to use it to acquire knowledge. My cinema then followed other avenues. Today, once again, a character appears that belongs to these latitudes even if the terrorist issue is addressed laterally.[95]

The film dares to deal with a delicate and complicated theme for Spanish culture. Imanol Uribe has already directed several films on problems related to Basque terrorism, such as The Burgos Trial (El proceso de Burgos, 1979), a documentary dealing with capital punishment and ETA terrorists who were sentenced to death during Francoism; ESCAPE FROM SEGOVIA (LA FUGA DE SEGO-VIA, 1981), a documentary about the breakout of ETA members from a prison in Segovia in 1976 and the fiction THE DEATH OF MIKEL (LA MUERTE DE MIKEL, 1983) that, with its recurring sequence of funerals, makes a gloomy backdrop of the topic. Another Basque filmmaker, Julio Medem, as we mentioned earlier, gave the public a voice in his 2003 documentary: THE BASQUE BALL. SKIN AGAINST STONE (LA PELOTA VASCA. LA PIEL CONTRA LA PIEDRA). The documentary is a compilation of interviews with hundreds of people who express their divergent opinions on the subject, thereby revealing the situation's complexity.

ETA is very present in Spain's collective memory; the public homage paid to the victims of attacks is not forgotten. Yet, it is a challenging task to give a concrete form to this problem; it is difficult to represent it through an image of the body. Critics commended the actors' performances yet showing on screen a terrorist character aroused numerous reactions. The filmmaker reacted in a neutral way to these kinds of commentaries, as he explains:

> I had the intention to tell a story about a crazy love (amour fou), a love on the border. I wanted to confront Charo-a drug addict who prostitutes herself- to a character that is equally marginal. I tracked down this character in Spanish reality. The 'ETA Terrorist' was the first to come to mind. I thought of a journalist or even a toreador, but I pushed them back because these would oblige me to tell in a certain way the character's past to place him in this marginality. In the end, I took the "ETA Terrorist" because he is archetypical, everyone knows that it is a character that plays with life and death, always at the margin and at the border.[96]

His comments reiterate that the story is a crazy love story (*amour fou*). Uribe adapted the eponymous novel by Juan Madrid changing the protagonist's profession: instead of being a photographer only, this character is also an ETA terrorist. The woman is an eighteen-year old prostitute who resembles the character in the myth of Carmen:

> What draws me to Juan Madrid's novel is Charo, the female character. She seems to me to be almost an archetypical character through some aspects that are very close to Mérimée's Carmen, through others completely different. In Carmen, the freedom she offers in her performance fascinates me, she adds her love to it and her fatalism, love guided by destiny like in a Greek tragedy. In Charo nevertheless, fatality is not substituted by superstition like in Carmen, but it has a stronger link to the reality of the end of this century in which she has lived. It is a more urban and cosmopolitan fatalism.[97]

The comparison of mythic Carmen to the character of Charo is original: a drug addict who also wants to live freely and independently embodies the archetype of the femme fatale. Imanol Uribe has directed a film about this evil inspired in a love story.

Montage of the bodies

The title reveals the image of the body: Running Out of Time (Días conta-dos). In resemblance to the films Hurry, Hurry (Deprisa, deprisa) and El Lute, Tomorrow I'll be Free (El Lute, mañana sere libre), there exists a direct relationship with the perception of time and the acquired freedom that can be described as non-traditional. In Días contados the uncertainty or the brevity of life characterises time; the days are counted. This is the literal meaning of "Días contados". The perpetual destruction, which distinguishes their environment, leads to their demise. The demolition of life is aimed at the body of others, through terrorism and onto their own bodies, through drugs and terrorism. The mythological story is based on the meeting of these inherently destructive and escapist worlds. Several characters go through multiple stages: first ETA body enters the town, then the encounter with Charo (drug addict) and finally the destruction of all these worlds. The body expresses the encounter, not by exploring the causes and the problems, but by illustrating the devastation.

Two mediators are in the foreground: firstly Antonio's body as a member of ETA. He enters a marginal world, meeting drug addicts and living intimately with them. By contrast, he gets on rather poorly with his two partners, who are also terrorist militants. Several conflicts between them are visualised. Antonio thus becomes the prototype of a mediator between several worlds bridging characters that are marked by different stereotyped features (drug addicts, terrorists) of clandestinity. The police also play a mediating role. A mediator can negotiate between different worlds, which often implies that the character incarnates characteristics of the opposed settings, for example the marginal world and society. The thought-image of the police body, supposed to maintain order and security for citizens, is here represented by a negative stereotype of this profession. The police is shown as overtly aggressive and verbally abusive with the marginalised. The mythological plot is created thanks to the main character, Antonio, who becomes a prototype among highly stereotyped bodies.

Updating the archetypes

The actualisation of these bodies relies on an archetype of liberty. Living in marginality, all the characters refer to an opposition to order, incarnating values that rely on an aspiration towards liberty. Escapism seems to be their chosen solution in order to create a world without constraints. Drug addicts and terrorists, the bodies realise their desire for boundless freedom in a distressing language. Visualising a marginal world that truly exists is not easy. The film director circumspectly chose the actors that eventually brought to life this sensitive topic. The terrorist is interpreted by the actor Carmelo Gómez who is well-known in Spanish cinema. Javier Bardem, who is also a well known and reputed actor accompanies him: he received an award for his performance as a drug addict. The rest of the casting also deserves a commentary since Uribe chose unknown actors: "To count on well-known faces to give an image to marginal characters seemed to me to take away the story's credibility. To find these new faces, I had to put some effort into it."[98]

A marginal prototype

A prototype is created of the terrorist body. Representing the image of such a body in Spanish society is a difficult task. At the airports and in the media, photos of terrorists are ubiquitous; the search to identify and find dangerous offenders is continuous. Describing a terrorist body as a prototype body deserves an explanation: even if he is a member of ETA, notorious for its brutality, he is shown as being vulnerable to his own doubts. Carmelo Gómez expresses through his body this prototype, actualising the archetype of evil in a terrorist body. This character has always provoked many reactions. Despite the difficulty of finding the right person, Carmelo Gómez is an excellent actor as the film director emphasises:

> Carmelo's character seems today, the film once released, impossible to imagine with another actor. It is an extremely difficult character. A complete picture. He resolved the problem with his immense quality and conviction. I am very proud of his work.[99]

Carmelo Gómez' mastery of his art enables him to express a mature image through his acting. Chris Perriam, in his book about Spanish stars, explains that this actor can be described as playing the same character across different films.[100] In the 1990s he played in many of Medem's films (COWS 1992, THE RED SQUIRREL 1993, EARTH 1995). Indeed, his fame is attributed to this kind of cinema. He is celebrated for his ability to merge into his surroundings.[101] This inveterate character, which can be found in several films, is sometimes a member of a distinct community, but as Perriam comments, he mostly represents a solid character, a man of action, a freedom fighter, detective, or policeman,[102] and at the same time an attractive and passionate lover.

In this film, the image of his body expresses his doubt about his actions even though he takes excessive risks. His faith in the terrorist cause starts to weaken. His uncertainties are not expressed by a long discourse but we keenly perceive that he moves away from his convictions through his behaviour. Moreover, his relationships with his partners are punctuated by misunderstandings and accentuated by his independent and autonomous attitude. Elvira Minguez (Lourdes) and Joseba Apaolaza (Carlos) take on the roles of his partners: with Lourdes, he had an affair that he wants to end; with Carlos, he disagrees. The team is divided and Antonio distances himself. It is indeed this behaviour of divergence concerning the principal enemy of Spanish society that allows him to be described as a prototype body.

The actor Javier Bardem, who interprets Lisardo, is as an actor most of all known for his macho roles, such as A TALE OF HAM AND PASSION (JAMÓN, JAMÓN, 1992) or GOLDEN BALLS (HUEVOS DE ORO, 1993) by Bigas Luna,[103] he recently illustrated his vast talents in other roles like THE SEA INSIDE (MAR ADENTRO, 2004) by Alejandro Amenábar, No COUNTRY FOR OLD MEN (2007), by E. and J. Coen, or VICKY CRISTINA BARCELONA (2008) by Woody Allen. In Uribe's 1994 film, he plays Lisardo, the drug addict, in a convincing way. He figures the stereotype of the drug addict: the thought-image of his body is amazing; he constructs the idea of a vague and cowardly person who doesn't hesitate to denounce his friends to the police to buy his drugs. His way of laughing, of moving, of talking, emphasises this idea. He is selfish and thinks about drugs only: all the preconceived opinions about drug addicts are represented by this stereotyped image.

Several other unknown actors in the panorama of Spanish cinema also create stereotyped images of marginality. These characters are damaged bodies at the margin that want to live life intensely. Charo, acted by Ruth Gabriel is submerged in the world of drugs and prostitution. She communicates an image of a woman who sells herself to obtain money to buy drugs. She sustains her habit and is Carmen as a junkie. Candela Peña plays the role of her friend Vanessa. To complete this picture one has to add the character of the cantankerous faced dealer, el Portugués, interpreted by Chacho Carreras. The thought-image of his body, far from being sympathetic, is disgraceful; he has a dirty face, with black teeth. He unscrupulously takes advantage of other people's weaknesses. Finally, Charo's husband is also immersed in the world of drugs; he traffics and is incarcerated at Carabanchel (a prison in Madrid). In the middle of this world, a policeman strolls along with his colleagues and exudes his own brand of violence and antipathy. Representing the mediator, he negotiates with violence and disdain. This marginal world represents doubtless recognisable stereotypes. These bodies are recognisable in their behaviour and surround Antonio's body; the protagonist, the terrorist, prey to his own doubts.

Reading the ritual

The ritual is situated in the frame of the marginalised. The ritualistic acts give the illusion of freedom but end in the destruction of the other through terrorism or drugs. The annihilation of life and the looming idea that days are limited are visualised by the constant provocation of death. The mise-en-scene puts it on the foreground by focusing on two bodies, Charo, a stereotyped body and Antonio, a prototype body. Charo injects her body with drugs; her whole body is framed in a lateral full shot, showing her to be in foetal position. We watch the effects of the drug on her body; this is a scene showcasing her self-destruction. The mise-en-scene foregrounds an image of the body that represents this dark myth: the needles, the curled up body, the eyes closed or completely stoned in a "trip", a long scar on her young body. To obtain heroin, the young woman flaunts her body, transforming it into a professional instrument or even a machine demanding injections. The image of drugs is harsh; this substance transforms the image of the body: Charo wants to escape, and in order to leave behind the everyday perception of the world she destroys herself, demolishes herself.

Another example of the destructive effect is shown and framed by a montage that unites the victims and the aggressors. They co-exist on the screen as at the background a cadaver is shown on television and Antonio is viewed in the foreground. Terrorism also questions the body language: killing a man in the street, from behind, terrorism provokes death; but the backdrop presents Spanish society without providing reasons for the attack. Murdering people is often perceived incidentally: only terrorists know their victim. At the end of the film all the characters are framed together in an immense fire that obliterates them in unison.

The scenes take place in sites that are symbols of the ephemeral; the bodies are filmed living on motorways, in bars, in cities. These are ephemeral sites for identities clearly living at the margin, outside societal norms. The places are often marked by a deliberate obscurity. Bodies are put into scene wrapped up in dim decors, or enveloped in the night. Enshrouding the characters in darkness incessantly foreshadows their ruin. This marginal milieu is stereotyped by a mark that draws attention to destruction. The bodies encounter each other inside a grey setting; their lifestyle is neither commented upon nor interrogated. They live their life, are carriers of an identity and they meet each other. That's all.

Introducing the team

The reunification of several marginal worlds in the same frame is realised up from the beginning of the film. The first sequence illustrates a car driving dangerously as it enters the city. A high angle long shot visualises a motorway. The camera approaches from the right on the car. The sound of a crescendo creates a tense rhythm. A close-up on the driver's face introduces us to Antonio. A car crosses his road, makes a sign with the headlights: Antonio turns around and follows them. A close-up on a woman's face introduces us to Lourdes and then to Carlos; the camera shows us two serious faces, they both look concentrated. They pass a prostitute, on the side of the road, who moves away. Antonio passes and stops: in a frontal medium close-up we see the hesitation on his face, then he moves back to let the prostitute get in.

Antonio, the prostitute, Carlos and Lourdes must pass a control. Antonio parks his car next to the others. Lourdes insults him because the prostitute's presence is a risk for all them. Lourdes and Carlos are waiting on the roadside to observe from afar. The camera follows their gaze. We see Antonio's car pass the control. Several of the next shots show in a high angle the car entering the city. This scene introduces one of the film's central themes: Antonio and his two partners have complicated internal relationships. They seem not to attach much importance to their acts. The discrepancy between his behaviour and that of the rest of the team is introduced by his imprudent decision to pick up the prostitute. Antonio's prototypical features, characteristics that differentiate him from his fellow terrorists, are delineated from the onset.

Encounter

Entering in his apartment Antonio hears knocking on a door and goes outside: he meets Charo who is knocking in a desperate way on his neighbour's door. An indecent image of her body is established by their exchange of gazes, the way that she speaks about her husband and the way she comments on the situation, particularly when she declares needing to "piss" (*mear*) immediately. He wavers, then, lets her into his apartment. The encounter continues inside the apartment: in a frontal medium close-up on Antonio's face handling his photo-camera, he looks at the bathroom. There is not a sound coming from behind the door; he begins to wonder what has happened. The camera follows him when he gets up and opens the door. The subjective point of view shot from Antonio who is in the right part of the shot. Beyond the medium close-up from behind on Antonio, we perceive Charo's body huddled up in the bathtub, dressed in a T-shirt only. A medium close-up shows the syringes, then Antonio's worried face. She gets up, looks at him with glazed over eyes and mumbles that she is not a junky but only feeling a bit nervous. He asks her to leave. Charo's reaction is typical, stereotypical for such a body: ready for anything to have her fix, a body readily becoming indecent to enjoy a fleeting moment of joy. Someone knocks on the door and interrupts their conversation: the neighbour, Vanessa, introduces herself. When he comes back in the bathroom, Charo takes a bath and smokes a joint. She confirms once again some stereotypes about drug addicts. Her attitude expresses her detached stance – she scoffs at everything; she couldn't care less about anything, she lives without a roof over her head and without any respect for the law. She satisfies herself with her drugs and other immediate pleasures, like taking a bath. They argue, calm down and when she notices that he is a photographer, she asks him to take pictures of her.

The next images present Charo's body in all its intimacy: in a frontal shot, she gets out of the bathtub; under her right breast a scar marks her skin. Without scruples she displays herself before him, content with her appearance. She lies down, spreads her legs vulgarly and asks him to take photos of her in this position. He asks her to close her eyes, approaches and puts his hand between her thighs. Charo withdraws immediately and says that she doesn't want to fuck as she is married. The situation is odd because she doesn't hesitate to provoke him. In a frontal close-up on his face Antonio apologises and gets out of the bathroom. Their encounter was brutal and direct; two marginal bodies, the female body exposing her sexuality. A scar damages the image of her skin and her presence is ethereal by the effect of drugs. This is a stereotyped image of a drug addict who attempts to mentally escape reality to find her earthly peace.

Carmen in hell

They meet up with other marginal identities, two girls, and they leave for a bar. A man enters, Lisardo (Javier Bardem): he is a drug addict and his appearance is marked with the appropriate clichés. He is dishevelled and while laughing in a pathetic way he shows us his rotten teeth. He asks for a little spoon to shoot up. This is a hackneyed version of the drug addict, who survives on the street, barely sustaining his life and habit. Charo lets Antonio enter and presents him to Lisardo. The latter shoots up in his neck, a close-up on the back accentuates his gesture (see photo). He enjoys the shock it produces, laughing in a mechanical way. He neighs like a horse, moving his shoulders, almost dying of laughter because of the drug-induced euphoria.

Antonio leaves. The encounter with the characters of the neighbourhood continues. Another mythical image intervenes, codified by the atmosphere of marginality: at the town square, a female street singer starts singing Bizet's Habenera from *Carmen*. In a medium close-up on the back, she holds her hand in the air and approaches the camera focusing on it. She is provocative, wildly moving her shoulders while singing *"L'amour est enfant de Bohème"*. With her face, then with her breasts moving brusquely, she expresses a macabre and sarcastic image of Carmen actualising by her body a rather gloomy adaptation of this famous myth. The camera moves backward and we discover José in a wheelchair next to her, with a disabled body. He wears a typical officer costume with big buttons. Together, they carry out a choreographed scene. José makes

Photo 34: Drug-addicted body exhibited

the same gestures as her, but the effect is ghastly: when she moves her arms, he does the same; when she moves to the right, he follows her. The powerlessness of this disabled man in front of this enormous woman is stressed when she puts herself on the wheelchair in an erotic position. Her enormous female body devours him by her physical presence, blocked together in this wheelchair as they continue to dance. Antonio takes a picture of them, then another of the police headquarters, the next target for an attack that he is preparing in this pitiable district that is so heavily branded by marginality.

All of the characters come together later in the same apartment: Charo and Vanessa turn on the television and Antonio sits next to them to read the newspaper. Lisardo enters in the living room pointing his pistol on Vanessa's friend's forehead. For him this potentially fatal scene is nothing more than a game, a banal act meant to amuse himself. Antonio intervenes; we see his imperious gaze facing that weak and cowardly man, an immoral drug addict, without feelings or compassion. Lisardo moves away, approaching the bedroom door. Turning around, he mimics killing Antonio with a pistol. He looks like a pathetic cowboy. Antonio looks away and Lisardo laughs in a sick way, whining and moving weakly, physically undermined by his drug habit.

Photo 35: A dependent body, Carmen as a junky

Carmen as a drug addict

Drugs destroy and weaken: Charo is a contemporary Carmen, one who is addicted to drugs, and who actualises an ancient mythical image of liberty of the female body attained through the intermediary of an intoxicated body. This is a sinister Carmen. The mythical resemblance is reinforced by the colour of Charo's clothes: black and red. Carmen had José or a bullfighter; Charo has her dealer, *el Portugués*, with an antipathetic face, a tough and rapacious look, incessantly asking for money. The two girls lie down and look at him. This scene is an uneasy exchange of strong images: *el Portugués* has all of the power. Charo is going to take her bag and notices that the money has disappeared. Medium close-up on Vanessa's face who is annoyed and who says she knows nothing about what happened to the money. She furrows her way under the sheets, annoyed, and says to their dealer that they are going to buy the drugs elsewhere. The *Portugués* stays impassive, he leaves, and Charo follows him. In a lateral full shot they are face to face. Charo is half naked, wearing only a red T-shirt, her usual outfit when home, whether she is alone or not.

The two girls are alone in their bed. Vanessa, like a little girl, puts herself in the arms of her "mummy". The camera approaches as Charo remembers that her mother had told her that she was going to prostitute herself to earn money. Vanessa raises her head to look at Charo, puts her hand under her head and says: "I am not a whore, am I?" And Charo replies: "Maybe we are finally." Vanessa turns her head abruptly, looking straight in front of her and says in a decisive way: "Don't say that, we are not whores." In their bed, they are in want of drugs, in need of money. Antonio enters, followed by policemen who are looking for *el Portugués*. The policemen are offensive: two of the three men wear sunglasses even inside the apartment, they have vulgar and brutal faces; they speak to the girls in a rude way "slut, whore, junky." The bodies resemble each other, they are all violent, representing the underworld: not one of the policemen is better educated than these marginal individuals and the confrontation is abrasive.

Coche bomba (Car bomb)

The destruction continues, the terrorists prepare an attack against the police headquarters but a meeting between them underlines their disagreement. Antonio has nevertheless planned with his partners a *coche bomba*, a car bomb. Lourdes parks the car and moves away. We see her coming back running, panicking, because she has forgotten her bag in the car. In a point of view long shot, the three characters observe the explosion, we perceive from far away a vagabond approaching the car: he sees the bag in the car, takes a stone and tries to break the window. The three terrorists cannot wait. A close-up of Carlos' contorted face precedes the image of the car that explodes; they escape in their vehicle. Seeing the consequences of their actions on televised news, Antonio remains indifferent before the pictures of children with bloody faces; he is unmoved by the victims of his crime (see photo).

He looks concentrated; his gaze stays fixed. This is followed by a shot on different screens showing the inert bodies, covered by sheets on the floor. In this frame, Antonio is in the background and we perceive the reflection of the covered bodies. He is their murderer and they are innocent victims of a covert cause. He enters a bar.

A dark picture

The different milieus meet and mix thanks to the love story between Charo and Antonio. The encounter, the intimacy and the birth of feelings are not without risks. Charo and Antonio live their love story at Granada where they go together in the middle of the night. Television images succeed the erotic images. While Charo hangs about the bathroom, Antonio is watching the news on television as they comment on the last attack. Lourdes's face appears on the screen and then his own face; at that moment Charo enters, watches the screen and immediately recognises Antonio as a member of ETA. She then hastily returns

Photo 36: Looking at destruction

to the bathroom. Antonio is conflicted because he has to kill her now. In contrast with the current situation, the television displays the classical and poised image of the royal Spanish family. This is followed by a close-up on a hand that holds a pistol. The camera frames Antonio's face that finds him in front of the television, tense, the arms turned down keeping the pistol prepared. These alternating shots expose several images of power: the classical image of the monarchy and Antonio's underground sort. In a medium close shot we see him hesitating before entering the bathroom. He is waiting in front of the door, enters, the camera precedes him in a close-up on his face then a close-up on the pistol; the camera films the entire bathroom then comes back in an extreme close-up on his face; he has to kill her, it is simply the way things must proceed.

Next to the bathtub, he sees Charo's lifeless body, in a medium close shot, in foetal position on the floor, a tight band still around her arm, the needles next to her, her eyes closed. She isn't there anymore. He drops his pistol. It is a thought-image of a body in destruction, a body in danger on two levels: drugs and terrorism. He takes her home to her place and doesn't kill her, refusing to adhere to the basic rules of prudence. The cause seems less important than his feelings for this woman; he becomes a humanised terrorist, not a blind killer. His body is marked by human feelings that are stronger than orders. These slightly positive features confer him the status of a prototype.

At the end of the film, all these protagonists of the marginal world come together. Lisardo informs the police about Antonio and the women are taken to the police station. Antonio prepares the assault against the police station where the women enter. The world of drug addicts, of justice and terrorism are reunited and create a dark picture of total destruction. A close-up on Antonio's face makes us comprehend that he recognises Charo entering into the police station slightly turning her head towards him. The look they give to one another translates their love in a place on the brink of exploding. Antonio starts running but his days are counted, returning to life is impossible. His partners are in the car, preparing the explosion. Lourdes points the pistol on Carlos' face then turns her head away and cries, her head down. Everything is finished. In a full shot on the back, Antonio runs to the police station, following the car. No noise, no sound. When the cataclysmic fire finally occurs, it is illustrated in complete silence. The fire is yellow, red, filling up the whole image, saturated by the silence. Drugs, police, terrorism, they are all destroyed.

Conclusion

In this film, the link between reality and fiction is not given through the bodies as it is in HURRY, HURRY, (DEPRISA, DEPRISA) or in the films about EL LUTE. The film director dedicates more attention to the choice of unknown actors to elaborate an image of marginality and appeals to some known actors to play delicate roles like the terrorist played by Carmelo Gómez.

The two first films of this chapter have inaugurated the filmic representations of new forms of societal violence (HURRY, HURRY) or depicted with a fresh perspective the plight of ethnic integration (LUTE). The film RUNNING OUT OF TIME (DÍAS CONTADOS), shows a groundbreaking myth about evil through bodies that assume two types of destruction: drug-use and terrorism. Uribe's film updates the archetypes on marginality with contemporary bodies: prostitutes, drug addicts, and terrorists. Through their own self-destruction or through their wilful destruction of others, these identities place themselves in an intimate and close relationship with death. The characters propagate a belief in a world without constraints. Within this world, these identities take on the allure of liberty. Their life can appear to be at times the result of a free choice based on a myth that freedom is accessed through marginality, through a declared opposition to the norm. This process is made clear through the parade of stereotyped bodies that runs through the film. We recognise the reference to the Carmen character, a femme fatale that wanted to live as she wishes. A perverse Carmen and a disabled José peruse the streets of the neighbourhood: the bodies that represent the myth are mutilated. Charo embodies this typical Spanish myth, in black and red, through the clothes that she wears during the film. Her body, shooting herself with drugs, gradually evades her cruel reality: we come to understand that she has chosen to escape the present moment to find her oblivion in intoxicated and transient detachment. Charo is a woman who lives in an imaginary bubble and destroys herself by using drugs. The stereotype of this destructive habit is confirmed as the idea of escaping is revealed to be temporary and illusory.

Inside this stereotyped frame Antonio displays some prototypical features of terrorism through behaviour that while contrasted to his terrorist counterparts, doesn't shed light on the motifs of his cause. He kills but not once explains the motifs of his acts. He seems distanced from his cause even while taking excessive risks. When he is obliged to kill Charo, he fails to do so. At the end of the film, he runs towards the police station trying to save Charo who is going inside of it, followed by the *coche bomba*, and he kills himself. Love is stronger than his ideals: his body is a prototype. The filmmaker highlights the terrorists' humanity by conveying his stance as distanced and by allowing his sentimental interest to override his terrorist inclinations. His unemotional face helps to create a convincing character. Stereotyping a marginal world by highlighting a terrorist's humanity necessitates a mythical construction; this kind of narrative effectively reduces the anxiety usually associated with terrorism.

IV. Conclusion: historicising evil through mythological figures

The aim of this chapter was to analyse the introduction of new mythological figures of delinquency in Spanish cinema since 1975. The three films studied illustrate how the body updates images about evil by depicting it through the characters of drug addicts, gypsies or terrorists. These figures represent three periods that differ in their political and cultural context. The democratic Transition (1975-1983) with the film HURRY, HURRY (1981) by Carlos Saura, the 1980s with EL LUTE by Vicente Aranda and the 1990s with RUNNING OUT OF TIME by Imanol Uribe. The first period is associated with the introduction of new images about drugs, relating the issue to violence in big cities; the 1980s and 1990s show groundbreaking myths about evil in Spanish culture, using gypsies, who already have a historical foothold in Spanish history. In the last film analysed, drugs are linked to the world of terrorism, the latter representing the most threatening problem for the Spanish population.

Drugs

In order to understand the novelty of these images during the Transition, one has to distinguish the three themes and illustrate their presence in Spanish contemporary cinema. For example, as we have already mentioned, the film THE DEATH OF MIKEL (LA MUERTE DE MIKEL) in 1983 was the last film to represent homosexuality as the main problem in the plot. Several studies of women have been carried out and many more may be done in future. However, our focal point was the new portrayals of the female identity with regard to work and sexuality. On the other hand, the drug addict and the terrorist are involved in violence, so films on delinquency still deal with worrying contemporary subjects. Moreover, the preponderant place of terrorism and the international consequences of this violence, confirm the political pertinence of the subject. Without claiming to provide a complete analysis of the representation of delinquency we mention some dominant tendencies, since 1975.

The body of the drug addict appears at the end of the 1970s through violent images related to youth delinquency. Then a new approach treats drugs comically, without any violence. The films by Pedro Almodóvar, which were released in the 1980s, are still the most memorable. The film director introduces this subject in DARK HABITS (ENTRE TINIEBLAS, 1983) and TIE ME UP! TIE ME DOWN! (¡ATAME!, 1989) to mention only two films. The topic is handled inside a comedy that is visualised in the auteur's typical language. He breaks through the taboos on drugs, dealing with them as if they were a commonplace occurrence; his presentation of drugs makes them even more provocative. Another comedy GOING DOWN IN MOROCCO (BAJARSE AL MORO, 1989) by the filmmaker Fernando Colomo shows characters who consume drugs and who are not at all marginalised. The dramatic aspect is completely absent.

The body of the drug addict is however still visualised in a dramatic setting in the 1990s. A well-known example is the film NEIGHBOURHOOD (BARRIO, 1998) by Fernando León. The story is about three boys who, having no money to go on holiday, spend the summer in Madrid. One of their brothers, according to the father's stories, seems to always be travelling to attend conferences. One day the young boy discovers the viaduct where his brother lives. He sees his brother injecting himself with a needle in the leg: the realistic aspect of these images is still disturbing. In summary, in recent decades, the body of the drug addict is still witnessed because, invisible in Francoist cinema, the junky becomes a protagonist during the Transition and a secondary character in the 1980s and 1990s. The phenomena's novelty enabled the creation of a new mythological figure of evil during the 1970s. Then, in the following decades (the 1980s and 1990s, the Transformation period), the stories present a social picture without either pity or the poignancy of the earlier periods. The aesthetics of the drug addict's body nevertheless remain disturbing.

The "domestic-Other"

The figure of the gypsy imposes also other readings in Spanish contemporary cinema. Representing exoticism and passion, often mise-en-scene by stereo-typed images, this body is updated through the image presented in a variety of films. The fiction about EL LUTE takes back a historical vision of Francoism ac-tualising it in the 1980s. The character Eleuterio Sánchez, alias EL LUTE, honours the myth through his sheer survival and his testament to social ascension, va-liantly begun during Francoism and resulting in his complete integration in the 1980s. Indeed, the rags-to-riches narrative terminates with Lute as a lawyer and writer. A recent publication by Isabel Santaolalla (2005)[104] offers interesting ana-lyses of the representation of ethnic differences in Spanish cinema. Exploring the image of the gypsies, she describes them as the "eternal domestic-Other", which is revealing for their place in Spanish culture. Concerning the period since 1975, she analyses gypsy aspects in the flamenco musical trilogy by Saura. Then, for the period of the 1990s until today, she notices the emergence of a new exoticism with Joaquín Cortés, actor and flamenco dancer, acting among others in THE FLOWER OF MY SECRET (LA FLOR DE MI SECRETO, 1996) by Pedro Almodó-var. She also notes the presence of the flamenco rock group Ketama in the film GYPSY SOUL (ALMA GITANA, 1995) by Chus Gutiérrez. This film is about the for-bidden love between a payo and a gypsy. The protagonist, Armara Carmona, is of gypsy origin.[105] Two other films cover this subject: I COME (VENGO, 2000) by Tony Gatliff and GYPSY (GITANO, 2000) by Manuel Palacios. The latter still pro-vokes lively debates among gypsies who denounce the stereotypical image pre-sented of their community.[106] The perseverance to react to degrading precon-ceived ideas can be noticed in the multiple reactions on the released films, now published in Santaolalla's book. A similar tendency was also confirmed in the same period in the exhaustive study by José Angel Garrido (2003) on their cine-matographic representation: scrutinising their filmic images, he concluded clearly that many realistic aspects about their life were rarely exposed.[107] It is therefore logical that this minority group still harshly questions the supposed realistic aspect of the transmitted images.

It also confirms the fact that the current debate is still continuing, because in the end the stereotyped idea is detected and condemned. Its function is to apply for a change by contrasting it with new images. The transmitted clichés of the robber, his exoticism and passion are accompanied by exemplary images (pro-totypical bodies) of the will to integrate and become a *payo* (EL LUTE). This film takes back Francoist images and modernises them by viewing that epoch from the current period. The cultural and historical context allows for the making of the reading of these images that refer to ancient clichés and update them at different moments through cinema. In short, as Santaolalla formulated it so well, the gypsy is still the Spanish "domestic-Other", being of another ethnicity, representing exoticism and passion within the culture.

Terrorism

Terrorism received a new wave of attention in Spanish society after the attack of the 11 March 2004. From the earliest days there have been attempts to illustrate this subject cinematographically. The period of the Transition shows films about the assassination of Carrero Blanco and documentaries by Imanol Uribe, THE BURGOS TRIAL (EL PROCESO DE BURGOS, 1979) and ESCAPE FROM SEGOVIA (LA FUGA DE SEGOVIA, 1981). In the 1980s and 1990s fiction films and documentaries were released, but their number was restricted, given the importance of the problem for Spanish society. RUNNING OUT OF TIME (DÍAS CONTADOS) shows terrorism discretely as an auto-destructive force. Several films outline this approach filming protagonists who regret their terrorist actions. Two examples mentioned in Carmona's book on ETA are: BLINDED (A CIEGAS, 1997), by Daniel Calparsoro and THE BEACH OF THE GREYHOUNDS (LA PLAYA DE LOS GALGOS, 2002), by Mario Camus (with the same actor, Carmelo Gómez).[108] In the 2000s, the political reactions testify to a continued preoccupation with the subject. Already quoted, the film by Medem THE BASQUE BALL: SKIN AGAINST STONE, (LA PELOTA VASCA. LA PIEL CONTRE LA PIEDRA, 2003), is still the most revealing as its release provoked a furious polemic.[109] Josetxo Cerdán recently published a convincing overview of Medem's contribution: he points out that Medem's film was new because of the identity of the filmmaker who had not previously dealt with the subject in a direct way.[110] Cerdán explains that, after the murder of Miguel Angel Blanco in 1997, this film exhibits some nationalistic statements.[111] But at the same time, politics are changing so rapidly, which means that he also considers this documentary to be a close-up on 2004, illustrated by the polemics within the film, which demonstrate how society and terrorism are closely intertwined.

Regarding ETA decisions, two periods of truce were fundamental: from 1998 to the beginning of 2000 (the 21st of January)[112] and a second one, from the 22nd of March 2006 to the end of the same year.[113] The number of victims has decreased since 2000 but terrorism is still present.[114] Regarding ETA terrorism and the number of victims, we notice that there is a different period between 2003 and 2006, because in 2004 Spain was struck by international terrorism. The current period since 2000 is completely different, so let us reconsider some filmic trends since the truce and since the international attack of 11 March 2004.

Some new films confirm a trend of revisiting the past. In 2000, filmmaker Helena Taberna released *Yoyes*. Played by Ana Torrent. Torrent is the well-known actress from Victor Erice's, THE SPIRIT OF THE BEEHIVE (EL ESPÍRITU DE LA COLMENA, 1973) and from Saura's RAISE RAVENS (CRÍA CUERVOS, 1975). Now an adult, her character narrates a real-life story about the first woman to be a member of the leading staff of ETA in the 1970s and who was murdered in the 1980s by her former comrades. After her exile she no longer wanted to continue her activities with ETA. As Elise Costa Villaverde points out, Helena Taberna's first feature film was well received in Spain, as it was in the period during which hope for peace was alive and well, considering the fact that ETA had just declared a truce. Helena Taberna's character was informed by psychological insight. Her character was formed out of her convictions, her life, showing her to be an individual and not a political or ideological icon.[115]

Two other films that revisited the past are THE WOLF (EL LOBO) from 2004 and GAL from 2006. Directed by the French filmmaker Miguel Courtois, who knew the Basque country very well as he grew up there. The project was first proposed to the Spanish director Fernando León de Aranao, but he was finishing his film PRINCESSES (PRINCESAS, 2005).[116] Courtois accepted the project and returned to the 1970s with the film THE WOLF (EL LOBO). It is an action thriller, with Eduardo Noriega as the protagonist. A handsome and popular actor, he is known internationally for films such as OPEN YOUR EYES (ABRE LOS OJOS) by Alejandro Amenábar. The story is about an undercover agent who helped the Francoist government denounce his ETA comrades: it led to the fall of some hundred ETA leaders.[117] His real name was Mikel Lejarza, who infiltrated ETA organisation between 1972 and 1975. The film shows how he was used by the government and then had to continue his life with a completely new identity. Plastic surgery, putting on gloves when he is filmed to cover his hands: he still lives in fear that his actions will be avenged as ETA calls for his assassination. The film GAL (2006) also represents a real-life aspect of terrorism. In the 1980s (from 1983 to 1989), the government infiltrated ETA, using violence to justify the operation politically.

The complexity of the relationship between the Spanish government and terrorism inspired other filmmakers to create new visions. From this viewpoint I would like to mention a recent film made by Jaime Rosales. The first title worth mentioning is SOLITARY FRAGMENTS (SOLEDAD, 2007) – a film that is not entirely based on terrorism, but nevertheless shows the consequences of losing someone subsequent to an attack. The film received a Goya award for Best Film and Best Mise-En-Scene. After this film, he immediately directed another one completely focused on the issue, entitled: BULLET IN THE HEAD (TIRO EN LA CABEZA, 2008). Rosales creates an artistic vision on the relationship between the viewer and an ETA terrorist.

The film is based on a real event that took place in the south of France in 2007 that resulted in the death of two policemen.[118] The protagonist played by Ion Arretxe represents everyday life in a sort of mute cinema, as through the images provided were the work of a surveillance camera. As a viewer we are in front of a screen, observing people over the course of a few hours, in their daily activities. The main characters come together, organise their crime, eat, make love, but no dialogue can be understood. At the end of the film, suddenly, the murdering takes place. The viewer is confronted with his own feelings toward this illegible world: images, daily scenes, human beings, but no explanation about what has happened. This film disturbed many spectators: the absence of dialogue, the lack of any intelligible explanation for the actions leaves the spectator dumbfounded.

The release of this film in Paris was quite an event. The actor and the film director came on stage afterwards and started commenting and explaining the film. It was a weird experience to hear them suddenly talking and explaining this artwork that we had just been watching. The main actor Ion Arretxe claims the power of no dialogue: the government and the Basque country use the same terms. They wish to have peace and a democracy. He considers that this dialogue of reconciliation is contaminated: it is no longer possible to talk about it. When there are too many words that lack a meaning or aim, it becomes like noise. This film creates this idea. Rosales comments that he as the filmmaker did not know what they were talking about: we as viewers are supposed to know something, but apparently they spoke about awkward issues. At the end of the film we hear: *chacurra*, which is a Basque term. It refers to a dog used by terrorists to detect policemen. As Ion Arretxe explains, when you hear this word in Basque, you know something awful will happen. Rosales once again provoked a polemic with this film as he had humanised the terrorist, something what is still difficult to do.

Spanish (international) politics and cinema since 1990s

Finishing this part on the impact of terrorism, the international attack of the 11 March 2004 was fundamental. Once again, how should we react to this event through cinema? How to visualise destruction that was so massive and cruel? In this context let us first consider the legendary documentary: WITH GOOD REASON (HAY MOTIVO) shot in February 2004, shortly before the elections of 14 March 2004, and therefore also made before the Al Qaeda terrorist attack. Many reputed film-directors participated in this project such as Icíar Bollaín, Isabel Coixet, Fernando Colomo, José Luis Cuerda, Julio Medem, Imanol Uribe, and so forth. These well-known filmmakers express their political discontent and denounce the government's lack of responsibility on several subjects. The Spanish government had engaged with the war in Iraq and the population had protested already several times. Other topics were treated (such as violence towards women, that with the Euro everything became more expensive, etc). However the events shortly after marked this film relating it to terrorism. The attack of 11 March 2004 caused 192 fatalities and more than 1400 injuries. The attack devastated the population. The government had lost all credibility by immediately accusing ETA in order to stay credible, given the elections that followed only some days later and given the country's commitment to the war in Iraq (that had already provoked numerous protests by the Spanish people, without result). It was clear for the population that Al Qaeda was responsible and WITH GOOD REASON (HAY MOTIVO) finishes with an epilogue made by Diego Galán illustrating the government's lies designed to win the elections. The government lost power during that election.

The terrorist attack of Al Qaeda inspired other films such as MADRID 11-M: WE ALL WENT ON THAT TRAIN (MADRID 11-M: TODOS ÍBAMOS EN ESE TREN, 2004) by Jaime Chávarri and Sergio Cabrera. This short film shows the travellers who took that train regularly. One day, the same train so often used by countless people, claimed the lives of so many and left countless others injured. In this context of terrorism and victims, another documentary is important THE FORGOTTEN (OLVIDADOS, 2004) by Iñaki Arteta. Interviewing family members sitting in front of the camera makes it an impressive document. The stories go back also to the earlier periods of ETA terrorism from the late 1970s, knowing that in 1979 and 1980 there were many victims. Often the family members felt ashamed that they were victims: there was a social shame that weighed upon them. Even if this document is particularly based on ETA terrorism, the perception of terrorism has of course changed. Conchita Martín's husband worked for the Army and was killed on 21 January 2000, the first victim after the truce. In the complete interview in the extras on the DVD, the widow Conchita Martín comments that people are nervous because of the events of 11 March 2004. They realise that it could happen to anyone. Paying attention to the victims continued. In 2005 the filmmaker Iñaki Arteta made THIRTEEN AMONG THOUSAND (TRECE ENTRE MIL), in which he films these thirteen families, knowing there were many more victims. This film about the victims of terrorism was nominated for the Goyas.

We cannot compare the two forms of terrorism even if they were politically related because of the elections in 2004. Another fact is that Spanish society has unquestionably been confronted with this phenomenon over the last several decades. In this book we went back to the 1970s by focusing on the change of film language, topics and style by creating new ideas. We notice therefore that new trends emerged in the 1990s as, because of international and national politics, Spanish filmmakers in particular engage with their social reality and their historical memory. WITH GOOD REASON (HAY MOTIVO) is one example of reflecting on Spanish reality and the political context. Román Gubern compares it with the American documentary FAHRENHEIT 9/11 (2004) by Michael Moore, emphasising the fact that the political circumstances in Spain were different when making this political statement.[119] Although the film was not screened to large audiences, its symbolic value is still of great importance.[120] Comparing it also to the American documentary, Jean Claude Seguin concludes that FAHRENHEIT 9/11 is the fight of a single man, while WITH GOOD REASON (HAY MOTIVO) is the fight of the entire population showing that cinema can still be a powerful weapon against an autistic government, veiled in lies, completely isolated by its politics.[121] New publications confirm that it was a much wider trend. Juan Miguel Company and José Javier Marzal refer to the famous phrase of President Aznar (1996-2004) stating that Spain was doing well. The strong reactions illustrate the uneasiness in Spanish society due to the disconnection that existed between politicians and social reality. Company and Marzal consider Fernando León's cinema, and in particular the fiction NEIGHBOURHOOD (BARRIO, 1998), as a good example for delivering an image of marginality in a country that is supposed to *va bien* (go well).[122] This phrase used by President Aznar became a national slogan. The intense relationship between Spanish cinema, the political context and reality is revived with a lot of conviction.

This trend is confirmed by several cineastes who previously filmed other themes. Current subjects on social issues renew their vision. I merely mention some well-known examples. The director Alejandro Amenábar uses another register with THE SEA INSIDE (MAR ADENTRO, 2004), inspired by a real-life story about euthanasia. For this film he received an Oscar in 2005. The film TAKE MY EYES (TE DOY MIS OJOS, 2003) by Icíar Bollaín, deals with domestic violence against women, a topic that received a lot of attention in the country. Also Fernando León's films continued to represent marginality, such as drugs, unemployment, prostitution in NEIGHBOURHOOD (BARRIO, 1998), MONDAYS IN THE SUN (LOS LUNES AL SOL, 2002) PRINCESAS (PRINCESSES, 2005) and AMADOR (2010). All of these films confirm the emergence of a new stream in Spanish cinema since the 1990s that witness a close relationship with society, culture, the political situation and historical memory.[123] The filmmakers feel committed to their own social reality and to their past, and create new images to express these issues. In this general overview, terrorism has found its place like a central event. It's impossible to marginalise, and still hard to create an image about the terrorist and its convictions. Maybe now the victim's family is the new protagonist, being faithful to Annette Wieviorka's thesis about the *Era of the Witness*.[124] There's also a trend in Spain to commemorate the Civil War and the Franco repression. Victims of terrorism form part of this violent past.

Concluding this chapter, before concluding the entire thesis of the book, I summarise the main trends. In this last chapter, we scrutinised the newly introduced images of violence and delinquency during the Transition periods. This allowed us to focus on the evolution of several identities that move from the Spanish cultural margin to the centre of the narration. The increase of drug-consumption related to violence to obtain it, the desire to change the social status of gypsies and the dominating presence of terrorism are typical Spanish themes that are related to precisely defined periods. Once again, myths show us how new phenomena are structured, while imposed on a society. Myths represent a constructed imaginary about its own culture. They are historicised over several decades and, thanks to the body image, we can analyse the meaning of their ideas on the screen. Comparing three chapters and three groups allows us to conclude with a number of methodological questions about myths and the body.

Conclusion

Novel representations of the body inform post-1975 Spanish film; after Franco, new images of the body began to reflect equally new thought-images, thereby revealing innovative choreographies of thought. While Pedro Almodóvar remains the most famous film director of the period, putting bodies that were dissident under Francoism at the centre of his cinema, he was nevertheless preceded and accompanied by other influential directors who also focused on taboos. Eloy de la Iglesia, Vicente Aranda, José Luis Garci, Imanol Uribe and Carlos Saura contributed to refreshing Spanish film by dealing directly with forbidden topics. Indeed, several foundational films exemplify this trend, such as POACHERS, (FURTIVOS, 1975) by José Luis Borau, MY DAUGHTER HILDEGART, (MI HIJA HILDEGART, 1977) by Fernando Fernán-Gómez, Pedro Olea's A MAN CALLED AUTUMN FLOWER, (UN HOMBRE LLAMADO FLOR DE OTOÑO, 1978), Bigas Luna's BILBAO, 1978, Josefina Molina's, NIGHT FUNCTION (FUNCIÓN DE NOCHE, 1981) and Jaime Chavarri's 1980 comedy THE THINGS OF LOVE, (LAS COSAS DEL QUERER, 1989). The transgression of taboos takes place through the transformation of bodies that, in their modified form, create new thought-images. Originally the characters represented dissident identities that were socially forbidden inside the historical context of dictatorship, as they were supposed to stay invisible. These "lost bodies" impose themselves in all of their fragility during the Transitory period, bolstered by a dialogue about life and death, emboldened by the portrayal of the norm and the forbidden. These identities construct themselves in a way that is conducive to the foundation of new mythical figures. As the body manifests a thought-image, it also expresses a kind of choreography of thoughts through its presence. To reflect on the history of Spanish film between the 1970s and the beginning of the 1990s is therefore also to study the changing representation of the body and its thought-image.

Visible bodies

Three focal interests guide this research. The first issue is the relationship between cinema as an institution and its culture. The second is the emergence of new myths and, finally, there is the study of the body. The interaction of these three elements is enlightening. Cinema, first and foremost, presents pre-existing prohibitions through the use of images and guides our view. It allows us to see new phenomena and societal realities through images.[1] This book explores the process of myth creation within a specific context, that of the Transition. This political period was particularly favourable to the creation of an imaginary on newly introduced forbidden topics of Spanish society. These images drew attention right after Franco's death because of the shock effect they created. "Cinema" *institutionalises* the view on these new myths that represent Francoism's Other. In this period, narratives dealing with the proscriptions regarding homosexuality, the independent woman and delinquency abound. The way the bodies are made visible allows one to understand their emergence within a specific timeframe. The body, therefore, becomes an agent of history; by identifying what can be shown and what cannot, the image meets the requirement of defining the nature of visibility.[2] The interaction between these three notions reveals a distanced reading of the new phenomena introduced in the Transition period, a conscientious examination of which has continued in spite of the displacement of this identity from the margin towards the centre.

With regard to societal institutions, archival research demonstrates a dichotomy between legal or judicial measures and the imaginary. As Spanish society had the ambition to rebuild itself, it modified some of its laws accordingly. A gulf is subsequently created between apparent myths and the legal actions taken by institutions. Filmic representations underline the marginality of women, the gypsy and the homosexual, even though these groups are legally defined as equal. Indeed, the imaginary part of a culture does not necessarily transform itself with the advent of new laws. In fact, the imaginary may be closer to a rendition of the then current reality than to the decrees of the penal code. Nevertheless, within this shifting environment, myths are established. Through the construction of belief systems, which are then projected onto new identities, myths are generated.

Ritual and mythological thought

Filmic representations bear witness to the emergence of new images, which reveal new mythical figures. The second chapter deals with the representation of women within the context of their newly acquired freedoms. The female body updates archetypal values of the mother-as-woman (FLUNKING OUT/ ASIGNATURA PENDIENTE), of the femme fatale (CARMEN) and of the bad working mother (HIGH HEELS/TACONES LEJANOS). In these narratives, these archetypes are presented as being liberated in imagination, but in reality the archetypes reproduce stereotypes that permeate traditional values. Laura Mulvey's famous text, *Visual pleasure and Narrative Cinema* (1975),[3] retains all of its pertinence in the analysis of these films. The gaze under which these women are brought to life is highly recognizable. The first two contain a masculine gaze on the female body. In FLUNKING OUT the woman asks José (José Sacristán) to listen to her life's narrative and in CARMEN, Gades' gaze is omnipresent. However, in HIGH HEELS, a public gaze on the female body is provided. She is glorified and questioned. This last mise-en-scene of the feminine body is constructed under a gaze that is directly related to the elaboration of a new mythical figure of freedom. The free woman is to be watched and followed.

To understand the symbolism of the corporal activity, one must first recognise that the body and the ritual are staged within a particular space. Marginalised during Francoism with regard to the public and professional realms, the female body translates the historical context in its way of actualising the archetypes. Accordingly, the woman in FLUNKING OUT (1977) is shown going through the motions of her alienating life within a domestic space. CARMEN (1983) is in a dance school, a site for public creation. Finally, the protagonist of HIGH HEELS (1991) is displayed in entirely public environments, such as aerodromes, television, courthouses and theatres. Women are therefore transferred from spaces characterised by their privacy and exclusion from the public, to sites for performance to end finally on the screen. The last film illustrates this progression in an original way: the selfish mother symbolises, at a certain latent level, the conflict between work and motherhood. This celebrity mother creates within the same body the antagonism between a successful career (one of a star no less) and her role as a mother. Despite her move towards the public, the stage, this character remains at the same time marked by strong recriminations. The underlying reproof of her behaviour points directly to archetypal values. Since freedom is made to be mythical in HIGH HEELS, it is fair to assume that freedom had yet to be completed integrated. After all, free human beings, by nature, do not need a stage to publicly proclaim their liberty.

Homosexuality, in the four films on this subject, is set on stage and portrayed through silly performances, such as the absurd, little dances in SEX CHANGE (CAMBIO DE SEXO) and THE DEATH OF MIKEL (LA MUERTE DE MIKEL). In THE DEPUTY (EL DIPUTADO), however, the homosexual protagonist ends up on a political podium, insist fully his next life mission. In LAW OF DESIRE (LA LEY DEL DESEO) homosexual love is central to the plot and is openly. Still, the amorous relations require the creation of a love discourse and so within the film a double mise-en-scene is created wherein the ideal form of love can flourish undeterred. This technique allows the focus to be placed on the formulation of the love discourse. Similarly, in the changing depiction of women, the margin comes to be replaced by the centre. Indeed, for women, the body moves from the domestic space to the stage and then to the screen. The homosexual, by contrast, moves in the opposite direction from the stage to the home. The ritual of introducing the homosexual identity takes place in obscure sites such as within the darkness of nightclubs or the covert locations of garages and basements and tents. With Almodóvar's, the homosexual identity is forcefully transported to the comfortable confines of the home. The change in location is characteristic of the issues surrounding homosexuality. Marginal or ephemeral sites are replaced by stable and uninhibited domestic spaces. The familial setting is the quintessential location of intimacy and in 1987 it is in this artless site that the homosexual is filmed.

Two archetypes are questioned with regard to homosexuality: new mythical representations of the family and of masculine sexuality are created. The archetype of masculinity is portrayed through the characteristics of virility and physical strength. The archetype of the family, a pillar of Francoist ideology that was understood as being the foundation of society and the proper setting for intimacy, loses its cloistered allure and is broken by ingenuous images of the homosexual identity. In SEX CHANGE the family rejects the protagonist, who ends up founding a new one: admonished by his relatives, the young protagonist nevertheless marries after having undergone a successful sex change. In THE DEPUTY, the archetype of the family is updated, situating the plot within a domestic setting. In order to keep the guise of a heterosexual household, a politician husband and his supportive wife decides to accept the husband's lover. The couple fabricates a cover-up story to explain the paramour's presence. THE DEATH OF MIKEL begins with a marriage's demise: the couple separates after a scene of domestic violence. LAW OF DESIRE updates the archetype of the family by constructing a new image of the familial bond, one dominated by emotion and multi-gendered bodies. Through their focus on an exemplary character, in terms of personality and physical beauty, all of these films confirm the protagonist's homosexual virility. The thought-image of femininity that is projected onto the homosexual body serves only to make homosexuality visible.

The third section also brings us to a distanced reading because, when framing society, the delinquent is placed outside the central focus. His identity is filmed at the margin rather than within the setting of conventional society. Therefore, a certain dualism is present in the construction of myths about this theme. Saura, Aranda and Uribe, carried out extensive research on their characters. Becoming extremely familiar with their subjects and the environments within which they live, the directors were able to reflect a specific understanding of the world, fuelled by its own myths. The characters are thus filmed living their life according to their free will and in accordance to their own ideas. Through their actions, they express their desire to break free from the strictures of society either because they cannot or do not want to obey its rules.

The filmic images created by the directors impose a distance that fragments space: the delinquents are exhibited in the midst of a marginal world, their milieu. This perceptible remoteness allows for the stereotyping of bodies as well as the construction of myths about bodies. The camera's perspective represents the centre. The camera is therefore viewing the location as a problematic site. Indeed, the space anchors the problem and permits the creation of an opposition between the centre and the margin. To sense that one is at the margin, one must, of course, understand where the centre is, but this perception of detachment is enough for the characters to create their own myths within their own frame and without constant juxtaposition to societal norms. The youths of HURRY, HURRY (DEPRISA, DEPRISA) express their convictions about freedom among themselves. When they cross into the realm of the mainstream, hoping impose their will, entering the city at full speed, the forces of order swiftly gun them down. The same punitive logic is explicit in RUNNING OUT OF TIME (DÍAS CONTADOS) in which drug addiction and terrorism are corollaries of freedom and independence; the heroes annihilate themselves and others in a dazzling combustion of the police station. EL LUTE, however, does succeed in being integrated and becomes a rags-to-riches hero. On a podium, he speaks about the marginality afflicting gypsies and of *quinquis*. The ambition to authentically portray social realities is buttressed by an observational approach. The observation approach allows the directors to project a belief system on the delinquents, thereby structuring the imaginary. In so doing, the directors reduce the anxiety commonly felt when faced with these images of civilian violence, which so forcefully impose themselves as of 1975.

The historicised body

Besides the mise-en-scene, which provides a certain point of view, another level of visibility is expressed through the bodies' contemporary language. By updating archetypal values, the body displays at a manifest level existing cultural models. In this way, the body's thought-image historicises the myth. The thought-image connects the body, at a latent level, to archetypal values. Translating the dominant values within the culture, these bodies are understood to be stereotyped or prototypical bodies, making the link visible at a manifest level. To introduce a new mythical figure, the stereotyped protagonist usually functions within a frame that is calling for change. Finally, the confrontation with the prototype fulfils an exemplary function. The prototypical body is typified by current traits that are inextricably bound to the present moment or to a future that is marked by an intense relationship with the present moment (the actor, the political ideas, both characteristic of the historical context).

Ruth Amossy (1991) has written about the link between the stereotype and the state of myth. She explains that the stereotype is negative whereas the mythical model is valorising.[4] According to Amossy, the construction of the stereotype constitutes the first step of myth creation. While this is a necessary step, it remains insufficient, as the model must be bestowed with an ideal model status.[5] The filmic analysis carried out in the preceding chapters demonstrates how the stereotypical body generates the first frame which functions as the starting point for myth creation. By following this reasoning, the stereotyped body is opposed to the prototype body to reach the ideal status. Carrying the signs of their period, their exchange is clearly marked by the historical context. Working with stereotypes instead of types can be explained by the pejorative connotation intrinsic to this concept. The stereotype is more recognisable than a social type because it calls for a change within society and a transfer from the margin towards the centre to make itself visible. The process of creating a stereotype in a society within a certain period relies on the ability to master the body, overcoming it and reducing it to a negative idea by imposing a marginal or distanced reading. This approach makes the body visible. Dyer (1977), with regard to the homosexual body, claims that distanced readings function hand in hand with marginalised understanding of the subject.[6] His book analyses the functioning of types, stereotypes and social groups with regard to homosexuality and lesbianism. Francesco Casetti also comments on the important process of the creation of the stereotype for the female body. His focus neither defines nor denounces the stereotype but rather concentrates on the function of the stereotype.[7] Nevertheless, the stereotype implies a remote view as well as a visibility.

In this conclusion I wish to mention other readings than the stereotype. First of all, Ruth Amossy not only emphasised a negative reading of this figure, but the way of relating this concept to myth construction interested me particularly for this historical context. Then, in this context, it is interesting to mention the book *Stéréotype et lecture. Essai sur la réception littéraire* (1994) by Jean-Louis Dufays. He also concentrates on the reading of stereotypes by introducing some variations. The playful aspect of the reading can, according to Dufays, also be transformed in new settings.[8] As in this book I focused on marginalised identities under Franco, this imposed reading the stereotype for these identities in the 1970s and 1980s particularly in terms of its negative prejudices, nevertheless openly applying for a change and introducing an example by the prototype body.

The concept of the stereotyped body becomes the starting point for a negative frame that is valid for all three observed identities The film FLUNKING OUT, discussed in the second chapter, introduces the female body, questioning the stereotype of the kitchen-bound housewife by paying particular attention to the repetitive nature of her movements and actions. CARMEN equally challenges an image, referring to Bizet, through a body that visualises the *españolada*. HIGH HEELS sets up the stereotype of the bad mother. Within these three films the body not only reflects a stereotype, but also demonstrates a will to change. The third chapter on the homosexual develops the stereotypical body on stage, one that is clearly visible in its marginality. In order to find the egress, to exit marginality, the prototypical body must intervene. The fourth chapter on the delinquent body also exposes the process of stereotype formulation. It exposes the process of the stereotype creation of marginality and also calls for a change through prototypical bodies, which play the protagonists (EL LUTE, RUNNING OUT OF TIME).

This interaction between the stereotype and the prototype expresses the conflicted binary opposition between them and allows for the introduction of new mythical figures within a confined historical period. In the analysis of women, the plot ends with the predominance of the stereotype. The introduction of homosexuality is realised through the meeting between two people that makes the relationship visible, taking it out of marginality. Through the love relationship the stereotyped body, in its femininity, renders the homosexual visible in comparison to another body that is not connoted by effete traits. The relation becomes visible thanks to this stereotyped identity. LAW OF DESIRE (1987) is an exception as the men are prototypes that create a myth within a universe heavily branded by Almodóvar's imaginative vision. The delinquent also testifies to this interaction. His image creates a stereotype, which makes it all the more comprehensible to watch Lute's transformation as he sheds the negative qualities to become the embodiment of prototypical ones. In the film RUNNING OUT OF TIME, we witness the same process of interaction but this time with regard to terrorism. The film illustrates a conversation between prototypical bodies, on the one hand and stereotyped bodies belonging to a marginal milieu, on the other. The dialogue between these bodies, though taking place in a pejoratively connoted environment right from the onset, does not always lead to a change within the plot. However, the exchange between thought-images allows for the understanding of myth construction; the body at once confronts and divulges the ideas of the time period.

The body therefore represents historicised cultural values. To mention only a few examples, Carmen, represents the thought image of the *españolada*. The actress is dressed in traditional garb, accompanied by Bizet's operatic soundtrack. This references a historical source dating back to 1875. The body therefore questions its creation in mythical time by incarnating the historical origin of the myth. The body incarnates the historical origin within a historicised body. The current language in CARMEN (1983) is expressed through the presence of contemporary dancers. In HIGH HEELS the tabloid press' language communicates the contemporary nature of the narrative. For homosexuality, the contemporary aspect is emphasised by the choice of actors, which contrasts with the stereotyped bodies. Finally, for the delinquent body, the contemporary angle is visualised at once through authentic characters and by the representation of socially pertinent problems through the thought-image of the body.

In general, the choice of a particular actor reflects certain cultural values. The homosexual theme clearly demonstrates how the cast is a means to make a political and cultural statement. The presence of actors such as Jose Sacristán, Imanol Arias and Antonio Banderas brings about a depiction of cultural values. They offer prototypes a new allure and merit by the sheer force of their reputations as stellar actors and by their astute choice in movies, preferring to play in politically progressive films (such as José Sacristán representing the *tercera vía*). They create universes emblematic of that period. Iglesia's cinema during the Transition, and then Almodóvar's since the 1980s, have emphasised the exemplary identity of the "good" homosexual: these film directors create recognisable universes that are directly related to a period and to the actors' choice. For the delinquent, the actors could not be more authentic, since they are genuinely representative of that group. With Eloy de la Iglesia, the actors such as Pirri (José Luis Fernández Pirri) or José Luis Manzano reappear frequently in films such as THE SHOOT (EL PICO,1983), THE SHOOT 2 (EL PICO 2, 1984), THE TOBACCONIST OF VALLECAS (LA ESTANQUERA DE VALLECAS 1986). Their physical appearance exposes the reality and the disastrous effects of drug addiction. Just as tragic as these true depictions of delinquency is the fact that they all died of overdoses.

Framing the margin

The different levels of the body's visibility underlines the distance, based on the introduction of a new phenomenon. As we have just explained, in the first instance, the mise-en-scene and the frame impose a gaze on women and on homosexuals by introducing them on stage with their new identities or by employing a double mise-en-scene. For the delinquents, by identifying settings that are conducive to marginality and that are dissociated from the centre, symbolising a location outside of society's norm. Secondly, visibility is translated in the process of stereotyping marginality, calling for a change. This idea of distance is fundamental also with regard to the construction of new myths on these themes. If the body were present at the centre, without assuming the perspective, it would preclude the possibility of creating myths on the topic as projecting belief systems in a phenomenon rarely concerns direct reality but rather the representation of a certain idea through this exposition of a certain body. This process obligates a distance that allows perhaps with time to establish myths at the centre of society. The concept of myths studied within this research confirms the function of introducing novel images. To cause the emergence of certain aspects of the body, within a certain frame, can help to understand how transformations are achieved. The period of the Transition introduced new mythical figures and the Transformation establishes them. But the underlying archetype is often updated within a traditional reading, which invites a vision of the body that is still stereotyped, thus maintaining a distance.

Cinema as an institution plays a fundamental role in orienting the gaze. It prefers, institutionalises, focuses on and mediates the transmission of these images that function as explanatory systems of the world with regard to the era in which they were created or to which they make reference. Thus, the images play an active and important role in the collective imaginary of a society. A paradox is revealed about the centre, subsequent to the duality dynamic. Firstly, within the image a distance is created between the centre and the margin. The mise-en-scene illustrates a gaze that maintains this distance, making the new phenomenon remote. Then, cinema concentrates our vision on certain images. The importance of film in a culture is emphasised by the mise-en-scene, which appears at the centre but which also brings to light marginality. Negotiations and polemics, among other discussions about culture, are brought to life on screen. Cinema is patently very effective in transmitting myths. In the light of myth's inbuilt power to affect the collective imagination, it is necessary to be critical of the transmission of images that are carriers of mythical values.

Notes

Acknowledgments

1. Pietsie Feenstra, *Les nouvelles figures mythiques du cinéma espagnol (1975-1995). A corps perdus*, Préface de Michèle Lagny. (Paris: Harmattan, Champs Visuels, 2006).
2. This book is based on my PhD study: "La Construction de Nouvelles Figures Mythiques dans le Cinéma Espagnol de l'Après-Franquisme (1975-1995)", (PhD diss., University of Paris III-Sorbonne Nouvelle, Film Studies, 12 November 2001).
3. I want to mention the book: *Mind the screen: media concepts according to Thomas Elsaesser*, edited by Jaap Kooijmann, Patricia Pisters, Wanda Strauven. (Amsterdam: Amsterdam University Press, 2008). They comment on the emergence of Film Studies in the Netherlands, explaining that it was in 1991 that Thomas Elsaesser was appointed to the first chair in Film and Television Studies at the University of Amsterdam. I have also analysed this emergence of Film Studies in my country as characterised by a constant relationship to Media Studies and the recent emergence of interest in Spanish cinema (see Pietsie Feenstra, "La enseñanza del cine en Holanda: la migración de la cinephilia y la emergencia del cine español/Filmstudies in the Netherlands: the migration of cinephilia and the emergence of Spanish cinema," in Javier Marzal (ed.), N°29, *La enseñanza del cine en la era de las mulipantallas/Cinema teaching in the age of screens, Comunicar* 29 (2007), 31-38.)

Preface

1. Pietsie Feenstra, *Les nouvelles figures mythiques du cinéma espagnol (1975-1995). A corps perdus*. Préface de Michèle Lagny.
2. Alain Corbin, Jean-Jacques Courtine, Georges Vigarello, *L'histoire du corps*, (Paris: Editions du Seuil, Tome I, 2005).
3. *Ibid.*, 12.
4. *Ibid.*, 9.
5. Antoine de Baecque, "Ecrans. Le corps au cinéma", in *L'histoire du corps, Tome III, Les mutations du regard. Le XXe siècle*, ed. Jean-Jacques Courtine, Georges Vigarellos et al. (Paris: Editions Seuil, 2006), 371.

Introduction

1. Pierre Sorlin, *European cinemas European societies 1939-1990*, London, (New York: Routledge, 1991) 20-21.

2. Marsha Kinder, *Blood cinema: The Reconstruction of National Identity in Spain*, (Los Angeles, London: University of California Press, 1993), 9.

3. The idea of the body as a "personal envelope" is often used in the French language to give particular attention to its aesthetic existence, entity and functioning.

4. Nicole Brenez, *De la figure en général et du corps en particulier. L'invention figurative au cinéma*. (Paris, Bruxelles: De Boeck & Larcier S.A., 1998). Vincent Amiel, *Le corps au cinéma*, (Paris: Presses Universitaires de France, 1998). Fabienne Costa, *Devenir corps. Passage de l'œuvre de Fellini*, (Paris: Harmattan, 2003).

5. Roland Barthes, *Mythologies*, (Paris: Editions Seuil, 1957).

6. I also studied the approaches and theoretical terms introduced by Carl-Gustav Jung, Claude Lévi-Strauss, Mircea Eliade, Gilbert Durand, Ruth Amossy and others.

7. Carl Gustav Jung, *Dialectique du Moi et de l'inconscient* (Paris: Gallimard, 1964), 46.

8. Gilbert Durand, *Introduction à la Mythodologie. Mythes et Sociétés* (Paris: Albin Michel, 1996) 45.

9. Even though censorship was officially abolished, the government had introduced some categories to control the access of audiences in terms of age or by putting an S rating on certain films, indicating violent and sexual images. We will come back to this point in the chapters on film analysis.

Chapter one

1. Román Gubern, "Los imaginarios del cine del franquismo", in *Un siglo de cine español*. (Madrid: Cuadernos de la Academia, Octubre, Nº 1, 1997), 157-158.

2. Román Gubern, *1936-1939: la guerra de España en la pantalla*, (Madrid: Filmoteca Española, 1986), 92-94.

3. Susan Martin-Márquez, *Feminist Discourse and Spanish Cinema, Sight Unseen*, (Oxford: Oxford University Press, 1999), 90-91.

4. In Spanish tradition it is common to share one's first name with one's parents and to take both surnames, that of the father and mother.

5. Román Gubern, *1936-1939: la guerra de España en la pantalla*, 100.

6. Concerning the framing of the image, we summarise the terminology defined by David Bordwell *in Film Art: an Introduction*, (New York, Mc Graw-Hill, Seventh Edition, 2004), 262 and the French terminology by Emmanuel Siety, *Le plan, au commencement du cinema*, (Paris: Editions Cahiers du Cinéma: 2001), 88-89. An extreme close-up: framing a detail (face, object, etc.), a close-up: showing just the face, hands or feet, emphasising details; a medium close-up: frames the body up from the chest (for example, the face and the shoulders); a medium close shot: the person is filmed from the knees up. A full shot: the person is filmed entirely; a medium long shot: the person is filmed entirely with a part of the background showing; a long shot: figures are prominent but the background still dominates; an extreme long shot: the human figure is barely visible, for example framing landscapes.

7. I examine this representation in my essay "Mémoires cinématographiques de la guerre civile espagnole", in *Caméra politique. Cinéma et stalinisme*, edited by Kristian Feigelson, (Théorème N° 5, Paris: Presses Sorbonne Nouvelle, 2005). Focusing on

the image of the International Brigades, I analyse the filmic representation of Communism inside Spanish national cinema since the 1940s. The dominating discourse was completely anti-Communist, sustained in the 1950s by the Cold War. The cinematographic memory considers that they had provoked the Civil War and threatened Spain. Franco presents himself as the person who saved the country, which is again illustrated in *Franco ese hombre* (1964), a film on Franco himself, also directed by José Luis Saenz de Heredia.

8. Nancy Berthier, *Le franquisme et son image. Cinéma et propagande.* (Toulouse: Presses Universitaires du Mirail, 1998), 51, 57.

9. Personal translations, as are all the quotes that will follow, the dialogues from the Spanish films, and the quotes of books published in French or Spanish which have not been translated into English.

10. We already mentioned Román Gubern's book, *1936-1939: la guerra de España en la pantalla,* 95-100. Other groundbreaking publications in France include: Nancy Berthier, *Le franquisme et son image. Cinéma et propagande,* (Toulouse: Presses Universitaires du Mirail, 1998). Emmanuel Larraz, "Raza et le mythe de la croisade dans le cinéma franquiste", in *Les mythologies hispaniques dans la seconde moitié du XXe siècle,* (Dijon: Hispanistica XX, Centre D'Etudes et de Recherches Hispaniques du XXe siècle, Université de Dijon, 1985), 133-140.

11. Virginia Higginbotham, *Spanish film under Franco,* (Austin: University of Texas Press, 1988), 10, 18-22.

12. Barry Jordan, Rikki Morgan-Tamosunas, *Contemporary Spanish Cinema* (Manchester: Manchester University Press, 1998), 17.

13. Roland Barthes, *Mythologies* (Paris: Editions du Seuil, 1957), 215.

14. Hans-Jörg Neuschafer, *Adiós a la España eterna. La dialéctica de la censura. Novela, teatro y cine bajo el franquismo,* (Barcelona: Editorial Anthropos, 1994), 9-10.

15. Steven Marsh, *Popular Spanish film under Franco. Comedy and the Weakening of the State* (New York: Palgrave MacMillan, 2006), 98-99. Referring to the classical study by John Hopewell, *El cine español después de Franco 1973-1988,* (Madrid: Ediciones el Arquero, 1989), and *Blood cinema. The Reconstruction of National Identity in Spain* (California: University of California Press, 1993), by Marsha Kinder.

16. Hans-Jörg Neuschafer, *Adiós a la España eterna. La dialéctica de la censura. Novela, teatro y cine bajo el franquismo,* 49.

17. Julián Juderias, *La leyenda negra: Estudios acerca del concepto de España en el extranjero* (Madrid: Editorial Nacional, 1967, 1st ed., Barcelona: Araluce, 1917).

18. Concerning the *españolada*, I wish to mention two groundbreaking books on this topic, analysing its function over several periods: the one by Valeria Camporesi, *Para grandes y chicos: Un cine para los españoles 1940-1990* (Madrid: Turfán, 1994), and the brilliant book by Nuria Triana-Toribio, *Spanish national cinema* (London: Routledge, 2003). In my research, I focus in this film on the purely stereotypical representation of the cliché.

19. A typical song related to flamenco, without really dancing: an established genre in Spain. I refer to some well-known personalities of the *copla* such as La Argentinita, Concha Piquer, Lola Sevilla, Miguel de Molina, etc.

20. Nancy Berthier, "Espagne folklorique et Espagne Eternelle; l'irrésistible ascension de l'Espagnolade" in *Bulletin d'Histoire Contemporaine de l'Espagne,* no. 24, décembre 1996, (Bordeaux: Maison des Pays Ibériques, Bordeaux III, 1996), 245-254.

21. *Ibid.*, 251-253.
22. Hans-Jörg Neuschafer, *Adiós a la España eterna. La dialéctica de la censura. Novela, tea-
     tro y cine bajo el franquismo*, 215.
23. Leandro Prados de la Escosura and Jorge C. Sanz, "Growth and Macroeconomic
     Performance in Spain 1939-1993", in *Economic Growth in Europe since 1945*, edited by
     Nicolas Crafts, 1996, (Cambridge: Cambridge University Press, 1996) 355-387. The
     Marshall Plan, the so-called European Recovery Program, did not include Spain
     after the Second World War, as it was under the reign of Franco. In 1951, when the
     European Recovery Program was finished, and due to the Cold War, and Franco's
     anti-communist policy, Spain received other financial support, but less than neigh-
     bouring countries.
24. Esteve Riambau, "El cine español durante la Transición (1973-1978): Una asignatura
     pendiente" in *Un siglo de cine español. Cuadernos de la Academia*, No. 1, October 1997,
     (Madrid: Academia de las Artes y las Ciencias Cinematograficas de España), 173.
25. Peter Besas, *Behind the Spanish Lens, Cinema under Fascism and Democracy* (Denver
     Colorado: Arden Press, 1985), 157.
26. Fernando Alonso Barahona, *Biografía del Cine Español* (Barcelona: C.I.L.E.H., 1992),
     103.
27. John Hopewell, *El cine español después de Franco* (Madrid: Ediciones el Arquero,
     1989), 141.
28. Eduardo Rodriguez Merchán, Concha Gomez, "El cine de la Democracia (1978-
     1995)", in *Un siglo de cine español. Cuadernos de la Academia*, no. 1 Octubre 1997, (Ma-
     drid: Academia de las Artes y las Ciencias Cinematográficas de España), 201.
29. Peter Besas, *Behind the Spanish Lens, Cinema under Fascism and Democracy*, 159.
30. Pietsie Feenstra, Hub Hermans, *Miradas sobre pasado y presente en el cine español 1990-
     2005*, (Amsterdam/New York: Rodopi, no. 32, 2008).
31. José Enrique Monterde, *Veinte años de cine español. Un cine bajo la paradoja (1973-
     1992)*, (Barcelona: Ediciones Paidós Ibérica S.A., 1993), 27 (my translation).
32. Paul Robert, *Le Nouveau Petit Robert, Dictionnaire alphabétique et analogique de la lan-
     gue française*, text reviewed and further developed under the direction of Josette
     Rey-Debove et Alain Rey, (Paris: Dictionnaire Le Robert, 1994), no. 2295.
33. I refer to the book by Françoise Heitz, *Pilar Miró: vingt ans de cinéma espagnol (1976-
     1996)*, (Arras: Artois Presses Université, 2001), 54-59. As Françoise Heitz empha-
     sises, it was only the filmmaker who had been accused: when the film was released
     in summer, to avoid problems, the opening credits were completed with e.g. a short
     comment stating that these historical facts from more than 65 years ago had been
     revised and re-assessed by the Appeals Court.
34. Arnold Van Gennep, *Rites de passage Etude systématique des rites*, 1ère Ed. 1909 (Paris:
     Editions A. et J.Picard, 1981). Van Gennep explains how human beings can pass
     from one stage to the other through initiation rituals. Cinema offers a discursive
     frame that visualise new ideas in order to pass to another stage, such as for example
     these films on homosexuality.
35. Judith Butler, *Trouble dans le genre. Pour un féminisme de la subversion*, (Paris: La Dé-
     couverte, 1990), 276.
36. Treating the transsexual character in Almodóvar's film is also a central issue in Isa-
     bel Maurer's book on Almodóvar's work, *Die Asthetik des Zwitters im filmischen Werk
     von Pedro Almodóvar*, (Frankfurt am Main, Vervuert Verlag, 2005). She introduces

the German term 'Zwitter', which means the hybridity of the gender, analysing it in different discourses such as religion, upper and lower class, etc. For this research I prefer the term multi-gender, because of the multiplicity of marginalised identities popping up in Spanish cinema after 1975.

37. Fernando Trueba, in *El País* 27 January 1979, "Sexo y política: un cóctel que vende."
38. Román Gubern, "Los imaginarios del cine del franquismo", in *Un siglo de cine español*, Madrid: Cuadernos de la Academia, (Octobre 1997, no. 1), 158-159.
39. Marsha Kinder (ed.). *Refiguring Spain. Cinema/Media/Representation*, (Durham and London: Duke University Press, 1997), 26-28.
40. Pierre Sorlin, *European Cinemas, European Societies 1939-1990*, (London, New York: Routledge), 200.
41. *Ibid.* 199-206, 215.
42. Michel Foucault, *Histoire de la sexualité I. La volonté de savoir*, (Paris: Gallimard, 1976), 143.
43. José Enrique Monterde, *Veinte años de cine español. Un cine bajo la paradoja (1973-1992)*, 25 (my translation).
44. *Código Penal y legislación de peligrosidad social*, (Madrid: Civitas, 1981), 22.
45. Juan Carlos Alfeo Alvarez, "La representación de la cuestión gay en el cine español," in *Cuadernos de la Academia*, (no. 5, Mayo 1999), 289.
46. Eduardo Rodriguez Merchán, Concha Gomez, "El cine de la Democracia (1978-1995)", 205.
47. Ramiro Gómez B. De Castro, *La producción cinematográfica española. De la Transición a la Democracia (1976-1986)*, (Bilbao: Ediciones Mensajero, 1989), 18, (my translation).
48. Titles in Spanish: CAMBIO DE SEXO (1977); UN HOMBRE LLAMADO FLOR DE OTOÑO (1978); EL DIPUTADO (1979); LA MUERTE DE MIKEL (1983); EL MATADOR (1986); LA LEY DEL DESEO (1987); LAS COSAS DEL QUERER (1989); HISTORIAS DEL KRONEN (1994), etc.
49. Vicente J. Benet, "Notas sobre el film policiaco español contemporáneo", in *Escritos sobre el cine español 1973-1987*, (Valencia: Ediciones Filmoteca Generalitat Valencia), 129.
50. I proposed this approach in my French edition *Mémoire du cinéma espagnol 1975-2007*, (Paris: Corlet, Cinémaction no. 130, 2009), inviting 25 international scholars to scrutinise the change in images over three decades. The period from 1975 until 2007, with the new Law on Historical Memory, is explored, confronting the way the political context changes with every government in relation to debates on this historical commemoration. Every chapter focuses on groundbreaking films dealing with this issue. A fourth chapter is dedicated to the international representation of the Civil War, also commenting on the Dutch television documentary *Franco fugitives on Ameland* (2004) by Paul Ruigrok and Carla Tromp, or by Pieter Jan Smit (2005), *L'ami hollandais Jef Last &, André Gide*.
51. Selecting and giving titles always involves a reduction; however we wish to mention the book by Román Gubern mentioned earlier, *1936-1939: la guerra de España en la pantalla (1936-1939)*, (Madrid: Filmoteca Española, 1986). A French edition by Marcel Oms, *La guerre d'Espagne au cinéma. Mythes et réalités*, (Paris: Editions Cerf, 1986), and a new Spanish edition by Vicente Sánchez Biosca, *Cine y Guerra civil española. Del mito a la memoria*, (Madrid: Alianza, 2006).

52. Ramiro Gómez B. de Castro, *La producción cinematográfica española. De la Transición a la Democracia (1976-1986)*, (Bilbao: Ediciones Mensajero, 1989), 224-226.

53. *Ibid.*, p. 226.

54. *Boletín Informativo. Películas Recaudaciones Espectadores*, Madrid: Ministerio de Cultura, Instituto de la Cinematografía y de las Artes Audiovisuales: Edition 1975-1995.

55. *Ibid.* FLUNKING OUT/ASIGNATURA PENDIENTE testifies by the statistics of a public success in the year of release, 1,873,850 spectators, reached on the period 1978-1987 the 2,200,100. The same tendency for HIGH HEELS/TACONES LEJANOS: in 1991: 1,688,135 (and from 1991 to 1993: 2,014,393).

56. Juan Carlos Alfeo Alvarez, "El enigma de la culpa: la homosexualidad en el cine español (1961-2000)," in *International Journal of Iberian Studies*, (Vol. 13, no. 3, 2000), 136-147.

57. Spanish titles: HISTORIAS DEL KRONEN, YO SOBREVIVIRÉ, PAJARICO.

58. *Boletín Informativo. Películas Recaudaciones Espectadores*, (Madrid: Ministerio de Cultura, Instituto de la Cinematografía y de las Artes Audiovisuales: Edition de 1975-1995). In 1978: 222,789, and in 1979 34,228 spectators.

59. *Ibid.* In 1979: 556,592, in 1980: 671,099 (and until 1984 from a total of 1,231,493).

60. *Ibid.* In 1983: 1,080,891 after LOS SANTOS INOCENTES: 1,756,311 and LAS BICICLETAS SON PARA EL VERANO: 1 135 532.

61. *Ibid.* Spectators: 638 646: after EL LUTE, CAMINA O REVIENTA: 1,117,973 and LA VIDA ALEGRE: 741,894. I wish to mention another film of the Transition period: UN HOMBRE LLAMADO FLOR DE OTOÑO (1980) also about homosexuality with the actor José Sacristán. This film took second place with 784,917 spectators (after VIAJE AL CENTRO DE LA TIERRA: 1,212,025).

62. *Ibid.* DEPRISA, DEPRISA: in 1981: 749,798 (from 1981 to 1990: about 1,022,796). EL LUTE, CAMINA O REVIENTA: 1987: 1,117,973 (1987-1990: 1,317,627). EL LUTE II, MAÑANA SERÉ LIBRE: in 1988: 347,324. DÍAS CONTADOS: 1994-1995: 659,176.

63. *Ibid.*

64. Ramiro Gómez B. de Castro, *La producción cinematográfica española. De la Transición a la Democracia (1976-1986)*, 224-226.

65. Francesco Casetti, *Les Théories du cinéma depuis 1945*, (Paris: Editions Nathan, 1999), 44 (my translation).

66. Pierre Sorlin, *European Cinemas European Societies 1939-1990*, 20.

67. Emile Durkheim, *Les formes élémentaires de la vie religieuse*, (Paris: Presses Universitaires de France/Quadrige, 1ère Ed: 1960, 3e 1994), 89-91, (my translation).

68. Ruth Friedberg, *Window Shopping, Cinema and the Postmodern culture*, (Berkeley, Los Angeles: University of California Press, 1992).

69. Emile Durkheim, *Les formes élémentaires de la vie religieuse*, 89-91.

70. Michèle Lagny, *De l'Histoire du cinéma. Méthode historique et histoire du cinéma*, (Paris: Editions Armand Colin, 1992), 181-182 (my translation).

71. Paul Julian Smith, *Laws of desire. Questions of homosexuality in Spanish Writing and Film 1960-1990*, (Oxford: Clarendon Press, 1992), 130 .

72. Carlos Aguilar, Francisco Llinas, "Visceralidad y Autoría. Entrevista con Eloy de la Iglesia", in *Conocer a Eloy de la Iglesia*, Carlos Aguilar, Dolores Devesa, Francisco Llinas, et al., (San Sebastian, Filmoteca Vasca, 1996), 171 (my translation).

73. Casimiro Torreiro, "Del cineasta como cronista airado: historia e ideología" in *Ibid.*, 16.

74. Paul Julian Smith, *op. cit.*, p. 2 in George De Stefano Post-Franco Frankness, FC 22 (junio 1986), 58-60.

75. Mark Allinson, *Un laberinto español. Las películas de Pedro Almodóvar*, (Madrid: Ocho y medio, Libros de Cine, 2003), 12. Allinson bases this interpretation on a publication from 1611 by Covarrubias, Tesoro de la Lengua Castellana o Española (1943: 99).

76. Antonio Holguin, *Pedro Almodóvar*, (Madrid: Cátedra, 1994), 26.

77. Claude Murcia defines the *"Movida"* as a colourful reaction against imposed culture, creating sites for fashion and ways of expression, in *Femmes au bord de la crise des nerfs. Pedro Almodóvar*, (Paris: Edition Nathan, 1995), 21.

78. María Antonia Garcia de Leon, Teresa Maldonado, *Pedro Almodóvar, la otra España cañi*, (Ciudad Real: Diputación Provincial, 1989), 55.

79. See: Nuria Vidal, *The films of Pedro Almodóvar*, (Madrid, Instituto de la Cinematografia y las Artes Audiovisuales), 1988, 301-302. Spanish titles: Dos PUTAS, O HISTORIA DE AMOR QUE TERMINA EN BODA, 1974, FILM POLITICO, 1974, LA CAÍDA DE SODOMA, 1975, HOMENAJE, 1975, EL SUEÑO OR LA ESTRELLA, 1975, BLANCOR, 1975, WHO'S AFRAID OF VIRGINIA WOOLF, 1976, SEA CARITATIVO, 1976, LAS TRES VENTAJAS DE PONTE, 1977, SEXO VA, SEXO VIENE, 1977, COMPLEMENTOS, 1977, FOLLE, FOLLE, FOLLEME, TIM, 1978, SALOMÉ, 1978.

80. *Ibid.* Spanish titles: PEPI, LUCI, BOM Y OTRAS CHICAS DEL MONTÓN, 1980, LABERINTO DE PASIONES, 1982, ENTRE TINIEBLAS, 1983, ¿QUÉ HE HECHO YO PARA MERECER ESTO?, 1984, MATADOR, 1986, LA LEY DEL DESEO, 1987, MUJERES AL BORDE DE UN ATAQUE DE NERVIOS, 1988, ¡ATAME!, 1989, TACONES LEJANOS, 1991, LA FLOR DE MI SECRETO, 1995, CARNE TRÉMULA, 1997, TODO SOBRE MI MADRE, 1998, HABLE CON ELLA, 2002, LA MALA EDUCACIÓN, 2004, VOLVER, 2006, ABRAZOS ROTOS, 2009.

81. María Antonia Garcia de Leon, Teresa Maldonado, *Pedro Almodóvar, la otra España cañi*, 63.

82. *Boletín Informativo. Películas Recaudaciones Espectadores*, (Madrid: Ministerio de Cultura, Instituto de la Cinematografía y de las Artes Audiovisuales: Edition de 1980-1995).

83. *Ibid.*, THE HEIFER (LA VAQUILLA) has received 1 793 999 entrances and WOMEN ON THE VERGE OF A NERVOUS BREAKDOWN (MUJERES AL BORDE DE UN ATAQUE DE NERVIOS) 1 784 697 in the same year.

84. In 1998, since ALL ABOUT MY MOTHER (TODO SOBRE MI MADRE), the Goyas have also been awarded to this filmmaker. In 2006 as best filmmaker, for TO RETURN (VOLVER). Often his actresses or actors received an Award, but not the film director himself. He received lots of awards from abroad (check the website of El Deseo).

85. Nuria Vidal, *El cine de Pedro Almodóvar*, (Barcelona: Edition Destinolibro, no. 285, 1988), 16-17, 245.

86. "LUZ CASAL edita un disco con las canciones de *Tacones lejanos"*, in *Pronto Madrid*, 7 December 1991.

87. Several scholars have already commented on the presence of new myths in the audiovisual media, I refer to (among others) the book *De Superman au Surhomme*, d'Umberto Eco, (Paris: Editions Grasset-Fasquelle, 1ère Ed. 1978). Concerning archetypes; James F. Iaccino, *Jungian Reflections within the Cinema. A psychological Analysis of Sci-Fi and Fantasy Archetypes*, (Road West: Greenwood Publishing Group, 1998); the author analyses the Jungian meaning of archetypes, focusing above all on

the structure of the narrative. The conference by Claudio Cifuentes Aldunate, "El mito del cuerpo en el cuerpo del mito: escritura e imagen", published in *Mitos*, Vol. I, (Zaragoza: Collección Trópica 4, 1998), 118-122, explained to us the particular link between the body and myth.

88. Paul Ricoeur, *Temps et récit. Tome III. Le temps raconté*, (Paris: Editions du Seuil, 1985), 189-193.
89. Mircea Eliade, *Aspects du mythe*, (Paris: Editions Gallimard, 1963), 26 (my translation).
90. Claude Lévi-Strauss, *Anthropologie structurale*, (Paris: Editions Plon, Ed. de 1956), 235-265.
91. *Ibid.*, 260.
92. Paul Valéry, *L'Ame et la danse*, (Paris: Editions Gallimard, 1944), 172 (my translation).
93. Michel Bernard, *Le corps*, (Paris: Editions du Seuil, 1995), 140 (my translation).
94. Ruth Amossy, *Les idées reçues. Sémiologie du stéréotype*, (Paris: Editions Nathan, 1991), 21 (my translation).
95. *Ibid.*, 103 (my translation).
96. Jacques Aumont, "Le point de vue", in *Enonciation et Cinéma, Communications,* (no. 38, 1983), 3-29.
97. Bill Moyers, *El poder del mito. Joseph Campbell en diálogo con Bill Moyers*, (Barcelona: Colleción reflexiones, Emecé Editores, 1998), 36.
98. José Gil, "Le corps, l'image, l'espace", in *La danse, naissance d'un mouvement de pensée, ou le complexe de Cunningham*. Ouvrage réalisé par la Biennale Nationale de Danse du Val-de-Marne, (Paris: Editions Armand Collin, 1989), 73 (my translation).

Chapter two

1. Pilar Escario, *Lo personal es político: el movimiento feminista en la transición*, (Madrid: Instituto de la Mujer, 1996), 74-75.
2. Elise Garrido Gonzalez, *Historia de las mujeres en España*, (Madrid: Síntesis, 1997), 528, 544-545.
3. Pilar Escario, *Lo personal es político: el movimiento feminista en la transición*, 88-90.
4. Elisa Garrido González, *Historia de las mujeres en España*, 495-496.
5. *Código Penal*, (Madrid: Civitas, 1996), 22.
6. Instituto de la Mujer, *Situación Social de la Mujer en España*, (Madrid: Instituto de la Mujer, 1986), 193.
7. *Ibid.*, 181, 189.
8. A. Blanes, F. Gil, J. Pérez, *Población y actividad en España: evolución y perspectivas*, (Barcelona: Colección Estudios e Informes, Caja de Aharros y pensiones, 1996), 7.
9. Elisa Garrido González, *Historia de las mujeres en España,* 562.
10. *Ibid.*, 47, 22.
11. *Ibid.* (my translation).
12. Laura Mulvey, "Visual pleasure and Narrative Cinema", in *Screen* (16), 3, 1975. Quoted or published in numerous books and magazines.

13. Ginette Vincendeau, "1973-199... Lectures féministes", in *Histoire des théories du cinéma*, edited by Joel Magny and Guy Hennebelle 116-129. (Paris: Cinémaction no. 60, 1991), 118.
14. *Ibid.* (my translation).
15. Francesco Casetti, *Les Théories du cinéma depuis 1945*, 247 (my translation).
16. John Hopewell, *El cine español después de Franco 1973-1988* (Madrid: Ediciones el Aquero, 1989), 243-244.
17. Agustin Sánchez Vidal, *Retrato de Carlos Saura* (Barcelona: Circulo de Lectores, Galaxia Gutenberg, 1994), 49 (my translation).
18. Susan Martin-Márquez, *Feminist Discourse and Spanish Cinema. Sight Unseen*, 3-4.
19. Barry Jordan and Rikki Morgan-Tamosunas, *Spanish Contemporary Cinema*, 114-117.
20. Hans Beerekamp: "Authenticiteit door siliconen en pikant melodrama" (Authenticity through silicon and spicy melodrama), in NRC Handelsblad, 01-03-2000, "Almodóvar toont zijn vrouwenhaat", in NRC Handelsblad, 25-09-2002, "Lady killer ontpopt zich als seriemoordenaar. Beelden van een 'hip' Spanje, Almodóvar toont zijn vrouwenhaat" (Lady killer becomes a serial killer. Images of a modern Spain; Almodóvar shows his hatred of women, 25-09-2002/07-02-2006, my translation).
21. Joris Henquet, "Almodóvar as a woman-hater: why Pedro Almodóvar is not unanimously described as a women's director." This is an unpublished essay, written for the masters course on Spanish cinema at the University of Amsterdam, 2008.
22. Mark Allinson, *Un laberinto español. Las películas de Pedro Almoóvar*, 99-100.
23. *Ibid*, 121.
24. Barry Jordan and Rikki Morgan-Tamosunas, *Spanish Contemporary Cinema*, Susan Martin Marquez, *Feminist Discourse and Spanish Cinema. Sight Unseen*.
25. Rodríguez, M.P., M.C. Ausan, E. Costa Villaverde, *Estudio cuantativo sobre la igualdad de género en el panorama de la ficción audiovisual*, (Madrid: Instituto de la Mujer, Ministerio de Trabajo y Asuntos Sociales, 2007).
26. Barry Jordan, Rikki Morgan-Tamosunas, *Spanish Contemporary Cinema*, 124.
27. Susan Martin-Márquez, *Feminist Discourse and Spanish Cinema. Sight Unseen*, 280.
28. Fatima Arranz, Esperanza Roquero, Pilar Aguilar, Pilar Pardo, Blanca Rilova, Olaya Alvarez, *La situación de las mujeres y los hombres en el audiovisual español: estudios sociológico y legislativo.* (Madrid: Universidad Complutense, 2008), 56-57.
29. The 28th of March 2008, Patricia Ferreira delivered a conference about women directors in Colegio de España in 2008-2009, Paris.
30. Carlos E. Heredero (ed.), *La mitad del cielo. Directoras españolas de los años 90*, (Málaga: Festival de Cine de Málaga, 1998).
31. Fátima Arranz et al *La situación de las mujeres y los hombres en el audiovisual español: estudios sociológico y legislativo.* 14.
32. Maria Cami-Vela, *Mujeres detrás de la cámara. Entrevistas con cineastas españolas 1990-2004*, (Madrid: Ocho y Medio, 2005).
33. CIMA: Asociación de mujeres cineastas y de medios audiovisuales
34. Susan Martin-Márquez, *Feminist Discourse and Spanish Cinema. Sight Unseen*, 213.
35. Jaume Martí-Olivella, "Regendering Spain's Political Bodies: Nationality and Gender in the Films of Pilar Miró and Arantxa Lazcano", in Marsha Kinder (ed.) *Refiguring Spain. Cinema/ Media/ Representation*, (Durham and London: Duke University Press, 1997) 215-238.

36. Pilar Aguilar, *Mujer, amor y sexo en el cine español de los '90* (Madrid: Editorial Fundamentos Colección Arte, 1998).
37. *Ibid.*, 131.
38. María Donapetry *La otra mirada. La mujer y el cine en la cultura española*, (New York: UPS, 1998).
39. *Ibid.*, 34.
40. Thomas Elsaesser, (1985, 1ª ed. 1972), '"Tales of Sound and Fury: Observation on the Family Melodrama," in *Movies and Methods II*, edited by Bill Nichols (Berkeley, Los Angeles, London: University of California Press), 165-189.
41. *Arriba*, 21 March 1978, "La primera película de José Luis Garci, *Asignatura pendiente*, 300 millones de pesetas de recaudación".
42. Angeles Masó, "Cinematografia Astoria "*Asignatura pendiente*" de Angeles MASO" in *La Vanguardia Española*, 01 May 1977.
43. Peter Besas, *Behind the Spanish Lens, Cinema under Fascism and Democracy*, 166.
44. In my article: "Les mémoires cinématographiques de la Guerre civile espagnole", I analyse some myths regarding communism and Stalinism during the Franco periods, in *Cinéma et Stalinisme, la caméra politique*, Théorème no. 8, (Paris: Presses Sorbonne Nouvelle, 2005), 164-179. As Francoist censorship dominated the visual representations of its national cinema, a total rejection of communism was felt in Spanish cinema. Or, for example, portraying the international brigades on the screen, no positive remark on them was allowed: censorship obliged them to suppress it.
45. *Ya*, 20 October 1978, "Prohibida *Asignatura pendiente*".
46. In my article: "La Carmen espagnole de Carlos Saura: construire une nouvelle figure mythique par le flamenco", in *Images et Divinités*, Actes de Colloque Grimh, no. 2, (Lyon: Les Cahiers du Grimh, 2000), 161-169, I comment on three adaptations in Spain: *Carmen, la de Triana* (1938) by Florián Rey, *Carmen de la Ronda* (1959) by Tulio Demichelli, *La Carmen* (1975) by Julio Diamante. There is also a silent film version, made earlier in the twentieth century. In 1998 the musical *La niña de tus ojos*, by Fernando Trueba, refers to this adaptation of 1938 in Germany. In 2003, Vicente Aranda makes a new adaptation of *Carmen*. See also: *Carmen on Screen. An Annotated Filmography and Bibliography*, edited by Phil Powrie and Ann Davies, Tamesis, Woodbridge, 2006, V-VIII.
47. *La Vanguardía*, 28 mai 1983, "Saura: Carmen, estampa de la libertad. Los españoles hemos sido los primeros en llevar adelante la Carmen de los 80". Saura explains that the Spaniards were the first to adapt Carmen in film in the 1980s, thus before the adaptation by Godard and by Rosi in the same period. In her research: *Le personnage mythique au cinéma. Etude des représentations de Carmen*, (Lille: Editions Septentrion, 1997), Anita Leandro analyses the adaptations abroad focusing on the structure of the narration of the actualisations; the stereotype receives particular attention in relationship with this mythological aspect of the character.
48. *El Correo Catalan*, Barcelona, 15 May 1983, "*Carmen* de Carlos Saura" (my translation).
49. Carlos Saura, Prosper Mérimée, *Carmen: el sueño del amor absoluto*, (Barcelona: Círculo de Lectores, 1984), 169 (my translation).

50.   Peter Evans, Robin W. Fiddian, "The Europeanization of Carmen", in *Challenges to authority: fiction and film in contemporary Spain*, (London, Tamesis Book Limited, 1988), 83-94.

51.   Elisabeth Ravoux-Rallo, "De la nouvelle de Mérimée au livret de Meilhac et Halévy: ressemblances et différences", in *Carmen. Figures mythiques*, (Paris: Editions Autrement, 1997), 12.

52.   Spanish title: *Carmen: el sueño del amor absoluto*. Carlos Saura, Prosper Mérimée, *op. cit.*

53.   Carlos García Gual, *Diccionario de mitos*, Barcelona: Editorial Planeta, 1997, pp. 96-99. Since then, new research has been done like the PhD by Gloria F.Vilches on the Carmen adaptations in American cinema, "La representación de Carmen en el cine norteamericano 1915-1954", (PhD diss., University of Valencia, Spain, 2007); or a special edition of the magazine Archivos, no. 51, October 2005: *Carmen en Hollywood*, as well as publications from the English research group on Carmen: *Carmen. From Silent Film to MTV*, edited by Ann Davies and Chris Perriam, Amsterdam/New York, 2005 Bruce Babington, et al., *Carmen on Film. A Cultural History*. Bloomington: Indiana University Press, 2007. These publications represent the same tendency in relation to Carmen, like a fashion.

54.   Ministerio de Cultura, *Boletín Informativo del Control de Taquilla. Películas, Recaudaciones, Espectadores*, (Madrid: Ministerio de la Educación, 1983, 1984).

55.   Marvin D'Lugo, *The Films of Carlos Saura. The Practice of Seeing*, (Princeton, New Jersey: Princeton University Press, 1991), 192.

56.   Fernando Jordan Pemán, *Religiosidad y moralidad de los gitanos en España*, (Madrid: Asociación Secretariado General Gitano, 1991), 18.

57.   Alicia Mederos, *El Flamenco*, (Madrid: Acento Editorial, 1996), 22-24.

58.   Edith Hamilton, *La mythologie*, (Marabout: Editions Hamilton, 1978), 126-128.

59.   Roger Odin, "Le film documentaire, lecture documentarisante", in *Cinémas et réalités*, Saint Etienne: Cierec, 1984.

60.   *El País*, 18 June 1993. "En danza por *Amor de Dios*. Asociacion y penas flamencas protestan contra el cierre de la academia de baile ¿A dónde iran los balaores?". The dance school: "*Escuela Amor de Dios*" is a professional flamenco dance school in Madrid that still exists today and is one of the most highly reputed in Spain.

61.   For the interpretations of the dance terminology, I refer to Donn E. Pohren, *The art of flamenco*, (Madrid: Society of Spanish Studies, 1990), 107. Even if there are different interpretations of these terms, all flamenco aficionados certainly recognise substantial differences between for instance a buleria, an allegria, or a farruca, etc. These more common interpretations, stemming from my personal encounters with the flamenco scene, sustain my reading, confirmed by the terminology used by Pohren.

62.   Prosper Mérimée, *Carmen*, (Saint-Amand Montrond: Bussière, 1996), 33.

63.   *Ibid.*

64.   *Ibid.*, p. 45.

65.   Susan Martin-Márquez, *Feminist Discourse and Spanish Cinema, Sight Unseen*, 248-259 analyses this metaphor in several films, relating it to the studies by Pedro A. Fuertes Oliveira, *Mujer, lenguaje y sociedad: los estereotipos de género en inglés y en español*, (Valladolid: Universidad de Valladolid, 1992). In the film LA GATA (THE SHE-CAT, 1956) by Bautista the animal metaphor draws out the human quality of Maria's sexuality. In other films by Erice, THE SPIRIT OF THE BEEHIVE (EL ESPIRITU DE LA

COLMENA, 1973) the comparison is made between female sexuality and felines, even though it is used in a different way, as Martin-Márquez comments.

66. Jacques Aumont, *L'Image*, (Paris: Editions Nathan, 1990), 116. The over framing is defined as a presence of a frame in the frame, for example by a mirror or a window. This serves as a materialisation of a point of view. Double framing or over framing is defined as the presence of a frame of reference within a frame of reference, such as through the use of a mirror or window. This technique allows for the expression of multiple points of view.

67. Donn E. Phoren, *The art of flamenco*, 158.

68. *El periodico*, 30 October 1991, "Tacones lejanos bate todos los récords. La película de Almodóvar recauda 123 millones en su primer fin de semana en cartel."

69. Carlos Aguilar, Jaume Genover, *El cine español en sus interpretes*, (Madrid: Ed. Verdoux S.L., 1992), 124, 143-144, 346. Amparo Rivelles stayed there for many years; certainly several trips have taken her to this continent, where she was extremely sucessful.

70. Frédéric Strauss, "A cœur ouvert. Entretien avec Pedro Almodóvar", in *Cahiers du cinéma*, no. 535, p. 36.

71. *El mundo*, 26 October 1991, "Visiones, glamour y espectáculo en el estreno, ayer en Madrid, del filme *Tacones lejanos*".

72. *Ibid.* (my translation)

73. *El mundo*, 26 October 1991, "Los placeres y los días de Fransisco UMBRAL" (my translation).

74. *El Independiente*, 22 October 1991, "La estética del fragmentarismo".

75. *Expansión Madrid*, 02 November 1991, "*Tacones lejanos:* el último saldo", Eduardo Torres-Dulce.

76. *Ibid.* (my translation).

77. I refer to the Anglo-American publications on this topic: S. Martin Marquez, *Feminist Discourse and Spanish Cinema, Sight Unseen*, 232-245. Marsha Kinder,"The Spanish Oedipal narrative and its subversion", in *Blood Cinema*, 197-275, Paul Julian Smith, *Desire Unlimited. The cinema of Pedro Almodóvar*, (London: Verso, 1994), 121-134.

78. Barry Jordan, and Rikki Tamosunas, *Spanish National Cinema*, 132.

79. Marsha Kinder interviewed the filmmaker: "Interview with Pedro Almodóvar", 131-144, in Marvin D'Lugo, *Pedro Almodóvar*, (Chicago and Urbana: University of Illinois Press, 2006), 142. Originally published in 1987: Marsha Kinder, "Pleasure and the New Spanish Mentality. A conversation with Pedro Almodóvar." In *Film Quarterly* no; 41 (Fall 1987): 33-44.

80. *Ibid.* 143.

81. *El mundo*, 26 October 1991, "Los placeres y los días de Fransisco UMBRAL"

82. Mark Allinson, *Un laberinto español. Las películas de Pedro Almodóvar*, 94-95.

83. Michel Bernard, *Le corps*, (Paris: Editions du Seuil, 1995), 140.

Chapter three

1. Luis María Gallego Sanz, *Breve estudio sobre la Ley de peligrosidad y rehabilitación social*, (Gallego: Ed. S.L. L.M., 1986), 7.
2. Victoriano Domingo Loren, *Los homosexuales frente a la ley: los juristas opinan. La homosexualidad. ¿es un vicio o es una enfermedad?*, (Esplugas de Llobregat (Barcelona): Plaza § Janés, 1978), 44.
3. *Ibid.*
4. *Ibid.*, p. 48.
5. *Código Penal y lesgislación de peligrosidad social*, (Año 1970, Madrid: Civitas, partie 23487).
6. *Ibid.*
7. *Ibid.*
8. *Ibid.*
9. Carlos María Romeo Casabona, *Peligrosidad y derecho penal preventivo*, (Barcelona: Bosche, 1986), 21.
10. *Constitución Española de 27 de Diciembre de 1978*, (3e ed. actualizada noviembre 1997, 10).
11. *Appendice 1975-1985*, al nuevo diccionario de legislación XIII, (1988, 1072).
12. Irene Pelayo comments in her PhD that a law on public scandal was maintained until 1988. While homosexuality was no longer illegal, it remained restricted, especially with regard to public displays of affection. Irene Pelayo, "Imagen fílmica del lesbianismo a través de los personajes protagonistas en el cine español", (diss. PhD Madrid, Universidad Complutense, 19 de mayo 2009), 39.
13. Richard Dyer, "Estereotipos", in *Cine y homosexualidad*, edited by Richard Dyer et al, 69-94. Barcelona: Ed. Laertes, 1982. (Original title: *Gays and Film*, London: British Film Institute, 1977) Paul Julian Smith, *Laws of Desire. Questions of Homosexuality in Spanish Writing and Film 1960-1990*, (Oxford: Clarendon Press, 1992).
14. Juan Carlos Alfeo Alvarez, "El enigma de la culpa: la homosexualidad en el cine español (1961-2000)", in *International Journal of Iberian Studies*, (Vol. 13, no.3, 2000), 136-147, 136.
15. Richard Dyer, "Estereotipos", 80 (my translation).
16. *Ibid.*, p. 69.
17. Paul Julian Smith, *Laws of Desire. Questions of Homosexuality in Spanish Writing and Film 1960-1990*, 134.
18. Juan Carlos Alfeo Alvarez, "La imagen del personaje homosexual masculino como protagonista en la cinematografía española", (PhD diss., Universidad Complutense Madrid, Departamento de Comunicacion Audiovisuel y Publicidad II, 1997), 15.
19. Chris Perriam, *Stars and masculinities in Spanish cinema*, (Oxford: Oxford University Press, 2003).
20. *Ibid.*, 6.
21. John Hopewell, *El cine español después de Franco 1973-1988*, 421-422.
22. Casimiro Torreiro, "Del tardofranquismo a la democracia (1969-1982)", in *Historia del cine español*, Román Gubern, José Enrique Monterde, Casimiro Torreiro, et al., 364. (Madrid: Ediciones Cátedra S.A., 1995), my translation.

23. See the film NEW SPANIARDS (LOS NUEVOS ESPAÑOLES, 1974) by R. Bodegas, it refers to the creation of new human models, inspired by the American formula but who, in the end, prefer to stay Spanish, less dynamic but authentic.

24. Juan Carlos Alfeo Alvarez, "Convergencias y divergencias discursivas en la representación de los valores asociados a la experiencia gay y lésbica a través de las películas españolas". Conferencia dictada por encargo de la Fundación Isonomía-Universidad Jaime I en el curso "Interculturalidad género y coeducación". (Castellón, 15 de julio de 2007).

25. Paul Julian Smith, "Cine, historia y homosexualidad. FAR FROM HEAVEN (LEJOS DEL CIELO, 2002) de Todd Haynes y LA MALA EDUCACIÓN (2004) de Almodóvar", in *La mirada homosexual*, edited by Alberto Mira (Archivos, no. 54 Octubre 2006), 101.

26. Alberto Mira, *La mirada homosexual*, (Archivos, no. 54, Octubre 2006, Valencia: Filmoteca de Valencia).

27. *Ibid.*

28. Jack Babuscio, "Lo camp y la sensibilidad homosexual", in *La mirada homosexual*, ed. Alberto Mira (Archivos, no. 54 Octubre 2006), 170-195.

29. www.coc.nl/. LGBT Rights in Germany: Wikipedia. L'homosexualité n'est plus un délit, le 27 Juillet 1982, Internaute Histoire. Comparing different countries is difficult, but I would like to mention some important changes. In France laws on homosexuality were modified under Mitterand in 1982. The PACS (Pacte Civil de Solidarité) has only been valid since 1999 making it possible for the French administration to recognise a same-sex couple. Marriage between homosexuals is still forbidden in that country, while it was legalised in Spain in 2005 and in the Netherlands in 2001. Decriminalized in the Netherlands since 1971, there are nonetheless distinct periods: until 1973 the institutions for mental health stopped treating it as an illness, but beforehand it was treated as such. In Germany homosexuality was legalised in 1968 in East Germany and in 1969 in West Germany. In the United Kingdom it has been legal since 1967. These are just some legal and historical facts, but the cultural consequences are of course another issue.

30. Irene Pelayo, "Imagen fílmica del lesbianismo a través de los personajes protagonistas en el cine español", (diss. PhD Madrid, Universidad Complutense, 19 de mayo 2009).

31. Juan Carlos Alfeo Alvarez, "El enigma de la culpa: la homosexualidad en el cine español (1961-2000)," in *International Journal of Iberian Studies*, (Vol. 13, no. 3, 2000), 136-147. Other periods have been commented on by Julio Perez Perucha and V. Ponce defining several periods for the Transition: Postfranquismo from 1974-1976, the Democratic Transition (1977-1982), the Democracy 1983-1986 in PÉREZ PERUCHA, J. y V. PONCE: "Algunas instrucciones para evitar naufragios metodológicos y rastrear la transición democrática en el cine español" en *El cine y la transición española*, (Valencia, Filmoteca Valenciana y Consellería de Cultura, Educació i Ciencia de la Generalitat Valenciana, 1985). Another period is mentioned by Alberto Mira in *La mirada homosexual*, Archivos de la Filmoteca de Valencia, (no. 54, Octubre 2006) comments in "El significante inexistente. Cinco calas en la representación de la homosexualidad en el cine español", 71-95. He comments on the presence of homosexual relationships during Francoism situating the male relationship in a homosexual spectrum. Mira's periodisation is absolutely fascinating and important, but for this research we focus on an explicitly named relationship that is homosexual. We

cite therefore the Alfeo Alvarez' periodisation as he relates it to the stereotyped character, directly used in our research by focusing on the stereotyped body.

32. Jean Claude Seguin discusses in *Histoire du cinéma espagnol,* (Paris, Nathan, 1994), 61, how exacting censorship was especially with regard to displays of sexuality. Yet, despite references to Garcia Lorca and Oscar Wilde, this film was accepted. Emmanuel Le Vagueresse analysis is noteworthy, "*Diferente* (1961) de Luis María Delgado: un regard 'différent' sur l'homosexuel en plein franquisme," in *Image et Corps,* (Lyon, Editions du Grimh-LCE, 2007), 463-470, 469. He analyses the theatrical performance in this musical and the main actor as victim, without making explicit what or who is victimising the actor.

33. Irene Pelayo, "Imagen fílmica del lesbianismo a través de los personajes protagonistas en el cine español," 308.

34. *Ibid.*

35. Daniel Kowalsky, "Rated S: softcore pornography and the Spanish transition to democracy, 1977-1982." In *Spanish Popular Cinema (Inside Popular Film),* edited by Antonio Lázarro Reboll and Andrew Willis, 188-208, (Manchester: Manchester University Press, 2004).

36. Irene Pelayo, "Imagen fílmica del lesbianismo a través de los personajes protagonistas en el cine español", 43: like: Las vampiras (1973) Emmanuelle y Carol (1978) – Silvia ama a Raquel (1979) La caliente niña Julietta (1980), La frígida y la viciosa (1981), Mi conejo es el mejor (1982).

37. *Ibid.,* 45: like: Me siento extraña (1977), Carne apaleada (1978), Entre Tinieblas (1983), Extramuros (1985), A mi madre le gustan las mujeres (2002), Sevigné Júlia Berkowitz (2004).

38. *Ibid,* 48: like: La noche del terror ciego (1972), Pepi, Luci, Bom y otras chicas del montón(1980), Calé (1985), Sauna (1990), Costa Brava (Family album) (1995), Pasajes (1996), El pájaro de la felicidad (1993).

39. *Ibid.* 50: like: Todo me pasa a mí (2000), En la ciudad (2003), Los 2 lados de la cama (2005).

40. Jacques-Louis Delpal, *Los travestís y el enigma de los cambios de sexo,* (Título original en francés: les travestís), (Madrid: Ed. Marsiega, Tropos editora, prensa underground, 1974).

41. Marsha Kinder, "Sex Change and Cultural Transformation in Aranda and Abril's *Cambio de Sexo* (1977)", in *Spanish Cinema. The Auteurist Tradition,* edited by Peter Evans, (New York: Oxford University Press, 1999), 128-146.

42. Marsha Kinder, "From Matricide to Motherlove in Almodóvar's High Heels", in *Post-Franco, Postmodernism, The films of Pedro Almodóvar,* (Vol. 43, edited by Kathleen M.Vernon and Barbara Morris, Greenwood Press, 1995), 151-152.

43. *La Vanguardia Española,* 25 June 1977, "*Cambio de sexo*". (my translation)

44. *Sábado Gráfico,* 28 Mayo 1977. "Comentario C7. "Cuando el "cambio" es… de sexo."

45. *Ibid.* (my translation).

46. The first sex changes took place in Europe in the twentieth century, in the 1940s in Denmark. In: Jacques-Louis Delpal, *Los travestís y el enigma de los cambios de sexo,* 83-84. I cite the next article in Spanish, explaining the change in legislation for transsexuals in Spain. Montilla Valerio, Javier, "Las dificultades sociales de las personas transexuales", in Pinyana Garl, Carme/Gil Gómez, Alicia, *Identidad de género vs. Identidad sexual,* (Actas 4º Congreso Estatal Isonomía sobre identidad de género vs

identidad sexual, Universitat Jaume I, Publicacions de la Universitat Jaume I, 2008), 122-131.

47. *Informaciones*, 19 Mayo 1977, "*Cambio de sexo.*"

48. *Ibid.*

49. Juan Eslava Galán, *El sexo de nuestros padres*, (Barcelona: Editorial Planeta, 1993), 289.

50. Vicente Molina Foix, "*¡Quiero llamarme Bibiana Fernández!*" in *El Pais Semanal*, (Número 1.110, Domingo 4 de enero 1998), 24-29.

51. Like Marsha Kinder comments, this actor must be related to Fassbinder's cinema. Marsha Kinder, "Sex Change and Cultural Transformation in Aranda and Abril's *Cambio de Sexo* (1977)," in ed. Peter Evans. *Spanish Cinema. The Auteurist Tradition*, (New York: Oxford University Press, 1999), 128-146.

52. Marsha Kinder, "Sex Change and Cultural Transformation in Aranda and Abril's *Cambio de Sexo* (1977)," 135.

53. Michel Poizat, *L'Opéra ou le cri de l'ange. Essai sur la jouissance de l'amateur d'opéra*, (Paris: Editions Métailié, 1986), 161-185. This wonderful essay explains the enormous impact of the angelic voices for the Catholic Church. Apparently this practice of castration started in Spain and was often executed in Italy to save these beautiful angelic voices. In the film this air is sung by the soprano Marí Fleta.

54. Jacques-Louis Delpal, *Los travestís y el enigma de los cambios de sexo.*

55. Peter Besas, *Behind the Spanish Lens, Cinema under Fascism and Democracy*, 175.

56. The party's real identity is not revealed but there are several Marxist references.

57. Javier Pradera Santos Julia y Joaquín Prieto, *Memoria de la Transición*, (Madrid: Taurus, 1996).

58. Pietsie Feenstra, "Mémoires cinématographiques de la Guerre civile espagnole", in edited by Kristian Feigelson, Théorème no. 8, *Cinéma et Stalinisme: Caméra politique*, (Paris: Presses Sorbonne Nouvelle, 2005), 164-179.

59. *ABC* 09 February 1979, "*El Diputado, de Eloy de la Iglesia*". (my translation)

60. *El Pais* 27 January 1979, "Sexo y política, un cóctel que vende". (my translation)

61. *Pueblo* 24 January 1979, "Real Cinema *El diputado*". (my translation)

62. *La Vanguardia*, 24 October 1978, "Llegó con *El diputado*. Eloy de la Iglesia: ." (my translation)

63. *Periódico*, 19 October 1979. "*El diputado;* político y homosexual". (my translation)

64. *La Calle*, Madrid 30 January 1979, "A por los 300 millones. 'Que *El diputado* es un éxito de taquilla, nadie lo pone en duda: ahí están los carteles de "No hay entradas" en los cines donde se proyecta." (my translation)

65. *Diario 16*, 23 February 1979: "Existe un divorcio claro entre crítica y público. 'Trece largometrajes son bastantes para un hombre de treinta y cinco años. Largometrajes frecuentemente rechazados por la crítica y casi siempre, como contrapunto, con enorme éxito de público." (my translation)

66. *El Pais*, 15 November 1985, "Política y homosexualidad." (my translation)

67. This idea has also been confirmed in two recent articles that explore this relationship between different kinds of marginality, which makes of homosexuality a political issue: Stephen Tropiano, "Out of the cinematic closet. Homosexuality in Films of Eloy de la Iglesia", in ed. Marsha Kinder, *Refiguring Spain: Cinema/Media/Representation*, (Durham, London: Duke University Press, 1997), 159-177. Alejandro Melero Salvador, "New Sexual Politics in the Cinema of the Transition to Democracy: de la

Iglesia's *El diputado* (1978)," in *Gender and Spanish Cinema*, edited by Steven Marsh, Nair Parvati, (New York, Oxford: Ed. Berg, 2004), 87-102.

68. I refer to Bénédicte Brémard's article, "Le métissage des cultures dans le cinema espagnol homosexuel contemporain: Pedro Almodóvar/Ventura Pons", in *Littératures, Arts, homosexualités. Dossier bilingue de Littératures Hispaniques*, edited by Patrick Dubuis, Nicolas Balutet, (Inverses 5/2005, Avril 2005), 53-80, and a recent article on Ventura Pons by Jorg Thurschmann: "La vida de lo teatral: actrices/actrius (1996) de Ventura Pons," in Verena Berger, Mercè Aumell, *Escenarios compartidos: cine y teatro en España en el umbral del siglo XXI*, (Wien: Lit Verlag, 2009), 75-86. See also "Chapter 6, Transformed Bodies," in *Live Flesh. The Male Body in Contemporary Spanish Cinema*, Santiago Fouz-Hernandez, Alfredo Martínez-Expósito, (London/ New York: I.B. Taurus, 2007), 135-160.

69. Juan Carlos Alfeo Alvarez, "La imagen del personaje homosexual masculino como protagonista en la cinematografía española," 77.

70. Marvin D'Lugo, "Re-imaging the Community: Imanol Uribe's La muerte de Mikel (1983) and the Cinema of Transition", 194-209, in *Spanish cinema. The auteurist cinema*, edited by Peter Evans, (Oxford: Oxford University Press, 1999). Another text to cite is Ann Davies, "Male sexuality and Basque Separatism in Two Films by Imanol Uribe", Hispanic Research Journal (Vol. 4, no. 2, June 2003), 121-132, who innovatively analyses communities and male sexuality using Slavoj Zizek and Jonathan Dollimore's theories. Davies compares Uribe's DIAS CONTADOS to LA MUERTE DE MIKEL.

71. Antonio Garcia Martin, Andrés Lopez Fernández, *Imagen social de la homosexualidad en España*, (Madrid: Asociación Pro Derechos Humanos, 1985).

72. *Ibid.*, p. 19.

73. *El Pais*, 18 February 1984, "Hermosa y arriesgada denuncia. La repercusión en Euskadi."

74. *El Pais*, 15 November 1983, "La nueva película de Imanol Uribe pretende reflejar la acual realidad interna de Euskadi."

75. Chris Perriam, *Stars and masculinities in Spanish cinema*, 19.

76. *Ibid.*, 17-22.

77. *Segre Lerida*, 06 May 1984, "La consagración de Arias. Una historia de un militante de izquierda homosexual". (my translation)

78. Marvin D'Lugo, "Re-imaging the Community: Imanol Uribe's *La muerte de Mikel* (1983) and the Cinema of Transition," 203.

79. *Fiesta de los gansos, information de Société d'études Basques*. Nowadays these village parties no longer use real animals. In Basque culture, several feasts exist which underline the physical force of man, such as hitting a button with a huge hammer to test one's force, or, in this case, to pull a rope with a goose tied at the other end, to display force.

80. In a revealing article Dagmar Schmelzer analyses this sequence about violence: the slow motion is the only one in the film, creating at the same time a distance toward the viewer. "La violencia enfocada: tres visiones cinematográficas españolas. LA MUERTE DE MIKEL (1983) de Imanol Uribe, HISTORIAS DEL KRONEN (1994) de Montxo Armendáriz, y EL BOLA (2000) de Achero Mañas", in *Miradas glocales. Cine español en el cambio de milenio*, edited by Burkhard Pohl, Jörg Thurschmann (Frankfurt am Main: Ed. Vervuert, 2007), 73-87.

81. Written by Rafael de León, this song is often quoted.

82. Manuel Vázquez Montalbán, *Crónica Sentimental de España*, (Barcelona: Ediciones Bruguera, 1980, first edition: 1971).

83. *Segre Lerida*, 07 June 1987, *"La ley del deseo.* Desde la butaca." (my translation)

84. Several newspapers react the same way: *ABC*, 08 February 1987, "LA LEY DEL DESEO, un desahogo en la carrera de Pedro Almodóvar. Desorbitada melodrama, con triángulo, celos, asesinato y desenlace fatal." The journalist points to Almodovar's typical universe; his provocative and changing cinematographic personality and his 'underground' mission scandalised the "bourgeois" audience. *Diario 16*, 24 January 1987, "Deseos, invitados y policies." This article emphasises the Almodóvarian approach to homosexuality, which characterises this filmmaker's cinema. *YA*, 13 October 1988, Madrid *"La ley del deseo*, récord en festivales."

85. Frédéric Strauss, *Conversations avec Pedro Almodóvar*, (Paris: Editions Cahiers du Cinéma, 2000), 64.

86. Paul Julian Smith, *Desire Unlimited. The Cinema of Pedro Almodóvar.* (First Ed. 1994, London: Verso, Second Edition, 2000), 79-92.

87. Paul Julian Smith, *Las leyes del deseo. La homosexualidad en la literatura y el cine español 1960-1990*, (Barcelona: Ediciones de Tempestad, 1998), 171.

88. Juan Carlos Alfeo Alvarez, "La imagen del personaje homosexual masculino como protagonista en la cinematografía española", 80.

89. Paul Julian Smith, *Laws of desire. Questions of homosexuality in Spanish writing and Film 1960-1990*, (Oxford: Clarendon Press, 1992), p. 12.

90. Other filmmakers like Ventura Pons also created a challenging discourse on these issues, but Iglesia's politically charged films made of him a more provocative force.

91. Jean Cocteau, *La voix humaine. Pièce en un acte.* (Stock: Editions Stock et Jean Cocteau, 1930).

92. Frédéric Strauss, *Conversations avec Pedro Almodóvar*, 178.

93. Susan Sontag, "Notes on 'Camp'." (First published in 1964 in *Partisan Review*). In: *Against Interpretation and other essays*, New York: Picador USA, (2001), 275-292.

94. Frédéric Strauss, *Conversations avec Pedro Almodóvar*, 127.

95. Santíago Fouz-Hernández, Chris Perriam, "El deseo sin ley: la representación de "la homosexualidad" en el cine español de los años noventa" in *Cultura, homosexualidad y homofobia*, editado por Félix González Rodríguez, (Vol. 1, Perspectivas gays, Barcelona: Ed. Laertes, 2007), 61-80.

96. Richard Dyer, *Now you see it. Studies on Lesbian and Gay film*, (London, New York, Routledge, 1990).

Chapter four

1. Juan Carlos Usó, *Drogas y cultura de masas: España (1855-1995)*, (Madrid: Taurus, 1996), 323.

2. Ministerio de la Gobernación, *Delincuencia Juvenil. Estudio de su problemática en España*, (Madrid: Ministerio de la Gobernación, Collección Estudios 14, 1972).

3. Eugenio Gonzalez Gonzalez, *Bandas Juveniles*, (Barcelona: Editorial Herder, 1982), 108, 183.

4. Ministerio de la Gobernación, *Delincuencia Juvenil. Estudio de su problemática en España*, 15-16, 33.

5. Juan Carlos Usó, *Drogas y cultura de masas: España (1855-1995)*, 308-309.

6. *Ibid.* 308-309, 322.

7. *Ibid.*, 224.

8. *Ibid.*, 188-200. Figures show that in 1961, 4 people were imprisoned; in 1962, 2 people; in 1963: 14, in 1964: 12, in 1965: 23, in 1966: 18. All with between 20 and 100 kilograms of marihuana in their possession.

9. *Ibid.*, 260.

10. *Ibid.*, 324.

11. *Ibid.*, 327.

12. *Ibid.*, 336-337.

13. *Ibid.*, 345.

14. "Toxicomanía y delincuencia," in *IV Simposium Europeo Regional de la AIDSM, 25 y 26 de enero*, Facultad de Medicina, (Barcelona: Casanova 143, 1991), 246.

15. *Ibid.*, 311.

16. Bato Tomasevic, Nebojsa, Rajko Djuric, et al., *Gypsies of the world* (London, Flint River Press, 1989).

17. Fernando Jordan Pemán, *Religiosidad y moralidad de los gitanos en España* (Madrid, Asociación Secretariado General Gitano, D.L., 1991), 18.

18. *Ibid.*, 19-22.

19. *Ibid.*, 21 (my translation).

20. *Ibid.*

21. Asociación Pro Derechos Humanos de España, *Actas de las primeras jornadas sobre problemática del pueblo gitano*, (Madrid: Asociación Pro Derechos Humanos con la colaboración del Ministerio de Trabajo y Seguridad Social, 1987), 5, (my translation).

22. Christopher J. Ross, *Contemporary Spain. A Handbook*, (London/New York: Ed. Arnold, 1997), 211-212.

23. *Ibid.*, 87-89.

24. Gurutz Jáuregui, "La cuestión vasca durante el franquismo", in *La cuestión vasca. Una mirada desde la Historia*, edited by Mercedes Arbaíza Vilallonga, 144-145 (Bilbao: Editiorial del País Vasco, 2001).

25. *Ibid.*, 148, 151.

26. Luis Miguel Carmona, *El terrorismo y E.T.A. en el cine*, (Madrid: Cacitel, S.L., 2004), 64.

27. Manuel Vidal Estevez, "La trilogía vasca del cine español," in *Entre el documental y la ficción. El cine de Imanol Uribe*, ed. Jesus Angulo, Carlos F. Heredero, (San Sebastian: Editorial Filmoteca vasca, 1994), 35.

28. Sagrario Morán Blanco, *ETA entre España y Francia*, (Madrid: Editorial Complutense, 1997).

29. Website AVT: Acociación Victimas del Terrorismo and Fundación Victimas del Terrorismo. This graphic includes the victims killed by the GRAPO founded in the 1970s as a revolutionary group. For a precise overview of the terrorist organizations responsible, I refer to the website of the Asociación de Victimas del Terrorismo, founded in 1981, which lists all of the victims before this date.

30. This radical group was inspired by Maoism, Marxism and Leninism, and was anti-capitalist. They are less known but still have caused many victims: this can all be checked on AVT's website.

31. Christopher J. Ross, *Contemporary Spain. A Handbook*, (London/New York: Ed. Arnold, 1997), 89.

32. Luis Miguel Carmona, *El terrorismo y E.T.A. en el cine*, 79.

33. Juan Carlos Usó, *Drogas y cultura de masas: España (1855-1995)*, 365.

34. Luis Miguel Carmona, *El terrorismo y E.T.A. en el cine*, 30-32.

35. *Ibid.*, 110-156.

36. Spanish titles: VACAS (1991), LA ARDILLA ROJA (1993), TIERRA (1996), LOS AMANTES DEL CÍRCULO POLAR (1998), LUCÍA Y EL SEXO (2001), CAÓTICA ANA (2007), HABITACION EN ROMA, (2010).

37. Luis Miguel Carmona, *El terrorismo y E.T.A. en el cine*, 150-156.

38. In this context I should mention Nekane Parejo Jiménez's PhD, "Fotografía y muerte: representación gráfica de los atentados de ETA (1968-1997)", (Diss PhD Universidad del Pais Vasco, 2003), p. 509. He analyses the representation of the ETA attacks in the press: in the 1970s there was a kind of censorship: the pictures of the bloody attacks were not yet shown, identity pictures of the victims were, however, displayed. In the 1980s the new protagonist was the corpse, the dead body frontally shown. In the 1990s once again there was a new kind of censorship, allowing for a distanced view of attacks.

39. Vicente José Benet, "Cuerpos en serie", in: *Cuerpos en serie*, edited by Vicente J. Benet, Eloísa Nos, (Jaume: Universitat Jaume-I, 1999), 9-14 .

40. Marvin D'Lugo, *The films of Carlos Saura. The practice of seeing*, (Princeton, New Jersey: Princeton University Press, 1991), 15 in: Enrique Brasó, *Carlos Saura: una introducción incompleta*, (Madrid: Taller de Ediciones Josefina Betantor, 1974).

41. *Ibid.*

42. *Ibid.*, p. 21. in: Emmanuel Laraz, "El cine español. Textos escogidos y presentados por." Regards sur le monde hispanique. (Paris: Ed. Masson, 1973), 47.

43. Francisco Perales, *Luis García Berlanga*, (Madrid: Ediciones Cátedra, 1997), 250.

44. *Diario de Barcelona*, 10 April 1981, "Rueda de prensa de Carlos Saura en Barcelona. *Deprisa, deprisa*, una historia de amor".

45. *Diario 16*, 20 February 1981, "*Deprisa, deprisa* causó cierta decepción en Berlín."

46. *El Pais*, 21 September 1980, "*Deprisa*, un documento sobre la delincuencia. "

47. *Diario de Barcelona*, 10 April 1981, "Rueda de prensa de Carlos Saura en Barcelona. *Deprisa, deprisa*, una historia de amor"..

48. *Diario 16*, 20 February 1981, "*Deprisa, deprisa* causó cierta decepción en Berlín."

49. *Semana*, no. 897, 1981, "Confesiones de Genoveva López: 'Creo que mi marido cometió el atraco influido por la película de Saura'."

50. *Diario de Barcelona*, 10 April 1981, Rueda de prensa de Carlos Saura en Barcelona. *Deprisa, deprisa*, una historia de amor".

51. *Diario 16*, 12 March 1981, "El protagonista de la última película de Saura, capturado, *Deprisa, deprisa*. José Antonio Valdelomar se acababa de llevar 170 000 pesetas de un banco de la calle Ríos Rosas". (my translation).

52. Julian Marias, "Señoritismo" in *Gaceta Ilustrada*, no. 837, 1981 (my translation).

53. *Ibid.* (my translation).

54. *Diario 16*, 12 March 1981, "El protagonista de la última película de Saura, capturado *Deprisa, deprisa*". (my translation).

55. *Cambio 16*, 23 March 1981, "La loca carrera de EL Mini", *Diario 16*, 12 mars 1981, *op. cit.*

56. *Diario 16*, 04 August 1981, "*Deprisa, deprisa,...* a la cárcel, a la cárcel" .

57. *Pueblo*, 06 September 1983, "Otro de los protagonistas de *Deprisa, deprisa*, detenido."

58. J.M. Caparros Lera, *El cine español de la democracia. De la muerte de Franco al "cambio" socialista (1975-1989)*, (Barcelona: Editorial Anthropos, 1992).

59. *Ibid.*

60. Agustín Sánchez Vidal, *Retrato de Carlos Saura*, (Barcelona: Círculo de Lectores, Galaxia Gutenberg, 1994), 84.

61. *El País*, 28 March 1981, "El lento y complicado rodaje de *Deprisa, deprisa*."

62. *El País*, 21 September 1980, "*Deprisa*, un documento sobre la delincuencia."

63. Chris Ealham, Michael Richards, *The splintering of Spain: cultural history and the Spanish Civil War, 1936-1939*, (Cambridge: Cambridge University Press, 2005), 80, 168.

64. Vicente Sánchez-Biosca, *Cine y Guerra Civil Española del mito a la memoria*, (Madrid: Alianza, 2006), 212, comments on why Saura puts this sequence in the film as talking about the past is not at all represented in this story. The filmmaker illustrates the silence about the past, but also shows how this generation lacked knowledge about the past in the first period of Democracy. Marcel Oms, *La Guerre civile espagnole au cinema*, (Paris: Editions Cerf 7ème Art, 1986), 200-201, shows also this image as a symbol of how the young generation turns the back to the past.

65. Cáritas Española, *Dossier Droga*, (Madrid: Servicio de documentacion de Cáritas, Febrero 1985), 63. The rate of unemployment among young people was important in Spain in the beginning of the 1980s. 'Cáritas Española' relates it directly to the increase of drug use.

66. In regards to these laws, I recommend a chapter of Josep Sánchez Cervella's work, "Capítulo 1. El contexto nacional e internacional de la resistencia (1939-1952)", in *El último Frente. La resistencia armada antifranquista en España 1939-1952*, edited by Julio Aróstegui y Jorge Marco, (Madrid: Los libros de la Catarata, 2008).

67. There are many articles on the subject, such as: "El Lute pide que la Ley de Memoria Histórica anule el proceso franquista que le condenó a muerte", ADN.ESPOLITICA, 3 January 2009. www.20minutos.ES: "'El Lute' pide que la Ley de Memoria Histórica anule su proceso franquista", 3 January 2009.

68. The song recounts the story of his life and I have quoted only a short part of it. The song's title is: "El Lute Gotta Go Home": This is the story of El Lute, A man who was born to be hunted like a wild animal. Because he was poor. But he refused to accept his fate. And today his honor has been restored. He was only nineteen. And he was sentenced to die. For something that somebody else did. And blamed on El Lute.

69. Eleuterio Sánchez, *Mañana seré libre: mémorias de "El Lute"*, 2a parte, (Barcelona: Círculo de Lectores; D.L., 1988, 1ère Ed. 1979), 10.

70. *Ibid.*, 75-76.

71. Barry Jordan, Rikki Morgan-Tamosunas, *Contemporary Spanish Cinema*, 26.

72. Laureano Montero, "El cine quinqui o el lado oscuro de la Transición", in *De la zarzuela al cine. Los medios de comunicación populares y su traducción de la voz marginal*, edited by Max Doppelbauer, Kathrin Sartringen, 123-138. (München: Martin Meidenbauer, 2010).

73. *El País,* 06 November 1987, "La ex esposa de Euleterio Sánchez pide el secuestro del filme sobre *El Lute"*.

74. *Semana,* Madrid, 07 April 1988, "La actriz Silvia Rodriguez se casó por el rito gitano con Imanol Arias".

75. Eleuterio Sánchez, *Mañana seré libre: mémorias de "El Lute",* 2a parte, 11 (my translation).

76. *Ibid.,* 475.

77. *Boletín Informativo, Películas, Recaudaciones, Espectadores,* (Madrid: Ministerio de Cultura, Instituto de la Cinematografía y de las Artes Audiovisuales, Ed. de 1987 à 1988).

78. *El País,* 06 November, 1987, "La ex esposa de Euleterio Sánchez pide el secuestro del filme sobre *El Lute"*.

79. *Hola,* 22 October 1987, "Consuelo Garcia Chelo, se ha querellado contra toda el equipo de *Camina o revienta". Diez minutos,* 20 October 1987, "Consuelo Garcia fírmo la denuncia contra la película *El Lute, Camina o revienta"*.

80. *Lecturas, Vivir para ver,* 18 November 1987, "Eleuterio Sánchez lamenta que su exmujer se haya querellado contra su película" *ABC,* Madrid, Oct. 1987. "Euleterio Sánchez habla de *El Lute* en su salida al camino de las pantallas".

81. *El País,* 21 July 1990, "Rechazado el recurso de la ex-mujer de El Lute contra un filme de Aranda" .

82. Fernando Jordan Pemán, *Reliogidad y moralidad de los gitanos en España,* (Madrid: Orinoco A.G., 1991), 33.

83. *Ibid.,* p. 26. (my translation).

84. Chris Perriam, *Stars and masculinities in Spanish cinema,* 17-22.

85. José Angel Garrido, *La etnia gitana en la pantalla. Minorías en el cine,* (Barcelona: Publicaciones de la Universitat de Barcelona, 2003), 184-185. Garrido scrutinises the representation of gypsies across different national cinemas. He emphasises the failure to authentically represent the social economic situation of gypsies. Their persecution during the Second World War and their drug addiction problems are seldom treated, for example.

86. *El Independiente,* Madrid, 13 Mayo 1988, "Vicente Aranda: El Lute fue la cabeza de turco, un chivo expiatoria". (my translation).

87. *Ya,* Madrid, 22 April 1988, "Imanol Arias: *"El Lute* ha acabado definitivamente con mi imagen de galán". Se acaba de estrenar la segunda parte: *Mañana seré libre."* (my translation).

88. John Hopewell, *El cine español después de Franco 1973-1988,* 105-111.

89. Eduardo Rodriguez, Concha Gómez, "El Cine de la Democracia (1978-1995)", 187.

90. *Ya,* 16 October 1987, "La historia de un quinqui que llegó a mito". (my translation)

91. *Segre Lerida,* 15 November 1987, "El Lute, camina o revienta". (my translation)

92. *Ya,* Madrid, 10 November 1987, "La dura crónica de un hombre perseguido."(my translation).

93. *Segre Lerida,* 14 October 1987, "El Lute, en las charlas sobre la marginación ."

94. *Diario de Leon,* Leon, 18 October 1994, "Imanol Uribe. Director de *Días contados,* última Concha de Oro." *La Información de Madrid,* Madrid, 19 September 1994, "*Días contados,* de Imanol Uribe, una crítica feroz al terrorisme y la droga. El segundo filme español a concurso en San Sebastián tuvo un frío recibimiento".

95. *Ibid.* (my translation).

96. *Ibid.* (my translation).
97. *EL Mundo*, Madrid, 10 September 1994, "Cinelandia. Punto de partida. Imanol Uribe". (my translation).
98. *Diario de Leon*, 18 octobre 1994. "Imanol Uribe. Director de *Días contados*, última Concha de Oro". (my translation).
99. *Ibid.* (my translation).
100. Chris Perriam, *Stars and masculinities in Spanish cinema*, 71.
101. *Ibid.*, 71-72.
102. *Ibid.*, 76.
103. *Ibid.*, 97.
104. Isabel Santaolalla, *Los "Otros". Ethnicidad y "raza" en el cine español contemporáneo*, (Zaragoza: Prensa Universitarias de Zaragoza, 2005).
105. *Ibid.*, 100.
106. *Ibid.*
107. We have already cited José Angel Garrido's book, *La etnia gitana en la pantalla. Minorías en el cine*, 184-189, in which the analysis of Lute's stereotypes and the representation of gypsy culture through stereotypes. Cinema in general fails to represent their real social situation, as he concluded.
108. Luis Miguel Carmona, *El terrorismo y E.T.A. en el cine*, 133-137.
109. Josetxo Cerdán, "Desplazamiento centrífugo en tres movimientos sobre la geografía del documental español," in *Doc 21. Panorama del reciente cine documental en España*. Prólogo de Román Gubern, edited by Inmaculada Sánchez, Marta Díaz 68 (Spain: Junta de Andalucía, Editorial Galibo, 2009).
110. Josetxo Cerdán, "Volar sobre el conflicto vasco: La pelota vasca. La piel contra la piedra /Euskal Pilota. Larrua Harriaren Kontre (Julio Medem, 2003)," *Miradas sobre pasado y presente en el cine español (1990-2005)*, edited by Pietsie Feenstra, Hub Hermans, 219-230. (Amsterdam/New York: Rodopi, no. 32, 2008).
111. *Ibid*, 223.
112. Florencio Domínguez Iribarren, "Tercera parte. El enfrentamiento de ETA con la democracia. Capítulo XII. La herencia de la crisis de Bidart", 375-435. in *La Historia de ETA*, edited by Antonio Elorza. (Madrid: Temas de Hoy, 2000), 408.
113. *Ibid.*, 435.
114. *Ibid.* 412. In 2000: there were 70 attacks and 23 people killed, in 2001: there were 59 attacks and 15 people killed, in 2002: there were 35 attacks and 5 people killed, in 2003: there were 23 attacks and three people killed until the truce of 22 March 2006.
115. Elisa Costa Villaverde, "La bonne nouvelle: les films de guerre ne sont pas l'apanage des hommes. Entretien avec la réalisatrice Helena Taberna" in *Mémoire du cinéma espagnol 1975-2007*, edited by Pietsie Feenstra, 139, (Paris: Corlet, 2009, no. 130).
116. Diario de Avisos Dtrulenque, 05 November 2004. Cine. "Un 'Lobo' pone en Jaque a ETA".
117. Luis Miguel Carmona, *El terrorismo y E.T.A. en el cine*, 141.
118. El País, 03 October 2008, "Tiro en la cabeza', todo un multiestreno inédito. El filme de Rosales llega a las salas, a Internet y al museo". El País on Madrid, 03 October 2008 (David Bernal), Tiro en la cabeza, Jaime Rosales no deja indiferente con su impactante recreación de un asesinato etarra. Diario de Navarra, 06 October 2008, La ventana, Tiro en la cabeza. Canarías 7, 02 October 2008, Cine. La película de la semana. Tiro en la cabeza.

119. Román Gubern, "¡Hay motivo! (2004) Un macrotexto de cine militante", Miradas sobre pasado y presente en el cine español (1990-2005), edited by Pietsie Feenstra, Hub Hermans, 213-217. (Amsterdam/New York: Rodopi, no. 32, 2008).

120. Ibid. 217.

121. Jean Claude Seguin, "El documental español del tercer milenio: las formas de transgresión," in Miradas glocales. Cine español en el cambio de milenio, edited by Burckhard. Pohl and Jörg Türschmann, 68 (Frankfurt am Main: Edition Vervuert, 2007). Another text to cite: Jean-Claude Seguin, "ETA y el nacionalismo vasco en el cine", in Hispanismo y Cine, edited by Cristina Martínez-Carazo, Javier Herrera, 421-436, (Madrid: Ed. Iberoamericana, 2007).

122. Juan Miguel Company, José Javier Marzal, La mirada cautiva. Formas de ver en el cine contemporáneo, (Valencia: Filmoteca, Generalitat Valenciana, 1999), 86.

123. Recent publications have focused on the relationship between the political context and its national cinema, for instance, Angel Quintana, "Modelos realistas en un tiempo de emergencias de lo político, " in El último cine español en perspectiva, edited by Vicente Sánchez-Biosca, 10-31. (Archivos de la filmoteca de Valencia, no. 49, Febrero 2005) and in two European editions: Miradas glocales. Cine español en el cambio de milenio, edited by Burckhard. Pohl and Jörg Türschmann, (Frankfurt am Main: Edition Vervuert, 2006); Miradas sobre pasado y presente en el cine español (1990-2005), edited by Pietsie Feenstra, Hub Hermans, (Amsterdam/New York: Edition Rodopi, no. 32, 2008). See also: Ann Davies, Daniel Calporsoro, (Manchester: Manchester University Press, 2009) on the representation of Basque themes in the filmmaker's work.

124. Annette Wieviorka, L'ère du témoin, (Paris: Editions Plon, 1998).

Conclusion

1. Pierre Sorlin, European cinemas, European societies 1939-1990, 12.

2. The importance of making something visible in a certain historical context has already been emphasised by Marc Ferro, in Cinéma et Histoire, (Paris: Editions Denoël /Gonthier, 1977).

3. Laura Mulvey "Visual pleasure and Narrative Cinema".

4. Ruth Amossy, Les idées reçues. Sémiologie du stéréotype, 101.

5. Ibid, 103.

6. Richard Dyer et al., Cine y homosexualidad, 69-70.

7. Fransesco Casetti, Les Théories du cinéma depuis 1945, 247.

8. Recently Nadia Lie, Silvana Mandolessi, Dagmar Vandebosch, Brigitte Adriaensen, and others from the University of Leuven organised a groundbreaking conference about the Spanish stereotypes, questioning new and particularly, contemporary readings. (Playing with stereotypes. Redefining Hispanic Identity in Post-national Literature and Film/El juego con los estereotipos. La redefinición de la identidad hispánica en la literatura y el cine postnacionales (Frankfurt: Peter Lang, 2011). Including contemporary cinema, it was fascinating to observe that current readings of stereotypes were transformed into playful and comical settings.

Bibliography

Film Studies

Amiel, Vincent, *Le corps au cinéma*. Paris: Presses Universitaires de France, 1998.

Aumont, Jacques, "Le 'point de vue'." *Enonciation et Cinéma, Communications*, no. 38 (1983): 3-29.

—, *L'Image*. Paris: Editions Nathan, 1990.

Baecque, Antoine de, "Ecrans. Le corps au cinéma". In *Histoire du corps, Tome III, Les mutations du regard. Le XXe siècle*, edited by Jean-Jacques Courtine, 371-391. Paris: Editions Seuil, 2006.

Benet, Vicente José,"Cuerpos en serie". In *Cuerpos en serie*, edited by Vicente J. Benet, Eloísa Nos, 9-14. Jaume: Universitat Jaume-I, 1999.

Bordwell, David *Film Art: an Introduction*. New York: Mc Graw-Hill, 2004, (Seventh Edition).

Brenez, Nicole, *De la figure en général et du corps en particulier. L'invention figurative au cinéma*. Paris, Bruxelles: De Boeck & Larcier S.A., 1998.

Casetti, Francesco, *Les Théories du cinéma depuis 1945*. Paris: Editions Nathan, 1999.

Costa, Fabienne, *Devenir corps. Passage de l'œuvre de Fellini*. Paris: Harmattan, 2003.

Dyer Richard et al. *Cine y homosexualidad, (English title: Gays and Film)*. London: British Film Institute, 1ère Ed. 1977, Barcelona: Laertus, 1982.

—, "Estereotipos". In: *Cine y homosexualidad, (English title: Gays and Film)* edited by Richard Dyer et al., 69-94. London: British Film Institute, 1ère Ed. 1977, Barcelona: Ed. Laertus, 1982.

—, *Now you see it. Studies on Lesbian and Gay film*, London, New York: Routledge, 1990.

Elsaesser, Thomas, "Tales of Sound and Fury: Observation on the Family Melodrama." In *Movies and Methods II*, edited by Bill Nichols, 165-189. Berkeley, Los Angeles, London: University of California Press, 1985 (1ª ed.1972).

Ferro, Marc, *Cinéma et Histoire*. Paris: Editions Denoël/Gauthier, 1977.

Friedberg, Ruth, *Window Shopping, Cinema and the Postmodern culture*. Berkeley, Los Angeles: University of California Press, 1992.

Lagny, Michèle, *De l'Histoire du cinéma. Méthode historique et histoire du cinéma*. Paris: Editions Armand Colin, 1992.

Mulvey, Laura, "Visual pleasure and Narrative Cinema". *Screen* 16, no. 3 (1975), 6-18.

Odin, Roger, "Le film documentaire, lecture documentarisante". In *Cinémas et réalités*, (CIEREC, TravauxNo XLI), Saint-Étienne, Université de Saint-Étienne, (1984): 263-278.

Sorlin, Pierre, *European cinemas, European societies 1939-1990*. London: Routledge, 1991.

Siety, Emmanuel, *Le plan, au commencement du cinema*. Paris: Editions Cahiers du Cinéma, 2001.

Vincendeau, Ginette, "1973-199... Lectures féministes". In *Histoire des théories du cinéma*, edited by Joel Magny and Guy Hennebelle 116-129. Cinémaction no. 60, Paris: Ed. Corlet, 1991.

Body and myths

Amossy, Ruth, *Les idées reçues. Sémiologie du stéréotype.* Paris: Editions Nathan, 1991.

Babuscio, Jack,

—, "Lo "camp" y la sensibilidad homosexual". In: *Cine y homosexualidad, (English title: Gays and Film),* edited by Richard Dyer et al. 95-127. London: British Film Institute, 1ère Ed. 1977, Barcelona: Ed. Laertus, 1982.

—, "Lo camp y la sensibilidad homosexual". *La mirada homosexual,* edited by Alberto Mira 170-195, Archivos, Filmoteca de Valencia, no 54, 2006.

Barthes, Roland, *Mythologies.* Paris: Editions du Seuil, 1957.

Bernard, Michel, *Le corps.* Paris: Editions du Seuil, 1995.

Butler, Judith, *Trouble dans le genre. Pour un féminisme de la subversion.* Paris: La Découverte, 1990.

Cifuentes Aldunate, Claudio, "El mito del cuerpo en el cuerpo del mito: escritura e imagen." Actes de Colloque *Mitos,* no 1. (Zaragoza: Colección Trópica 4, 1998): 118-122.

Cocteau, Jean, *La voix humaine. Pièce en un acte.* Stock: Editions Stock et Jean Cocteau, 1930.

Corbin, Alain, Jean-Jacques Courtine, Georges Vigarelleo, *Histoire du corps,* Tome I, Paris: Editions du Seuil, 2005

Dufays, Jean-Louis, *Stéréotype et lecture. Essai sur la réception littéraire.* Liège: Pierre Mardage, 1994.

Durand, Gilbert, *Introduction à la Mythodologie. Mythes et sociétés.* Paris: Albin Michel, 1996.

Durkheim, Emile, *Les formes élémentaires de la vie religieuse.* Paris: Presses Universitaires de France/Quadrige, 1ère Ed: 1960, 3e, 1994.

Eco, Umberto, *De Superman au Surhomme.* Paris: Editions Grasset-Fasquelle, 1ère Ed. 1978.

Eliade, Mircea, *Aspects du mythe.* Paris: Editions Gallimard, 1963.

Garcia Gual, Carlos, *Diccionario de mitos.* Barcelona: Editorial Planeta, 1997.

Gil, José, "Le corps, l'image, l'espace." In *La danse, naissance d'un mouvement de pensée, ou le complexe de Cunningham,* edited by the Biennale Nationale de Danse du Val-de-Marne, 70-77. Paris: Editions Armand Collin, 1989.

Hamilton, Edith, *La mythologie.* Marabout: Editions Hamilton, 1978.

Iaccino, James F., *Jungian Reflections within the Cinema. A psychological Analysis of Sci-Fi and Fantasy Archetypes.* Road West: Greenwood Publishing Group, 1998.

Jung, Carl Gustav, *Dialectique du Moi et de l'inconscient.* Paris: Gallimard, 1964.

Levi-Strauss, Claude, *Anthropologie structurale.* Paris: Editions Plon, Ed. de 1956.

Mérimée, Prosper, *Carmen.* Saint-Amand Montrond: Bussière, 1996.

Moyers, Bill, *El poder del mito. Joseph Campbell en diálogo con Bill Moyers.* Barcelona: Colección Reflexiones, Emecé Editores, 1998.

Ravoux-Rallo, Elisabeth, "De la nouvelle de Mérimée au livret de Meilhac et Halévy: ressemblances et différences". In *Carmen. Figures mythiques,* edited by Elisabeth Ravoux Rallo, 10-13. Paris: Editions Autrement, 1997.

Ricoeur, Paul, *Temps et récit. Tome III. Le temps raconté.* Paris: Editions du Seuil, 1985.

Sontag, Susan, "Notes on "Camp". In *Against Interpretation and other essays,* New York: Picador USA, (2001), 275-292. Originally published in 1964: *Partisan Review.*

Valery, Paul, *L'Ame et la danse.* Paris: Editions Gallimard, 1944.

Van Gennep, Arnold, *Rites de passage Etude systématique des rites*. 1ère Ed. 1909, Paris: Editions A. et J. Picard, 1981.

Spanish cinema

Aguilar, Carlos, Jaume Genover, *El cine español en sus interpretes*. Madrid: Ed. Verdoux S. L., 1992.

—, Carlos, Francisco Llinas, "Visceralidad y Autoría. Entrevista con Eloy de la Iglesia." In *Conocer a Eloy de la Iglesia*, edited by Carlos Aguilar, Dolores Devesa, Francisco Llinas, et al. 97-173. San Sebastián: Filmoteca Vasca, 1996.

Aguilar, Pilar, *Mujer, amor y sexo en el cine español de los '90*. Madrid: Editorial Fundamentos Colección Arte, 1998.

Alfeo Alvarez, Juan Carlos, *"La imagen del personaje homosexual masculino como protagonista en la cinematografía española."* PhD diss., Universidad Complutense Madrid, Departamento de Comunicacion Audiovisuel y Publicidad II, 1997.

—, "La representación de la cuestión gay en el cine español." *Cuadernos de la Academia*, no. 5, (Mayo 1999): 287-301.

—, "El enigma de la culpa: la homosexualidad en el cine español (1961-2000)." *International Journal of Iberian Studies*, Vol. 13, no 3, (2000): 136-147.

—, "Convergencias y divergencias discursivas en la representación de los valores asociados a la experiencia gay y lésbica a través de las películas españolas". Paper presented at the meeting "Interculturalidad género y coeducación" for the Fundación Isonomía-Universidad Jaime I. Castellón, 15 de julio de 2007.

Allinson, Mark, *A Spanish Labyinth. The films of Pedro Almodóvar*. London/New York: I.B. Tauris Publishers, 2001.

—, *Un laberinto español. Las películas de Pedro Almoóvar*. Madrid: Ocho y Medio, Libros de Cine, 2003.

Babington, Bruce, Ann Davies, Chris Perriam, Phil Powrie, *Carmen on Film. A Cultural History*. Bloomington: Indiana University Press, 2007.

Barahona, Fernando Alonso, *Biografía del Cine Español*. Barcelona: C.I.L.E.H., 1992.

Benet, Vicente J., "Notas sobre el film policiaco español contemporáneo." In *Escritos sobre el cine español 1973-1987*, edited by José A. Hurtado and Francisco M. Picó, 125-131. Valencia: Filmoteca Generalitat Valencia, 1989.

Berthier, Nancy, *Le franquisme et son image. Cinéma et propagande*. Toulouse: Presses Universitaires du Mirail, 1998.

—, "Espagne folklorique et Espagne Eternelle; l'irrésistible ascension de l'Espagnolade ". *Bulletin d'Histoire Contemporaine de l'Espagne*, Bordeaux: Maison des Pays Ibériques, Bordeaux III, no. 24, (décembre 1996): 245-254.

Besas, Peter, *Behind the Spanish Lens, Cinema under Fascism and Democracy*. Denver, Colorado: Arden Press, 1985.

Brasó, Enrique *Carlos Saura: una introducción incompleta*, Madrid: Taller de Ediciones Josefina Betantor, 1974.

Brémard, Bénédicte, "Le métissage des cultures dans le cinema espagnol homosexuel contemporain: Pedro Almodóvar/Ventura Pons". *Littératures, Arts, homosexualités. Dossier bilingue de Littératures Hispaniques*, edited by Patrick Dubuis, Nicolas Balutet, Inverses 5/2005, (Avril 2005), 53-80.

Cami-Vela, María, *Mujeres detrás de la cámara. Entrevistas con cineastas españolas 1900-2004*. Madrid: Ocho y Medio, 2005.

Camporesi, Valeria, *Para grandes y chicos: Un cine para los españoles 1940-1990*. Madrid ; Turfán, 1994.

Caparros Lera, J.M, *El cine español de la democracia. De la muerte de Franco al 'cambio' socialista (1975-1989)*. Barcelona: Editorial Anthropos, 1992.

Carmona, Luis Miguel, *El terrorismo y E.T.A. en el cine*. Madrid: Cacitel, S. L., 2004.

Cerdan, Josetxo, "Volar sobre el conflicto vasco: La pelota vasca. La piel contra la piedra /Euskal Pilota. Larrua Harriaren Kontre (Julio Medem, 2003)." In *Miradas sobre pasado y presente en el cine español (1990-2005)*, edited by Pietsie Feenstra, Hub. Hermans, 219-230. Amsterdam/New York NY: Rodopi, no. 32, 2008.

—, "Desplazamiento centrífugo en tres movimientos sobre la geografía del documental español". In *Doc 21. Panorama del reciente cine documental en España. Prólogo de Román Gubern*, edited by Inmaculada Sánchez, Marta Díaz, 67-80. Spain: Junta de Andalucía, Editorial Galibo, 2009.

Company, Juan Miguel, José Javier Marzal, *La mirada cautiva. Formas de ver en el cine contemporáneo*. Valencia: Filmoteca, Generalitat Valenciana, 1999.

Costa, Villaverde, Elisa, "*La bonne nouvelle*: les films de guerre ne sont pas l'apanage des hommes. Entretien avec la réalisatrice Helena Taberna." In *Mémoire du cinéma espagnol 1975-2007*, edited by P. Feenstra, 139-145. Cinémaction no. 130, Paris: Ed. Corlet, 2009.

Davies, Ann, Chris Perriam (ed.), *Carmen. From Silent Film to MTV*. Amsterdam/New York NY: Rodopi, Critical Studies, vol. 24, 2005.

Davies, Ann, "Male sexuality and Basque Separatism in Two Films by Imanol Uribe", *Hispanic Research Journal*, vol. 4, no. 2, (June 2003), 121-132.

—, *Daniel Calporsoro*, Manchester: Manchester University Press, 2009.

Donapetry, María, *La otra mirada. La mujer y el cine en la cultura española*. New York: UPS, 1998.

D'Lugo, Marvin, *The Films of Carlos Saura. The Practice of Seeing*, Princeton, New Jersey: Princeton University Press, 1991.

—, "Re-imaging the Community: Imanol Uribe's *La muerte de Mikel* (1983) and the Cinema of Transition." In *Spanish cinema. The auteurist cinema*, edited by Peter Evans, 194-209, Oxford: Oxford University Press, 1999.

—, *Pedro Almodóvar*, Series: Contemporary Film Directors, Chicago and Urbana: University of Illinois Press, 2006.

Evans, Peter (ed.), *Spanish cinema. The Auteurist Tradition*. Oxford: Oxford University Press, 1999.

—, Robin W. Fiddian, "The Europeanization of Carmen." In *Challenges to authority: fiction and film in contemporary Spain*, edited by Peter Evans and Robin W.Fiddian, 83-94. London, Tamesis Book Limited, 1988.

Feenstra, Pietsie, "La Carmen espagnole de Carlos Saura: construire une nouvelle figure mythique par le flamenco." In *Images et Divinités*, Actes de Colloque Grimh, Lyon: Les Cahiers du Grimh, no. 2, 2000, 161-169.

—, "La construction des nouvelles figures mythiques dans le cinéma espagnol de l'après-franquisme (1975-1995)." PhD diss., Université de Paris III-Sorbonne Nouvelle, Département des Etudes Cinématographiques et Audiovisuelles, 12 November 2001.

—, "Les mémoires cinématographiques de la Guerre civile espagnole." In *Cinéma et Stalinisme, la caméra politique*, edited by Kristian Feigelson, 164-179. Théorème no. 8, Paris: Presses Sorbonne Nouvelle, 2005.

—, "Mitos "españoles" y cuerpos exóticos: *Carmen Jones* (1954) y *Carmen: a Hip Hopera* (2001). " In *Carmen en Hollywood*, edited by Gloria F. Vilches and Vicente Sánchez-Biosca, 84-93, *Archivos* no. 51, Valencia: Ed. Filmoteca Valencia, October 2005.

—, *Les nouvelles figures mythiques du cinéma espagnol. A corps perdus*. Préface de Michèle Lagny. Paris: Harmattan, Collection Champs Visuels, 2006.

—, "Fernando León de Aranoa, autor de un género: cámaras intimistas sobre la marginalidad en el cine español. " In *Miradas glocales. Cine español en el cambio de milenio*, edited by Burckhard. Pohl and Jorg Tuerschmann, 201-217, Frankfurt am Main: Edition Vervuert/Iberoamericana, 2006.

—, Feenstra, Pietsie, Hub Hermans, *Miradas sobre pasado y presente en el cine español 1990-2005*. Amsterdam/New York: Rodopi, no. 32, 2008.

—, Feenstra, Pietsie (ed.), *Mémoire du cinéma espagnol 1975-2007*, Cinémaction no. 130, Paris: Editions Corlet, 2009.

Fereira, Patricia, The 28th of March 2008, Patricia Ferreira delivered a conference about women directors in Colegio de España in 2008-2009, Paris.

Fouz-Hernandez, Santíago, Chris Perriam, "El deseo sin ley: la representación de 'la homosexualidad' en el cine español de los años noventa." In *Cultura, homosexualidad y homofobia*, edited by Félix González Rodríguez, 61-80. Vol. 1, Perspectivas Gays, Barcelona: Ed. Laertes, 2007.

Fouz-Hernandez, Santiago, Alfredo Martínez-Expósito, *Live Flesh. The Male Body in Contemporary Spanish Cinema*, London/New York: I.B. Taurus, 2007.

F. Vilches, Gloria, "La representación de Carmen en el cine norteamericano 1915-1954." PhD diss., Universidad de Valencia, 2007.

F. Vilches, Gloria, Vicente Sánchez-Biosca, (ed.), *Carmen en Hollywood*, Archivos de la Filmoteca de Valencia, no. 51, October 2005.

Garcia de Leon, María Antonia, Teresa Maldonado, *Pedro Almodóvar, la otra España cañi*. Ciudad Real: Diputación Provincial, 1989.

Garrido, José Angel, *La etnia gitana en la pantalla. Minorías en el cine*. Barcelona: Publicaciones de la Universitat de Barcelona, 2003.

Gomez B De Castro, Ramiro, *La producción cinematográfica española. De la Transición a la Democracia (1976-1986)*. Bilbao: Ediciones Mensajero, 1989.

Gubern, Román, *1936-1939: la guerra de España en la pantalla*. Madrid: Filmoteca Española, 1986.

—, "la guerra civil y Los imaginarios del cine del franquismo." In *Un siglo de cine español*, edited by Román Gubern, 157-168. Madrid: Cuadernos de la Academia, Octubre, no. 1, 1997.

—, "¡Hay motivo! (2004) Un macrotexto de cine militante." In *Miradas sobre pasado y presente en el cine español (1990-2005)*, edited by Pietsie Feenstra and Hub Hermans, 213-217. Amsterdam/New York: Rodopi, no. 32, 2008.

Heitz, Françoise, *Pilar Miró: vingt ans de cinéma espagnol (1976-1996)*. Arras: Artois Presses Université, 2001.

Henguet, Joris, "Almodóvar as a women-hater: why Pedro Almodóvar is not unanimously described as a women-director." This is an unpublished essay, written for the masters course on Spanish cinema, at the University of Amsterdam, 2008.

Heredero, Carlos F. (ed.), *La mitad del cielo. Directoras españolas de los años 90*. Festival de Cine de Malaga: Malaga, 1998.

Herrera, Javier, Cristina Martínez-Carazo, *Hispanismo y Cine*, Madrid: Ed. Iberoamericana, 2007.

Higginbotham, Virginia, *Spanish film under Franco*. Austin: University of Texas Press, 1988.

Holguin, Antonio, *Pedro Almodóvar*. Madrid: Cátedra, 1994.

Hopewell, John, *El cine español después de Franco 1973-1988*. Madrid: Ediciones el Arquero, 1989.

Jordan, Barry, Rikki Morgan-Tamosunas, *Contemporary Spanish Cinema*. Manchester: Manchester University Press, 1998.

Kinder, Marsha,

—, *Blood cinema: The Reconstruction of National Identity in Spain*. Los Angeles, London: University of California Press, 1993.

—, "From Matricide to Motherlove in Almodóvar's *High Heels*." In *Post-Franco, Postmodern: The Films of Pedro Almodóvar*, edited by Kathleen M. Vernon and Barbara Morris, 144-153. Vol. 43, Greenwood: Greenwood Press, 1995.

—, Marsha Kinder (ed.), *Refiguring Spain, Cinema/Media/Representation*. Durham and London: Duke University Press, 1997.

—, "Sex Change and Cultural Transformation in Aranda and Abril's *Cambio de Sexo* (1977)." In *Spanish Cinema. The Auteurist Tradition*, edited by Peter Evans, 128-146. New York: Oxford University Press, 1999.

—, "Interview with Pedro Almodóvar", pp. 131-144, in Marvin D'Lugo, *Pedro Almodóvar*, Series: Contemporary Film Directors, Chicago and Urbana: University of Illinois Press, 2006. Originally published in 1987: Marsha Kinder, "Pleasure and the New Spanish Mentality. A conversation with Pedro Almodóvar." In *Film Quarterly* no. 41 (Fall 1987): 33-44.

Kowalsky, Daniel, "Rated S: softcore pornography and the Spanish transition to democracy, 1977-1982." In *Spanish Popular Cinema (Inside Popular Film)*, edited by Antonio Lázarro Reboll and Andrew Willis, 188-208. Manchester: Manchester University Press, 2004.

Larraz, Emmanuel, "El cine español. Textos escogidos y presentados por." (Regards sur le monde hispanique). Paris: Ed. Masson, 1973.

—, "Raza et le mythe de la croisade dans le cinéma franquiste." In *Les mythologies hispaniques dans la seconde moitié du XXe siècle*. Dijon: Hispanistica XX, Centre D'Etudes et de Recherches Hispaniques du XXe siècle, Université de Dijon, (1985), 133-140.

—, *Le cinéma espagnol dès origines à nos jours*. Paris: Edition Cerf 7ème Art, 1986.

Leandro, Anita, *Le personnage mythique au cinéma. Etude des représentations de Carmen*. Lille: Editions Septentrion, 1997.

Le Vagueresse, Emmanuel, "*Diferente* (1961) de Luis María Delgado: un regard 'différent' sur l'homosexuel en plein franquisme." In *Image et Corps*, Lyon: Editions du Grimh-LCE, 2007, 463-470.

Lie, Nadia, Silvana Mandolessi, Dagmar Vandebosch, *El juego con los estereotipos. La redefinición de la identidad hispánica en la literature y el cine postnacionales (Playing with stereotypes. Redefining Hispanic Identity in Post-national Literature and Film)*, Frankfurt am Main: Peter Lang, 2011.

Manuel Vidal, Estevez, "La trilogía vasca del cine español." In: *Entre el documental y la ficción. El cine de Imanol Uribe,* edited by Jesus Angulo, Carlos F. Heredero, 31-44. San Sebastian: Editorial Filmoteca vasca, 1994.

Marsh, Steven, *Popular Spanish film under Franco. Comedy and the Weakening of the State.* New York: Palgrave MacMillan, 2006.

Marsh, Steven, Parvati Nair (ed.), *Gender and Spanish Cinema.* New York, Oxford: Ed. Berg, 2004.

Marti-Olivella, Jaume, "Regendering Spain's Political Bodies: Nationality and Gender in the Films of Pilar Miró and Arantxa Lazcano." In *Refiguring Spain. Cinema/Media/Representation,* edited by Marsha Kinder, 215-238, Durham and London: Duke University Press, 1997.

Martin-Marquez, Susan, *Feminist Discourse and Spanish Cinema, Sight Unseen.* Oxford: Oxford University Press, 1999.

Maurer, Isabel, *Die Asthetik des Zwitters im filmischen Werk von Pedro Almodóvar.* Frankfurt am Main: Ed. Vervuert, 2005.

Merchán, Eduardo Rodriguez, Concha Gómez, "El cine de la Democracia (1978-1995). " In *Un siglo de cine español* edited by Román Gubern, 185-224. Madrid: Cuadernos de la Academia, Octubre, no. 1, 1997.

Mira, Alberto (ed.), *La mirada homosexual,* Archivos de la Filmoteca, no. 54, Octubre, Valencia: Ed. Filmoteca de Valencia, 2006.

—, "El significante inexistente. Cinco calas en la representación de la homosexualidad en el cine español." In *La mirada homosexual,* edited by Alberto Mira, 71-95. Archivos de la Filmoteca de Valencia, no. 54, Octubre 2006.

Monterde, José Enrique, *Veinte años de cine español. Un cine bajo la paradoja (1973-1992).* Barcelona: Ediciones Paidós Ibérica S.A., 1993.

Montero, Laureano, "El cine quinqui o el lado oscuro de la Transición." In *De la zarzuela al cine. Los medios de comunicación populares y su traducción de la voz marginal,* edited by Max Doppelbauer, Kathrin Sartringen, 123-138. München: Martin Meidenbauer, 2010.

Murcia, Claude, *Femmes au bord de la crise des nerfs. Pedro Almodóvar,* Paris: Edition Nathan, 1995.

Neuschafer, Hans-Jörg, *Adiós a la España eterna. La dialéctica de la censura. Novela, teatro y cine bajo el franquismo.* Barcelona: Editorial Anthropos, 1994.

Oms, Marcel, *La guerre d'Espagne au cinéma. Mythes et réalités.* Paris: Editions Cerf, 1986.

Pavlovic, Tatjana, *Despotic Bodies and Transgressive Bodies. Spanish Culture from Francisco Franco to Jesús Franco.* Albany: SUNY (State University of New York Press), 2003.

Pelayo, Irene, "Imagen fílmica del lesbianismo a través de los personajes protagonistas en el cine español." PhD diss., Universidad Complutense Madrid, 19 de mayo 2009.

Perales, Francisco, *Luis García Berlanga.* Madrid: Ediciones Cátedra, 1997.

Perez Perucha, Julio, Vicente Ponce, "Algunas instrucciones para evitar naufragios metodológicos y rastrear la transición democrática en el cine español". In *El cine y la transición política española,* 34-45. Valencia: Filmoteca Valenciana y Consellería de Cultura, Educació i Ciencia de la Generalitat Valenciana, 1985.

Perriam, Chris, *Stars and masculinities in Spanish cinema.* Oxford: Oxford University Press, 2003.

Pohl, Burkhard, Jörg Türschmann, *Miradas glocales. Cine español en el cambio de milenio.* Frankfurt am Main: Edition Vervuert, 2006.

Quintana, Angel, "Modelos realistas en un tiempo de emergencias de lo político." In *El último cine español en perspectiva*, edited by Vicente Sánchez-Biosca, 10-31. Archivos de la Filmoteca de Valencia, no. 49, Febrero 2005.

Riambau, Esteve, "El cine español durante la Transición (1973-1978): Una asignatura pendiente." In *Un siglo de cine español*, edited by Román Gubern, 173-184. *Cuadernos de la Academia*, no. 1 Octubre, Madrid: Academia de las Artes y las Ciencias Cinematográficas de España, 1997.

Salvador, Alejandro Melero, "New Sexual Politics in the Cinema of the Transition to Democracy: de la Iglesia's *El diputado* (1978). " In *Gender and Spanish Cinema*, edited by Steven Marsh, Parvati Nair, 87-102. New York, Oxford: Ed. Berg, 2004.

Sánchez-Biosca, Vicente, "La Ficcionalización de la historia por el nuevo cine español: de *La vaquilla* (1985) a *Madregilda* (1994)." In: *Revista Canadiense de Estudios Hispánicos*, Vol. XX, 1, Otoño (1995), 179-193.

—, *Cine y Guerra civil española. Del mito a la memoria*. Madrid: Alianza, 2006.

Sánchez Vidal, Agustín, *Retrato de Carlos Saura*. Barcelona: Circulo de Lectores, Galaxia Gutenberg, 1994.

Santaolalla, Isabel, *Los 'Otros'. Ethnicidad y 'raza' en el cine español contemporáneo*. Zaragoza: Prensa Universitarias de Zaragoza, 2005.

Saura, Carlos, Prosper Mérimée, *Carmen: el sueño del amor absoluto*. Barcelona: Círculo de Lectores, 1984.

Schmelzer, Dagmar, "La violencia enfocada: tres visiones cinematográficas españolas. *La muerte de Mikel* (1983) de Imanol Uribe, *Historias del Kronen* (1994) de Montxo Armendáriz, y *El Bola* (2000) de Achero Mañas." In *Miradas glocales. Cine español en el cambio de milenio*, edited by Burkhard Pohl and Jörg Türschmann, 73-87. Frankfurt am Main: Ed. Vervuert/Iberoamericana, 2007.

Seguin, Jean Claude, *Histoire du cinéma espagnol*. Paris: Nathan, 1994.

—, "El documental español del tercer milenio: las formas de transgresión". In *Miradas glocales. Cine español en el cambio de milenio*, edited by Burckhard Pohl and Jörg Türschmann, 55-69. Frankfurt am Main: Edition Vervuert/Iberoamericana, 2007.

—, "ETA y el nacionalismo vasco en el cine", in *Hispanismo y Cine*, edited by Cristina Martínez-Carazo, Javier Herrera, 421-436, Madrid: Ed. Iberoamericana, 2007.

Smith, Paul Julian, In George De Stefano Post-Franco Frankness, FC 22 (Junio 1986), 58-60.

—, *Laws of Desire. Questions of homosexuality in Spanish Writing and Film 1960-1990*. Oxford: Clarendon Press, 1992.

—, *Desire Unlimited. The Cinema of Pedro Almodóvar*. London: Verso, 1994 (Second Ed. 2000).

—, *Las leyes del deseo. La homosexualidad en la literatura y el cine español 1960-1990*. Barcelona: Ediciones de la Tempestad, 1998.

—, "Cine, historia y homosexualidad. *Far from Heaven (Lejos del cielo*, 2002) de Todd Haynes y *La mala educación* (2004) de Almodóvar." In *La mirada homosexual*, edited by Alberto Mira 98-109, Archivos no. 54, Octubre 2006.

Strauss, Frédéric, *Conversations avec Pedro Almodóvar*. Paris: Editions Cahiers du Cinéma, 2000.

Torreiro, Casimiro, "Del tardofranquismo a la democracia (1969-1982)." In *Historia del cine español*, Román Gubern, José Enrique Monterde, Casimiro Torreiro, et al., 341-398. Madrid: Ediciones Cátedra S.A., 1995.

—, "Del cineasta como cronista airado: historia e ideología." In *Conocer a Eloy de la Iglesia*, Carlos Aguilar, Dolores Devesa, Francisco Llinas et al., 15-47. San Sebastián: Filmoteca Vasca, 1996.

Triana-Toribio, Nuria, *Spanish national cinema.* London: Routledge, 2003.

Tropiano, Stephen, "Out of the cinematic closet. Homosexuality in Films of Eloy de la Iglesia." In *Refiguring Spain: Cinema/Media/Representation*: edited by Marsha Kinder, 159-177. Durham, London: Duke University Press, 1997.

Türschmann, Jörg, "La vida de lo teatral: actrices/actrius (1996) de Ventura Pons." In: *Escenarios compartidos: cine y teatro en España en el umbral del siglo XXI*, edited by Verena Berger and Mercè Aumell, 75-86. Wien: Lit Verlag, 2009.

Vidal Estevez, Manuel, "La trilogía vasca del cine español." In *Entre el documental y la ficción. El cine de Imanol Uribe*, edited by Jesus Angulo, Carlos F. Heredero, 31-44. San Sebastian: Editorial Filmoteca vasca, 1994.

Vidal, Nuria, *El cine de Pedro Almodóvar.* Barcelona: Edition Destinolibro, no. 285, 1988.

—, *The Films of Pedro Almodóvar.* Madrid: Instituto de la Cinematografía y las Artes Audiovisuales, Ministerio de Cultura, 1988.

Political and sociological studies, juridical documents

Arranz, Fátima, Esperanza Roquero, Pilar Aguilar, Pilar Pardo, Blanca Rilova, Olaya Alvarez, *La situación de las mujeres y los hombres en el audiovisual español: estudios sociológico y legislativo.* Madrid: Universidad Complutense, 2008.

AVT: Asociación Víctimas del Terrorismo (www.avt.org)

Asociación Pro Derechos Humanos de España, *Actas de las primeras jornadas sobre problemática del pueblo gitano.* Madrid: Asociación Pro Derechos Humanos con la colaboración del Ministerio de Trabajo y Seguridad Social, 1987.

Bato Tomasevic, Nebojsa, Rajko Djuric, et al., *Gypsies of the world.* London: Flint River Press, 1989.

Blanes, A., F. Gil, J. Perez, *Población y actividad en España: evolución y perspectivas.* Barcelona: Colección Estudios e Informes, Caja de Aharros y pensiones, 1996.

Caritas Española, *Dossier Droga.* Madrid: Servicio de documentacion de Cáritas, Febrero 1985.

Código Penal, *Código Penal y legislación de peligrosidad social.* Madrid: Civitas, partie 23487, 1970.

Código Penal, *Código Penal y legislación de peligrosidad social.* Madrid: Civitas, 1981.

— Penal, *Appendice 1975-1985*, al nuevo diccionario de legislación XIII, 1988.

Constitución Española, *Constitución Española de 27 de Diciembre de 1978.* 3e Ed actualizada noviembre 1997.

Delpal, Jacques-Louis, *Los travestís y el enigma de los cambios de sexo.* Madrid: Ed. Marsiega, Tropos editora, prensa underground, 1974.

Domínguez Iribarren, Florencio, "Tercera parte. El enfrentamiento de ETA con la democracia. Capítulo XII. La herencia de la crisis de Bidart", in *La Historia de ETA*, edited by Antonio Elorza, Madrid: Temas de Hoy, 2000, 375-435.

Domingo Loren, Victoriano, *Los homosexuales frente a la ley: los juristas opinan. La homosexualidad. ¿es un vicio o es una enfermedad?* Esplugas de Llobregat (Barcelona): Plaza § Janés, 1978.

Ealham, Chris, Michael Richards, *The splintering of Spain: cultural history and the Spanish Civil War, 1936-1939.* Cambridge: Cambridge University Press, 2005.

Elorza, Antonio (ed.), *La Historia de ETA.* Madrid: Temas de Hoy, 2000.

Escario, Pilar, *Lo personal es político: el movimiento feminista en la transición.* Madrid: Instituto de la Mujer, 1996.

Eslava Galán, Juan, *El sexo de nuestros padres.* Barcelona: Editorial Planeta, 1993.

Foucault, Michel, *Histoire de la sexualité I. La volonté de savoir.* Paris: Gallimard, 1976.

Fuertes Oliveira, Pedro A, *Mujer, lenguaje y sociedad: los estereotipos de género en inglés y en español.* Valladolid: Universidad de Valladolid, 1992.

Gallego Sanz, Luis María, *Breve estudio sobre la Ley de peligrosidad y rehabilitación social.* Gallego: Ed. S.L. L.M., 1986.

Garcia Martin, Antonio, Andrés López Fernández, *Imagen social de la homosexualidad en España.* Madrid: Asociación Pro Derechos Humanos, 1985.

Garrido Gonzalez, Elisa, *Historia de las mujeres en España.* Madrid: Síntesis, 1997.

Gonzalez Gonzalez, Eugenio, *Bandas Juveniles.* Barcelona: Editorial Herder, 1982.

Gurutz Jáuregui, "La cuestión vasca durante el franquismo." In *La cuestión vasca. Una mirada desde la Historia,* edited by Mercedes Arbaíza Vilallonga , 139-154. Bilbao: Editiorial del País Vasco, 2001.

Instituto de la Mujer, *Situación Social de la Mujer en España.* Madrid: Instituto de la Mujer, 1986.

Jauregui, Gurutz, "La cuestión vasca durante el franquismo". In *La cuestión vasca. Una mirada desde la Historia,* edited by Mercedes Arbaíza Vilallonga, 139-154. Bilbao: Editiorial del País Vasco.

Jordan Pemán, Fernando, *Religiosidad y moralidad de los gitanos en España.* Madrid: Asociación Secretariado General Gitano, D.L., 1991.

Juderías, Julián, *La leyenda negra: Estudios acerca del concepto de España en el extranjero.* Madrid: Editorial Nacional, 1967, primera ed., Barcelona: Araluce, 1917.

Medero, Alicia, *El Flamenco.* Madrid: Acento Editorial, 1996.

Ministerio de la Cultura, *Boletín Informativo del Control de Taquilla. Películas, Recaudaciones, Espectadores,* Madrid: Ministerio de Cultura, Instituto de la Cinematografía y de las Artes Audiovisuales: Ed. 1975-1995.

Ministerio de la Gobernación, *Delincuencia Juvenil. Estudio de su problemática en España.* Madrid: Ministerio de la Gobernación, Colleción Estudios 14, 1972.

Molina Foix, Vicente, "¡Quiero llamarme Bibiana Fernández! ". In *El País Semanal,* Número 1 110, Domingo 4 de enero (1998), 24-29.

Montilla Valerio, Javier, "Las dificultades sociales de las personas transexuales." In *Identidad de género vs. Identidad sexual,* Carme Pinyana Garl, Alicia Gil Gómez. Actas 4º Congreso Estatal Isonomía sobre identidad de género vs identidad sexual, Universitat Jaume I, Publicacions de la Universitat Jaume I, 2008, 122-131.

Morán Blanco, Sagrario, *ETA entre España y Francia.* Madrid: Editorial Complutense, 1997.

Parejo, Jimenez Nekane, "Fotografía y muerte: representación gráfica de los atentados de ETA (1968-1997)." PhD diss., Universidad del Pais Vasco, 2003.

Pohren, Donn E., *The art of flamenco.* Madrid: Society of Spanish Studies, 1990.

Poizat, Michel, *L'Opéra ou le cri de l'ange. Essai sur la jouissance de l'amateur d'opéra.* Paris: Editions Métailié, 1986.

Prados de la Escosura, Leandro, Sanz, Jorge C., "Growth and Macroeconomic Performance in Spain 1939-1993." In: *Economic Growth in Europe since 1945*, edited by Nicolas Crafts, 355-387. Cambridge: Cambridge University Press, 1996.

Rodriguez, M.P., M.C. Ausan, E. Costa Villaverde, *Estudio cuantativo sobre la igualdad de género en el panorama de la ficción audiovisual*. Madrid: Instituto de la Mujer, Ministerio de Trabajo y Asuntos Sociales, 2007.

Romeo Casabona, Carlos María, *Peligrosidad y derecho penal preventive*. Barcelona: Bosche, 1986.

Ross, Christopher J., *Contemporary Spain. A Handbook*. London/New York: Ed. Arnold, 1997.

Sánchez, Euleterio, *Mañana seré libre: mémorias de "El Lute"*. 2a parte, Barcelona: Círculo de Lectores, D.L., 1988, 1ère Ed., 1979.

Sánchez Cervella, Josep, "El contexto nacional e internacional de la resistencia (1939-1952)." In: *El último Frente. La resistencia armada antifranquista en España 1939-1952*, edited by Julio Aróstegui and Jorge Marco, 17-38. Madrid: Los libros de la Catarata, 2008.

Santos, Julio, Javier Pradera, Joaquín Prieto, *Memoria de la Transición*. Madrid: Taurus, 1996.

Sociedad de Estudios Vascos, *Fiesta de los gansos, information de l'Association de la culture basque*.

"Toxicomanía y delincuencia". In: *IV Simposium Europeo Regional de la AIDSM, 25 y 26 de enero*, Facultad de Medicina, Barcelona: Casanova 143, 1991.

Usó, Juan Carlos, *Drogas y cultura de masas: España (1855-1995)*. Madrid: Taurus, 1996.

Vázquez Montalbán, Manuel, *Crónica Sentimental de España*. Barcelona: Ediciones Bruguera, 1980 (first edition: 1971).

Wieviorka, Annette, *L'ère du témoin*. Paris: Editions Plon, 1998.

Websites (last checked 15 December 2010)

Asociacion de mujeres cineastas y de medios audiovisuales (CIMA):
http://www.cimamujerescineastas.es/

Fiesta de los gansos:
http://www.elmundo.es/elmundo/2010/09/05/paisvasco/1283706019.html
Homosexuality:
www.coc.nl

Victims of Terrorism:
http://www.avt.org/
http://www.fundacionvt.org/

Magazines and newspapers

Press articles

Flunking Out/Asignatura pendiente, Carmen, High Heels/Tacones lejanos

Arriba, 21 March 1978, "La primera película de José Luis Garci, *Asignatura pendiente*, 300 millones de pesetas de recaudación." *Ya*, 20 October 1978, "Prohibida *Asignatura pendiente*."

La Vanguardia Española, 01 May 1977, "Cinematografia Astoria "*Asignatura pendiente*" de Angeles MASO."

La Vanguardía, 28 May 1983, "Saura: *Carmen*, estampa de la libertad. Los españoles hemos sido los primeros en llevar adelante la *Carmen* de los 80."

El País, 16 August 1984, "Gades define el personaje de Carmen como una mujer libre."

El Correo Catalan, 15 May 1983, "*Carmen* de Carlos Saura."

El periodico, 30 October 1991, "*Tacones lejanos* bate todos los récords. La película de Almodóvar recauda 123 millones en su primer fin de semana en cartel."

El mundo, 26 October 1991, "Visiones, glamour y espectáculo en el estreno, ayer en Madrid, del filme *Tacones lejanos*."

El mundo, 26 October 1991, "Los placeres y los días de Fransisco UMBRAL."

El Independiente, 22 October 1991, "La estética del fragmentarismo."

Expansión Madrid, 02 November 1991, "*Tacones lejanos*: el último saldo, Eduardo Torres-Dulce."

Pronto Madrid, 7 December 1991, "LUZ CASAL edita un disco con las canciones de *Tacones lejanos*."

El País, 18 June 1993, "En danza por Amor de Dios. Asociacion y penas flamencas protestan contra el cierre de la academia de baile. ?A dónde iran los balaores ?"

Press articles

SEX CHANGE/CAMBIO DE SEXO, THE DEPUTY/EL DIPUTADO, THE DEATH OF MIKEL/LA MUERTE DE MIKEL, LAW OF DESIRE/LA LEY DEL DESEO

La Vanguardia Española, 25 June 1977, "*Cambio de sexo*."

Sábado Gráfico, 28 May 1977, "Comentario C7. "Cuando el 'cambio' es… de sexo."

Informaciones, 19 May 1977, "*Cambio de sexo*."

La Vanguardia, 24 October 1978, "Llegó con *El diputado*. Eloy de la Iglesia: "La izquierda ha heredado una moral que no es la suya."

ABC, 09 February 1979 , "*El diputado*, de Eloy de la Iglesia."

El País, 27 January 1979, "*Sexo y política*: un cóctel que vende," Fernando Treuba.

Pueblo, 24 January 1979, "Real Cinema *El Diputado*."

Periódico, 19 January 1979, "*El diputado*; político y homosexual."

La Calle, Madrid 30 January 1979, "A por los 300 millones'. Que *El diputado* es un éxito de taquilla, nadie lo pone en duda: ahí están los carteles de "No hay entradas" en los cines donde se proyecta."

Diario 16, 23 February 1979, "Existe un divorcio claro entre crítica y público."

El País, 18 February 1984, "Hermosa y arriesgada denuncia. La repercusión en Euskadi."

El País, 15 November 1983, "La nueva película de Imanol Uribe pretende reflejar la acual realidad interna de Euskadi."

Segre Lerida, 06 May 1984, "La consagración de Arias. Una historia de un militante de izquierda homosexual."

El País, 15 November 1985, "Política y homosexualidad."

Segre Lerida, 07 June 1987, "*La ley del deseo*. Desde la butaca."

ABC, 08 February 1987, "*La ley del deseo*, un desahogo en la carrera de Pedro Almodóvar. Desorbitada melodrama, con triángulo, celos, asesinato y desenlace fatal."

Diario 16, 24 January 1987, "Deseos, invitados y policías."
YA, 13 October 1988, Madrid, *"La ley del deseo,* récord en festivales."

Press articles

Hurry, Hurry/Deprisa, deprisa, El Lute, Running Out of Time/Días contados
El País, 21 September 1980, *"Deprisa,* un documento sobre la delincuencia."
Diario de Barcelona, 10 April 1981, "Rueda de prensa de Carlos Saura en Barcelona. *Deprisa, Deprisa,* una historia de amor."
Diario 16, 20 February 1981, *"Deprisa, deprisa* causó cierta decepción en Berlín."
Semana, nr 897, 1981, "Confesiones de Genoveva López: Creo que mi marido cometió el atraco influido por la película de Saura."
Diario 16, 12 March 1981, "El protagonista de la última película de Saura, capturado *Deprisa, deprisa."*
Cambio 16, 23 March 1981, "La loca carrera de El Mini."
Diario 16, 04 August 1981, *"Deprisa, deprisa,…* a la cárcel, a la cárcel."
El País, 28 March 1981, "El lento y complicado rodaje de *Deprisa, deprisa.* Carlos Saura habla de su última película, que se estrena el miércoles."
Gaceta Ilustrada, no. 837, 1981, "MARIAS, Julian, Señoritismo."
Pueblo, 06 September 1983, "Otro de los protagonistas de *Deprisa, deprisa,* detenido."
ABC, Madrid, October 1987, "Euleterio Sánchez habla de *El Lute* en su salida al camino de las pantallas."
El País, 06 October 1987, "La ex esposa de Euleterio Sánchez pide el secuestro del filme sobre *El Lute."*
Segre Lerida, 14 October 1987, "El Lute, en las charlas sobre la marginación."
Ya, 16 October 1987, "La historia de un quinqui que llegó a mito."
Diez minutos, 20 October 1987, "Consuelo Garcia fírmo la denuncia contra la película El Lute, *Camina o revienta."*
Hola, 22 October 1987, "Consuelo Garcia Chelo, se ha querellado contra toda el equipo de *Camina o revienta."*
Ya, Madrid, 10 November 1987, "La dura crónica de un hombre perseguido."
Segre Lerida, 15 November 1987, *"El Lute, camina o revienta."*
Lecturas, Vivir para ver, 18 November 1987, "Eleuterio Sánchez lamenta que su ex-mujer se haya querellado contra su película."
Semana, Madrid, 07 April 1988, "La actriz Silvia Rodriguez se casó por el rito gitano con Imanol Arias."
El Independiente, Madrid, 13 May 1988, "Vicente Aranda: El Lute fue la cabeza de turco, un chivo expiatoria."
Ya, Madrid, 22 April 1988, "Imanol Arias: El Lute ha acabado definitivamente con mi imagen de galán."
El País, 21 July 1990, "Rechazado el recurso de la ex-mujer de El Lute contra un filme de Aranda."
Diario de Leon, Leon, 18 October 1994, "Imanol Uribe. Director de *Días contados,* última Concha de Oro."
La Información de Madrid, Madrid, 19 September 1994, *"Días contados,* de Imanol Uribe, una crítica feroz al terrorisme y la droga. El segundo filme español a concurso en San Sebastián tuvo un frío recibimiento."

Diario de Leon, Leon, 18 October 1994, "Imanol Uribe. Director de *Días contados*, última Concha de Oro."

El Mundo, Madrid, 10 September 1994, "Cinelandia. Punto de partida. Imanol Uribe."

Other press articles

Beerekamp, Hans. In *NRC Handelsblad*,

– 1 March 2000. "Authenticiteit door siliconen en pikant melodrama." "(Authenticity through silicon and spicy melodrama.")

– 25 September 2002, "Almodóvar toont zijn vrouwenhaat." (Almodóvar shows his hatred of women")

– 7 February 2006: Lady killer ontpopt zich als seriemoordenaar. Beelden van een 'hip' Spanje." ("Lady killer becomes a serrial killer. Images of a modern Spain.")

Diario de Avisos Dtrulenque, 05 November 2004. "Cine. Un 'Lobo' pone en Jaque a ETA."

El País, 03 October 2008, "Tiro en la cabeza, todo un multiestreno inédito. El filme de Rosales llega a las salas, a Internet y al museo."

El País on Madrid, 03 October 2008 (David Bernal), "Tiro en la cabeza, Jaime Rosales no deja indiferente con su impactante recreación de un asesinato etarra."

Diario de Navarra, 06 October 2008, "La ventana, Tiro en la cabeza."

Canarias 7, 02 October 2008, "Cine. La película de la semana. Tiro en la cabeza."

Dictionary

Le Nouveau Petit Robert, Dictionnaire alphabétique et analogique de la langue française, de Paul Robert, texte remanié et amplifié sous la direction de Josette Rey-Debove et Alain Rey, Paris, Dictionnaire Le Robert, 1994.

Photography

1. RACE (RAZA, 1941) by José Luis Saenz de Heredia
2. *Ibid.*
3. WELCOME MR MARSHALL! ¡BIENVENIDO, MR MARSHALL! (1953) by Luis García Berlanga
4. *Ibid.*
5. FLUNKING OUT (ASIGNATURA PENDIENTE, 1977) by José Luis Garci
6. *Ibid.*
7. *Ibid.*
8. CARMEN (1983) by Carlos Saura
9. *Ibid.*
10. *Ibid.*
11. *Ibid.*
12. HIGH HEELS (TACONES LEJANOS, 1991) by Pedro Almodóvar
13. *Ibid.*
14. *Ibid.*
15. *Ibid.*
16. SEX CHANGE (CAMBIO DE SEXO, 1977) by Vicente Aranda
17. *Ibid.*
18. THE DEPUTY (EL DIPUTADO, 1979) by Eloy de la Iglesia
19. *Ibid.*
20. THE DEATH OF MIKEL (LA MUERTE DE MIKEL, 1983) by Imanol Uribe
21. *Ibid.*
22. *Ibid.*
23 LAW OF DESIRE (LA LEY DEL DESEO, 1987) by Pedro Almodóvar
24 *Ibid.*
25 HURRY, HURRY (DEPRISA, DEPRISA, 1981) by Carlos Saura
26 *Ibid.*
27. *Ibid.*
28. *Ibid.*
29. EL LUTE: RUN FOR YOUR LIFE (EL LUTE: CAMINA O REVIENTA, 1987) by Vicente Aranda
30. *Ibid.*
31. EL LUTE, TOMORROW I'LL BE FREE (EL LUTE: MAÑANA SERÉ LIBRE, 1988) by Vicente Aranda
32. *Ibid.*
33. *Ibid.*
34. RUNNING OUT OF TIME (DÍAS CONTADOS, 1994) by Imanol Uribe
35. *Ibid.*
36. *Ibid.*

Index of Names

Film Culture in Transition

General Editor: *Thomas Elsaesser*

Thomas Elsaesser, Robert Kievit and Jan Simons (eds.)
Double Trouble: Chiem van Houweninge on Writing and Filming, 1994
ISBN paperback 978 90 5356 025 9

Thomas Elsaesser, Jan Simons and Lucette Bronk (eds.)
Writing for the Medium: Television in Transition, 1994
ISBN paperback 978 90 5356 054 9

Karel Dibbets and Bert Hogenkamp (eds.)
Film and the First World War, 1994
ISBN paperback 978 90 5356 064 8

Warren Buckland (ed.)
The Film Spectator: From Sign to Mind, 1995
ISBN paperback 978 90 5356 131 7; ISBN hardcover 978 90 5356 170 6

Egil Törnqvist
Between Stage and Screen: Ingmar Bergman Directs, 1996
ISBN paperback 978 90 5356 137 9; ISBN hardcover 978 90 5356 171 3

Thomas Elsaesser (ed.)
A Second Life: German Cinema's First Decades, 1996
ISBN paperback 978 90 5356 172 0; ISBN hardcover 978 90 5356 183 6

Thomas Elsaesser
Fassbinder's Germany: History Identity Subject, 1996
ISBN paperback 978 90 5356 059 4; ISBN hardcover 978 90 5356 184 3

Thomas Elsaesser and Kay Hoffmann (eds.)
Cinema Futures: Cain, Abel or Cable? The Screen Arts in the Digital Age, 1998
ISBN paperback 978 90 5356 282 6; ISBN hardcover 978 90 5356 312 0

Siegfried Zielinski
Audiovisions: Cinema and Television as Entr'Actes in History, 1999
ISBN paperback 978 90 5356 313 7; ISBN hardcover 978 90 5356 303 8

Kees Bakker (ed.)
Joris Ivens and the Documentary Context, 1999
ISBN paperback 978 90 5356 389 2; ISBN hardcover 978 90 5356 425 7

Egil Törnqvist
Ibsen, Strindberg and the Intimate Theatre: Studies in TV Presentation, 1999
ISBN paperback 978 90 5356 350 2; ISBN hardcover 978 90 5356 371 7

Michael Temple and James S. Williams (eds.)
The Cinema Alone: Essays on the Work of Jean-Luc Godard 1985-2000, 2000
ISBN paperback 978 90 5356 455 4; ISBN hardcover 978 90 5356 456 1

Patricia Pisters and Catherine M. Lord (eds.)
Micropolitics of Media Culture: Reading the Rhizomes of Deleuze and Guattari, 2001
ISBN paperback 978 90 5356 472 1; ISBN hardcover 978 90 5356 473 8

William van der Heide
Malaysian Cinema, Asian Film: Border Crossings and National Cultures, 2002
ISBN paperback 978 90 5356 519 3; ISBN hardcover 978 90 5356 580 3

Bernadette Kester
Film Front Weimar: Representations of the First World War in German Films of the Weimar Period (1919-1933), 2002
ISBN *paperback 978 90 5356 597 1;* ISBN *hardcover 978 90 5356 598 8*

Richard Allen and Malcolm Turvey (eds.)
Camera Obscura, Camera Lucida: Essays in Honor of Annette Michelson, 2003
ISBN paperback 978 90 5356 494 3

Ivo Blom
Jean Desmet and the Early Dutch Film Trade, 2003
ISBN paperback 978 90 5356 463 9; ISBN hardcover 978 90 5356 570 4

Alastair Phillips
City of Darkness, City of Light: Émigré Filmmakers in Paris 1929-1939, 2003
ISBN paperback 978 90 5356 634 3; ISBN hardcover 978 90 5356 633 6

Thomas Elsaesser, Alexander Horwath and Noel King (eds.)
The Last Great American Picture Show: New Hollywood Cinema in the 1970s, 2004
ISBN paperback 978 90 5356 631 2; ISBN hardcover 978 905356 493 6

Thomas Elsaesser (ed.)
Harun Farocki: Working on the Sight-Lines, 2004
ISBN paperback 978 90 5356 635 0; ISBN hardcover 978 90 5356 636 7

Kristin Thompson
Herr Lubitsch Goes to Hollywood: German and American Film after World War I, 2005
ISBN paperback 978 90 5356 708 1; ISBN hardcover 978 90 5356 709 8

Marijke de Valck and Malte Hagener (eds.)
Cinephilia: Movies, Love and Memory, 2005
ISBN paperback 978 90 5356 768 5; ISBN hardcover 978 90 5356 769 2

Thomas Elsaesser
European Cinema: Face to Face with Hollywood, 2005
ISBN paperback 978 90 5356 594 0; ISBN hardcover 978 90 5356 602 2

Michael Walker
Hitchcock's Motifs, 2005
ISBN paperback 978 90 5356 772 2; ISBN hardcover 978 90 5356 773 9

Nanna Verhoeff
The West in Early Cinema: After the Beginning, 2006
ISBN paperback 978 90 5356 831 6; ISBN hardcover 978 90 5356 832 3

Anat Zanger
Film Remakes as Ritual and Disguise: From Carmen to Ripley, 2006
ISBN paperback 978 90 5356 784 5; ISBN hardcover 978 90 5356 785 2

Wanda Strauven
The Cinema of Attractions Reloaded, 2006
ISBN paperback 978 90 5356 944 3; ISBN hardcover 978 90 5356 945 0

Malte Hagener
*Moving Forward, Looking Back: The European Avant-garde and the Invention of Film
    Culture, 1919-1939*, 2007
ISBN paperback 978 90 5356 960 3; ISBN hardcover 978 90 5356 961 0

Tim Bergfelder, Sue Harris and Sarah Street
*Film Architecture and the Transnational Imagination: Set Design in 1930s European
    Cinema*, 2007
ISBN paperback 978 90 5356 984 9; ISBN hardcover 978 90 5356 980 1

Jan Simons
Playing the Waves: Lars von Trier's Game Cinema, 2007
ISBN paperback 978 90 5356 991 7; ISBN hardcover 978 90 5356 979 5

Marijke de Valck
Film Festivals: From European Geopolitics to Global Cinephilia, 2007
ISBN paperback 978 90 5356 192 8; ISBN hardcover 978 90 5356 216 1

Asbjørn Grønstad
Transfigurations: Violence, Death, and Masculinity in American Cinema, 2008
ISBN paperback 978 90 8964 010 9; ISBN hardcover 978 90 8964 030 7

Vinzenz Hediger and Patrick Vonderau (eds.)
Films that Work: Industrial Film and the Productivity of Media, 2009
ISBN paperback 978 90 8964 013 0; ISBN hardcover 978 90 8964 012 3

Pasi Väliaho
Mapping the Moving Image: Gesture, Thought and Cinema circa 1900, 2010
ISBN paperback 978 90 8964 140 3; ISBN hardcover 978 90 8964 141 0